Edited by

Marc Stier, Grant Ward, Joan McCord, Mark Haller, Daniel P. Tompkins, and Istvan Varkonyi

Temple University

Intellectual Heritage 52

Fourth Edition

Key readings

The Enlightenment and the Tradition of Natural Rights

The Romantic Rebellion

Revolutionary Thinkers

Nonviolent Struggle and Anticolonialism

Imagining the World

Temple University Press / Philadelphia

Temple University Press
1601 North Broad Street
Philadelphia, PA 19122
www.temple.edu/tempress

Published 2004

Printed in the United States of America

♾ The paper used in this publication meets the requirements of the American National Standard for Information Sciences—Permanence of Paper for Printed Library Materials, ANSI Z39.48-1992

Acknowledgments
Grateful acknowledgment is made to the following sources for permission to reprint material copyrighted or controlled by them:

"What is Enlightenment?" reprinted from *The Philosophy of Kant* by Immanuel Kant, translated by Carl Friedrich, copyright © 1949 by Random House, Inc. Used by permission of Random House, Inc.

Emily Dickinson poems reprinted by permission of the publishers and the Trustees of Amherst College from *The Poems of Emily Dickinson: Variorum Edition,* Ralph W. Franklin, ed., Cambridge, Mass.: The Belknap Press of Harvard University Press, copyright © 1998 by the President and Fellows of Harvard College. Copyright © 1951, 1955, 1979 by the President and Fellows of Harvard College.

"I, Too" reprinted from *Selected Poems of Langston Hughes* by Langston Hughes, copyright © 1927 by Alfred A. Knopf, Inc. and renewed 1955 by Langston Hughes. Used by permission of Alfred A. Knopf, a division of Random House, Inc.

"Untouchability" reprinted from *For the Well-Being of the Nation: The Message of Mahatma Gandhi* by Mahatma Gandhi (New Delhi, 1943), edited by U.S. Mohan Ran, Ministry of Information and Broadcasting. Copyright © Navajivan Trust.

"Introduction" reprinted from *The Second Sex* by Simone De Beauvoir, translated by H.M. Parshley, copyright © 1952 and renewed 1980 by Alfred A. Knopf, a division of Random House, Inc. Used by permission of Alfred A. Knopf, a division of Random House, Inc.

"Letter from Birmingham Jail," by Dr. Martin Luther King Jr., reprinted by arrangement with the Estate of Martin Luther King Jr., c/o Writers House, as agent for the proprietor New York, NY. Copyright © 1963 Martin Luther King Jr. Copyright renewed 1991 Coretta Scott King.

ISBN 1-59213-104-2

2 4 6 8 9 7 5 3 1

Contents

PART III
Revolutionary Thinkers

PART IV
Nonviolent Struggle and Anticolonialism

Introduction

Key Readings I and *II* are the official collections of readings for Temple University's Intellectual Heritage Program as of the fall semester, 2001. The editors compiled these readings with specific goals in mind. They sought faculty consensus in developing readings that would be used by a large number of instructors and that students could buy at reasonable prices. Finally, they included a document that students must have access to, the Temple University Policy on Academic Dishonesty passed by the Faculty Senate.

Faculty commentary on these readings can now be found on the Intellectual Heritage Program website:

http://courses.temple.edu/ih

The existence of this rich and handy supportive material means that the current volume can be dedicated to the readings themselves, along with timelines and maps.

The editors express their gratitude to the large number of Temple University faculty who offered suggestions about the readings, to the staff of Temple University Press, and to the Intellectual Heritage Program Office Manager, Ms. Linda Tribune, for her unfailing good will and steady assistance throughout this process.

PART I

The Enlightenment and Civil and Political Rights

John Locke

Selections from The Second Treatise of Government (1690)

Chapter I

Of Political Power

1. It having been shown in the foregoing discourse:

Firstly. That Adam had not, either by natural right of fatherhood or by positive donation from God, any such authority over his children, nor dominion over the world, as is pretended.

Secondly. That if he had, his heirs yet had no right to it.

Thirdly. That if his heirs had, there being no law of Nature nor positive law of God that determines which is the right heir in all cases that may arise, the right of succession, and consequently of bearing rule, could not have been certainly determined.

Fourthly. That if even that had been determined, yet the knowledge of which is the eldest line of Adam's posterity being so long since utterly lost, that in the races of mankind and families of the world, there remains not to one above another the least pretence to be the eldest house, and to have the right of inheritance.

All these promises having, as I think, been clearly made out, it is impossible that the rulers now on earth should make any benefit, or derive any the least shadow of authority from that which is held to be the fountain of all power, "Adam's private dominion and paternal jurisdiction"; so that he that will not give just occasion to think that all government in the world is the product only of force and violence, and that men live together by no other rules but that of beasts, where the strongest carries it, and so lay a foundation for perpetual disorder and mischief, tumult, sedition, and rebellion (things that the followers of that hypothesis so loudly cry out against), must of necessity find out another rise of government, another original of political power, and another way of designing and knowing the persons that have it than what Sir Robert Filmer hath taught us.

2. To this purpose, I think it may not be amiss to set down what I take to be political power. That the power of a magistrate over a subject may be distinguished from that of a father over his children, a master over his servant, a husband over his wife, and a lord over his slave. All which distinct powers happening sometimes together in the same man, if he be considered under these different relations, it may help us to distinguish these powers one from another, and show the difference betwixt a ruler of a commonwealth, a father of a family, and a captain of a galley.

3. Political power, then, I take to be a right of making laws, with penalties of death, and consequently all less penalties for the regulating and preserving of property, and of employing the force of the community in the execution of such laws, and in the defense of the commonwealth from foreign injury, and all this only for the public good.

Chapter II

Of the State of Nature

4. To understand political power aright, and derive it from its original, we must consider what estate all men are naturally in, and that is, a state of perfect freedom to order their actions, and dispose of their possessions and persons as they think fit, within the bounds of the law of Nature, without asking leave or depending upon the will of any other man.

A state also of equality, wherein all the power and jurisdiction is reciprocal, no one having more than another, there being nothing more evident than that creatures of the same species and rank, promiscuously born to all the same advantages of Nature, and the use of the same faculties, should also be equal one amongst another, without subordination or subjection, unless the lord and master of them all should, by any manifest declaration of his will, set one above another, and confer on him, by an evident and clear appointment, an undoubted right to dominion and sovereignty.

5. This equality of men by Nature, the judicious Hooker looks upon as so evident in itself, and beyond all question, that he makes it the foundation of that obligation to mutual love amongst men on which he builds the duties they owe one another, and from whence he derives the great maxims of justice and charity. His words are:

> "The like natural inducement hath brought men to know that it is no less their duty to love others than themselves, for seeing those things which are equal, must needs all have one measure; if I cannot but wish to receive good, even as much at every man's hands, as any man can wish unto his own soul, how

> should I look to have any part of my desire herein satisfied, unless myself be careful to satisfy the like desire, which is undoubtedly in other men weak, being of one and the same nature: to have anything offered them repugnant to this desire must needs, in all respects, grieve them as much as me; so that if I do harm, I must look to suffer, there being no reason that others should show greater measure of love to me than they have by me showed unto them; my desire, therefore, to be loved of my equals in Nature, as much as possible may be, imposes upon me a natural duty of bearing to them-ward fully the like affection. From which relation of equality between ourselves and them that are as ourselves, what several rules and canons natural reason hath drawn for direction of life no man is ignorant." (*Eccl. Pol.* i.)

6. But though this be a state of liberty, yet it is not a state of license; though man in that state have an uncontrollable liberty to dispose of his person or possessions, yet he has not liberty to destroy himself, or so much as any creature in his possession, but where some nobler use than its bare preservation calls for it. The state of Nature has a law of Nature to govern it, which obliges every one, and reason, which is that law, teaches all mankind who will but consult it, that being all equal and independent, no one ought to harm another in his life, health, liberty or possessions; for men being all the workmanship of one omnipotent and infinitely wise Maker; all the servants of one sovereign Master, sent into the world by His order and about His business; they are His property, whose workmanship they are made to last during His, not one another's pleasure. And, being furnished with like faculties, sharing all in one community of Nature, there cannot be supposed any such subordination among us that may authorize us to destroy one another, as if we were made for one another's uses, as the inferior ranks of creatures are for ours. Every one as he is bound to preserve himself, and not to quit his station wilfully, so by the like reason, when his own preservation comes not in competition, ought he as much as he can to preserve the rest of mankind, and not unless it be to do justice on an offender, take away or impair the life, or what tends to the preservation of the life, the liberty, health, limb, or goods of another.

7. And that all men may be restrained from invading others' rights, and from doing hurt to one another, and the law of Nature be observed, which wills the peace and preservation of all mankind, the execution of the law of Nature is in that state put into every man's hands, whereby every one has a right to punish the transgressors of that law to such a degree as may hinder its violation. For the law of Nature would, as all other laws that concern men in this world, be in vain if there were nobody that in the state of Nature had a power to execute that law, and thereby preserve the innocent and restrain offenders; and if any one in the state of Nature may punish another for any evil he has done, every one may do so. For in that state of perfect equality, where naturally there is no superiority or jurisdiction of one over another, what any may do in prosecution of that law, every one must needs have a right to do.

8. And thus, in the state of Nature, one man comes by a power over another, but yet no absolute or arbitrary power to use a criminal, when he has got him in his hands, according to the passionate heats or boundless extravagancy of his own will, but only to retribute to him so far as calm reason and conscience dictate, what is proportionate to his transgression, which is so much as may serve for reparation and restraint. For these two are the only reasons why one man may lawfully do harm to another, which is that we call punishment. In transgressing the law of Nature, the offender declares himself to live by another rule than that of reason and common equity, which is that measure God has set to the actions of men for their mutual security, and so he becomes dangerous to mankind; the tie which is to secure them from injury and violence being slighted and broken by him, which being a trespass against the whole species, and the peace and safety of it, provided for by the law of Nature, every man upon this score, by the right he hath to preserve mankind in general, may restrain, or where it is necessary, destroy things noxious to them, and so may bring such evil on any one who hath transgressed that law, as may make him repent the doing of it, and thereby deter him, and, by his example, others from doing the like mischief. And in this case, and upon this ground, *every man hath a right to punish the offender, and be executioner of the law of Nature.*

9. I doubt not but this will seem a very strange doctrine to some men; but before they condemn it, I desire them to resolve me by what right any prince or state can put to death or punish an alien for any crime he commits in their country? It is certain their laws, by virtue of any sanction they receive from the promulgated will of the legislature, reach not a stranger. They speak not to him, nor, if they did, is he bound to hearken to them. The legislative authority by which they are in force over the subjects of that commonwealth hath no power over him. Those who have the supreme power of making laws in England, France, or Holland are, to an Indian, but like the rest of the world—men without authority. And therefore, if by the law of Nature every man hath not a power to punish offences against it, as he soberly judges the case to require, I see not how the magistrates of any community can punish an alien of another country, since, in reference to him, they can have no more power than what every man naturally may have over another.

10. Besides the crime which consists in violating the laws, and varying from the right rule of reason, whereby a man so far becomes degenerate, and declares himself to quit the principles of human nature and to be a noxious creature, there is commonly injury done, and some person or other, some other man, receives damage by his transgression; in which case, he who hath received any damage has (besides the right of punishment common to him, with other men) a particular right to seek reparation from him that hath done it. And any other person who finds it just may also join with him that is injured, and assist him in recovering from the offender so much as may make satisfaction for the harm he hath suffered.

11. From these two distinct rights (the one of punishing the crime, for restraint and preventing the like offence, which right of punishing is in everybody, the other of taking reparation, which belongs only to the injured party) comes it to pass that the magistrate, who by being magistrate hath the common right of punishing put into his hands,

can often, where the public good demands not the execution of the law, remit the punishment of criminal offences by his own authority, but yet cannot remit the satisfaction due to any private man for the damage he has received. That he who hath suffered the damage has a right to demand in his own name, and he alone can remit. The damnified person has this power of appropriating to himself the goods or service of the offender by right of self-preservation, as every man has a power to punish the crime to prevent its being committed again, by the right he has of preserving all mankind, and doing all reasonable things he can in order to that end. And thus it is that every man in the state of Nature has a power to kill a murderer, both to deter others from doing the like injury (which no reparation can compensate) by the example of the punishment that attends it from everybody, and also to secure men from the attempts of a criminal who, having renounced reason, the common rule and measure God hath given to mankind, hath, by the unjust violence and slaughter he hath committed upon one, declared war against all mankind, and therefore may be destroyed as a lion or a tiger, one of those wild savage beasts with whom men can have no society nor security. And upon this is grounded that great law of nature, "Whoso sheddeth man's blood, by man shall his blood be shed." And Cain was so fully convinced that every one had a right to destroy such a criminal, that, after the murder of his brother, he cries out, "Every one that findeth me shall slay me," so plain was it writ in the hearts of all mankind.

12. By the same reason may a man in the state of Nature punish the lesser breaches of that law, it will, perhaps, be demanded, with death? I answer: Each transgression may be punished to that degree, and with so much severity, as will suffice to make it an ill bargain to the offender, give him cause to repent, and terrify others from doing the like. Every offence that can be committed in the state of Nature may, in the state of Nature, be also punished equally, and as far forth, as it may, in a commonwealth. For though it would be beside my present purpose to enter here into the particulars of the law of Nature, or its measures of punishment, yet it is certain there is such a law, and that too as intelligible and plain to a rational creature and a studier of that law as the positive laws of commonwealths, nay, possibly plainer; as much as reason is easier to be understood than the fancies and intricate contrivances of men, following contrary and hidden interests put into words; for truly so are a great part of the municipal laws of countries, which are only so far right as they are founded on the law of Nature, by which they are to be regulated and interpreted.

13. To this strange doctrine—viz., That in the state of Nature every one has the executive power of the law of Nature—I doubt not but it will be objected that it is unreasonable for men to be judges in their own cases, that self-love will make men partial to themselves and their friends; and, on the other side, ill-nature, passion, and revenge will carry them too far in punishing others, and hence nothing but confusion and disorder will follow, and that therefore God hath certainly appointed government to restrain the partiality and violence of men. I easily grant that civil government is the proper remedy for the inconveniences of the state of Nature, which must certainly be great where men may be judges in their own case, since it is easy to be imagined that he who was so unjust as to do his brother an injury will scarce be so just as to condemn himself for it. But I shall de-

sire those who make this objection to remember that absolute monarchs are but men; and if government is to be the remedy of those evils which necessarily follow from men being judges in their own cases, and the state of Nature is therefore not to be endured, I desire to know what kind of government that is, and how much better it is than the state of Nature, where one man commanding a multitude has the liberty to be judge in his own case, and may do to all his subjects whatever he pleases without the least question or control of those who execute his pleasure? and in whatsoever he doth, whether led by reason, mistake, or passion, must be submitted to? which men in the state of Nature are not bound to do one to another. And if he that judges, judges amiss in his own or any other case, he is answerable for it to the rest of mankind.

14. It is often asked as a mighty objection, where are, or ever were, there any men in such a state of Nature? To which it may suffice as an answer at present, that since all princes and rulers of "independent" governments all through the world are in a state of Nature, it is plain the world never was, nor never will be, without numbers of men in that state. I have named all governors of "independent" communities, whether they are, or are not, in league with others; for it is not every compact that puts an end to the state of Nature between men, but only this one of agreeing together mutually to enter into one community, and make one body politic; other promises and compacts men may make one with another, and yet still be in the state of Nature. The promises and bargains for truck, etc., between the two men in Soldania, in or between a Swiss and an Indian, in the woods of America, are binding to them, though they are perfectly in a state of Nature in reference to one another for truth, and keeping of faith belongs to men as men, and not as members of society.

15. To those that say there were never any men in the state of Nature, I will not oppose the authority of the judicious Hooker (*Eccl. Pol.* i. 10), where he says, "the laws which have been hitherto mentioned"—i.e., the laws of Nature—"do bind men absolutely, even as they are men, although they have never any settled fellowship, never any solemn agreement amongst themselves what to do or not to do; but for as much as we are not by ourselves sufficient to furnish ourselves with competent store of things needful for such a life as our Nature doth desire, a life fit for the dignity of man, therefore to supply those defects and imperfections which are in us, as living single and solely by ourselves, we are naturally induced to seek communion and fellowship with others; this was the cause of men uniting themselves as first in politic societies." But I, moreover, affirm that all men are naturally in that state, and remain so till, by their own consents, they make themselves members of some politic society, and I doubt not, in the sequel of this discourse, to make it very clear.

Chapter III

Of the State of War

16. The state of war is a state of enmity and destruction; and therefore declaring by word or action, not a passionate and hasty, but sedate, settled design upon another

man's life puts him in a state of war with him against whom he has declared such an intention, and so has exposed his life to the other's power to be taken away by him, or any one that joins with him in his defense, and espouses his quarrel; it being reasonable and just I should have a right to destroy that which threatens me with destruction; for by the fundamental law of Nature, man being to be preserved as much as possible, when all cannot be preserved, the safety of the innocent is to be preferred, and one may destroy a man who makes war upon him, or has discovered an enmity to his being, for the same reason that he may kill a wolf or a lion, because they are not under the ties of the common law of reason, have no other rule but that of force and violence, and so may be treated as a beast of prey, those dangerous and noxious creatures that will be sure to destroy him whenever he falls into their power.

17. And hence it is that he who attempts to get another man into his absolute power does thereby put himself into a state of war with him; it being to be understood as a declaration of a design upon his life. For I have reason to conclude that he who would get me into his power without my consent would use me as he pleased when he had got me there, and destroy me too when he had a fancy to it; for nobody can desire to have me in his absolute power unless it be to compel me by force to that which is against the right of my freedom—i.e. make me a slave. To be free from such force is the only security of my preservation, and reason bids me look on him as an enemy to my preservation who would take away that freedom which is the fence to it; so that he who makes an attempt to enslave me thereby puts himself into a state of war with me. He that in the state of Nature would take away the freedom that belongs to any one in that state must necessarily be supposed to have a design to take away everything else, that freedom being the foundation of all the rest; as he that in the state of society would take away the freedom belonging to those of that society or commonwealth must be supposed to design to take away from them everything else, and so be looked on as in a state of war.

18. This makes it lawful for a man to kill a thief who has not in the least hurt him, nor declared any design upon his life, any farther than by the use of force, so to get him in his power as to take away his money, or what he pleases, from him; because using force, where he has no right to get me into his power, let his pretence be what it will, I have no reason to suppose that he who would take away my liberty would not, when he had me in his power, take away everything else. And, therefore, it is lawful for me to treat him as one who has put himself into a state of war with me—i.e., kill him if I can; for to that hazard does he justly expose himself whoever introduces a state of war, and is aggressor in it.

19. And here we have the plain difference between the state of Nature and the state of war, which however some men have confounded, are as far distant as a state of peace, goodwill, mutual assistance, and preservation; and a state of enmity, malice, violence and mutual destruction are one from another. Men living together according to reason without a common superior on earth, with authority to judge between them, is properly the state of Nature. But force, or a declared design of force upon the person of another, where there is no common superior on earth to appeal to for relief, is the state of war; and it is the want of such an appeal gives a man the right of war even against an aggressor, though

he be in society and a fellow-subject. Thus, a thief whom I cannot harm, but by appeal to the law, for having stolen all that I am worth, I may kill when he sets on me to rob me but of my horse or coat, because the law, which was made for my preservation, where it cannot interpose to secure my life from present force, which if lost is capable of no reparation, permits me my own defense and the right of war, a liberty to kill the aggressor, because the aggressor allows not time to appeal to our common judge, nor the decision of the law, for remedy in a case where the mischief may be irreparable. Want of a common judge with authority puts all men in a state of Nature; force without right upon a man's person makes a state of war both where there is, and is not, a common judge.

20. But when the actual force is over, the state of war ceases between those that are in society and are equally on both sides subject to the judge; and, therefore, in such controversies, where the question is put, "Who shall be judge?" it cannot be meant who shall decide the controversy; every one knows what Jephtha here tells us, that "the Lord the Judge" shall judge. Where there is no judge on earth the appeal lies to God in Heaven. That question then cannot mean who shall judge, whether another hath put himself in a state of war with me, and whether I may, as Jephtha did, appeal to Heaven in it? Of that I myself can only judge in my own conscience, as I will answer it at the great day to the Supreme Judge of all men.

Chapter IV

Of Slavery

21. The natural liberty of man is to be free from any superior power on earth, and not to be under the will or legislative authority of man, but to have only the law of Nature for his rule. The liberty of man in society is to be under no other legislative power but that established by consent in the commonwealth, nor under the dominion of any will, or restraint of any law, but what that legislative shall enact according to the trust put in it. Freedom, then, is not what Sir Robert Filmer tells us: "A liberty for every one to do what he lists, to live as he pleases, and not to be tied by any laws"; but freedom of men under government is to have a standing rule to live by, common to every one of that society, and made by the legislative power erected in it. A liberty to follow my own will in all things where that rule prescribes not, not to be subject to the inconstant, uncertain, unknown, arbitrary will of another man, as freedom of nature is to be under no other restraint but the law of Nature.

22. This freedom from absolute, arbitrary power is so necessary to, and closely joined with, a man's preservation, that he cannot part with it but by what forfeits his preservation and life together. For a man, not having the power of his own life, cannot by compact or his own consent enslave himself to any one, nor put himself under the absolute, arbitrary power of another to take away his life when he pleases. Nobody can give more power than he has himself, and he that cannot take away his own life cannot give anoth-

er power over it. Indeed, having by his fault forfeited his own life by some act that deserves death, he to whom he has forfeited it may, when he has him in his power, delay to take it, and make use of him to his own service; and he does him no injury by it. For, whenever he finds the hardship of his slavery outweigh the value of his life, it is in his power, by resisting the will of his master, to draw on himself the death he desires.

23. This is the perfect condition of slavery, which is nothing else but the state of war continued between a lawful conqueror and a captive, for if once compact enter between them, and make an agreement for a limited power on the one side, and obedience on the other, the state of war and slavery ceases as long as the compact endures; for, as has been said, no man can by agreement pass over to another that which he hath not in himself—a power over his own life.

I confess, we find among the Jews, as well as other nations, that men did sell themselves; but it is plain this was only to drudgery, not to slavery; for it is evident the person sold was not under an absolute, arbitrary, despotical power, for the master could not have power to kill him at any time, whom at a certain time he was obliged to let go free out of his service; and the master of such a servant was so far from having an arbitrary power over his life that he could not at pleasure so much as maim him, but the loss of an eye or tooth set him free (Exod. 21.).

Chapter V

Of Property

24. Whether we consider natural reason, which tells us that men, once being born, have a right to their preservation, and consequently to meat and drink and such other things as Nature affords for their subsistence, or "revelation," which gives us an account of those grants God made of the world to Adam, and to Noah and his sons, it is very clear that God, as King David says (Psalm 115. 16), "has given the earth to the children of men," given it to mankind in common. But, this being supposed, it seems to some a very great difficulty how any one should ever come to have a property in anything, I will not content myself to answer, that, if it be difficult to make out "property" upon a supposition that God gave the world to Adam and his posterity in common, it is impossible that any man but one universal monarch should have any "property" upon a supposition that God gave the world to Adam and his heirs in succession, exclusive of all the rest of his posterity; but I shall endeavor to show how men might come to have a property in several parts of that which God gave to mankind in common, and that without any express compact of all the commoners.

25. God, who hath given the world to men in common, hath also given them reason to make use of it to the best advantage of life and convenience. The earth and all that is therein is given to men for the support and comfort of their being. And though all the fruits it naturally produces, and beasts it feeds, belong to mankind in common, as they are

produced by the spontaneous hand of Nature, and nobody has originally a private dominion exclusive of the rest of mankind in any of them, as they are thus in their natural state, yet being given for the use of men, there must of necessity be a means to appropriate them some way or other before they can be of any use, or at all beneficial, to any particular men. The fruit or venison which nourishes the wild Indian, who knows no enclosure, and is still a tenant in common, must be his, and so his—i.e., a part of him, that another can no longer have any right to it before it can do him any good for the support of his life.

26. Though the earth and all inferior creatures be common to all men, yet every man has a "property" in his own "person." This nobody has any right to but himself. The "labor" of his body and the "work" of his hands, we may say, are properly his. Whatsoever, then, he removes out of the state that Nature hath provided and left it in, he hath mixed his labor with it, and joined to it something that is his own, and thereby makes it his property. It being by him removed from the common state Nature placed it in, it hath by this labor something annexed to it that excludes the common right of other men. For this "labor" being the unquestionable property of the laborer, no man but he can have a right to what that is once joined to, at least where there is enough, and as good left in common for others.

27. He that is nourished by the acorns he picked up under an oak, or the apples he gathered from the trees in the wood, has certainly appropriated them to himself. Nobody can deny but the nourishment is his. I ask, then, when did they begin to be his? when he digested? or when he ate? or when he boiled? or when he brought them home? or when he picked them up? And it is plain, if the first gathering made them not his, nothing else could. That labor put a distinction between them and common. That added something to them more than Nature, the common mother of all, had done, and so they became his private right. And will any one say he had no right to those acorns or apples he thus appropriated because he had not the consent of all mankind to make them his? Was it a robbery thus to assume to himself what belonged to all in common? If such a consent as that was necessary, man had starved, notwithstanding the plenty God had given him. We see in commons, which remain so by compact, that it is the taking any part of what is common, and removing it out of the state Nature leaves it in, which begins the property, without which the common is of no use. And the taking of this or that part does not depend on the express consent of all the commoners. Thus, the grass my horse has bit, the turfs my servant has cut, and the ore I have digged in any place, where I have a right to them in common with others, become my property without the assignation or consent of anybody. The labor that was mine, removing them out of that common state they were in, hath fixed my property in them.

28. By making an explicit consent of every commoner necessary to any one's appropriating to himself any part of what is given in common, children or servants could not cut the meat which their father or master had provided for them in common without assigning to every one his peculiar part. Though the water running in the fountain be every one's, yet who can doubt but that in the pitcher is his only who drew it out? His labor hath taken it out of the hands of Nature where it was common, and belonged equally to all her children, and hath thereby appropriated it to himself.

29. Thus this law of reason makes the deer that Indian's who hath killed it; it is allowed to be his goods who hath bestowed his labor upon it, though, before, it was the common right of every one. And amongst those who are counted the civilized part of mankind, who have made and multiplied positive laws to determine property, this original law of Nature for the beginning of property, in what was before common, still takes place, and by virtue thereof, what fish any one catches in the ocean, that great and still remaining common of mankind; or what amber-gris any one takes up here is by the labor that removes it out of that common state Nature left it in, made his property who takes that pains about it. And even amongst us, the hare that any one is hunting is thought his who pursues her during the chase. For being a beast that is still looked upon as common, and no man's private possession, whoever has employed so much labor about any of that kind as to find and pursue her has thereby removed her from the state of Nature wherein she was common, and hath begun a property.

30. It will, perhaps, be objected to this, that if gathering the acorns or other fruits of the earth, etc., makes a right to them, then any one may engross as much as he will. To which I answer, Not so. The same law of Nature that does by this means give us property, does also bound that property too. "God has given us all things richly." Is the voice of reason confirmed by inspiration? But how far has He given it us—"to enjoy"? As much as any one can make use of to any advantage of life before it spoils, so much he may by his labor fix a property in. Whatever is beyond this is more than his share, and belongs to others. Nothing was made by God for man to spoil or destroy. And thus considering the plenty of natural provisions there was a long time in the world, and the few spenders, and to how small a part of that provision the industry of one man could extend itself and engross it to the prejudice of others, especially keeping within the bounds set by reason of what might serve for his use, there could be then little room for quarrels or contentions about property so established.

31. But the chief matter of property being now not the fruits of the earth and the beasts that subsist on it, but the earth itself, as that which takes in and carries with it all the rest, I think it is plain that property in that too is acquired as the former. As much land as a man tills, plants, improves, cultivates, and can use the product of, so much is his property. He by his labor does, as it were, enclose it from the common. Nor will it invalidate his right to say everybody else has an equal title to it, and therefore he cannot appropriate, he cannot enclose, without the consent of all his fellow-commoners, all mankind. God, when He gave the world in common to all mankind, commanded man also to labor, and the penury of his condition required it of him. God and his reason commanded him to subdue the earth—i.e., improve it for the benefit of life and therein lay out something upon it that was his own, his labor. He that, in obedience to this command of God, subdued, tilled, and sowed any part of it, thereby annexed to it something that was his property, which another had no title to, nor could without injury take from him.

32. Nor was this appropriation of any parcel of land, by improving it, any prejudice to any other man, since there was still enough and as good left, and more than the yet unprovided could use. So that, in effect, there was never the less left for others because of

his enclosure for himself. For he that leaves as much as another can make use of does as good as take nothing at all. Nobody could think himself injured by the drinking of another man, though he took a good draught, who had a whole river of the same water left him to quench his thirst. And the case of land and water, where there is enough of both, is perfectly the same.

33. God gave the world to men in common, but since He gave it them for their benefit and the greatest conveniencies of life they were capable to draw from it, it cannot be supposed He meant it should always remain common and uncultivated. He gave it to the use of the industrious and rational (and labor was to be his title to it); not to the fancy or covetousness of the quarrelsome and contentious. He that had as good left for his improvement as was already taken up needed not complain, ought not to meddle with what was already improved by another's labor; if he did it is plain he desired the benefit of another's pains, which he had no right to, and not the ground which God had given him, in common with others, to labor on, and whereof there was as good left as that already possessed, and more than he knew what to do with, or his industry could reach to.

34. It is true, in land that is common in England or any other country, where there are plenty of people under government who have money and commerce, no one can enclose or appropriate any part without the consent of all his fellow-commoners; because this is left common by compact—i.e., by the law of the land, which is not to be violated. And, though it be common in respect of some men, it is not so to all mankind, but is the joint propriety of this country, or this parish. Besides, the remainder, after such enclosure, would not be as good to the rest of the commoners as the whole was, when they could all make use of the whole; whereas in the beginning and first peopling of the great common of the world it was quite otherwise. The law man was under was rather for appropriating. God commanded, and his wants forced him to labor. That was his property, which could not be taken from him wherever he had fixed it. And hence subduing or cultivating the earth and having dominion, we see, are joined together. The one gave title to the other. So that God, by commanding to subdue, gave authority so far to appropriate. And the condition of human life, which requires labor and materials to work on, necessarily introduce private possessions.

35. The measure of property Nature well set, by the extent of men's labor and the conveniency of life. No man's labor could subdue or appropriate all, nor could his enjoyment consume more than a small part; so that it was impossible for any man, this way, to entrench upon the right of another or acquire to himself a property to the prejudice of his neighbor, who would still have room for as good and as large a possession (after the other had taken out his) as before it was appropriated. Which measure did confine every man's possession to a very moderate proportion, and such as he might appropriate to himself without injury to anybody in the first ages of the world, when men were more in danger to be lost, by wandering from their company, in the then vast wilderness of the earth than to be straitened for want of room to plant in.

36. The same measure may be allowed still, without prejudice to anybody, full as the world seems. For, supposing a man or family, in the state they were at first, peopling

of the world by the children of Adam or Noah, let him plant in some inland vacant places of America. We shall find that the possessions he could make himself, upon the measures we have given, would not be very large, nor, even to this day, prejudice the rest of mankind or give them reason to complain or think themselves injured by this man's encroachment, though the race of men have now spread themselves to all the corners of the world, and do infinitely exceed the small number was at the beginning. Nay, the extent of ground is of so little value without labor that I have heard it affirmed that in Spain itself a man may be permitted to plough, sow, and reap, without being disturbed, upon land he has no other title to, but only his making use of it. But, on the contrary, the inhabitants think themselves beholden to him who, by his industry on neglected, and consequently waste land, has increased the stock of corn, which they wanted. But be this as it will, which I lay no stress on, this I dare boldly affirm, that the same rule of propriety—viz., that every man should have as much as he could make use of, would hold still in the world, without straitening anybody, since there is land enough in the world to suffice double the inhabitants, had not the invention of money, and the tacit agreement of men to put a value on it, introduced (by consent) larger possessions and a right to them; which, how it has done, I shall by and by show more at large.

37. This is certain, that in the beginning, before the desire of having more than men needed had altered the intrinsic value of things, which depends only on their usefulness to the life of man, or had agreed that a little piece of yellow metal, which would keep without wasting or decay, should be worth a great piece of flesh or a whole heap of corn, though men had a right to appropriate by their labor, each one to himself, as much of the things of Nature as he could use, yet this could not be much, nor to the prejudice of others, where the same plenty was still left, to those who would use the same industry.

Before the appropriation of land, he who gathered as much of the wild fruit, killed, caught, or tamed as many of the beasts as he could—he that so employed his pains about any of the spontaneous products of Nature as any way to alter them from the state Nature put them in, by placing any of his labor on them, did thereby acquire a propriety in them; but if they perished in his possession without their due use—if the fruits rotted or the venison putrefied before he could spend it, he offended against the common law of Nature, and was liable to be punished: he invaded his neighbor's share, for he had no right farther than his use called for any of them, and they might serve to afford him conveniencies of life.

38. The same measures governed the possession of land, too. Whatsoever he tilled and reaped, laid up and made use of before it spoiled, that was his peculiar right; whatsoever he enclosed, and could feed and make use of, the cattle and product was also his. But if either the grass of his enclosure rotted on the ground, or the fruit of his planting perished without gathering and laying up, this part of the earth, notwithstanding his enclosure, was still to be looked on as waste, and might be the possession of any other. Thus, at the beginning, Cain might take as much ground as he could till and make it his own land, and yet leave enough to Abel's sheep to feed on: a few acres would serve for both their possessions. But as families increased and industry enlarged their stocks, their possessions en-

larged with the need of them; but yet it was commonly without any fixed property in the ground they made use of till they incorporated, settled themselves together, and built cities, and then, by consent, they came in time to set out the bounds of their distinct territories and agree on limits between them and their neighbors, and by laws within themselves settled the properties of those of the same society. For we see that in that part of the world which was first inhabited, and therefore like to be best peopled, even as low down as Abraham's time, they wandered with their flocks and their herds, which was their substance, freely up and down—and this Abraham did in a country where he was a stranger; whence it is plain that, at least, a great part of the land lay in common, that the inhabitants valued it not, nor claimed property in any more than they made use of; but when there was not room enough in the same place for their herds to feed together, they, by consent, as Abraham and Lot did (Gen. xiii. 5), separated and enlarged their pasture where it best liked them. And for the same reason, Esau went from his father and his brother, and planted in Mount Seir (Gen. 36. 6).

39. And thus, without supposing any private dominion and property in Adam over all the world, exclusive of all other men, which can no way be proved, nor any one's property be made out from it, but supposing the world, given as it was to the children of men in common, we see how labor could make men distinct titles to several parcels of it for their private uses, wherein there could be no doubt of right, no room for quarrel.

40. Nor is it so strange as, perhaps, before consideration, it may appear, that the property of labor should be able to overbalance the community of land, for it is labor indeed that puts the difference of value on everything; and let any one consider what the difference is between an acre of land planted with tobacco or sugar, sown with wheat or barley, and an acre of the same land lying in common without any husbandry upon it, and he will find that the improvement of labor makes the far greater part of the value. I think it will be but a very modest computation to say, that of the products of the earth useful to the life of man, nine-tenths are the effects of labor. Nay, if we will rightly estimate things as they come to our use, and cast up the several expenses about them—what in them is purely owing to Nature and what to labor—we shall find that in most of them ninety-nine hundredths are wholly to be put on the account of labor.

41. There cannot be a clearer demonstration of anything than several nations of the Americans are of this, who are rich in land and poor in all the comforts of life; whom Nature, having furnished as liberally as any other people with the materials of plenty—i.e., a fruitful soil, apt to produce in abundance what might serve for food, raiment, and delight; yet, for want of improving it by labor, have not one hundredth part of the conveniencies we enjoy, and a king of a large and fruitful territory there feeds, lodges, and is clad worse than a day laborer in England.

42. To make this a little clearer, let us but trace some of the ordinary provisions of life, through their several progresses, before they come to our use, and see how much they receive of their value from human industry. Bread, wine, and cloth are things of daily use and great plenty; yet notwithstanding acorns, water, and leaves, or skins must be our bread, drink and clothing, did not labor furnish us with these more useful commodities. For

whatever bread is more worth than acorns, wine than water, and cloth or silk than leaves, skins or moss, that is wholly owing to labor and industry. The one of these being the food and raiment which unassisted Nature furnishes us with; the other provisions which our industry and pains prepare for us, which how much they exceed the other in value, when any one hath computed, he will then see how much labor makes the far greatest part of the value of things we enjoy in this world; and the ground which produces the materials is scarce to be reckoned in as any, or at most, but a very small part of it; so little, that even amongst us, land that is left wholly to nature, that hath no improvement of pasturage, tillage, or planting, is called, as indeed it is, waste; and we shall find the benefit of it amount to little more than nothing.

43. An acre of land that bears here twenty bushels of wheat, and another in America, which, with the same husbandry, would do the like, are, without doubt, of the same natural, intrinsic value. But yet the benefit mankind receives from one in a year is worth five pounds, and the other possibly not worth a penny; if all the profit an Indian received from it were to be valued and sold here, at least I may truly say, not one thousandth. It is labor, then, which puts the greatest part of value upon land, without which it would scarcely be worth anything; it is to that we owe the greatest part of all its useful products; for all that the straw, bran, bread, of that acre of wheat, is more worth than the product of an acre of as good land which lies waste is all the effect of labor. For it is not barely the ploughman's pains, the reaper's and thresher's toil, and the baker's sweat, is to be counted into the bread we eat; the labor of those who broke the oxen, who digged and wrought the iron and stones, who felled and framed the timber employed about the plough, mill, oven, or any other utensils, which are a vast number, requisite to this corn, from its sowing to its being made bread, must all be charged on the account of labor, and received as an effect of that; Nature and the earth furnished only the almost worthless materials as in themselves. It would be a strange catalogue of things that industry provided and made use of about every loaf of bread before it came to our use if we could trace them; iron, wood, leather, bark, timber, stone, bricks, coals, lime, cloth, dyeing-drugs, pitch, tar, masts, ropes, and all the materials made use of in the ship that brought any of the commodities made use of by any of the workmen, to any part of the work, all which it would be almost impossible, at least too long, to reckon up.

44. From all which it is evident, that though the things of Nature are given in common, man (by being master of himself, and proprietor of his own person, and the actions or labor of it) had still in himself the great foundation of property; and that which made up the great part of what he applied to the support or comfort of his being, when invention and arts had improved the conveniences of life, was perfectly his own, and did not belong in common to others.

45. Thus labor, in the beginning, gave a right of property, wherever any one was pleased to employ it, upon what was common, which remained a long while, the far greater part, and is yet more than mankind makes use of. Men at first, for the most part, contented themselves with what unassisted Nature offered to their necessities; and though afterwards, in some parts of the world, where the increase of people and stock, with the use of money,

had made land scarce, and so of some value, the several communities settled the bounds of their distinct territories, and, by laws, within themselves, regulated the properties of the private men of their society, and so, by compact and agreement, settled the property which labor and industry began. And the leagues that have been made between several states and kingdoms, either expressly or tacitly disowning all claim and right to the land in the other's possession, have, by common consent, given up their pretences to their natural common right, which originally they had to those countries; and so have, by positive agreement, settled a property amongst themselves, in distinct parts of the world; yet there are still great tracts of ground to be found, which the inhabitants thereof, not having joined with the rest of mankind in the consent of the use of their common money, lie waste, and are more than the people who dwell on it, do, or can make use of, and so still lie in common; though this can scarce happen amongst that part of mankind that have consented to the use of money.

46. The greatest part of things really useful to the life of man, and such as the necessity of subsisting made the first commoners of the world look after—as it doth the Americans now—are generally things of short duration, such as—if they are not consumed by use—will decay and perish of themselves. Gold, silver, and diamonds are things that fancy or agreement hath put the value on, more than real use and the necessary support of life. Now of those good things which Nature hath provided in common, every one hath a right (as hath been said) to as much as he could use; and had a property in all he could effect with his labor; all that his industry could extend to, to alter from the state Nature had put it in, was his. He that gathered a hundred bushels of acorns or apples had thereby a property in them; they were his goods as soon as gathered. He was only to look that he used them before they spoiled, else he took more than his share, and robbed others. And, indeed, it was a foolish thing, as well as dishonest, to hoard up more than he could make use of. If he gave away a part to anybody else, so that it perished not uselessly in his possession, these he also made use of. And if he also bartered away plums that would have rotted in a week, for nuts that would last good for his eating a whole year, he did no injury; he wasted not the common stock; destroyed no part of the portion of goods that belonged to others, so long as nothing perished uselessly in his hands. Again, if he would give his nuts for a piece of metal, pleased with its color or exchange his sheep for shells, or wool for a sparkling pebble or a diamond, and keep those by him all his life, he invaded not the right of others; he might heap up as much of these durable things as he pleased; the exceeding of the bounds of his just property not lying in the largeness of his possession, but the perishing of anything uselessly in it.

47. And thus came in the use of money; some lasting thing that men might keep without spoiling, and that, by mutual consent, men would take in exchange for the truly useful but perishable supports of life.

48. And as different degrees of industry were apt to give men possessions in different proportions, so this invention of money gave them the opportunity to continue and enlarge them. For supposing an island, separate from all possible commerce with the rest of the world, wherein there were but a hundred families, but there were sheep, horses, and cows, with other useful animals, wholesome fruits, and land enough for corn for a hun-

dred thousand times as many, but nothing in the island, either because of its commonness or perishableness, fit to supply the place of money. What reason could any one have there to enlarge his possessions beyond the use of his family, and a plentiful supply to its consumption, either in what their own industry produced, or they could barter for like perishable, useful commodities with others? Where there is not something both lasting and scarce, and so valuable to be hoarded up, there men will not be apt to enlarge their possessions of land, were it ever so rich, ever so free for them to take. For I ask, what would a man value ten thousand or an hundred thousand acres of excellent land, ready cultivated and well stocked, too, with cattle, in the middle of the inland parts of America, where he had no hopes of commerce with other parts of the world, to draw money to him by the sale of the product? It would not be worth the enclosing, and we should see him give up again to the wild common of Nature whatever was more than would supply the conveniences of life, to be had there for him and his family.

49. Thus, in the beginning, all the world was America, and more so than that is now; for no such thing as money was anywhere known. Find out something that hath the use and value of money amongst his neighbors, you shall see the same man will begin presently to enlarge his possessions.

50. But, since gold and silver, being little useful to the life of man, in proportion to food, raiment, and carriage, has its value only from the consent of men—whereof labor yet makes in great part the measure—it is plain that the consent of men have agreed to a disproportionate and unequal possession of the earth—I mean out of the bounds of society and compact; for in governments the laws regulate it; they having, by consent, found out and agreed in a way how a man may, rightfully and without injury, possess more than he himself can make use of by receiving gold and silver, which may continue long in a man's possession without decaying for the overplus, and agreeing those metals should have a value.

51. And thus, I think, it is very easy to conceive, without any difficulty, how labor could at first begin a title of property in the common things of Nature, and how the spending it upon our uses bounded it; so that there could then be no reason of quarrelling about title, nor any doubt about the largeness of possession it gave. Right and conveniency went together. For as a man had a right to all he could employ his labor upon, so he had no temptation to labor for more than he could make use of. This left no room for controversy about the title, nor for encroachment on the right of others. What portion a man carved to himself was easily seen; and it was useless, as well as dishonest, to carve himself too much, or take more than he needed.

Chapter VI

Of Paternal Power

52. It may perhaps be censured as an impertinent criticism in a discourse of this nature to find fault with words and names that have obtained in the world. And yet possibly

it may not be amiss to offer new ones when the old are apt to lead men into mistakes, as this of paternal power probably has done, which seems so to place the power of parents over their children wholly in the father, as if the mother had no share in it; whereas if we consult reason or revelation, we shall find she has an equal title, which may give one reason to ask whether this might not be more properly called parental power? For whatever obligation Nature and the right of generation lays on children, it must certainly bind them equal to both the concurrent causes of it. And accordingly we see the positive law of God everywhere joins them together without distinction, when it commands the obedience of children: "Honor thy father and thy mother" (Exod. 20. 12); "Whosoever curseth his father or his mother" (Lev. 20. 9); "Ye shall fear every man his mother and his father" (Lev. 19. 3); "Children, obey your parents" (Eph. 6. 1), etc., is the style of the Old and New Testament.

53. Had but this one thing been well considered without looking any deeper into the matter, it might perhaps have kept men from running into those gross mistakes they have made about this power of parents, which however it might without any great harshness bear the name of absolute dominion and regal authority, when under the title of "paternal" power, it seemed appropriated to the father; would yet have sounded but oddly, and in the very name shown the absurdity, if this supposed absolute power over children had been called parental, and thereby discovered that it belonged to the mother too. For it will but very ill serve the turn of those men who contend so much for the absolute power and authority of the fatherhood, as they call it, that the mother should have any share in it. And it would have but ill supported the monarchy they contend for, when by the very name it appeared that that fundamental authority from whence they would derive their government of a single person only was not placed in one, but two persons jointly. But to let this of names pass.

54. Though I have said above (Chap. II) "That all men by nature are equal," I cannot be supposed to understand all sorts of "equality." Age or virtue may give men a just precedency. Excellency of parts and merit may place others above the common level. Birth may subject some, and alliance or benefits others, to pay an observance to those to whom Nature, gratitude, or other respects, may have made it due; and yet all this consists with the equality which all men are in respect of jurisdiction or dominion one over another, which was the equality I there spoke of as proper to the business in hand, being that equal right that every man hath to his natural freedom, without being subjected to the will or authority of any other man.

55. Children, I confess, are not born in this full state of equality, though they are born to it. Their parents have a sort of rule and jurisdiction over them when they come into the world, and for some time after, but it is but a temporary one. The bonds of this subjection are like the swaddling clothes they are wrapt up in and supported by in the weakness of their infancy. Age and reason as they grow up loosen them, till at length they drop quite off, and leave a man at his own free disposal.

56. Adam was created a perfect man, his body and mind in full possession of their strength and reason, and so was capable from the first instance of his being to provide for his own support and preservation, and govern his actions according to the dictates of the

law of reason God had implanted in him. From him the world is peopled with his descendants, who are all born infants, weak and helpless, without knowledge or understanding. But to supply the defects of this imperfect state till the improvement of growth and age had removed them, Adam and Eve, and after them all parents were, by the law of Nature, under an obligation to preserve, nourish and educate the children they had begotten, not as their own workmanship, but the workmanship of their own Maker, the Almighty, to whom they were to be accountable for them.

57. The law that was to govern Adam was the same that was to govern all his posterity, the law of reason. But his offspring having another way of entrance into the world, different from him, by a natural birth, that produced them ignorant, and without the use of reason, they were not presently under that law. For nobody can be under a law that is not promulgated to him; and this law being promulgated or made known by reason only, he that is not come to the use of his reason cannot be said to be under this law; and Adam's children being not presently as soon as born under this law of reason, were not presently free. For law, in its true notion, is not so much the limitation as the direction of a free and intelligent agent to his proper interest, and prescribes no farther than is for the general good of those under that law. Could they be happier without it, the law, as a useless thing, would of itself vanish; and that ill deserves the name of confinement which hedges us in only from bogs and precipices. So that however it may be mistaken, the end of law is not to abolish or restrain, but to preserve and enlarge freedom. For in all the states of created beings, capable of laws, where there is no law there is no freedom. For liberty is to be free from restraint and violence from others, which cannot be where there is no law; and is not, as we are told, "a liberty for every man to do what he lists." For who could be free, when every other man's humor might domineer over him? But a liberty to dispose and order freely as he lists his person, actions, possessions, and his whole property within the allowance of those laws under which he is, and therein not to be subject to the arbitrary will of another, but freely follow his own.

58. The power, then, that parents have over their children arises from that duty which is incumbent on them, to take care of their offspring during the imperfect state of childhood. To inform the mind, and govern the actions of their yet ignorant nonage, till reason shall take its place and ease them of that trouble, is what the children want, and the parents are bound to. For God having given man an understanding to direct his actions, has allowed him a freedom of will and liberty of acting, as properly belonging thereunto within the bounds of that law he is under. But whilst he is in an estate wherein he has no understanding of his own to direct his will, he is not to have any will of his own to follow. He that understands for him must will for him too; he must prescribe to his will, and regulate his actions, but when he comes to the estate that made his father a free man, the son is a free man too.

59. This holds in all the laws a man is under, whether natural or civil. Is a man under the law of Nature? What made him free of that law? What gave him a free disposing of his property, according to his own will, within the compass of that law? I answer, an estate wherein he might be supposed capable to know that law, that so he might keep his ac-

tions within the bounds of it. When he has acquired that state, he is presumed to know how far that law is to be his guide, and how far he may make use of his freedom, and so comes to have it; till then, somebody else must guide him, who is presumed to know how far the law allows a liberty. If such a state of reason, such an age of discretion made him free, the same shall make his son free too. Is a man under the law of England? what made him free of that law—that is, to have the liberty to dispose of his actions and possessions, according to his own will, within the permission of that law? a capacity of knowing that law. Which is supposed, by that law, at the age of twenty-one, and in some cases sooner. If this made the father free, it shall make the son free too. Till then, we see the law allows the son to have no will, but he is to be guided by the will of his father or guardian, who is to understand for him. And if the father die and fail to substitute a deputy in this trust, if he hath not provided a tutor to govern his son during his minority, during his want of understanding, the law takes care to do it: some other must govern him and be a will to him till he hath attained to a state of freedom, and his understanding be fit to take the government of his will. But after that the father and son are equally free, as much as tutor and pupil, after nonage, equally subjects of the same law together, without any dominion left in the father over the life, liberty, or estate of his son, whether they be only in the state and under the law of Nature, or under the positive laws of an established government.

60. But if through defects that may happen out of the ordinary course of Nature, any one comes not to such a degree of reason wherein he might be supposed capable of knowing the law, and so living within the rules of it, he is never capable of being a free man, he is never let loose to the disposure of his own will; because he knows no bounds to it, has not understanding, its proper guide, but is continued under the tuition and government of others all the time his own understanding is incapable of that charge. And so lunatics and idiots are never set free from the government of their parents: "Children who are not as yet come unto those years whereat they may have, and innocents, which are excluded by a natural defect from ever having." Thirdly: "Madmen, which, for the present, cannot possibly have the use of right reason to guide themselves, have, for their guide, the reason that guideth other men which are tutors over them, to seek and procure their good for them," says Hooker (*Eccl. Pol.*, lib. i., s. 7). All which seems no more than that duty which God and Nature has laid on man, as well as other creatures, to preserve their offspring till they can be able to shift for themselves, and will scarce amount to an instance or proof of parents' regal authority.

61. Thus we are born free as we are born rational; not that we have actually the exercise of either: age that brings one, brings with it the other too. And thus we see how natural freedom and subjection to parents may consist together, and are both founded on the same principle. A child is free by his father's title, by his father's understanding, which is to govern him till he hath it of his own. The freedom of a man at years of discretion, and the subjection of a child to his parents, whilst yet short of it, are so consistent and so distinguishable that the most blinded contenders for monarchy, "by right of fatherhood," cannot miss of it; the most obstinate cannot but allow of it. For were their doctrine all true, were the right heir of Adam now known, and, by that title, settled a monarch in his

throne, invested with all the absolute unlimited power Sir Robert Filmer talks of, if he should die as soon as his heir were born, must not the child, notwithstanding he were never so free, never so much sovereign, be in subjection to his mother and nurse, to tutors and governors, till age and education brought him reason and ability to govern himself and others? The necessities of his life, the health of his body, and the information of his mind would require him to be directed by the will of others and not his own; and yet will any one think that this restraint and subjection were inconsistent with, or spoiled him of, that liberty or sovereignty he had a right to, or gave away his empire to those who had the government of his nonage? This government over him only prepared him the better and sooner for it. If anybody should ask me when my son is of age to be free, I shall answer, just when his monarch is of age to govern. "But at what time," says the judicious Hooker (*Eccl. Pol.*, lib. i., s. 6), "a man may be said to have attained so far forth the use of reason as sufficeth to make him capable of those laws whereby he is then bound to guide his actions; this is a great deal more easy for sense to discern than for any one, by skill and learning, to determine."

62. Commonwealths themselves take notice of, and allow that there is a time when men are to begin to act like free men, and therefore, till that time, require not oaths of fealty or allegiance, or other public owning of, or submission to, the government of their countries.

63. The freedom then of man, and liberty of acting according to his own will, is grounded on his having reason, which is able to instruct him in that law he is to govern himself by, and make him know how far he is left to the freedom of his own will. To turn him loose to an unrestrained liberty, before he has reason to guide him, is not the allowing him the privilege of his nature to be free, but to thrust him out amongst brutes, and abandon him to a state as wretched and as much beneath that of a man as theirs. This is that which puts the authority into the parents' hands to govern the minority of their children. God hath made it their business to employ this care on their offspring, and hath placed in them suitable inclinations of tenderness and concern to temper this power, to apply it as His wisdom designed it, to the children's good as long as they should need to be under it.

64. But what reason can hence advance this care of the parents due to their offspring into an absolute, arbitrary dominion of the father, whose power reaches no farther than by such a discipline as he finds most effectual to give such strength and health to their bodies, such vigor and rectitude to their minds, as may best fit his children to be most useful to themselves and others, and, if it be necessary to his condition, to make them work when they are able for their own subsistence; but in this power the mother, too, has her share with the father.

65. Nay, this power so little belongs to the father by any peculiar right of Nature, but only as he is guardian of his children, that when he quits his care of them he loses his power over them, which goes along with their nourishment and education, to which it is inseparably annexed, and belongs as much to the foster-father of an exposed child as to the natural father of another. So little power does the bare act of begetting give a

man over his issue, if all his care ends there, and this be all the title he hath to the name and authority of a father. And what will become of this paternal power in that part of the world where one woman hath more than one husband at a time? or in those parts of America where, when the husband and wife part, which happens frequently, the children are all left to the mother, follow her, and are wholly under her care and provision? And if the father die whilst the children are young, do they not naturally everywhere owe the same obedience to their mother, during their minority, as to their father, were he alive? And will any one say that the mother hath a legislative power over her children that she can make standing rules which shall be of perpetual obligation, by which they ought to regulate all the concerns of their property, and bound their liberty all the course of their lives, and enforce the observation of them with capital punishments? For this is the proper power of the magistrate, of which the father hath not so much as the shadow. His command over his children is but temporary, and reaches not their life or property. It is but a help to the weakness and imperfection of their nonage, a discipline necessary to their education. And though a father may dispose of his own possessions as he pleases when his children are out of danger of perishing for want, yet his power extends not to the lives or goods which either their own industry, or another's bounty, has made theirs, nor to their liberty neither when they are once arrived to the enfranchisement of the years of discretion. The father's empire then ceases, and he can from thenceforward no more dispose of the liberty of his son than that of any other man. And it must be far from an absolute or perpetual jurisdiction from which a man may withdraw himself, having license from Divine authority to "leave father and mother and cleave to his wife."

66. But though there be a time when a child comes to be as free from subjection to the will and command of his father as he himself is free from subjection to the will of anybody else, and they are both under no other restraint but that which is common to them both, whether it be the law of Nature or municipal law of their country, yet this freedom exempts not a son from that honor which he ought, by the law of God and Nature, to pay his parents, God having made the parents instruments in His great design of continuing the race of mankind and the occasions of life to their children. As He hath laid on them an obligation to nourish, preserve, and bring up their offspring, so He has laid on the children a perpetual obligation of honoring their parents, which, containing in it an inward esteem and reverence to be shown by all outward expressions, ties up the child from anything that may ever injure or affront, disturb or endanger the happiness or life of those from whom he received his, and engages him in all actions of defense, relief, assistance, and comfort of those by whose means he entered into being and has been made capable of any enjoyments of life. From this obligation no state, no freedom, can absolve children. But this is very far from giving parents a power of command over their children, or an authority to make laws and dispose as they please of their lives or liberties. It is one thing to owe honor, respect, gratitude, and assistance; another to require an absolute obedience and submission. The honor due to parents a monarch on his throne owes his mother, and yet this lessens not his authority nor subjects him to her government.

67. The subjection of a minor places in the father a temporary government which terminates with the minority of the child; and the honor due from a child places in the parents a perpetual right to respect, reverence, support, and compliance, to more or less, as the father's care, cost, and kindness in his education has been more or less, and this ends not with minority, but holds in all parts and conditions of a man's life. The want of distinguishing these two powers which the father hath, in the right of tuition, during minority, and the right of honor all his life, may perhaps have caused a great part of the mistakes about this matter. For, to speak properly of them, the first of these is rather the privilege of children and duty of parents than any prerogative of paternal power. The nourishment and education of their children is a charge so incumbent on parents for their children's good, that nothing can absolve them from taking care of it. And though the power of commanding and chastising them go along with it, yet God hath woven into the principles of human nature such a tenderness for their offspring, that there is little fear that parents should use their power with too much rigor; the excess is seldom on the severe side, the strong bias of nature drawing the other way. And therefore God Almighty, when He would express His gentle dealing with the Israelites, He tells them that though He chastened them, "He chastened them as a man chastens his son" (Deut. 8. 5)—i.e., with tenderness and affection, and kept them under no severer discipline than what was absolutely best for them, and had been less kindness, to have slackened. This is that power to which children are commanded obedience, that the pains and care of their parents may not be increased or ill-rewarded.

68. On the other side, honor and support all that which gratitude requires to return; for the benefits received by and from them is the indispensable duty of the child and the proper privilege of the parents. This is intended for the parents' advantage, as the other is for the child's; though education, the parents' duty, seems to have most power, because the ignorance and infirmities of childhood stand in need of restraint and correction, which is a visible exercise of rule and a kind of dominion. And that duty which is comprehended in the word "honor" requires less obedience, though the obligation be stronger on grown than younger children. For who can think the command, "Children, obey your parents," requires in a man that has children of his own the same submission to his father as it does in his yet young children to him, and that by this precept he were bound to obey all his father's commands, if, out of a conceit of authority, he should have the indiscretion to treat him still as a boy?

69. The first part, then, of paternal power, or rather duty, which is education, belongs so to the father that it terminates at a certain season. When the business of education is over it ceases of itself, and is also alienable before. For a man may put the tuition of his son in other hands; and he that has made his son an apprentice to another has discharged him, during that time, of a great part of his obedience, both to himself and to his mother. But all the duty of honor, the other part, remains nevertheless entire to them; nothing can cancel that. It is so inseparable from them both, that the father's authority cannot dispossess the mother of this right, nor can any man discharge his son from honoring her that bore him. But both these are very far from a power to make laws, and en-

forcing them with penalties that may reach estate, liberty, limbs, and life. The power of commanding ends with nonage, and though after that honor and respect, support and defense, and whatsoever gratitude can oblige a man to, for the highest benefits he is naturally capable of be always due from a son to his parents, yet all this puts no sceptre into the father's hand, no sovereign power of commanding. He has no dominion over his son's property or actions, nor any right that his will should prescribe to his son's in all things; however, it may become his son in many things, not very inconvenient to him and his family, to pay a deference to it.

70. A man may owe honor and respect to an ancient or wise man, defense to his child or friend, relief and support to the distressed, and gratitude to a benefactor, to such a degree that all he has, all he can do, cannot sufficiently pay it. But all these give no authority, no right of making laws to any one over him from whom they are owing. And it is plain all this is due, not to the bare title of father, not only because as has been said, it is owing to the mother too, but because these obligations to parents, and the degrees of what is required of children, may be varied by the different care and kindness trouble and expense, is often employed upon one child more than another.

71. This shows the reason how it comes to pass that parents in societies, where they themselves are subjects, retain a power over their children and have as much right to their subjection as those who are in the state of Nature, which could not possibly be if all political power were only paternal, and that, in truth, they were one and the same thing; for then, all paternal power being in the prince, the subject could naturally have none of it. But these two powers, political and paternal, are so perfectly distinct and separate, and built upon so different foundations, and given to so different ends, that every subject that is a father has as much a paternal power over his children as the prince has over his. And every prince that has parents owes them as much filial duty and obedience as the meanest of his subjects do to theirs, and can therefore contain not any part or degree of that kind of dominion which a prince or magistrate has over his subject.

72. Though the obligation on the parents to bring up their children, and the obligation on children to honor their parents, contain all the power, on the one hand, and submission on the other, which are proper to this relation, yet there is another power ordinarily in the father, whereby he has a tie on the obedience of his children, which, though it be common to him with other men, yet the occasions of showing it, almost constantly happening to fathers in their private families and in instances of it elsewhere being rare, and less taken notice of, it passes in the world for a part of "paternal jurisdiction." And this is the power men generally have to bestow their estates on those who please them best. The possession of the father being the expectation and inheritance of the children ordinarily, in certain proportions, according to the law and custom of each country, yet it is commonly in the father's power to bestow it with a more sparing or liberal hand, according as the behavior of this or that child hath comported with his will and humor.

73. This is no small tie to the obedience of children; and there being always annexed to the enjoyment of land a submission to the government of the country of which that land is a part, it has been commonly supposed that a father could oblige his posteri-

ty to that government of which he himself was a subject, that his compact held them; whereas, it being only a necessary condition annexed to the land which is under that government, reaches only those who will take it on that condition, and so is no natural tie or engagement, but a voluntary submission; for every man's children being, by Nature, as free as himself or any of his ancestors ever were, may, whilst they are in that freedom, choose what society they will join themselves to, what commonwealth they will put themselves under. But if they will enjoy the inheritance of their ancestors, they must take it on the same terms their ancestors had it, and submit to all the conditions annexed to such a possession. By this power, indeed, fathers oblige their children to obedience to themselves even when they are past minority, and most commonly, too, subject them to this or that political power. But neither of these by any peculiar right of fatherhood, but by the reward they have in their hands to enforce and recompense such a compliance, and is no more power than what a Frenchman has over an Englishman, who, by the hopes of an estate he will leave him, will certainly have a strong tie on his obedience; and if when it is left him, he will enjoy it, he must certainly take it upon the conditions annexed to the possession of land in that country where it lies, whether it be France or England.

74. To conclude, then, though the father's power of commanding extends no farther than the minority of his children, and to a degree only fit for the discipline and government of that age; and though that honor and respect, and all that which the Latins called piety, which they indispensably owe to their parents all their lifetime, and in all estates, with all that support and defense, is due to them, gives the father no power of governing—i.e., making laws and exacting penalties on his children; though by this he has no dominion over the property or actions of his son, yet it is obvious to conceive how easy it was, in the first ages of the world, and in places still where the thinness of people gives families leave to separate into unpossessed quarters, and they have room to remove and plant themselves in yet vacant habitations, for the father of the family to become the prince of it; he had been a ruler from the beginning of the infancy of his children; and when they were grown up, since without some government it would be hard for them to live together, it was likeliest it should, by the express or tacit consent of the children, be in the father, where it seemed, without any change, barely to continue. And when, indeed, nothing more was required to it than the permitting the father to exercise alone in his family that executive power of the law of Nature which every free man naturally hath, and by that permission resigning up to him a monarchical power whilst they remained in it. But that this was not by any paternal right, but only by the consent of his children, is evident from hence, that nobody doubts but if a stranger, whom chance or business had brought to his family, had there killed any of his children, or committed any other act, he might condemn and put him to death, or otherwise have punished him as well as any of his children. which was impossible he should do by virtue of any paternal authority over one who was not his child, but by virtue of that executive power of the law of Nature which, as a man, he had a right to; and he alone could punish him in his family where the respect of his children had laid by the exercise of such a power, to give way to the dignity and authority they were willing should remain in him above the rest of his family.

75. Thus it was easy and almost natural for children, by a tacit and almost natural consent, to make way for the father's authority and government. They had been accustomed in their childhood to follow his direction, and to refer their little differences to him; and when they were men, who was fitter to rule them? Their little properties and less covetousness seldom afforded greater controversies; and when any should arise, where could they have a fitter umpire than he, by whose care they had every one been sustained and brought up. and who had a tenderness for them all? It is no wonder that they made no distinction betwixt minority and full age, nor looked after one-and-twenty, or any other age, that might make them the free disposers of themselves and fortunes, when they could have no desire to be out of their pupilage. The government they had been under during it continued still to be more their protection than restraint; and they could nowhere find a greater security to their peace, liberties, and fortunes than in the rule of a father.

76. Thus the natural fathers of families, by an insensible change, became the politic monarchs of them too; and as they chanced to live long, and leave able and worthy heirs for several successions or otherwise, so they laid the foundations of hereditary or elective kingdoms under several constitutions and manors, according as chance, contrivance, or occasions happened to mould them. But if princes have their titles in the father's right, and it be a sufficient proof of the natural right of fathers to political authority, because they commonly were those in whose hands we find, *de facto*, the exercise of government, I say, if this argument be good, it will as strongly prove that all princes, nay, princes only, ought to be priests, since it is as certain that in the beginning "the father of the family was priest, as that he was ruler in his own household."

Chapter VII

Of Political or Civil Society

77. God, having made man such a creature that, in His own judgment, it was not good for him to be alone, put him under strong obligations of necessity, convenience, and inclination, to drive him into society, as well as fitted him with understanding and language to continue and enjoy it. The first society was between man and wife, which gave beginning to that between parents and children, to which, in time, that between master and servant came to be added. And though all these might, and commonly did, meet together, and make up but one family, wherein the master or mistress of it had some sort of rule proper to a family, each of these, or all together, came short of "political society," as we shall see if we consider the different ends, ties, and bounds of each of these.

78. Conjugal society is made by a voluntary compact between man and woman, and though it consist chiefly in such a communion and right in one another's bodies as is necessary to its chief end, procreation, yet it draws with it mutual support and assistance, and a communion of interests too, as necessary not only to unite their care and affection,

but also necessary to their common offspring, who have a right to be nourished and maintained by them till they are able to provide for themselves.

79. For the end of conjunction between male and female being not barely procreation, but the continuation of the species, this conjunction betwixt male and female ought to last, even after procreation, so long as is necessary to the nourishment and support of the young ones, who are to be sustained by those that got them till they are able to shift and provide for themselves. This rule, which the infinite wise Maker hath set to the works of His hands, we find the inferior creatures steadily obey. In those vivaporous animals which feed on grass the conjunction between male and female lasts no longer than the very act of copulation, because the teat of the dam being sufficient to nourish the young till it be able to feed on grass. the male only begets, but concerns not himself for the female or young, to whose sustenance he can contribute nothing. But in beasts of prey the conjunction lasts longer because the dam, not being able well to subsist herself and nourish her numerous offspring by her own prey alone (a more laborious as well as more dangerous way of living than by feeding on grass), the assistance of the male is necessary to the maintenance of their common family, which cannot subsist till they are able to prey for themselves, but by the joint care of male and female. The same is observed in all birds (except some domestic ones, where plenty of food excuses the cock from feeding and taking care of the young brood), whose young, needing food in the nest, the cock and hen continue mates till the young are able to use their wings and provide for themselves.

80. And herein, I think, lies the chief, if not the only reason, why the male and female in mankind are tied to a longer conjunction than other creatures—viz., because the female is capable of conceiving, and, *de facto*, is commonly with child again, and brings forth too a new birth, long before the former is out of a dependency for support on his parents' help and able to shift for himself and has all the assistance due to him from his parents, whereby the father, who is bound to take care for those he hath begot, is under an obligation to continue in conjugal society with the same woman longer than other creatures, whose young, being able to subsist of themselves before the time of procreation returns again, the conjugal bond dissolves of itself, and they are at liberty till Hymen, at his usual anniversary season, summons them again to choose new mates. Wherein one cannot but admire the wisdom of the great Creator, who, having given to man an ability to lay up for the future as well as supply the present necessity, hath made it necessary that society of man and wife should be more lasting than of male and female amongst other creatures, that so their industry might be encouraged, and their interest better united, to make provision and lay up goods for their common issue, which uncertain mixture, or easy and frequent solutions of conjugal society, would mightily disturb.

81. But though these are ties upon mankind which make the conjugal bonds more firm and lasting in a man than the other species of animals, yet it would give one reason to inquire why this compact, where procreation and education are secured and inheritance taken care for, may not be made determinable, either by consent, or at a certain time, or upon certain conditions, as well as any other voluntary compacts, there being no necessity, in the nature of the thing, nor to the ends of it, that it should always be for life—I

mean, to such as are under no restraint of any positive law which ordains all such contracts to be perpetual.

82. But the husband and wife, though they have but one common concern, yet having different understandings, will unavoidably sometimes have different wills too. It therefore being necessary that the last determination (i.e., the rule) should be placed somewhere, it naturally falls to the man's share as the abler and the stronger. But this, reaching but to the things of their common interest and property, leaves the wife in the full and true possession of what by contract is her peculiar right, and at least gives the husband no more power over her than she has over his life; the power of the husband being so far from that of an absolute monarch that the wife has, in many cases, a liberty to separate from him where natural right or their contract allows it, whether that contract be made by themselves in the state of Nature or by the customs or laws of the country they live in, and the children, upon such separation, fall to the father or mother's lot as such contract does determine.

83. For all the ends of marriage being to be obtained under politic government, as well as in the state of Nature, the civil magistrate doth not abridge the right or power of either, naturally necessary to those ends—viz., procreation and mutual support and assistance whilst they are together, but only decides any controversy that may arise between man and wife about them. If it were otherwise, and that absolute sovereignty and power of life and death naturally belonged to the husband, and were necessary to the society between man and wife, there could be no matrimony in any of these countries where the husband is allowed no such absolute authority. But the ends of matrimony requiring no such power in the husband, it was not at all necessary to it. The condition of conjugal society put it not in him; but whatsoever might consist with procreation and support of the children till they could shift for themselves—mutual assistance, comfort, and maintenance—might be varied and regulated by that contract which first united them in that society, nothing being necessary to any society that is not necessary to the ends for which it is made.

84. The society betwixt parents and children, and the distinct rights and powers belonging respectively to them, I have treated of so largely in the foregoing chapter that I shall not here need to say anything of it; and I think it is plain that it is far different from a politic society.

85. Master and servant are names as old as history, but given to those of far different condition; for a free man makes himself a servant to another by selling him for a certain time the service he undertakes to do in exchange for wages he is to receive; and though this commonly puts him into the family of his master, and under the ordinary discipline thereof, yet it gives the master but a temporary power over him, and no greater than what is contained in the contract between them. But there is another sort of servant which by a peculiar name we call slaves, who being captives taken in a just war are, by the right of Nature, subjected to the absolute dominion and arbitrary power of their masters. These men having, as I say, forfeited their lives and, with it, their liberties, and lost their estates, and being in the state of slavery, not capable of any property, cannot in that state be considered as any part of civil society, the chief end whereof is the preservation of property.

86. Let us therefore consider a master of a family with all these subordinate relations of wife, children, servants and slaves, united under the domestic rule of a family, with what resemblance soever it may have in its order, offices, and number too, with a little commonwealth, yet is very far from it both in its constitution, power, and end; or if it must be thought a monarchy, and the paterfamilias the absolute monarch in it, absolute monarchy will have but a very shattered and short power, when it is plain by what has been said before, that the master of the family has a very distinct and differently limited power both as to time and extent over those several persons that are in it; for excepting the slave (and the family is as much a family, and his power as paterfamilias as great, whether there be any slaves in his family or no) he has no legislative power of life and death over any of them, and none too but what a mistress of a family may have as well as he. And he certainly can have no absolute power over the whole family who has but a very limited one over every individual in it. But how a family, or any other society of men, differ from that which is properly political society, we shall best see by considering wherein political society itself consists.

87. Man being born, as has been proved, with a title to perfect freedom and an uncontrolled enjoyment of all the rights and privileges of the law of Nature, equally with any other man, or number of men in the world, hath by nature a power not only to preserve his property—that is, his life, liberty, and estate, against the injuries and attempts of other men, but to judge of and punish the breaches of that law in others, as he is persuaded the offence deserves, even with death itself, in crimes where the heinousness of the fact, in his opinion, requires it. But because no political society can be, nor subsist, without having in itself the power to preserve the property, and in order thereunto punish the offences of all those of that society, there, and there only, is political society where every one of the members hath quitted this natural power, resigned it up into the hands of the community in all cases that exclude him not from appealing for protection to the law established by it. And thus all private judgment of every particular member being excluded, the community comes to be umpire, and by understanding indifferent rules and men authorized by the community for their execution, decides all the differences that may happen between any members of that society concerning any matter of right, and punishes those offences which any member hath committed against the society with such penalties as the law has established; whereby it is easy to discern who are, and are not, in political society together. Those who are united into one body, and have a common established law and judicature to appeal to, with authority to decide controversies between them and punish offenders, are in civil society one with another; but those who have no such common appeal, I mean on earth, are still in the state of Nature, each being where there is no other, judge for himself and executioner; which is, as I have before showed it, the perfect state of Nature.

88. And thus the commonwealth comes by a power to set down what punishment shall belong to the several transgressions they think worthy of it, committed amongst the members of that society (which is the power of making laws), as well as it has the power to punish any injury done unto any of its members by any one that is not of it (which is the power of war and peace); and all this for the preservation of the property of all the

members of that society, as far as is possible. But though every man entered into society has quitted his power to punish offences against the law of Nature in prosecution of his own private judgment, yet with the judgment of offences which he has given up to the legislative, in all cases where he can appeal to the magistrate, he has given up a right to the commonwealth to employ his force for the execution of the judgments of the commonwealth whenever he shall be called to it, which, indeed, are his own judgements, they being made by himself or his representative. And herein we have the original of the legislative and executive power of civil society, which is to judge by standing laws how far offences are to be punished when committed within the commonwealth; and also by occasional judgments founded on the present circumstances of the fact, how far injuries from without are to be vindicated, and in both these to employ all the force of all the members when there shall be need.

89. Wherever, therefore, any number of men so unite into one society as to quit every one his executive power of the law of Nature, and to resign it to the public, there and there only is a political or civil society. And this is done wherever any number of men, in the state of Nature, enter into society to make one people one body politic under one supreme government: or else when any one joins himself to, and incorporates with any government already made. For hereby he authorizes the society, or which is all one, the legislative thereof, to make laws for him as the public good of the society shall require, to the execution whereof his own assistance (as to his own decrees) is due. And this puts men out of a state of Nature into that of a commonwealth, by setting up a judge on earth with authority to determine all the controversies and redress the injuries that may happen to any member of the commonwealth, which judge is the legislative or magistrates appointed by it. And wherever there are any number of men, however associated, that have no such decisive power to appeal to, there they are still in the state of Nature.

90. And hence it is evident that absolute monarchy, which by some men is counted for the only government in the world, is indeed inconsistent with civil society, and so can be not form of civil government at all. For the end of civil society being to avoid and remedy those inconveniences of the state of Nature which necessarily follow from every man's being judge in his own case, by setting up a known authority to which every one of that society may appeal upon any injury received, or controversy that may arise, and which every one of the society ought to obey. Wherever any persons are who have not such an authority to appeal to, and decide any difference between them there, those persons are still in the state of Nature. And so is every absolute prince in respect of those who are under his dominion.

91. For he being supposed to have all, both legislative and executive, power in himself alone, there is no judge to be found, no appeal lies open to any one, who may fairly and indifferently, and with authority decide, and from whence relief and redress may be expected of any injury or inconveniency that may be suffered from him, or by his order. So that such a man, however entitled, Czar, or Grand Signior, or how you please, is as much in the state of Nature, with all under his dominion, as he is with the rest of mankind. For wherever any two men are, who have no standing rule and common judge to appeal to on

earth, for the determination of controversies of right betwixt them, there they are still in the state of Nature, and under all the inconveniencies of it, with only this woeful difference to the subject, or rather slave of an absolute prince. That whereas, in the ordinary state of Nature, he has a liberty to judge of his right, according to the best of his power to maintain it; but whenever his property is invaded by the will and order of his monarch, he has not only no appeal, as those in society ought to have, but, as if he were degraded from the common state of rational creatures, is denied a liberty to judge of, or defend his right, and so is exposed to all the misery and inconveniencies that a man can fear from one, who being in the unrestrained state of Nature, is yet corrupted with flattery and armed with power.

92. For he that thinks absolute power purifies men's blood, and corrects the baseness of human nature, need read but the history of this, or any other age, to be convinced to the contrary. He that would have been insolent and injurious in the woods of America would not probably be much better on a throne, where perhaps learning and religion shall be found out to justify all that he shall do to his subjects, and the sword presently silence all those that dare question it. For what the protection of absolute monarchy is, what kind of fathers of their countries it makes princes to be, and to what a degree of happiness and security it carries civil society, where this sort of government is grown to perfection, he that will look into the late relation of Ceylon may easily see.

93. In absolute monarchies, indeed, as well as other governments of the world, the subjects have an appeal to the law, and judges to decide any controversies, and restrain any violence that may happen betwixt the subjects themselves, one amongst another. This every one thinks necessary, and believes; he deserves to be thought a declared enemy to society and mankind who should go about to take it away. But whether this be from a true love of mankind and society, and such a charity as we owe all one to another, there is reason to doubt. For this is no more than what every man, who loves his own power, profit, or greatness, may, and naturally must do, keep those animals from hurting or destroying one another who labor and drudge only for his pleasure and advantage; and so are taken care of, not out of any love the master has for them, but love of himself, and the profit they bring him. For if it be asked what security, what fence is there in such a state against the violence and oppression of this absolute ruler, the very question can scarce be borne. They are ready to tell you that it deserves death only to ask after safety. Betwixt subject and subject, they will grant, there must be measures, laws, and judges for their mutual peace and security. But as for the ruler, he ought to be absolute, and is above all such circumstances; because he has a power to do more hurt and wrong, it is right when he does it. To ask how you may be guarded from harm or injury on that side, where the strongest hand is to do it, is presently the voice of faction and rebellion. As if when men, quitting the state of Nature, entered into society, they agreed that all of them but one should be under the restraint of laws; but that he should still retain all the liberty of the state of Nature, increased with power, and made licentious by impunity. This is to think that men are so foolish that they take care to avoid what mischiefs may be done them by polecats or foxes, but are content, nay, think it safety, to be devoured by lions.

94. But, whatever flatterers may talk to amuse people's understandings, it never hinders men from feeling; and when they perceive that any man, in what station soever, is out of the bounds of the civil society they are of, and that they have no appeal, on earth, against any harm they may receive from him, they are apt to think themselves in the state of Nature, in respect of him whom they find to be so; and to take care, as soon as they can, to have that safety and security, in civil society, for which it was first instituted, and for which only they entered into it. And therefore, though perhaps at first, as shall be showed more at large hereafter, in the following part of this discourse, some one good and excellent man having got a pre-eminency amongst the rest, had this deference paid to his goodness and virtue, as to a kind of natural authority, that the chief rule, with arbitration of their differences, by a tacit consent devolved into his hands, without any other caution but the assurance they had of his uprightness and wisdom; yet when time giving authority, and, as some men would persuade us, sacredness to customs, which the negligent and unforeseeing innocence of the first ages began, had brought in successors of another stamp, the people finding their properties not secure under the government as then it was (whereas government has no other end but the preservation of property), could never be safe, nor at rest, nor think themselves in civil society, till the legislative was so placed in collective bodies of men, call them senate, parliament, or what you please, by which means every single person became subject equally with other the meanest men, to those laws, which he himself, as part of the legislative, had established; nor could any one, by his own authority, avoid the force of the law, when once made, nor by any pretence of superiority plead exemption, thereby to license his own, or the miscarriages of any of his dependants. No man in civil society can be exempted from the laws of it. For if any man may do what he thinks fit and there be no appeal on earth for redress or security against any harm he shall do, I ask whether he be not perfectly still in the state of Nature, and so can be no part or member of that civil society, unless any one will say the state of Nature and civil society are one and the same thing, which I have never yet found any one so great a patron of anarchy as to affirm.

Chapter VIII

Of the Beginning of Political Societies

95. Men being, as has been said, by nature all free, equal, and independent, no one can be put out of this estate and subjected to the political power of another without his own consent, which is done by agreeing with other men, to join and unite into a community for their comfortable, safe, and peaceable living, one amongst another, in a secure enjoyment of their properties, and a greater security against any that are not of it. This any number of men may do, because it injures not the freedom of the rest; they are left, as they were, in the liberty of the state of Nature. When any number of men have so consented to make one community or government, they are thereby presently incorporated, and make one body politic, wherein the majority have a right to act and conclude the rest.

96. For, when any number of men have, by the consent of every individual, made a community, they have thereby made that community one body, with a power to act as one body, which is only by the will and determination of the majority. For that which acts any community, being only the consent of the individuals of it, and it being one body, must move one way, it is necessary the body should move that way whither the greater force carries it, which is the consent of the majority, or else it is impossible it should act or continue one body, one community, which the consent of every individual that united into it agreed that it should; and so every one is bound by that consent to be concluded by the majority. And therefore we see that in assemblies empowered to act by positive laws where no number is set by that positive law which empowers them, the act of the majority passes for the act of the whole, and of course determines as having, by the law of Nature and reason, the power of the whole.

97. And thus every man, by consenting with others to make one body politic under one government, puts himself under an obligation to every one of that society to submit to the determination of the majority, and to be concluded by it; or else this original compact, whereby he with others incorporates into one society, would signify nothing, and be no compact if he be left free and under no other ties than he was in before in the state of Nature. For what appearance would there be of any compact? What new engagement if he were no farther tied by any decrees of the society than he himself thought fit and did actually consent to? This would be still as great a liberty as he himself had before his compact, or any one else in the state of Nature, who may submit himself and consent to any acts of it if he thinks fit.

98. For if the consent of the majority shall not in reason be received as the act of the whole, and conclude every individual, nothing but the consent of every individual can make anything to be the act of the whole, which, considering the infirmities of health and avocations of business, which in a number though much less than that of a commonwealth, will necessarily keep many away from the public assembly; and the variety of opinions and contrariety of interests which unavoidably happen in all collections of men, it is next impossible ever to be had. And, therefore, if coming into society be upon such terms, it will be only like Cato's coming into the theatre, *tantum ut exiret.* Such a constitution as this would make the mighty leviathan of a shorter duration than the feeblest creatures, and not let it outlast the day it was born in, which cannot be supposed till we can think that rational creatures should desire and constitute societies only to be dissolved. For where the majority cannot conclude the rest, there they cannot act as one body, and consequently will be immediately dissolved again.

99. Whosoever, therefore, out of a state of Nature unite into a community, must be understood to give up all the power necessary to the ends for which they unite into society to the majority of the community, unless they expressly agreed in any number greater than the majority. And this is done by barely agreeing to unite into one political society, which is all the compact that is, or needs be, between the individuals that enter into or make up a commonwealth. And thus, that which begins and actually constitutes any political society is nothing but the consent of any number of freemen capable of majority,

to unite and incorporate into such a society. And this is that, and that only, which did or could give beginning to any lawful government in the world.

100. To this I find two objections made:

First, that there are no instances to be found in story of a company of men, independent and equal one amongst another, that met together, and in this way began and set up a government.

Secondly, it is impossible of right that men should do so, because all men, being born under government, they are to submit to that, and are not at liberty to begin a new one.

101. To the first there is this to answer: That it is not at all to be wondered that history gives us but a very little account of men that lived together in the state of Nature. The inconveniencies of that condition, and the love and want of society, no sooner brought any number of them together, but they presently united and incorporated if they designed to continue together. And if we may not suppose men ever to have been in the state of Nature, because we hear not much of them in such a state, we may as well suppose the armies of Salmanasser or Xerxes were never children, because we hear little of them till they were men and embodied in armies. Government is everywhere antecedent to records, and letters seldom come in amongst a people till a long continuation of civil society has, by other more necessary arts, provided for their safety, ease, and plenty. And then they begin to look after the history of their founders, and search into their original when they have outlived the memory of it. For it is with commonwealths as with particular persons, they are commonly ignorant of their own births and infancies; and if they know anything of it, they are beholding for it to the accidental records that others have kept of it. And those that we have of the beginning of any polities in the world, excepting that of the Jews, where God Himself immediately interposed, and which favors not at all paternal dominion, are all either plain instances of such a beginning as I have mentioned, or at least have manifest footsteps of it.

102. He must show a strange inclination to deny evident matter of fact, when it agrees not with his hypothesis, who will not allow that the beginning of Rome and Venice were by the uniting together of several men, free and independent one of another, amongst whom there was no natural superiority or subjection. And if Josephus Acosta's word may be taken, he tells us that in many parts of America there was no government at all. "There are great and apparent conjectures," says he, "that these men [speaking of those of Peru] for a long time had neither kings nor commonwealths, but lived in troops, as they do this day in Florida—the Cheriquanas, those of Brazil, and many other nations, which have no certain kings, but, as occasion is offered in peace or war, they choose their captains as they please" (lib. i. cap. 25). If it be said, that every man there was born subject to his father, or the head of his family, that the subjection due from a child to a father took away not his freedom of uniting into what political society he thought fit, has been already proved; but be that as it will, these men, it is evident, were actually free; and whatever superiority some politicians now would place in any of them, they themselves claimed it not; but, by consent, were all equal, till, by the same consent, they set rulers over themselves. So that their

politic societies all began from a voluntary union, and the mutual agreement of men freely acting in the choice of their governors and forms of government.

103. And I hope those who went away from Sparta, with Palantus, mentioned by Justin, will be allowed to have been freemen independent one of another, and to have set up a government over themselves by their own consent. Thus I have given several examples out of history of people, free and in the state of Nature, that, being met together, incorporated and began a commonwealth. And if the want of such instances be an argument to prove that government were not nor could not be so begun, I suppose the contenders for paternal empire were better let it alone than urge it against natural liberty; for if they can give so many instances out of history of governments begun upon paternal right, I think (though at least an argument from what has been to what should of right be of no great force) one might, without any great danger, yield them the cause. But if I might advise them in the case, they would do well not to search too much into the original of governments as they have begun *de facto*, lest they should find at the foundation of most of them something very little favorable to the design they promote, and such a power as they contend for.

104. But, to conclude: reason being plain on our side that men are naturally free; and the examples of history showing that the governments of the world, that were begun in peace, had their beginning laid on that foundation, and were made by the consent of the people; there can be little room for doubt, either where the right is, or what has been the opinion or practice of mankind about the first erecting of governments.

105. I will not deny that if we look back, as far as history will direct us, towards the original of commonwealths, we shall generally find them under the government and administration of one man. And I am also apt to believe that where a family was numerous enough to subsist by itself, and continued entire together, without mixing with others, as it often happens, where there is much land and few people, the government commonly began in the father. For the father having, by the law of Nature, the same power, with every man else, to punish, as he thought fit, any offences against that law, might thereby punish his transgressing children, even when they were men, and out of their pupilage; and they were very likely to submit to his punishment, and all join with him against the offender in their turns, giving him thereby power to execute his sentence against any transgression, and so, in effect, make him the law-maker and governor over all that remained in conjunction with his family. He was fittest to be trusted; paternal affection secured their property and interest under his care, and the custom of obeying him in their childhood made it easier to submit to him rather than any other. If, therefore, they must have one to rule them, as government is hardly to be avoided amongst men that live together, who so likely to be the man as he that was their common father, unless negligence, cruelty, or any other defect of mind or body, made him unfit for it? But when either the father died—and left his next heir—for want of age, wisdom, courage, or any other qualities—less fit for rule, or where several families met and consented to continue together, there, it is not to be doubted, but they used their natural freedom to set up him whom they judged the ablest and most likely to rule well over them. Conformable hereunto we find the people of America, who—living out of the reach of the conquering swords and spreading domination of

the two great empires of Peru and Mexico—enjoyed their own natural freedom, though, *caeteris paribus*, they commonly prefer the heir of their deceased king; yet, if they find him any way weak or incapable, they pass him by, and set up the stoutest and bravest man for their ruler.

106. Thus, though looking back as far as records give us any account of peopling the world, and the history of nations, we commonly find the government to be in one hand, yet it destroys not that which I affirm—viz., that the beginning of politic society depends upon the consent of the individuals to join into and make one society, who, when they are thus incorporated, might set up what form of government they thought fit. But this having given occasion to men to mistake and think that, by Nature, government was monarchical, and belonged to the father, it may not be amiss here to consider why people, in the beginning, generally pitched upon this form, which, though perhaps the father's pre-eminency might, in the first institution of some commonwealths, give a rise to and place in the beginning the power in one hand, yet it is plain that the reason that continued the form of government in a single person was not any regard or respect to paternal authority, since all petty monarchies—that is, almost all monarchies, near their original, have been commonly, at least upon occasion, elective.

107. First, then, in the beginning of things, the father's government of the childhood of those sprung from him having accustomed them to the rule of one man, and taught them that where it was exercised with care and skill, with affection and love to those under it, it was sufficient to procure and preserve men (all the political happiness they sought for in society), it was no wonder that they should pitch upon and naturally run into that form of government which, from their infancy, they had been all accustomed to, and which, by experience, they had found both easy and safe. To which if we add, that monarchy being simple and most obvious to men, whom neither experience had instructed in forms of government, nor the ambition or insolence of empire had taught to beware of the encroachments of prerogative or the inconveniencies of absolute power, which monarchy, in succession, was apt to lay claim to and bring upon them; it was not at all strange that they should not much trouble themselves to think of methods of restraining any exorbitances of those to whom they had given the authority over them, and of balancing the power of government by placing several parts of it in different hands. They had neither felt the oppression of tyrannical dominion, nor did the fashion of the age, nor their possessions or way of living, which afforded little matter for covetousness or ambition, give them any reason to apprehend or provide against it; and, therefore, it is no wonder they put themselves into such a frame of government as was not only, as I said, most obvious and simple, but also best suited to their present state and condition, which stood more in need of defense against foreign invasions and injuries than of multiplicity of laws where there was but very little property, and wanted not variety of rulers and abundance of officers to direct and look after their execution where there were but few trespassers and few offenders. Since, then, those who liked one another so well as to join into society cannot but be supposed to have some acquaintance and friendship together, and some trust one in another, they could not but have greater apprehensions of others than of one another;

and, therefore, their first care and thought cannot but be supposed to be, how to secure themselves against foreign force. It was natural for them to put themselves under a frame of government which might best serve to that end, and choose the wisest and bravest man to conduct them in their wars and lead them out against their enemies, and in this chiefly be their ruler.

108. Thus we see that the kings of the Indians, in America, which is still a pattern of the first ages in Asia and Europe, whilst the inhabitants were too few for the country, and want of people and money gave men no temptation to enlarge their possessions of land or contest for wider extent of ground, are little more than generals of their armies; and though they command absolutely in war, yet at home, and in time of peace, they exercise very little dominion, and have but a very moderate sovereignty, the resolutions of peace and war being ordinarily either in the people or in a council, though the war itself, which admits not of pluralities of governors, naturally evolves the command into the king's sole authority.

109. And thus, in Israel itself, the chief business of their judges and first kings seems to have been to be captains in war and leaders of their armies, which (besides what is signified by "going out and in before the people," which was, to march forth to war and home again at the heads of their forces) appears plainly in the story of Jephtha. The Ammonites making war upon Israel, the Gileadites, in fear, send to Jephtha, a bastard of their family, whom they had cast off, and article with him, if he will assist them against the Ammonites, to make him their ruler, which they do in these words: "And the people made him head and captain over them" (Judges 11. 11), which was, as it seems, all one as to be judge. "And he judged Israel" (Judges 12. 7)—that is, was their captain-general—"six years." So when Jotham upbraids the Shechemites with the obligation they had to Gideon, who had been their judge and ruler, he tells them: "He fought for you, and adventured his life for, and delivered you out of the hands of Midian" (Judges 9. 17). Nothing mentioned of him but what he did as a general, and, indeed, that is all is found in his history, or in any of the rest of the judges. And Abimelech particularly is called king, though at most he was but their general. And when, being weary of the ill-conduct of Samuel's sons, the children of Israel desired a king, "like all the nations, to judge them, and to go out before them, and to fight their battles" (1 Sam. 8. 20), God, granting their desire, says to Samuel, "I will send thee a man, and thou shalt anoint him to be captain over my people Israel, that he may save my people out of the hands of the Philistines" (ch. 9. 16). As if the only business of a king had been to lead out their armies and fight in their defense; and, accordingly, at his inauguration, pouring a vial of oil upon him, declares to Saul that "the Lord had anointed him to be captain over his inheritance" (ch. 10. 1). And therefore those who, after Saul being solemnly chosen and saluted king by the tribes at Mispah, were unwilling to have him their king, make no other objection but this, "How shall this man save us?" (ch. 10. 27), as if they should have said: "This man is unfit to be our king, not having skill and conduct enough in war to be able to defend us." And when God resolved to transfer the government to David, it is in these words: "But now thy kingdom shall not continue: the Lord hath sought Him a man after His own heart, and the Lord hath commanded him to be

captain over His people" (ch. 13. 14.). As if the whole kingly authority were nothing else but to be their general; and therefore the tribes who had stuck to Saul's family, and opposed David's reign, when they came to Hebron with terms of submission to him, they tell him, amongst other arguments, they had to submit to him as to their king, that he was, in effect, their king in Saul's time, and therefore they had no reason but to receive him as their king now. "Also," say they, "in time past, when Saul was king over us, thou wast he that leddest out and broughtest in Israel, and the Lord said unto thee, Thou shalt feed my people Israel, and thou shalt be a captain over Israel."

110. Thus, whether a family, by degrees, grew up into a commonwealth, and the fatherly authority being continued on to the elder son, every one in his turn growing up under it tacitly submitted to it, and the easiness and equality of it not offending any one, every one acquiesced till time seemed to have confirmed it and settled a right of succession by prescription; or whether several families, or the descendants of several families, whom chance, neighborhood, or business brought together, united into society; the need of a general whose conduct might defend them against their enemies in war, and the great confidence the innocence and sincerity of that poor but virtuous age, such as are almost all those which begin governments that ever come to last in the world, gave men one of another, made the first beginners of commonwealths generally put the rule into one man's hand, without any other express limitation or restraint but what the nature of the thing and the end of government required. It was given them for the public good and safety, and to those ends, in the infancies of commonwealths, they commonly used it; and unless they had done so, young societies could not have subsisted. Without such nursing fathers, without this care of the governors, all governments would have sunk under the weakness and infirmities of their infancy, the prince and the people had soon perished together.

111. But the golden age (though before vain ambition, and *amor sceleratus habendi*, evil concupiscence had corrupted men's minds into a mistake of true power and honor) had more virtue, and consequently better governors, as well as less vicious subjects; and there was then no stretching prerogative on the one side to oppress the people, nor, consequently, on the other, any dispute about privilege, to lessen or restrain the power of the magistrate; and so no contest betwixt rulers and people about governors or government. Yet, when ambition and luxury, in future ages, would retain and increase the power, without doing the business for which it was given, and aided by flattery, taught princes to have distinct and separate interests from their people, men found it necessary to examine more carefully the original and rights of government, and to find out ways to restrain the exorbitances and prevent the abuses of that power, which they having entrusted in another's hands, only for their own good, they found was made use of to hurt them.

112. Thus we may see how probable it is that people that were naturally free, and, by their own consent, either submitted to the government of their father, or united together, out of different families, to make a government, should generally put the rule into one man's hands, and choose to be under the conduct of a single person, without so much, as by express conditions, limiting or regulating his power, which they thought safe enough in his honesty and prudence; though they never dreamed of monarchy being *jure Divi-*

no, which we never heard of among mankind till it was revealed to us by the divinity of this last age, nor ever allowed paternal power to have a right to dominion or to be the foundation of all government. And thus much may suffice to show that, as far as we have any light from history, we have reason to conclude that all peaceful beginnings of government have been laid in the consent of the people. I say "peaceful," because I shall have occasion, in another place, to speak of conquest, which some esteem a way of beginning of governments.

The other objection, I find, urged against the beginning of polities, in the way I have mentioned, is this, viz.:

113. "That all men being born under government, some or other, it is impossible any of them should ever be free and at liberty to unite together and begin a new one, or ever be able to erect a lawful government." If this argument be good, I ask, How came so many lawful monarchies into the world? For if anybody, upon this supposition, can show me any one man, in any age of the world, free to begin a lawful monarchy, I will be bound to show him ten other free men at liberty, at the same time, to unite and begin a new government under a regal or any other form. It being demonstration that if any one born under the dominion of another may be so free as to have a right to command others in a new and distinct empire, every one that is born under the dominion of another may be so free too, and may become a ruler or subject of a distinct separate government. And so, by this their own principle, either all men, however born, are free, or else there is but one lawful prince, one lawful government in the world; and then they have nothing to do but barely to show us which that is, which, when they have done, I doubt not but all mankind will easily agree to pay obedience to him.

114. Though it be a sufficient answer to their objection to show that it involves them in the same difficulties that it doth those they use it against, yet I shall endeavor to discover the weakness of this argument a little farther. "All men," say they, "are born under government, and therefore they cannot be at liberty to begin a new one. Every one is born a subject to his father or his prince, and is therefore under the perpetual tie of subjection and allegiance." It is plain mankind never owned nor considered any such natural subjection that they were born in, to one or to the other, that tied them, without their own consents, to a subjection to them and their heirs.

115. For there are no examples so frequent in history, both sacred and profane, as those of men withdrawing themselves and their obedience from the jurisdiction they were born under, and the family or community they were bred up in, and setting up new governments in other places, from whence sprang all that number of petty commonwealths in the beginning of ages, and which always multiplied as long as there was room enough, till the stronger or more fortunate swallowed the weaker; and those great ones, again breaking to pieces, dissolved into lesser dominions; all which are so many testimonies against paternal sovereignty, and plainly prove that it was not the natural right of the father descending to his heirs that made governments in the beginning; since it was impossible, upon that ground, there should have been so many little kingdoms but only one universal monarchy if men had not been at liberty to separate themselves from their families and

their government, be it what it will that was set up in it, and go and make distinct commonwealths and other governments as they thought fit.

116. This has been the practice of the world from its first beginning to this day; nor is it now any more hindrance to the freedom of mankind, that they are born under constituted and ancient polities that have established laws and set forms of government, than if they were born in the woods amongst the unconfined inhabitants that run loose in them. For those who would persuade us that by being born under any government we are naturally subjects to it, and have no more any title or pretence to the freedom of the state of Nature, have no other reason (bating that of paternal power, which we have already answered) to produce for it, but only because our fathers or progenitors passed away their natural liberty, and thereby bound up themselves and their posterity to a perpetual subjection to the government which they themselves submitted to. It is true that whatever engagements or promises any one made for himself, he is under the obligation of them, but cannot by any compact whatsoever bind his children or posterity. For his son, when a man, being altogether as free as the father, any act of the father can no more give away the liberty of the son than it can of anybody else. He may, indeed, annex such conditions to the land he enjoyed, as a subject of any commonwealth, as may oblige his son to be of that community, if he will enjoy those possessions which were his father's, because that estate being his father's property, he may dispose or settle it as he pleases.

117. And this has generally given the occasion to the mistake in this matter; because commonwealths not permitting any part of their dominions to be dismembered, nor to be enjoyed by any but those of their community, the son cannot ordinarily enjoy the possessions of his father but under the same terms his father did, by becoming a member of the society, whereby he puts himself presently under the government he finds there established, as much as any other subject of that commonweal. And thus the consent of free men, born under government, which only makes them members of it, being given separately in their turns, as each comes to be of age, and not in a multitude together, people take no notice of it, and thinking it not done at all, or not necessary, conclude they are naturally subjects as they are men.

118. But it is plain governments themselves understand it otherwise; they claim no power over the son because of that they had over the father; nor look on children as being their subjects, by their fathers being so. If a subject of England have a child by an Englishwoman in France, whose subject is he? Not the King of England's; for he must have leave to be admitted to the privileges of it. Nor the King of France's, for how then has his father a liberty to bring him away, and breed him as he pleases; and whoever was judged as a traitor or deserter, if he left, or warred against a country, for being barely born in it of parents that were aliens there? It is plain, then, by the practice of governments themselves, as well as by the law of right reason, that a child is born a subject of no country nor government. He is under his father's tuition and authority till he come to age of discretion, and then he is a free man, at liberty what government he will put himself under, what body politic he will unite himself to. For if an Englishman's son born in France be at liberty, and may do so, it is evident there is no tie upon him by his father being a subject of that king-

dom, nor is he bound up by any compact of his ancestors; and why then hath not his son, by the same reason, the same liberty, though he be born anywhere else? Since the power that a father hath naturally over his children is the same wherever they be born, and the ties of natural obligations are not bounded by the positive limits of kingdoms and commonwealths.

119. Every man being, as has been showed, naturally free, and nothing being able to put him into subjection to any earthly power, but only his own consent, it is to be considered what shall be understood to be a sufficient declaration of a man's consent to make him subject to the laws of any government. There is a common distinction of an express and a tacit consent, which will concern our present case. Nobody doubts but an express consent of any man, entering into any society, makes him a perfect member of that society, a subject of that government. The difficulty is, what ought to be looked upon as a tacit consent, and how far it binds—i.e., how far any one shall be looked on to have consented, and thereby submitted to any government, where he has made no expressions of it at all. And to this I say, that every man that hath any possession or enjoyment of any part of the dominions of any government doth hereby give his tacit consent, and is as far forth obliged to obedience to the laws of that government, during such enjoyment, as any one under it, whether this his possession be of land to him and his heirs for ever, or a lodging only for a week; or whether it be barely traveling freely on the highway; and, in effect, it reaches as far as the very being of any one within the territories of that government.

120. To understand this the better, it is fit to consider that every man when he at first incorporates himself into any commonwealth, he, by his uniting himself thereunto, annexes also, and submits to the community those possessions which he has, or shall acquire, that do not already belong to any other government. For it would be a direct contradiction for any one to enter into society with others for the securing and regulating of property, and yet to suppose his land, whose property is to be regulated by the laws of the society, should be exempt from the jurisdiction of that government to which he himself, and the property of the land, is a subject. By the same act, therefore, whereby any one unites his person, which was before free, to any commonwealth, by the same he unites his possessions, which were before free, to it also; and they become, both of them, person and possession, subject to the government and dominion of that commonwealth as long as it hath a being. Whoever therefore, from thenceforth, by inheritance, purchases permission, or otherwise enjoys any part of the land so annexed to, and under the government of that commonweal, must take it with the condition it is under—that is, of submitting to the government of the commonwealth, under whose jurisdiction it is, as far forth as any subject of it.

121. But since the government has a direct jurisdiction only over the land and reaches the possessor of it (before he has actually incorporated himself in the society) only as he dwells upon and enjoys that, the obligation any one is under by virtue of such enjoyment to submit to the government begins and ends with the enjoyment; so that whenever the owner, who has given nothing but such a tacit consent to the government will, by donation, sale or otherwise, quit the said possession, he is at liberty to go and incorporate

himself into any other commonwealth, or agree with others to begin a new one *in vacuis locis*, in any part of the world they can find free and unpossessed; whereas he that has once, by actual agreement and any express declaration, given his consent to be of any commonweal, is perpetually and indispensably obliged to be, and remain unalterably a subject to it, and can never be again in the liberty of the state of Nature, unless by any calamity the government he was under comes to be dissolved.

122. But submitting to the laws of any country, living quietly and enjoying privileges and protection under them, makes not a man a member of that society; it is only a local protection and homage due to and from all those who, not being in a state of war, come within the territories belonging to any government, to all parts whereof the force of its law extends. But this no more makes a man a member of that society, a perpetual subject of that commonwealth, than it would make a man a subject to another in whose family he found it convenient to abide for some time, though, whilst he continued in it, he were obliged to comply with the laws and submit to the government he found there. And thus we see that foreigners, by living all their lives under another government, and enjoying the privileges and protection of it, though they are bound, even in conscience, to submit to its administration as far forth as any denizen, yet do not thereby come to be subjects or members of that commonwealth. Nothing can make any man so but his actually entering into it by positive engagement and express promise and compact. This is that which, I think, concerning the beginning of political societies, and that consent which makes any one a member of any commonwealth.

Chapter IX

Of the Ends of Political Society and Government

123. If man in the state of Nature be so free as has been said, if he be absolute lord of his own person and possessions, equal to the greatest and subject to nobody, why will he part with his freedom, this empire, and subject himself to the dominion and control of any other power? To which it is obvious to answer, that though in the state of Nature he hath such a right, yet the enjoyment of it is very uncertain and constantly exposed to the invasion of others; for all being kings as much as he, every man his equal, and the greater part no strict observers of equity and justice, the enjoyment of the property he has in this state is very unsafe, very insecure. This makes him willing to quit this condition which, however free, is full of fears and continual dangers; and it is not without reason that he seeks out and is willing to join in society with others who are already united, or have a mind to unite for the mutual preservation of their lives, liberties and estates, which I call by the general name—property.

124. The great and chief end, therefore, of men uniting into commonwealths, and putting themselves under government, is the preservation of their property; to which in the state of Nature there are many things wanting.

Firstly, there wants an established, settled, known law, received and allowed by common consent to be the standard of right and wrong, and the common measure to decide all controversies between them. For though the law of Nature be plain and intelligible to all rational creatures, yet men, being biased by their interest, as well as ignorant for want of study of it, are not apt to allow of it as a law binding to them in the application of it to their particular cases.

125. Secondly, in the state of Nature there wants a known and indifferent judge, with authority to determine all differences according to the established law. For every one in that state being both judge and executioner of the law of Nature, men being partial to themselves, passion and revenge is very apt to carry them too far, and with too much heat in their own cases, as well as negligence and unconcernedness, make them too remiss in other men's.

126. Thirdly, in the state of Nature there often wants power to back and support the sentence when right, and to give it due execution. They who by any injustice offended will seldom fail where they are able by force to make good their injustice. Such resistance many times makes the punishment dangerous, and frequently destructive to those who attempt it.

127. Thus mankind, notwithstanding all the privileges of the state of Nature, being but in an ill condition while they remain in it are quickly driven into society. Hence it comes to pass, that we seldom find any number of men live any time together in this state. The inconveniencies that they are therein exposed to by the irregular and uncertain exercise of the power every man has of punishing the transgressions of others, make them take sanctuary under the established laws of government, and therein seek the preservation of their property. It is this that makes them so willingly give up every one his single power of punishing to be exercised by such alone as shall be appointed to it amongst them, and by such rules as the community, or those authorized by them to that purpose, shall agree on. And in this we have the original right and rise of both the legislative and executive power as well as of the governments and societies themselves.

128. For in the state of Nature to omit the liberty he has of innocent delights, a man has two powers. The first is to do whatsoever he thinks fit for the preservation of himself and others within the permission of the law of Nature; by which law, common to them all, he and all the rest of mankind are one community, make up one society distinct from all other creatures, and were it not for the corruption and viciousness of degenerate men, there would be no need of any other, no necessity that men should separate from this great and natural community, and associate into lesser combinations. The other power a man has in the state of Nature is the power to punish the crimes committed against that law. Both these he gives up when he joins in a private, if I may so call it, or particular political society, and incorporates into any commonwealth separate from the rest of mankind.

129. The first power—viz., of doing whatsoever he thought fit for the preservation of himself and the rest of mankind, he gives up to be regulated by laws made by the society, so far forth as the preservation of himself and the rest of that society shall require; which laws of the society in many things confine the liberty he had by the law of Nature.

130. Secondly, the power of punishing he wholly gives up, and engages his natural force, which he might before employ in the execution of the law of Nature, by his own single authority, as he thought fit, to assist the executive power of the society as the law thereof shall require. For being now in a new state, wherein he is to enjoy many conveniencies from the labor, assistance, and society of others in the same community, as well as protection from its whole strength, he is to part also with as much of his natural liberty, in providing for himself, as the good, prosperity, and safety of the society shall require, which is not only necessary but just, since the other members of the society do the like.

131. But though men when they enter into society give up the equality, liberty, and executive power they had in the state of Nature into the hands of the society, to be so far disposed of by the legislative as the good of the society shall require, yet it being only with an intention in every one the better to preserve himself, his liberty and property (for no rational creature can be supposed to change his condition with an intention to be worse), the power of the society or legislative constituted by them can never be supposed to extend farther than the common good, but is obliged to secure every one's property by providing against those three defects above mentioned that made the state of Nature so unsafe and uneasy. And so, whoever has the legislative or supreme power of any commonwealth, is bound to govern by established standing laws, promulgated and known to the people, and not by extemporary decrees, by indifferent and upright judges, who are to decide controversies by those laws; and to employ the force of the community at home only in the execution of such laws, or abroad to prevent or redress foreign injuries and secure the community from inroads and invasion. And all this to be directed to no other end but the peace, safety, and public good of the people.

Chapter X

Of the Forms of a Commonwealth

132. The majority having, as has been showed, upon men's first uniting into society, the whole power of the community naturally in them, may employ all that power in making laws for the community from time to time, and executing those laws by officers of their own appointing, and then the form of the government is a perfect democracy; or else may put the power of making laws into the hands of a few select men, and their heirs or successors, and then it is an oligarchy; or else into the hands of one man, and then it is a monarchy; if to him and his heirs, it is a hereditary monarchy; if to him only for life, but upon his death the power only of nominating a successor, to return to them, an elective monarchy. And so accordingly of these make compounded and mixed forms of government, as they think good. And if the legislative power be at first given by the majority to one or more persons only for their lives, or any limited time, and then the supreme power to revert to them again, when it is so reverted the community may dispose of it again anew into what hands they please, and so constitute a new form of government; for the

form of government depending upon the placing the supreme power, which is the legislative, it being impossible to conceive that an inferior power should prescribe to a superior, or any but the supreme make laws, according as the power of making laws is placed, such is the form of the commonwealth.

133. By "commonwealth" I must be understood all along to mean not a democracy, or any form of government, but any independent community which the Latins signified by the word *civitas*, to which the word which best answers in our language is "commonwealth," and most properly expresses such a society of men which "community" does not (for there may be subordinate communities in a government), and "city" much less. And therefore, to avoid ambiguity, I crave leave to use the word "commonwealth" in that sense, in which sense I find the word used by King James himself, which I think to be its genuine signification, which, if anybody dislike, I consent with him to change it for a better.

Chapter XI

Of the Extent of the Legislative Power

134. The great end of men's entering into society being the enjoyment of their properties in peace and safety, and the great instrument and means of that being the laws established in that society, the first and fundamental positive law of all commonwealths is the establishing of the legislative power, as the first and fundamental natural law which is to govern even the legislative itself is the preservation of the society and (as far as will consist with the public good) of every person in it. This legislative is not only the supreme power of the commonwealth, but sacred and unalterable in the hands where the community have once placed it. Nor can any edict of anybody else, in what form soever conceived, or by what power soever backed, have the force and obligation of a law which has not its sanction from that legislative which the public has chosen and appointed; for without this the law could not have that which is absolutely necessary to its being a law, the consent of the society, over whom nobody can have a power to make laws but by their own consent and by authority received from them; and therefore all the obedience, which by the most solemn ties any one can be obliged to pay, ultimately terminates in this supreme power, and is directed by those laws which it enacts. Nor can any oaths to any foreign power whatsoever, or any domestic subordinate power, discharge any member of the society from his obedience to the legislative, acting pursuant to their trust, nor oblige him to any obedience contrary to the laws so enacted or farther than they do allow, it being ridiculous to imagine one can be tied ultimately to obey any power in the society which is not the supreme.

135. Though the legislative, whether placed in one or more, whether it be always in being or only by intervals, though it be the supreme power in every commonwealth, yet, first, it is not, nor can possibly be, absolutely arbitrary over the lives and fortunes of the people. For it being but the joint power of every member of the society given up to that person or assembly which is legislator, it can be no more than those persons had in a

state of Nature before they entered into society, and gave it up to the community. For nobody can transfer to another more power than he has in himself, and nobody has an absolute arbitrary power over himself, or over any other, to destroy his own life, or take away the life or property of another. A man, as has been proved, cannot subject himself to the arbitrary power of another; and having, in the state of Nature, no arbitrary power over the life, liberty, or possession of another, but only so much as the law of Nature gave him for the preservation of himself and the rest of mankind, this is all he doth, or can give up to the commonwealth, and by it to the legislative power, so that the legislative can have no more than this. Their power in the utmost bounds of it is limited to the public good of the society. It is a power that hath no other end but preservation, and therefore can never have a right to destroy, enslave, or designedly to impoverish the subjects; the obligations of the law of Nature cease not in society, but only in many cases are drawn closer, and have, by human laws, known penalties annexed to them to enforce their observation. Thus the law of Nature stands as an eternal rule to all men, legislators as well as others. The rules that they make for other men's actions must, as well as their own and other men's actions, be conformable to the law of Nature—i.e., to the will of God, of which that is a declaration, and the fundamental law of Nature being the preservation of mankind, no human sanction can be good or valid against it.

136. Secondly, the legislative or supreme authority cannot assume to itself a power to rule by extemporary arbitrary decrees, but is bound to dispense justice and decide the rights of the subject by promulgated standing laws, and known authorized judges. For the law of Nature being unwritten, and so nowhere to be found but in the minds of men, they who, through passion or interest, shall miscite or misapply it, cannot so easily be convinced of their mistake where there is no established judge; and so it serves not as it aught, to determine the rights and fence the properties of those that live under it, especially where every one is judge, interpreter, and executioner of it too, and that in his own case; and he that has right on his side, having ordinarily but his own single strength, hath not force enough to defend himself from injuries or punish delinquents. To avoid these inconveniencies which disorder men's properties in the state of Nature, men unite into societies that they may have the united strength of the whole society to secure and defend their properties, and may have standing rules to bound it by which every one may know what is his. To this end it is that men give up all their natural power to the society they enter into, and the community put the legislative power into such hands as they think fit, with this trust, that they shall be governed by declared laws, or else their peace, quiet, and property will still be at the same uncertainty as it was in the state of Nature.

137. Absolute arbitrary power, or governing without settled standing laws, can neither of them consist with the ends of society and government, which men would not quit the freedom of the state of Nature for, and tie themselves up under, were it not to preserve their lives, liberties, and fortunes, and by stated rules of right and property to secure their peace and quiet. It cannot be supposed that they should intend, had they a power so to do, to give any one or more an absolute arbitrary power over their persons and estates, and put a force into the magistrate's hand to execute his unlimited will arbitrarily upon

them; this were to put themselves into a worse condition than the state of Nature, wherein they had a liberty to defend their right against the injuries of others, and were upon equal terms of force to maintain it, whether invaded by a single man or many in combination. Whereas by supposing they have given up themselves to the absolute arbitrary power and will of a legislator, they have disarmed themselves, and armed him to make a prey of them when he pleases; he being in a much worse condition that is exposed to the arbitrary power of one man who has the command of a hundred thousand than he that is exposed to the arbitrary power of a hundred thousand single men, nobody being secure, that his will who has such a command is better than that of other men, though his force be a hundred thousand times stronger. And, therefore, whatever form the commonwealth is under, the ruling power ought to govern by declared and received laws, and not by extemporary dictates and undetermined resolutions, for then mankind will be in a far worse condition than in the state of Nature if they shall have armed one or a few men with the joint power of a multitude, to force them to obey at pleasure the exorbitant and unlimited decrees of their sudden thoughts, or unrestrained, and till that moment, unknown wills, without having any measures set down which may guide and justify their actions. For all the power the government has, being only for the good of the society, as it ought not to be arbitrary and at pleasure, so it ought to be exercised by established and promulgated laws, that both the people may know their duty, and be safe and secure within the limits of the law, and the rulers, too, kept within their due bounds, and not be tempted by the power they have in their hands to employ it to purposes, and by such measures as they would not have known, and own not willingly.

138. Thirdly, the supreme power cannot take from any man any part of his property without his own consent. For the preservation of property being the end of government, and that for which men enter into society, it necessarily supposes and requires that the people should have property, without which they must be supposed to lose that by entering into society which was the end for which they entered into it; too gross an absurdity for any man to own. Men, therefore, in society having property, they have such a right to the goods, which by the law of the community are theirs, that nobody hath a right to take them, or any part of them, from them without their own consent; without this they have no property at all. For I have truly no property in that which another can by right take from me when he pleases against my consent. Hence it is a mistake to think that the supreme or legislative power of any commonwealth can do what it will, and dispose of the estates of the subject arbitrarily, or take any part of them at pleasure. This is not much to be feared in governments where the legislative consists wholly or in part in assemblies which are variable, whose members upon the dissolution of the assembly are subjects under the common laws of their country, equally with the rest. But in governments where the legislative is in one lasting assembly, always in being, or in one man as in absolute monarchies, there is danger still, that they will think themselves to have a distinct interest from the rest of the community, and so will be apt to increase their own riches and power by taking what they think fit from the people. For a man's property is not at all secure, though there be good and equitable laws to set the bounds of it between him and his fel-

low-subjects, if he who commands those subjects have power to take from any private man what part he pleases of his property, and use and dispose of it as he thinks good.

139. But government, into whosesoever hands it is put, being as I have before shown, entrusted with this condition, and for this end, that men might have and secure their properties, the prince or senate, however it may have power to make laws for the regulating of property between the subjects one amongst another, yet can never have a power to take to themselves the whole, or any part of the subjects' property, without their own consent; for this would be in effect to leave them no property at all. And to let us see that even absolute power, where it is necessary, is not arbitrary by being absolute, but is still limited by that reason and confined to those ends which required it in some cases to be absolute, we need look no farther than the common practice of martial discipline. For the preservation of the army, and in it of the whole commonwealth, requires an absolute obedience to the command of every superior officer, and it is justly death to disobey or dispute the most dangerous or unreasonable of them; but yet we see that neither the sergeant that could command a soldier to march up to the mouth of a cannon, or stand in a breach where he is almost sure to perish, can command that soldier to give him one penny of his money; nor the general that can condemn him to death for deserting his post, or not obeying the most desperate orders, cannot yet with all his absolute power of life and death dispose of one farthing of that soldier's estate, or seize one jot of his goods; whom yet he can command anything, and hang for the least disobedience. Because such a blind obedience is necessary to that end for which the commander has his power—viz., the preservation of the rest, but the disposing of his goods has nothing to do with it.

140. It is true governments cannot be supported without great charge, and it is fit every one who enjoys his share of the protection should pay out of his estate his proportion for the maintenance of it. But still it must be with his own consent—i.e., the consent of the majority, giving it either by themselves or their representatives chosen by them; for if any one shall claim a power to lay and levy taxes on the people by his own authority, and without such consent of the people, he thereby invades the fundamental law of property, and subverts the end of government. For what property have I in that which another may by right take when he pleases to himself?

141. Fourthly. The legislative cannot transfer the power of making laws to any other hands, for it being but a delegated power from the people, they who have it cannot pass it over to others. The people alone can appoint the form of the commonwealth, which is by constituting the legislative, and appointing in whose hands that shall be. And when the people have said, "We will submit, and be governed by laws made by such men, and in such forms," nobody else can say other men shall make laws for them; nor can they be bound by any laws but such as are enacted by those whom they have chosen and authorized to make laws for them.

142. These are the bounds which the trust that is put in them by the society and the law of God and Nature have set to the legislative power of every commonwealth, in all forms of government. First: They are to govern by promulgated established laws, not to be varied in particular cases, but to have one rule for rich and poor, for the favorite at

Court, and the countryman at plough. Secondly: These laws also ought to be designed for no other end ultimately but the good of the people. Thirdly: They must not raise taxes on the property of the people without the consent of the people given by themselves or their deputies. And this properly concerns only such governments where the legislative is always in being, or at least where the people have not reserved any part of the legislative to deputies, to be from time to time chosen by themselves. Fourthly: Legislative neither must nor can transfer the power of making laws to anybody else, or place it anywhere but where the people have.

Chapter XII

The Legislative, Executive, and Federative Power of the Commonwealth

143. The legislative power is that which has a right to direct how the force of the commonwealth shall be employed for preserving the community and the members of it. Because those laws which are constantly to be executed, and whose force is always to continue, may be made in a little time, therefore there is no need that the legislative should be always in being, not having always business to do. And because it may be too great temptation to human frailty, apt to grasp at power, for the same persons who have the power of making laws to have also in their hands the power to execute them, whereby they may exempt themselves from obedience to the laws they make, and suit the law, both in its making and execution, to their own private advantage, and thereby come to have a distinct interest from the rest of the community, contrary to the end of society and government. Therefore in well-ordered commonwealths, where the good of the whole is so considered as it ought, the legislative power is put into the hands of divers persons who, duly assembled, have by themselves, or jointly with others, a power to make laws, which when they have done, being separated again, they are themselves subject to the laws they have made; which is a new and near tie upon them to take care that they make them for the public good.

144. But because the laws that are at once, and in a short time made, have a constant and lasting force, and need a perpetual execution, or an attendance thereunto, therefore it is necessary there should be a power always in being which should see to the execution of the laws that are made, and remain in force. And thus the legislative and executive power come often to be separated.

145. There is another power in every commonwealth which one may call natural, because it is that which answers to the power every man naturally had before he entered into society. For though in a commonwealth the members of it are distinct persons, still, in reference to one another, and, as such, are governed by the laws of the society, yet, in reference to the rest of mankind, they make one body, which is, as every member of it before was, still in the state of Nature with the rest of mankind, so that the controversies that

happen between any man of the society with those that are out of it are managed by the public, and an injury done to a member of their body engages the whole in the reparation of it. So that under this consideration the whole community is one body in the state of Nature in respect of all other states or persons out of its community.

146. This, therefore, contains the power of war and peace, leagues and alliances, and all the transactions with all persons and communities without the commonwealth, and may be called federative if any one pleases. So the thing be understood, I am indifferent as to the name.

147. These two powers, executive and federative, though they be really distinct in themselves, yet one comprehending the execution of the municipal laws of the society within itself upon all that are parts of it, the other the management of the security and interest of the public without with all those that it may receive benefit or damage from, yet they are always almost united. And though this federative power in the well or ill management of it be of great moment to the commonwealth, yet it is much less capable to be directed by antecedent, standing, positive laws than the executive, and so must necessarily be left to the prudence and wisdom of those whose hands it is in, to be managed for the public good. For the laws that concern subjects one amongst another, being to direct their actions, may well enough precede them. But what is to be done in reference to foreigners depending much upon their actions, and the variation of designs and interests, must be left in great part to the prudence of those who have this power committed to them, to be managed by the best of their skill for the advantage of the commonwealth.

148. Though, as I said, the executive and federative power of every community be really distinct in themselves, yet they are hardly to be separated and placed at the same time in the hands of distinct persons. For both of them requiring the force of the society for their exercise, it is almost impracticable to place the force of the commonwealth in distinct and not subordinate hands, or that the executive and federative power should be placed in persons that might act separately, whereby the force of the public would be under different commands, which would be apt some time or other to cause disorder and ruin.

Chapter XVIII

Of Tyranny

199. As usurpation is the exercise of power which another hath a right to, so tyranny is the exercise of power beyond right, which nobody can have a right to; and this is making use of the power any one has in his hands, not for the good of those who are under it, but for his own private, separate advantage. When the governor, however entitled, makes not the law, but his will, the rule, and his commands and actions are not directed to the preservation of the properties of his people, but the satisfaction of his own ambition, revenge, covetousness, or any other irregular passion.

200. If one can doubt this to be truth or reason because it comes from the obscure hand of a subject, I hope the authority of a king will make it pass with him. King James, in his speech to the Parliament, 1603, tells them thus:

> "I will ever prefer the weal of the public and of the whole commonwealth, in making of good laws and constitutions, to any particular and private ends of mine, thinking ever the wealth and weal of the commonwealth to be my greatest weal and worldly felicity—a point wherein a lawful king doth directly differ from a tyrant; for I do acknowledge that the special and greatest point of difference that is between a rightful king and an usurping tyrant is this—that whereas the proud and ambitious tyrant doth think his kingdom and people are only ordained for satisfaction of his desires and unreasonable appetites, the righteous and just king doth, by the contrary, acknowledge himself to be ordained for the procuring of the wealth and property of his people."

And again, in his speech to the Parliament, 1609, he hath these words:

> "The king binds himself, by a double oath, to the observation of the fundamental laws of his kingdom—tacitly, as by being a king, and so bound to protect, as well the people as the laws of his kingdom; and expressly by his oath at his coronation; so as every just king, in a settled kingdom, is bound to observe that paction made to his people, by his laws, in framing his government agreeable thereunto, according to that paction which God made with Noah after the deluge: 'Hereafter, seed-time, and harvest, and cold, and heat, and summer, and winter, and day, and night, shall not cease while the earth remaineth.' And therefore a king, governing in a settled kingdom, leaves to be a king, and degenerates into a tyrant, as soon as he leaves off to rule according to his laws."

And a little after:

> "Therefore, all kings that are not tyrants, or perjured, will be glad to bound themselves within the limits of their laws, and they that persuade them the contrary are vipers, pests, both against them and the commonwealth."

Thus, that learned king, who well understood the notions of things, makes the difference betwixt a king and a tyrant to consist only in this: that one makes the laws the bounds of his power and the good of the public the end of his government; the other makes all give way to his own will and appetite.

201. It is a mistake to think this fault is proper only to monarchies. Other forms of government are liable to it as well as that; for wherever the power that is put in any hands for the government of the people and the preservation of their properties is applied to other ends, and made use of to impoverish, harass, or subdue them to the arbitrary and

irregular commands of those that have it, there it presently becomes tyranny, whether those that thus use it are one or many. Thus we read of the thirty tyrants at Athens, as well as one at Syracuse; and the intolerable dominion of the *Decemviri* at Rome was nothing better.

202. Wherever law ends, tyranny begins, if the law be transgressed to another's harm; and whosoever in authority exceeds the power given him by the law, and makes use of the force he has under his command to compass that upon the subject which the law allows not, ceases in that to be a magistrate, and acting without authority may be opposed, as any other man who by force invades the right of another. This is acknowledged in subordinate magistrates. He that hath authority to seize my person in the street may be opposed as a thief and a robber if he endeavors to break into my house to execute a writ, notwithstanding that I know he has such a warrant and such a legal authority as will empower him to arrest me abroad. And why this should not hold in the highest, as well as in the most inferior magistrate, I would gladly be informed. Is it reasonable that the eldest brother, because he has the greatest part of his father's estate, should thereby have a right to take away any of his younger brothers' portions? Or that a rich man, who possessed a whole country, should from thence have a right to seize, when he pleased, the cottage and garden of his poor neighbor? The being rightfully possessed of great power and riches, exceedingly beyond the greatest part of the sons of Adam, is so far from being an excuse, much less a reason for rapine and oppression, which the endamaging another without authority is, that it is a great aggravation of it. For exceeding the bounds of authority is no more a right in a great than a petty officer, no more justifiable in a king than a constable. But so much the worse in him as that he has more trust put in him, is supposed, from the advantage of education and counsellors, to have better knowledge and less reason to do it, having already a greater share than the rest of his brethren.

203. May the commands, then, of a prince be opposed? May he be resisted, as often as any one shall find himself aggrieved, and but imagine he has not right done him? This will unhinge and overturn all polities, and instead of government and order, leave nothing but anarchy and confusion.

204. To this I answer: That force is to be opposed to nothing but to unjust and unlawful force. Whoever makes any opposition in any other case draws on himself a just condemnation, both from God and man; and so no such danger or confusion will follow, as is often suggested.

205. First. As in some countries the person of the prince by the law is sacred, and so whatever he commands or does, his person is still free from all question or violence, not liable to force, or any judicial censure or condemnation. But yet opposition may be made to the illegal acts of any inferior officer or other commissioned by him, unless he will, by actually putting himself into a state of war with his people, dissolve the government, and leave them to that defense, which belongs to every one in the state of Nature. For of such things, who can tell what the end will be? And a neighbor kingdom has showed the world an odd example. In all other cases the sacredness of the person exempts him from all inconveniencies, whereby he is secure, whilst the government stands, from all violence and harm

whatsoever, than which there cannot be a wiser constitution. For the harm he can do in his own person not being likely to happen often, nor to extend itself far, nor being able by his single strength to subvert the laws nor oppress the body of the people, should any prince have so much weakness and ill-nature as to be willing to do it. The inconveniency of some particular mischiefs that may happen sometimes when a heady prince comes to the throne are well recompensed by the peace of the public and security of the government in the person of the chief magistrate, thus set out of the reach of danger; it being safer for the body that some few private men should be sometimes in danger to suffer than that the head of the republic should be easily and upon slight occasions exposed.

206. Secondly. But this privilege, belonging only to the king's person, hinders not but they may be questioned, opposed, and resisted, who use unjust force, though they pretend a commission from him which the law authorizes not; as is plain in the case of him that has the king's writ to arrest a man which is a full commission from the king, and yet he that has it cannot break open a man's house to do it, nor execute this command of the king upon certain days nor in certain places, though this commission have no such exception in it; but they are the limitations of the law, which, if any one transgress, the king's commission excuses him not. For the king's authority being given him only by the law, he cannot empower any one to act against the law, or justify him by his commission in so doing. The commission or command of any magistrate where he has no authority, being as void and insignificant as that of any private man, the difference between the one and the other being that the magistrate has some authority so far and to such ends, and the private man has none at all; for it is not the commission but the authority that gives the right of acting, and against the laws there can be no authority. But notwithstanding such resistance, the king's person and authority are still both secured, and so no danger to governor or government.

207. Thirdly. Supposing a government wherein the person of the chief magistrate is not thus sacred, yet this doctrine of the lawfulness of resisting all unlawful exercises of his power will not, upon every slight occasion, endanger him or embroil the government; for where the injured party may be relieved and his damages repaired by appeal to the law, there can be no pretence for force, which is only to be used where a man is intercepted from appealing to the law. For nothing is to be accounted hostile force but where it leaves not the remedy of such an appeal. and it is such force alone that puts him that uses it into a state of war, and makes it lawful to resist him. A man with a sword in his hand demands my purse on the highway, when perhaps I have not 12 pence in my pocket. This man I may lawfully kill. To another I deliver 100 pounds to hold only whilst I alight, which he refuses to restore me when I am got up again, but draws his sword to defend the possession of it by force. I endeavor to retake it. The mischief this man does me is a hundred, or possibly a thousand times more than the other perhaps intended me (whom I killed before he really did me any); and yet I might lawfully kill the one and cannot so much as hurt the other lawfully. The reason whereof is plain; because the one using force which threatened my life, I could not have time to appeal to the law to secure it, and when it was gone it was too late to appeal. The law could not restore life to my dead carcass. The loss was irreparable;

which to prevent the law of Nature gave me a right to destroy him who had put himself into a state of war with me and threatened my destruction. But in the other case, my life not being in danger, I might have the benefit of appealing to the law, and have reparation for my 100 pounds that way.

208. Fourthly. But if the unlawful acts done by the magistrate be maintained (by the power he has got), and the remedy, which is due by law, be by the same power obstructed, yet the right of resisting, even in such manifest acts of tyranny, will not suddenly, or on slight occasions, disturb the government. For if it reach no farther than some private men's cases, though they have a right to defend themselves, and to recover by force what by unlawful force is taken from them, yet the right to do so will not easily engage them in a contest wherein they are sure to perish; it being as impossible for one or a few oppressed men to disturb the government where the body of the people do not think themselves concerned in it, as for a raving madman or heady malcontent to overturn a well-settled state, the people being as little apt to follow the one as the other.

209. But if either these illegal acts have extended to the majority of the people, or if the mischief and oppression has lighted only on some few, but in such cases as the precedent and consequences seem to threaten all, and they are persuaded in their consciences that their laws, and with them, their estates, liberties, and lives are in danger, and perhaps their religion too, how they will be hindered from resisting illegal force used against them I cannot tell. This is an inconvenience, I confess, that attends all governments whatsoever, when the governors have brought it to this pass, to be generally suspected of their people, the most dangerous state they can possibly put themselves in; wherein they are the less to be pitied, because it is so easy to be avoided. It being as impossible for a governor, if he really means the good of his people, and the preservation of them and their laws together, not to make them see and feel it, as it is for the father of a family not to let his children see he loves and takes care of them.

210. But if all the world shall observe pretences of one kind, and actions of another, arts used to elude the law, and the trust of prerogative (which is an arbitrary power in some things left in the prince's hand to do good, not harm, to the people) employed contrary to the end for which it was given; if the people shall find the ministers and subordinate magistrates chosen, suitable to such ends, and favored or laid by proportionably as they promote or oppose them; if they see several experiments made of arbitrary power, and that religion underhand favored, though publicly proclaimed against, which is readiest to introduce it, and the operators in it supported as much as may be; and when that cannot be done, yet approved still, and liked the better, and a long train of acting show the counsels all tending that way, how can a man any more hinder himself from being persuaded in his own mind which way things are going; or, from casting about how to save himself, than he could from believing the captain of a ship he was in was carrying him and the rest of the company to Algiers, when he found him always steering that course, though cross winds, leaks in his ship, and want of men and provisions did often force him to turn his course another way for some time, which he steadily returned to again as soon as the wind, weather, and other circumstances would let him?

Chapter XIX

Of the Dissolution of Government

211. He that will, with any clearness, speak of the dissolution of government, ought in the first place to distinguish between the dissolution of the society and the dissolution of the government. That which makes the community, and brings men out of the loose state of Nature into one politic society, is the agreement which every one has with the rest to incorporate and act as one body, and so be one distinct commonwealth. The usual, and almost only way whereby this union is dissolved, is the inroad of foreign force making a conquest upon them. For in that case (not being able to maintain and support themselves as one entire and independent body) the union belonging to that body, which consisted therein, must necessarily cease, and so every one return to the state he was in before, with a liberty to shift for himself and provide for his own safety, as he thinks fit, in some other society. Whenever the society is dissolved, it is certain the government of that society cannot remain. Thus conquerors' swords often cut up governments by the roots, and mangle societies to pieces, separating the subdued or scattered multitude from the protection of and dependence on that society which ought to have preserved them from violence. The world is too well instructed in, and too forward to allow of this way of dissolving of governments, to need any more to be said of it; and there wants not much argument to prove that where the society is dissolved, the government cannot remain; that being as impossible as for the frame of a house to subsist when the materials of it are scattered and displaced by a whirlwind, or jumbled into a confused heap by an earthquake.

212. Besides this overturning from without, governments are dissolved from within:

First. When the legislative is altered, civil society being a state of peace amongst those who are of it, from whom the state of war is excluded by the umpirage which they have provided in their legislative for the ending all differences that may arise amongst any of them; it is in their legislative that the members of a commonwealth are united and combined together into one coherent living body. This is the soul that gives form, life, and unity to the commonwealth; from hence the several members have their mutual influence, sympathy, and connection; and therefore when the legislative is broken, or dissolved, dissolution and death follows. For the essence and union of the society consisting in having one will, the legislative, when once established by the majority, has the declaring and, as it were, keeping of that will. The constitution of the legislative is the first and fundamental act of society, whereby provision is made for the continuation of their union under the direction of persons and bonds of laws, made by persons authorized thereunto, by the consent and appointment of the people, without which no one man, or number of men, amongst them can have authority of making laws that shall be binding to the rest. When any one, or more, shall take upon them to make laws whom the people have not appointed so to do, they make laws without authority, which the people are not therefore bound to obey; by which means they come again to be out of subjection, and may constitute to themselves a new legislative, as they think best, being in full liberty to resist the force of those who, without authority, would impose anything upon them. Every one is at the disposure of his own will, when those who had, by the delegation of the society, the declaring of the public will, are excluded from it, and others usurp the place who have no such authority or delegation.

213. This being usually brought about by such in the commonwealth, who misuse the power they have, it is hard to consider it aright, and know at whose door to lay it, without knowing the form of government in which it happens. Let us suppose, then, the legislative placed in the concurrence of three distinct persons:—First, a single hereditary person having the constant, supreme, executive power, and with it the power of convoking and dissolving the other two within certain periods of time. Secondly, an assembly of hereditary nobility. Thirdly, an assembly of representatives chosen, *pro tempore*, by the people. Such a form of government supposed, it is evident:

214. First, that when such a single person or prince sets up his own arbitrary will in place of the laws which are the will of the society declared by the legislative, then the legislative is changed. For that being, in effect, the legislative whose rules and laws are put in execution, and required to be obeyed, when other laws are set up, and other rules pretended and enforced than what the legislative, constituted by the society, have enacted, it is plain that the legislative is changed. Whoever introduces new laws, not being thereunto authorized, by the fundamental appointment of the society, or subverts the old, disowns and overturns the power by which they were made, and so sets up a new legislative.

215. Secondly, when the prince hinders the legislative from assembling in its due time, or from acting freely, pursuant to those ends for which it was constituted, the legislative is altered. For it is not a certain number of men—no, nor their meeting, unless they have also freedom of debating and leisure of perfecting what is for the good of the society, wherein the legislative consists; when these are taken away, or altered, so as to deprive the society of the due exercise of their power, the legislative is truly altered. For it is not names that constitute governments, but the use and exercise of those powers that were intended to accompany them; so that he who takes away the freedom, or hinders the acting of the legislative in its due seasons, in effect takes away the legislative, and puts an end to the government.

216. Thirdly, when, by the arbitrary power of the prince, the electors or ways of election are altered without the consent and contrary to the common interest of the people, there also the legislative is altered. For if others than those whom the society hath authorized thereunto do choose, or in another way than what the society hath prescribed, those chosen are not the legislative appointed by the people.

217. Fourthly, the delivery also of the people into the subjection of a foreign power, either by the prince or by the legislative, is certainly a change of the legislative, and so a dissolution of the government. For the end why people entered into society being to be preserved one entire, free, independent society to be governed by its own laws, this is lost whenever they are given up into the power of another.

218. Why, in such a constitution as this, the dissolution of the government in these cases is to be imputed to the prince is evident, because he, having the force, treasure, and

offices of the State to employ, and often persuading himself or being flattered by others, that, as supreme magistrate, he is incapable of control; he alone is in a condition to make great advances towards such changes under pretence of lawful authority, and has it in his hands to terrify or suppress opposers as factious, seditious, and enemies to the government; whereas no other part of the legislative, or people, is capable by themselves to attempt any alteration of the legislative without open and visible rebellion, apt enough to be taken notice of, which, when it prevails, produces effects very little different from foreign conquest. Besides, the prince, in such a form of government, having the power of dissolving the other parts of the legislative, and thereby rendering them private persons, they can never, in opposition to him, or without his concurrence, alter the legislative by a law, his consent being necessary to give any of their decrees that sanction. But yet so far as the other parts of the legislative any way contribute to any attempt upon the government, and do either promote, or not, what lies in them, hinder such designs, they are guilty, and partake in this, which is certainly the greatest crime men can be guilty of one towards another.

219. There is one way more whereby such a government may be dissolved, and that is: When he who has the supreme executive power neglects and abandons that charge, so that the laws already made can no longer be put in execution; this is demonstratively to reduce all to anarchy, and so effectively to dissolve the government. For laws not being made for themselves, but to be, by their execution, the bonds of the society to keep every part of the body politic in its due place and function. When that totally ceases, the government visibly ceases, and the people become a confused multitude without order or connection. Where there is no longer the administration of justice for the securing of men's rights, nor any remaining power within the community to direct the force, or provide for the necessities of the public, there certainly is no government left. Where the laws cannot be executed it is all one as if there were no laws, and a government without laws is, I suppose, a mystery in politics inconceivable to human capacity, and inconsistent with human society.

220. In these, and the like cases, when the government is dissolved, the people are at liberty to provide for themselves by erecting a new legislative differing from the other by the change of persons, or form, or both, as they shall find it most for their safety and good. For the society can never, by the fault of another, lose the native and original right it has to preserve itself, which can only be done by a settled legislative and a fair and impartial execution of the laws made by it. But the state of mankind is not so miserable that they are not capable of using this remedy till it be too late to look for any. To tell people they may provide for themselves by erecting a new legislative, when, by oppression, artifice, or being delivered over to a foreign power, their old one is gone, is only to tell them they may expect relief when it is too late, and the evil is past cure. This is, in effect, no more than to bid them first be slaves, and then to take care of their liberty, and, when their chains are on, tell them they may act like free men. This, if barely so, is rather mockery than relief, and men can never be secure from tyranny if there be no means to escape it till they are perfectly under it; and, therefore, it is that they have not only a right to get out of it, but to prevent it.

221. There is, therefore, secondly, another way whereby governments are dissolved, and that is, when the legislative, or the prince, either of them act contrary to their trust.

For the legislative acts against the trust reposed in them when they endeavor to invade the property of the subject, and to make themselves, or any part of the community, masters or arbitrary disposers of the lives, liberties, or fortunes of the people.

222. The reason why men enter into society is the preservation of their property; and the end while they choose and authorize a legislative is that there may be laws made, and rules set, as guards and fences to the properties of all the society, to limit the power and moderate the dominion of every part and member of the society. For since it can never be supposed to be the will of the society that the legislative should have a power to destroy that which every one designs to secure by entering into society, and for which the people submitted themselves to legislators of their own making: whenever the legislators endeavor to take away and destroy the property of the people, or to reduce them to slavery under arbitrary power, they put themselves into a state of war with the people, who are thereupon absolved from any farther obedience, and are left to the common refuge which God hath provided for all men against force and violence. Whensoever, therefore, the legislative shall transgress this fundamental rule of society, and either by ambition, fear, folly, or corruption, endeavor to grasp themselves, or put into the hands of any other, an absolute power over the lives, liberties, and estates of the people, by this breach of trust they forfeit the power the people had put into their hands for quite contrary ends, and it devolves to the people, who have a right to resume their original liberty, and by the establishment of a new legislative (such as they shall think fit), provide for their own safety and security, which is the end for which they are in society. What I have said here concerning the legislative in general holds true also concerning the supreme executor, who having a double trust put in him, both to have a part in the legislative and the supreme execution of the law, acts against both, when he goes about to set up his own arbitrary will as the law of the society. He acts also contrary to his trust when he employs the force, treasure, and offices of the society to corrupt the representatives and gain them to his purposes, when he openly pre-engages the electors, and prescribes, to their choice, such whom he has, by solicitation, threats, promises, or otherwise, won to his designs, and employs them to bring in such who have promised beforehand what to vote and what to enact. Thus to regulate candidates and electors, and new model the ways of election, what is it but to cut up the government by the roots, and poison the very fountain of public security? For the people having reserved to themselves the choice of their representatives as the fence to their properties, could do it for no other end but that they might always be freely chosen, and so chosen, freely act and advise as the necessity of the commonwealth and the public good should, upon examination and mature debate, be judged to require. This, those who give their votes before they hear the debate, and have weighed the reasons on all sides, are not capable of doing. To prepare such an assembly as this, and endeavor to set up the declared abettors of his own will, for the true representatives of the people, and the law-makers of the society, is certainly as great a breach of trust, and as perfect a declaration of a design to subvert the government, as is possible to be met with. To which,

if one shall add rewards and punishments visibly employed to the same end, and all the arts of perverted law made use of to take off and destroy all that stand in the way of such a design, and will not comply and consent to betray the liberties of their country, it will be past doubt what is doing. What power they ought to have in the society who thus employ it contrary to the trust that along with it in its first institution, is easy to determine; and one cannot but see that he who has once attempted any such thing as this cannot any longer be trusted.

223. To this, perhaps, it will be said that the people being ignorant and always discontented, to lay the foundation of government in the unsteady opinion and uncertain humor of the people, is to expose it to certain ruin; and no government will be able long to subsist if the people may set up a new legislative whenever they take offence at the old one. To this I answer, quite the contrary. People are not so easily got out of their old forms as some are apt to suggest. They are hardly to be prevailed with to amend the acknowledged faults in the frame they have been accustomed to. And if there be any original defects, or adventitious ones introduced by time or corruption, it is not an easy thing to get them changed, even when all the world sees there is an opportunity for it. This slowness and aversion in the people to quit their old constitutions has in the many revolutions [that] have been seen in this kingdom, in this and former ages, still kept us to, or after some interval of fruitless attempts, still brought us back again to, our old legislative of king, lords and commons; and whatever provocations have made the crown be taken from some of our princes' heads, they never carried the people so far as to place it in another line.

224. But it will be said this hypothesis lays a ferment for frequent rebellion. To which I answer:

First: no more than any other hypothesis. For when the people are made miserable, and find themselves exposed to the ill usage of arbitrary power, cry up their governors as much as you will for sons of Jupiter, let them be sacred and divine, descended or authorized from Heaven; give them out for whom or what you please, the same will happen. The people generally ill treated, and contrary to right, will be ready upon any occasion to ease themselves of a burden that sits heavy upon them. They will wish and seek for the opportunity, which in the change, weakness, and accidents of human affairs, seldom delays long to offer itself He must have lived but a little while in the world, who has not seen examples of this in his time; and he must have read very little who cannot produce examples of it in all sorts of governments in the world.

225. Secondly: I answer, such revolutions happen not upon every little mismanagement in public affairs. Great mistakes in the ruling part, many wrong and inconvenient laws, and all the slips of human frailty will be borne by the people without mutiny or murmur. But if a long train of abuses, prevarications, and artifices, all tending the same way, make the design visible to the people, and they cannot but feel what they lie under, and see whither they are going, it is not to be wondered that they should then rouse themselves, and endeavor to put the rule into such hands which may secure to them the ends for which government was at first erected, and without which, ancient names and specious forms are so far from being better, that they are much worse than the state of Na-

ture or pure anarchy; the inconveniencies being all as great and as near, but the remedy farther off and more difficult.

226. Thirdly: I answer, that this power in the people of providing for their safety anew by a new legislative when their legislators have acted contrary to their trust by invading their property, is the best fence against rebellion, and the probable means to hinder it. For rebellion being an opposition, not to persons, but authority, which is founded only in the constitutions and laws of the government: those, whoever they be, who, by force, break through, and, by force, justify their violation of them, are truly and properly rebels. For when men, by entering into society and civil government, have excluded force, and introduced laws for the preservation of property, peace, and unity amongst themselves, those who set up force again in opposition to the laws, do *rebellare*—that is, bring back again the state of war, and are properly rebels, which they who are in power, by the pretence they have to authority, the temptation of force they have in their hands, and the flattery of those about them being likeliest to do, the proper way to prevent the evil is to show them the danger and injustice of it who are under the greatest temptation to run into it.

227. In both the forementioned cases, when either the legislative is changed, or the legislators act contrary to the end for which they were constituted, those who are guilty are guilty of rebellion. For if any one by force takes away the established legislative of any society, and the laws by them made, pursuant to their trust, he thereby takes away the umpirage which every one had consented to for a peaceable decision of all their controversies, and a bar to the state of war amongst them. They who remove or change the legislative take away this decisive power, which nobody can have but by the appointment and consent of the people, and so destroying the authority which the people did, and nobody else can, set up, and introducing a power which the people hath not authorized, actually introduce a state of war, which is that of force without authority; and thus by removing the legislative established by the society, in whose decisions the people acquiesced and united as to that of their own will, they untie the knot, and expose the people anew to the state of war. And if those, who by force take away the legislative, are rebels, the legislators themselves, as has been shown, can be no less esteemed so, when they who were set up for the protection and preservation of the people, their liberties and properties shall by force invade and endeavor to take them away; and so they putting themselves into a state of war with those who made them the protectors and guardians of their peace, are properly, and with the greatest aggravation, *rebellantes*, rebels.

228. But if they who say it lays a foundation for rebellion mean that it may occasion civil wars or intestine broils to tell the people they are absolved from obedience when illegal attempts are made upon their liberties or properties, and may oppose the unlawful violence of those who were their magistrates when they invade their properties, contrary to the trust put in them, and that, therefore, this doctrine is not to be allowed, being so destructive to the peace of the world; they may as well say, upon the same ground, that honest men may not oppose robbers or pirates, because this may occasion disorder or bloodshed. If any mischief come in such cases, it is not to be charged upon him who defends his own right, but on him that invades his neighbor's. If the innocent honest man

must quietly quit all he has for peace sake to him who will lay violent hands upon it, I desire it may be considered what kind of a peace there will be in the world which consists only in violence and rapine, and which is to be maintained only for the benefit of robbers and oppressors. Who would not think it an admirable peace betwixt the mighty and the mean, when the lamb, without resistance, yielded his throat to be torn by the imperious wolf? Polyphemus's den gives us a perfect pattern of such a peace. Such a government wherein Ulysses and his companions had nothing to do but quietly to suffer themselves to be devoured. And no doubt Ulysses, who was a prudent man, preached up passive obedience, and exhorted them to a quiet submission by representing to them of what concernment peace was to mankind, and by showing [what] inconveniencies might happen if they should offer to resist Polyphemus, who had now the power over them.

229. The end of government is the good of mankind; and which is best for mankind, that the people should be always exposed to the boundless will of tyranny, or that the rulers should be sometimes liable to be opposed when they grow exorbitant in the use of their power, and employ it for the destruction, and not the preservation, of the properties of their people?

230. Nor let any one say that mischief can arise from hence as often as it shall please a busy head or turbulent spirit to desire the alteration of the government. It is true such men may stir whenever they please, but it will be only to their own just ruin and perdition. For till the mischief be grown general, and the ill designs of the rulers become visible, or their attempts sensible to the greater part, the people, who are more disposed to suffer than right themselves by resistance, are not apt to stir. The examples of particular injustice or oppression of here and there an unfortunate man moves them not. But if they universally have a persuasion grounded upon manifest evidence that designs are carrying on against their liberties, and the general course and tendency of things cannot but give them strong suspicions of the evil intention of their governors, who is to be blamed for it? Who can help it if they, who might avoid it, bring themselves into this suspicion? Are the people to be blamed if they have the sense of rational creatures, and can think of things no otherwise than as they find and feel them? And is it not rather their fault who put things in such a posture that they would not have them thought as they are? I grant that the pride, ambition, and turbulency of private men have sometimes caused great disorders in commonwealths, and factions have been fatal to states and kingdoms. But whether the mischief hath oftener begun in the people's wantonness, and a desire to cast off the lawful authority of their rulers, or in the rulers' insolence and endeavors to get and exercise an arbitrary power over their people, whether oppression or disobedience gave the first rise to the disorder, I leave it to impartial history to determine. This I am sure, whoever, either ruler or subject, by force goes about to invade the rights of either prince or people, and lays the foundation for overturning the constitution and frame of any just government, he is guilty of the greatest crime I think a man is capable of, being to answer for all those mischiefs of blood, rapine, and desolation, which the breaking to pieces of governments bring on a country; and he who does it is justly to be esteemed the common enemy and pest of mankind, and is to be treated accordingly.

231. That subjects or foreigners attempting by force on the properties of any people may be resisted with force is agreed on all hands; but that magistrates doing the same thing may be resisted, hath of late been denied; as if those who had the greatest privileges and advantages by the law had thereby a power to break those laws by which alone they were set in a better place than their brethren; whereas their offence is thereby the greater, both as being ungrateful for the greater share they have by the law, and breaking also that trust which is put into their hands by their brethren.

232. Whosoever uses force without right—as every one does in society who does it without law—puts himself into a state of war with those against whom he so uses it, and in that state all former ties are cancelled, all other rights cease, and every one has a right to defend himself, and to resist the aggressor. This is so evident that Barclay himself—that great assertor of the power and sacredness of kings—is forced to confess that it is lawful for the people, in some cases, to resist their king, and that, too, in a chapter wherein he pretends to show that the Divine law shuts up the people from all manner of rebellion. Whereby it is evident, even by his own doctrine, that since they may, in some cases, resist, all resisting of princes is not rebellion. His words are these:

233. "But if any one should ask: Must the people, then, always lay themselves open to the cruelty and rage of tyranny—must they see their cities pillaged and laid in ashes, their wives and children exposed to the tyrant's lust and fury, and themselves and families reduced by their king to ruin and all the miseries of want and oppression, and yet sit still—must men alone be debarred the common privilege of opposing force with force, which Nature allows so freely to all other creatures for their preservation from injury? I answer: Self-defense is a part of the law of Nature; nor can it be denied the community, even against the king himself; but to revenge themselves upon him must, by no means, be allowed them, it being not agreeable to that law. Wherefore, if the king shall show an hatred, not only to some particular persons, but sets himself against the body of the commonwealth, whereof he is the head, and shall, with intolerable ill-usage, cruelly tyrannies over the whole, or a considerable part of the people; in this case the people have a right to resist and defend themselves from injury; but it must be with this caution, that they only defend themselves, but do not attack their prince. They may repair the damages received, but must not, for any provocation, exceed the bounds of due reverence and respect. They may repulse the present attempt, but must not revenge past violences. For it is natural for us to defend life and limb, but that an inferior should punish a superior is against nature. The mischief which is designed them the people may prevent before it be done, but, when it is done, they must not revenge it on the king, though author of the villany. This, therefore, is the privilege of the people in general above what any private person hath: That particular men are allowed, by our adversaries themselves (Buchanan only excepted), to have no other remedy but patience; but the body of the people may, with respect, resist intolerable tyranny, for when it is but moderate they ought to endure it."

234. Thus far that great advocate of monarchical power allows of resistance.

235. It is true, he has annexed two limitations to it, to no purpose:

First. He says it must be with reverence.

Secondly. It must be without retribution or punishment; and the reason he gives is, "because an inferior cannot punish a superior."

First. How to resist force without striking again, or how to strike with reverence, will need some skill to make intelligible. He that shall oppose an assault only with a shield to receive the blows, or in any more respectful posture, without a sword in his hand to abate the confidence and force of the assailant, will quickly be at an end of his resistance, and will find such a defense serve only to draw on himself the worse usage. This is as ridiculous a way of resisting as Juvenal thought it of fighting: *Ubi tu pulsas, ego vapulo tantum.* ["When you strike, I only beaten"] And the success of the combat will be unavoidably the same he there describes it:

> *Libertas pauperis haec est; Pulsatus rogat, et pugnis concisus, adorat, Ut liceat paucis cum dentibus inde reverti.*
>
> [This is the poor man's freedom: When he is beaten, he prays; when smitten he implores that he may be able to come home with a few teeth]

This will always be the event of such an imaginary resistance, where men may not strike again. He, therefore, who may resist must be allowed to strike. And then let our author, or anybody else, join a knock on the head or a cut on the face with as much reverence and respect as he thinks fit. He that can reconcile blows and reverence may, for aught I know, deserve for his pains a civil, respectful cudgelling wherever he can meet with it.

Secondly, as to his second: an inferior cannot punish a superior. That is true, generally speaking, whilst he is his superior. But to resist force with force, being the state of war that levels the parties, cancels all former relation of reverence, respect, and superiority; and then the odds that remains is that he who opposes the unjust aggressor has this superiority over him, that he has a right, when he prevails, to punish he offender, both for the breach of the peace and all the evils that followed upon it. Barclay, therefore, in another place, more coherently to himself, denies it to be lawful to resist a king in any case. But he there assigns two cases whereby a king may unking himself. His words are:

237. "What, then, can there no case happen wherein the people may of right, and by their own authority, help themselves, take arms, and set upon their king, imperiously domineering over them? None at all whilst he remains a king. 'Honor the king,' and 'he that resists the power, resists the ordinance of God,' are Divine oracles that will never permit it. The people, therefore, can never come by a power over him unless he does something that makes him cease to be a king; for then he divests himself of his crown and dignity, and returns to the state of a private man, and the people become free and superior; the power which they had in the interregnum, before they crowned him king, devolving to them again. But there are but few miscarriages which bring the matter to this state. After considering it well on all sides, I can find but two. Two cases there are, I say, whereby a king, *ipso facto*, becomes no king, and loses all power and regal authority over his people, which are also taken notice of by Winzerus. The first is, if he endeavor to overturn the gov-

ernment—that is, if he have a purpose and design to ruin the kingdom and commonwealth, as it is recorded of Nero that he resolved to cut off the senate and people of Rome, lay the city waste with fire and sword, and then remove to some other place; and of Caligula, that he openly declared that he would be no longer a head to the people or senate, and that he had it in his thoughts to cut off the worthiest men of both ranks, and then retire to Alexandria; and he wished that the people had but one neck that he might dispatch them all at a blow. Such designs as these, when any king harbors in his thoughts, and seriously promotes, he immediately gives up all care and thought of the commonwealth, and, consequently, forfeits the power of governing his subjects, as a master does the dominion over his slaves whom he hath abandoned.

238. "The other case is, when a king makes himself the dependent of another, and subjects his kingdom, which his ancestors left him, and the people put free into his hands, to the dominion of another. For however, perhaps, it may not be his intention to prejudice the people, yet because he has hereby lost the principal part of regal dignity, viz., to be next and immediately under God, supreme in his kingdom; and also because he betrayed or forced his people, whose liberty he ought to have carefully preserved, into the power and dominion of a foreign nation. By this, as it were, alienation of his kingdom, he himself loses the power he had in it before, without transferring any the least right to those on whom he would have bestowed it; and so by this act sets the people free, and leaves them at their own disposal. One example of this is to be found in the Scotch annals."

239. In these cases Barclay, the great champion of absolute monarchy, is forced to allow that a king may be resisted, and ceases to be a king. That is in short—not to multiply cases—in whatsoever he has no authority, there he is no king, and may be resisted: for wheresoever the authority ceases, the king ceases too, and becomes like other men who have no authority. And these two cases that he instances differ little from those above mentioned, to be destructive to governments, only that he has omitted the principle from which his doctrine flows, and that is the breach of trust in not preserving the form of government agreed on, and in not intending the end of government itself, which is the public good and preservation of property. When a king has dethroned himself, and put himself in a state of war with his people, what shall hinder them from prosecuting him who is no king, as they would any other man, who has put himself into a state of war with them, Barclay, and those of his opinion, would do well to tell us. Bilson, a bishop of our Church, and a great stickler for the power and prerogative of princes, does, if I mistake not, in his treatise of "Christian Subjection," acknowledge that princes may forfeit their power and their title to the obedience of their subjects; and if there needed authority in a case where reason is so plain, I could send my reader to Bracton, Fortescue, and the author of the "Mirror," and others, writers that cannot be suspected to be ignorant of our government, or enemies to it. But I thought Hooker alone might be enough to satisfy those men who, relying on him for their ecclesiastical polity, are by a strange fate carried to deny those principles upon which he builds it. Whether they are herein made the tools of cunninger workmen, to pull down their own fabric, they were best look. This I am

sure, their civil policy is so new, so dangerous, and so destructive to both rulers and people, that as former ages never could bear the broaching of it, so it may be hoped those to come, redeemed from the impositions of these Egyptian under-taskmasters, will abhor the memory of such servile flatterers, who, whilst it seemed to serve their turn, resolved all government into absolute tyranny, and would have all men born to what their mean souls fitted them—slavery.

240. Here it is like the common question will be made: Who shall be judge whether the prince or legislative act contrary to their trust? This, perhaps, ill-affected and factious men may spread amongst the people, when the prince only makes use of his due prerogative. To this I reply, The people shall be judge; for who shall be judge whether his trustee or deputy acts well and according to the trust reposed in him, but he who deputes him and must, by having deputed him, have still a power to discard him when he fails in his trust? If this be reasonable in particular cases of private men, why should it be otherwise in that of the greatest moment, where the welfare of millions is concerned and also where the evil, if not prevented, is greater, and the redress very difficult, dear, and dangerous?

241. But, farther, this question, Who shall be judge? cannot mean that there is no judge at all. For where there is no judicature on earth to decide controversies amongst men, God in heaven is judge. He alone, it is true, is judge of the right. But every man is judge for himself, as in all other cases so in this, whether another hath put himself into a state of war with him, and whether he should appeal to the supreme judge, as Jephtha did.

242. If a controversy arise betwixt a prince and some of the people in a matter where the law is silent or doubtful, and the thing be of great consequence, I should think the proper umpire in such a case should be the body of the people. For in such cases where the prince hath a trust reposed in him, and is dispensed from the common, ordinary rules of the law, there, if any men find themselves aggrieved, and think the prince acts contrary to, or beyond that trust, who so proper to judge as the body of the people (who at first lodged that trust in him) how far they meant it should extend? But if the prince, or whoever they be in the administration, decline that way of determination, the appeal then lies nowhere but to Heaven. Force between either persons who have no known superior on earth or, which permits no appeal to a judge on earth, being properly a state of war, wherein the appeal lies only to heaven; and in that state the injured party must judge for himself when he will think fit to make use of that appeal and put himself upon it.

243. To conclude. The power that every individual gave the society when he entered into it can never revert to the individuals again, as long as the society lasts, but will always remain in the community; because without this there can be no community—no commonwealth, which is contrary to the original agreement; so also when the society hath placed the legislative in any assembly of men, to continue in them and their successors, with direction and authority for providing such successors, the legislative can never revert to the people whilst that government lasts: because, having provided a legislative with power to continue for ever, they have given up their political power to the legislative, and cannot resume it. But if they have set limits to the duration of their legislative, and made this

supreme power in any person or assembly only temporary; or else when, by the miscarriages of those in authority, it is forfeited; upon the forfeiture of their rulers, or at the determination of the time set, it reverts to the society, and the people have a right to act as supreme, and continue the legislative in themselves or place it in a new form, or new hands, as they think good.

Thomas Jefferson et al.

The Declaration of Independence

In Congress, July 4, 1776.

The unanimous Declaration of the thirteen united States of America,

When in the Course of human events, it becomes necessary for one people to dissolve the political bands which have connected them with another, and to assume among the powers of the earth, the separate and equal station to which the Laws of Nature and of Nature's God entitle them, a decent respect to the opinions of mankind requires that they should declare the causes which impel them to the separation.

We hold these truths to be self-evident, that all men are created equal, that they are endowed by their Creator with certain unalienable Rights, that among these are Life, Liberty and the pursuit of Happiness.—That to secure these rights, Governments are instituted among Men, deriving their just powers from the consent of the governed—That whenever any Form of Government becomes destructive of these ends, it is the Right of the People to alter or to abolish it, and to institute new Government, laying its foundation on such principles and organizing its powers in such form, as to them shall seem most likely to effect their Safety and Happiness. Prudence, indeed, will dictate that Governments long established should not be changed for light and transient causes; and accordingly all experience hath shewn, that mankind are more disposed to suffer, while evils are sufferable, than to right themselves by abolishing the forms to which they are accustomed. But when a long train of abuses and usurpations, pursuing invariably the same Object evinces a design to reduce them under absolute Despotism, it is their right, it is their duty, to throw off such Government, and to provide new Guards for their future security.—Such has been the patient sufferance of these Colonies; and such is now the necessity which constrains them to alter their former Systems of Government. The history of the present King of Great Britain is a history of repeated injuries and usurpations, all having in direct object the establishment of an absolute Tyranny over these States. To prove this, let Facts be submitted to a candid world.

He has refused his Assent to Laws, the most wholesome and necessary for the public good.

He has forbidden his Governors to pass Laws of immediate and pressing importance, unless suspended in their operation till his Assent should be obtained; and when so suspended, he has utterly neglected to attend to them.

He has refused to pass other Laws for the accommodation of large districts of people, unless those people would relinquish the right of Representation in the Legislature, a right inestimable to them and formidable to tyrants only.

He has called together legislative bodies at places unusual, uncomfortable, and distant from the depository of their public Records, for the sole purpose of fatiguing them into compliance with his measures.

He has dissolved Representative Houses repeatedly, for opposing with manly firmness his invasions on the rights of the people.

He has refused for a long time, after such dissolutions, to cause others to be elected; whereby the Legislative powers, incapable of Annihilation, have returned to the People at large for their exercise; the State remaining in the mean time exposed to all the dangers of invasion from without, and convulsions within.

He has endeavoured to prevent the population of these States; for that purpose obstructing the Laws for Naturalization of Foreigners; refusing to pass others to encourage their migrations hither, and raising the conditions of new Appropriations of Lands.

He has obstructed the Administration of Justice, by refusing his Assent to Laws for establishing Judiciary powers.

He has made Judges dependent on his Will alone, for the tenure of their offices, and the amount and payment of their salaries.

He has erected a multitude of New Offices, and sent hither swarms of Officers to harrass our people, and eat out their substance.

He has kept among us, in times of peace, Standing Armies without the Consent of our legislatures.

He has affected to render the Military independent of and superior to the Civil power.

He has combined with others to subject us to a jurisdiction foreign to our constitution, and unacknowledged by our laws; giving his Assent to their Acts of pretended Legislation:

For Quartering large bodies of armed troops among us:

For protecting them, by a mock Trial, from punishment for any Murders which they should commit on the Inhabitants of these States:

For cutting off our Trade with all parts of the world:

For imposing Taxes on us without our Consent:

For depriving us in many cases, of the benefits of Trial by Jury:

For transporting us beyond Seas to be tried for pretended offences:

For abolishing the free System of English Laws in a neighbouring Province, establishing therein an Arbitrary government, and enlarging its Boundaries so as to render it at once an example and fit instrument for introducing the same absolute rule into these Colonies:

For taking away our Charters, abolishing our most valuable Laws, and altering fundamentally the Forms of our Governments:

For suspending our own Legislatures, and declaring themselves invested with power to legislate for us in all cases whatsoever.

He has abdicated Government here, by declaring us out of his Protection and waging War against us.

He has plundered our seas, ravaged our Coasts, burnt our towns, and destroyed the lives of our people.

He is at this time transporting large Armies of foreign Mercenaries to compleat the works of death, desolation and tyranny, already begun with circumstances of Cruelty & perfidy scarcely paralleled in the most barbarous ages, and totally unworthy the Head of a civilized nation.

He has constrained our fellow Citizens taken Captive on the high Seas to bear Arms against their Country, to become the executioners of their friends and Brethren, or to fall themselves by their Hands.

He has excited domestic insurrections amongst us, and has endeavoured to bring on the inhabitants of our frontiers, the merciless Indian Savages, whose known rule of warfare, is an undistinguished destruction of all ages, sexes and conditions.

In every stage of these Oppressions We have Petitioned for Redress in the most humble terms: Our repeated Petitions have been answered only by repeated injury. A Prince whose character is thus marked by every act which may define a Tyrant, is unfit to be the ruler of a free people.

Nor have We been wanting in attentions to our British brethren. We have warned them from time to time of attempts by their legislature to extend an unwarrantable jurisdiction over us. We have reminded them of the circumstances of our emigration and settlement here. We have appealed to their native justice and magnanimity, and we have conjured them by the ties of our common kindred to disavow these usurpations, which, would inevitably interrupt our connections and correspondence. They too have been deaf to the voice of justice and of consanguinity. We must, therefore, acquiesce in the necessity, which denounces our Separation, and hold them, as we hold the rest of mankind, Enemies in War, in Peace Friends.

We, therefore, the Representatives of the united States of America, in General Congress, Assembled, appealing to the Supreme Judge of the world for the rectitude of our intentions, do, in the Name, and by Authority of the good People of these Colonies, solemnly publish and declare, That these United Colonies are, and of Right ought to be Free and Independent States; that they are Absolved from all Allegiance to the British Crown, and that all political connection between them and the State of Great Britain, is and ought to be totally dissolved; and that as Free and Independent States, they have full Power to levy War, conclude Peace, contract Alliances, establish Commerce, and to do all other Acts and Things which Independent States may of right do. And for the support of this Declaration, with a firm reliance on the protection of divine Providence, we mutually pledge to each other our Lives, our Fortunes and our sacred Honor.

From The Constitution of the United States of America

Preamble

We the People of the United States, in Order to form a more perfect Union, establish Justice, insure domestic Tranquility, provide for the common defense, promote the general Welfare, and secure the Blessings of Liberty to ourselves and our Posterity, do ordain and establish this Constitution for the United States of America.

Articles of the Constitution of the United States Referring to Slavery and the Rights of Slaves

Article I, Section 2, Item 3

Representatives and direct taxes shall be apportioned among the several States which may be included within this Union, according to their respective numbers, which shall be determined by adding to the whole number of free persons, including those bound to Service for a Term of Years, and excluding Indians not taxed, three fifths of all other persons. The actual enumeration shall be made within three years after the first meeting of the Congress of the United States, and within every subsequent term of ten years, in such manner as they shall by law direct. The number of Representatives shall not exceed one for every thirty thousand, but each State shall have at least one Representative.

Article I, Section 9, Item 1

The migration or importation of such persons as any of the states now existing shall think proper to admit, shall not be prohibited by the Congress prior to the year one thousand eight hundred and eight, but a tax or duty may be imposed on such importation, not exceeding ten dollars for each person.

Article IV, Section 2, Item 3

No person held to service or labour in one state, under the laws thereof, escaping into another, shall, in consequence of any law or regulation therein, be discharged from such service or labour, but shall be delivered up on claim of the party to whom such service or labour may be due.

The Bill of Rights

(The first ten amendments resulted from an understanding arrived at during the controversy over the ratification of the Constitution. The advocates of immediate ratification won over some of those who originally preferred a second convention to revise the original draft before ratification. Twelve amendments were proposed by Congress in 1789; of the twelve, ten were ratified by the necessary number of states by the end of 1791.)

Resolved, by the Senate and House of Representatives of the United States of America, in Congress assembled, two-thirds of both Houses concurring, that the following articles be proposed to the Legislatures of the several States, as amendments to the Constitution of the United States; all or any of which articles, when ratified by three-fourths of the said Legislatures, to be valid to all intents and purposes as part of the said Constitution, namely:

Amendment I

Congress shall make no law respecting an establishment of religion, or prohibiting the free exercise thereof; or abridging the freedom of speech, or of the press; or the right of the people peaceably to assemble, and to petition the government for a redress of grievances.

Amendment II

A well regulated militia, being necessary to the security of a free state, the right of the people to keep and bear arms, shall not be infringed.

Amendment III

No soldier shall, in time of peace be quartered in any house, without the consent of the owner, nor in time of war, but in a manner to be prescribed by law.

Amendment IV

The right of the people to be secure in their persons, houses, papers, and effects, against unreasonable searches and seizures, shall not be violated, and no warrants shall issue, but upon probable cause, supported by oath or affirmation, and particularly describing the place to be searched, and the persons or things to be seized.

Amendment V

No person shall be held to answer for a capital, or otherwise infamous crime, unless on a presentment or indictment of a Grand Jury, except in cases arising in the land or naval forces, or in the Militia, when in actual service in time of War or public danger; nor shall any person be subject for the same offense to be twice put in jeopardy of life or limb; nor shall be compelled in any criminal case to be a witness against himself, nor be deprived of life, liberty, or property, without due process of law; nor shall private property be taken for public use, without just compensation.

Amendment VI

In all criminal prosecutions, the accused shall enjoy the right to a speedy and public trial, by an impartial jury of the State and district wherein the crime shall have been committed, which district shall have been previously ascertained by law, and to be informed of the nature and cause of the accusation; to be confronted with the witnesses against him; to have compulsory process for obtaining witnesses in his favor, and to have the Assistance of Counsel for his defense.

Amendment VII

In Suits at common law, where the value in controversy shall exceed twenty dollars, the right of trial by jury shall be preserved, and no fact tried by a jury, shall be otherwise reexamined in any Court of the United States, than according to the rules of the common law.

Amendment VIII

Excessive bail shall not be required, nor excessive fines imposed, nor cruel and unusual punishments inflicted.

Amendment IX

The enumeration in the Constitution, of certain rights, shall not be construed to deny or disparage others retained by the people.

Amendment X

The powers not delegated to the United States by the Constitution, nor prohibited by it to the States, are reserved to the states respectively, or to the people.

Other Amendments

Amendment XIII (The earliest of the three "Civil War amendments"; proposed in February and ratified by December, 1865.)

Amendment XIII

Section 1. Neither slavery nor involuntary servitude, except as a punishment for crime whereof the party shall have been duly convicted, shall exist within the United States, or any place subject to their jurisdiction.

Section 2. Congress shall have power to enforce this article by appropriate legislation.

Amendment XIV (From the standpoint of later interpretation the first section of this amendment is probably the most important historically of all the amendments. Proposed in 1866 and ratified by July, 1868.)

Amendment XIV

Section 1. All persons born or naturalized in the United States, and subject to the jurisdiction thereof, are citizens of the United States and of the state wherein they reside. No state shall make or enforce any law which shall abridge the privileges or immunities of citizens of the United States; nor shall any state deprive any person of life, liberty, or property, without due process of law; nor deny to any person within its jurisdiction the equal protection of the laws.

Section 2. Representatives shall be apportioned among the several states according to their respective numbers, counting the whole number of persons in each state, excluding Indians not taxed. But when the right to vote at any election for the choice of electors for President and Vice-President of the United States, Representatives in Congress, the executive and judicial officers of a state, or the members of the legislature thereof, is denied to any of the male inhabitants of such state, being twenty-one years of age, and citizens of the United States, or in any way abridged, except for participation in rebellion, or other crime, the basis of representation therein shall be reduced in the proportion which the number of such male citizens shall bear to the whole number of male citizens twenty-one years of age in such state.

Section 3. No person shall be a Senator or Representative in Congress, or elector of President and Vice-President, or hold any office, civil or military, under the United States, or under any state, who, having previously taken an oath, as a member of Congress, or as an officer of the United States, or as a member of any state legislature, or as an executive or judicial officer of any state, to support the Constitution of the United States, shall have engaged in insurrection or rebellion against the same, or given aid or comfort to the enemies thereof. But Congress may, by a vote of two-thirds of each House, remove such disability.

Section 4. The validity of the public debt of the United States, authorized by law, including debts incurred for payment of pensions and bounties for services in suppressing insurrection or rebellion, shall not be questioned. But neither the United States nor any state shall assume or pay any debt or obligation incurred in aid of insurrection or rebellion against the United States, or any claim for the loss or emancipation of any slave; but all such debts, obligations and claims shall be held illegal and void.

Section 5. The Congress shall have power to enforce, by appropriate legislation, the provisions of this article.

Amendment XV (Note the negative form of statement in this amendment. It was proposed in 1869 and ratified by early 1870.)

Amendment XV

Section 1. The right of citizens of the United States to vote shall not be denied or abridged by the United States or by any state on account of race, color, or previous condition of servitude.

Section 2. The Congress shall have power to enforce this article by appropriate legislation.

Amendment XIX (Proposed in 1919 and ratified in fifteen months)

Section 1. The right of citizens of the United States to vote shall not be denied or abridged by the United States or by any state on account of sex.

Section 2. Congress shall have power to enforce this article by appropriate legislation.

James Madison

Federalist Papers

Federalist 10 [1787]

Among the numerous advantages promised by a well-constructed Union, none deserves to be more accurately developed than its tendency to break and control the violence of faction. The friend of popular governments never finds himself so much alarmed for their character and fate, as when he contemplates their propensity to this dangerous vice. He will not fail, therefore, to set a due value on any plan which, without violating the principles to which he is attached, provides a proper cure for it. The instability, injustice, and confusion introduced into the public councils, have, in truth, been the mortal diseases under which popular governments have everywhere perished; as they continue to be the favorite and fruitful topics from which the adversaries to liberty derive their most specious declamations. The valuable improvements made by the American constitutions on the popular models, both ancient and modern, cannot certainly be too much admired; but it would be an unwarrantable partiality, to contend that they have as effectually obviated the danger on this side, as was wished and expected. Complaints are everywhere heard from our most considerate and virtuous citizens, equally the friends of public and private faith, and of public and personal liberty, that our governments are too unstable, that the public good is disregarded in the conflicts of rival parties, and that measures are too often decided, not according to the rules of justice and the rights of the minor party, but by the superior force of an interested and overbearing majority. However anxiously we may wish that these complaints had no foundation, the evidence, of known facts will not permit us to deny that they are in some degree true. It will be found, indeed, on a candid review of our situation, that some of the distresses under which we labor have been erroneously charged on the operation of our governments; but it will be found, at the same time, that other causes will not alone account for many of our heaviest misfortunes; and, particularly, for that prevailing and increasing distrust of public engagements, and alarm for private rights, which are echoed from one end of the continent to the other. These must be chiefly, if not wholly, effects of the unsteadiness and injustice with which a factious spirit has tainted our public administration.

By a faction, I understand a number of citizens, whether amounting to a majority or a minority of the whole, who are united and actuated by some common impulse of passion, or of interest, adverse to the rights of other citizens, or to the permanent and aggregate interests of the community.

There are two methods of curing the mischiefs of faction: the one, by removing its causes; the other, by controlling its effects.

There are again two methods of removing the causes of faction: the one, by destroying the liberty which is essential to its existence; the other, by giving to every citizen the same opinions, the same passions, and the same interests.

It could never be more truly said than of the first remedy, that it was worse than the disease. Liberty is to faction what air is to fire, an aliment without which it instantly expires. But it could not be less folly to abolish liberty, which is essential to political life, because it nourishes faction, than it would be to wish the annihilation of air, which is essential to animal life, because it imparts to fire its destructive agency.

The second expedient is as impracticable as the first would be unwise. As long as the reason of man continues fallible, and he is at liberty to exercise it, different opinions will be formed. As long as the connection subsists between his reason and his self-love, his opinions and his passions will have a reciprocal influence on each other; and the former will be objects to which the latter will attach themselves. The diversity in the faculties of men, from which the rights of property originate, is not less an insuperable obstacle to a uniformity of interests. The protection of these faculties is the first object of government. From the protection of different and unequal faculties of acquiring property, the possession of different degrees and kinds of property immediately results; and from the influence of these on the sentiments and views of the respective proprietors, ensues a division of the society into different interests and parties.

The latent causes of faction are thus sown in the nature of man; and we see them everywhere brought into different degrees of activity, according to the different circumstances of civil society. A zeal for different opinions concerning religion, concerning government, and many other points, as well of speculation as of practice; an attachment to different leaders ambitiously contending for preeminence and power; or to persons of other descriptions whose fortunes have been interesting to the human passions, have, in turn, divided mankind into parties, inflamed them with mutual animosity, and rendered them much more disposed to vex and oppress each other than to co-operate for their common good. So strong is this propensity of mankind to fall into mutual animosities, that where no substantial occasion presents itself, the most frivolous and fanciful distinctions have been sufficient to kindle their unfriendly passions and excite their most violent conflicts. But the most common and durable source of factions has been the various and unequal distribution of property. Those who hold and those who are without property have ever formed distinct interests in society. Those who are creditors, and those who are debtors, fall under a like discrimination. A landed interest, a manufacturing interest, a mercantile interest, a moneyed interest, with many lesser interests, grow up of necessity in civilized nations, and divide them into different classes, actuated by different sentiments and views. The regulation of these various and interfering interests forms the principal task of modern legislation, and involves the spirit of party and faction in the necessary and ordinary operations of the government.

No man is allowed to be a judge in his own cause, because his interest would certainly bias his judgment, and, not improbably, corrupt his integrity. With equal, nay with greater reason, a body of men are unfit to be both judges and parties at the same time; yet what are many of the most important acts of legislation, but so many judicial determinations, not indeed concerning the rights of single persons, but concerning the rights of large bodies of citizens? And what are the different classes of legislators but advocates and parties to the causes which they determine? Is a law proposed concerning private debts? It is a question to which the creditors are parties on one side and the debtors on the other. Justice ought to hold the balance between them. Yet the parties are, and must be, themselves the judges; and the most numerous party, or, in other words, the most powerful faction must be expected to prevail. Shall domestic manufactures be encouraged, and in what degree, by restrictions on foreign manufactures? are questions which would be differently decided by the landed and the manufacturing classes, and probably by neither with a sole regard to justice and the public good. The apportionment of taxes on the various descriptions of property is an act which seems to require the most exact impartiality; yet there is, perhaps, no legislative act in which greater opportunity and temptation are given to a predominant party to trample on the rules of justice. Every shilling with which they overburden the inferior number, is a shilling saved to their own pockets.

It is in vain to say that enlightened statesmen will be able to adjust these clashing interests, and render them all subservient to the public good. Enlightened statesmen will not always be at the helm. Nor, in many cases, can such an adjustment be made at all without taking into view indirect and remote considerations, which will rarely prevail over the immediate interest which one party may find in disregarding the rights of another or the good of the whole.

The inference to which we are brought is, that the *causes* of faction cannot be removed, and that relief is only to be sought in the means of controlling its *effects*.

If a faction consists of less than a majority, relief is supplied by the republican principle, which enables the majority to defeat its sinister views by regular vote. It may clog the administration, it may convulse the society; but it will be unable to execute and mask its violence under the forms of the Constitution. When a majority is included in a faction, the form of popular government, on the other hand, enables it to sacrifice to its ruling passion or interest both the public good and the rights of other citizens. To secure the public good and private rights against the danger of such a faction, and at the same time to preserve the spirit and the form of popular government, is then the great object to which our inquiries are directed. Let me add that it is the great desideratum by which this form of government can be rescued from the opprobrium under which it has so long labored, and be recommended to the esteem and adoption of mankind.

By what means is this object attainable? Evidently by one of two only. Either the existence of the same passion or interest in a majority at the same time must be prevented, or the majority, having such coexistent passion or interest, must be rendered, by their number and local situation, unable to concert and carry into effect schemes of oppression. If the impulse and the opportunity be suffered to coincide, we well know that neither moral nor religious motives can be relied on as an adequate control. They are not found to be such on the injustice and violence of individuals, and lose their efficacy in proportion to the number combined together, that is, in proportion as their efficacy becomes needful.

From this view of the subject it may be concluded that a pure democracy, by which I mean a society consisting of a small number of citizens, who assemble and administer the government in person, can admit of no cure for the mischiefs of faction. A common passion or interest will, in almost every case, be felt by a majority of the whole; a communication and concert result from the form of government itself; and there is nothing to check the inducements to sacrifice the weaker party or an obnoxious individual. Hence it is that such democracies have ever been spectacles of turbulence and contention; have ever been found incompatible with personal security or the rights of property; and have in general been as short in their lives as they have been violent in their deaths. Theoretic politicians, who have patronized this species of government, have erroneously supposed that by reducing mankind to a perfect equality in their political rights, they would, at the same time, be perfectly equalized and assimilated in their possessions, their opinions, and their passions.

A republic, by which I mean a government in which the scheme of representation takes place, opens a different prospect, and promises the cure for which we are seeking. Let us examine the points in which it varies from pure democracy, and we shall comprehend both the nature of the cure and the efficacy which it must derive from the Union.

The two great points of difference between a democracy and a republic are: first, the delegation of the government, in the latter, to a small number of citizens elected by the rest; secondly, the greater number of citizens and greater sphere of country over which the latter may be extended.

The effect of the first difference is, on the one hand, to refine and enlarge the public views by passing them through the medium of a chosen body of citizens, whose wisdom may best discern the true interest of their country and whose patriotism and love of justice will be least likely to sacrifice it to temporary or partial considerations. Under such a regulation, it may well happen that the public voice, pronounced by the representatives of the people, will be more consonant to the public good than if pronounced by the people themselves, convened for the purpose. On the other hand, the effect may be inverted. Men of factious tempers, of local prejudices, or of sinister designs, may, by intrigue, by corruption, or by other means, first obtain the suffrages, and then betray the interests, of the people. The question resulting is, whether small or extensive republics are more favorable to the election of proper guardians of the public weal; and it is clearly decided in favor of the latter by two obvious considerations:

In the first place, it is to be remarked that, however small the republic may be, the representatives must be raised to a certain number, in order to guard against the cabals of a few; and that, however large it may be, they must be limited to a certain number, in order to guard against the confusion of a multitude. Hence, the number of representatives in the two cases not being in proportion to that of the two constituents, and being proportionally greater in the small republic, it follows that, if the proportion of fit characters be not less in the large than in the small republic, the former will present a greater option, and consequently a greater probability of a fit choice.

In the next place, as each representative will be chosen by a greater number of citizens in the large than in the small republic, it will be more difficult for unworthy candidates to practice with success the vicious arts by which elections are too often carried; and the suffrages of the people being more free, will be more likely to centre in men who possess the most attractive merit and the most diffusive and established characters.

It must be confessed that in this, as in most other cases, there is a mean, on both sides of which inconveniences will be found to lie. By enlarging too much the number of electors, you render the representatives too little acquainted with all their local circumstances and lesser interests; as by reducing it too much, you render him unduly attached to these, and too little fit to comprehend and pursue great and national objects. The federal Constitution forms a happy combination in this respect; the great and aggregate interests being referred to the national, the local and particular to the State legislatures.

The other point of difference is, the greater number of citizens and extent of territory which may be brought within the compass of republican than of democratic government; and it is this circumstance principally which renders factious combinations less to be dreaded in the former than in the latter. The smaller the society, the fewer probably will be the distinct parties and interests composing it; the fewer the distinct parties and interests, the more frequently will a majority be found of the same party; and the smaller the number of individuals composing a majority, and the smaller the compass within which they are placed, the more easily will they concert and execute their plans of oppression. Extend the sphere, and you take in a greater variety of parties and interests; you make it less probable that a majority of the whole will have a common motive to invade the rights of other citizens; or if such a common motive exists, it will be more difficult for all who feel it to discover their own strength, and to act in unison with each other. Besides other impediments, it may be remarked that, where there is a consciousness of unjust or dishonorable purposes, communication is always checked by distrust in proportion to the number whose concurrence is necessary.

Hence, it clearly appears, that the same advantage which a republic has over a democracy, in controlling the effects of faction is enjoyed by a large over a small republic—is enjoyed by the Union over the States composing it. Does the advantage consist in the substitution of representatives whose enlightened views and virtuous sentiments render them superior to local prejudices and schemes of injustice? It will not be denied that the representation of the Union will be most likely to possess these requisite endowments. Does it consist in the greater security afforded by a greater variety of parties, against the event of any one party being able to outnumber and oppress the rest? In an equal degree does the increased variety of parties comprised within the Union, increase this security. Does it, in fine, consist in the greater obstacles opposed to the concert and accomplishment of the secret wishes of an unjust and interested majority? Here, again, the extent of the Union gives it the most palpable advantage.

The influence of factious leaders may kindle a flame within their particular States but will be unable to spread a general conflagration through the other States. A religious sect may degenerate into a political faction in a part of the Confederacy; but the variety of sects dispersed over the entire face of it must secure the national councils against any danger from that source. A rage for paper money, for an abolition of debts, for an equal division of property, or for any other improper or wicked project, will be less apt to pervade the whole body of the Union than a particular member of it, in the same proportion as such a malady is more likely to taint a particular county or district, than an entire State.

In the extent and proper structure of the Union, therefore, we behold a republican remedy for the diseases most incident to republican government. And according to the degree of pleasure and pride we feel in being republicans, ought to be our zeal in cherishing the spirit and supporting the character of Federalists.

PUBLIUS

Federalist 51 [1788]

To what expedient, then, shall we finally resort, for maintaining in practice the necessary partition of power among the several departments, as laid down in the Constitution? The only answer that can be given is that as all these exterior provisions are found to be inadequate the defect must be supplied, by so contriving the interior structure of the government as that its several constituent parts may, by their mutual relations, be the means of keeping each other in their proper places. Without presuming to undertake a full development of this important idea I will hazard a few general observations, which may perhaps place it in a clearer light, and enable us to form a more correct judgment of the principles and structure of the government planned by the convention.

In order to lay a due foundation for that separate and distinct exercise of the different powers of government, which to a certain extent is admitted on all hands to be essential to the preservation of liberty, it is evident that each department should have a will of its own; and consequently should be so constituted that the members of each should have as little agency as possible in the appointment of the members of the others. Were this principle rigorously adhered to, it would require that all the appointments for the supreme executive, legislative, and judiciary magistracies should be drawn from the same fountain of authority, the people, through channels having no communication whatever with one another. Perhaps such a plan of constructing the several departments would be less difficult in practice than it may in contemplation appear. Some difficulties, however, and some additional expense would attend the execution of it. Some deviations, therefore, from the principle must be admitted. In the constitution of the judiciary department in particular, it might be inexpedient to insist rigorously on the principle: first, because peculiar qualifications being essential in the members, the primary consideration ought to be to select that mode of choice which best secures these qualifications; secondly, because the permanent tenure by which the appointments are held in that department must soon destroy all sense of dependence on the authority conferring them.

It is equally evident, that the members of each department should be as little dependent as possible on those of the others for the emoluments annexed to their offices. Were the executive magistrate, or the judges, not independent of the legislature in this particular, their independence in every other would be merely nominal.

But the great security against a gradual concentration of the several powers in the same department consists in giving to those who administer each department the necessary constitutional means and personal motives to resist encroachments of the others. The provision for defense must in this, as in all other cases, be made commensurate to the danger of attack. Ambition must be made to counteract ambition. The interest of the man must be connected with the constitutional rights of the place. It may be a reflection on human nature that such devices should be necessary to control the abuses of government. But what is government itself but the greatest of all reflections on human nature? If men were angels, no government would be necessary. If angels were to govern men, neither external nor internal controls on government would be necessary. In framing a government which is to be administered by men over men, the great difficulty lies in this: you must first enable the government to control the governed; and in the next place oblige it to control itself. A dependence on the people is, no doubt, the primary control on the government; but experience has taught mankind the necessity of auxiliary precautions.

This policy of supplying, by opposite and rival interests, the defect of better motives, might be traced through the whole system of human affairs, private as well as public. We see it particularly displayed in all the subordinate distributions of power, where the constant aim is to divide and arrange the several offices in such a manner as that each may be a check on the other—that the private interest of every individual may be a sentinel over the public rights. These inventions of prudence cannot be less requisite in the distribution of the supreme powers of the State.

But it is not possible to give to each department an equal power of self-defense. In republican government, the legislative authority necessarily predominates. The remedy for this inconveniency is to divide the legislature into different branches; and to render them, by different modes of election and different principles of action, as little connected with each other as the nature of their common functions and their common dependence on the society will admit. It may even be necessary to guard against dangerous encroachments by still further precautions. As the weight of the legislative authority requires that it should be thus divided, the weakness of the executive may require, on the other hand, that it should be fortified. An absolute negative on the legislature appears, at first view, to be the natural defense with which the executive magistrate should be armed. But perhaps it would be neither altogether safe nor alone sufficient. On ordinary occasions it might not be exerted with the requisite firmness, and on extraordinary occasions it might be perfidiously abused. May not this defect of an absolute negative be supplied by some qualified connection between this weaker department and the weaker branch of the stronger department, by which the latter may be led to support the constitutional rights of the former, without being too much detached from the rights of its own department?

If the principles on which these observations are founded be just, as I persuade myself they are, and they be applied as a criterion to the several State constitutions, and to the federal Constitution it will be found that if the latter does not perfectly correspond with them, the former are infinitely less able to bear such a test.

There are, moreover, two considerations particularly applicable to the federal system of America, which place that system in a very interesting point of view.

First. In a single republic, all the power surrendered by the people is submitted to the administration of a single government; and the usurpations are guarded against by a division of the government into distinct and separate departments. In the compound republic of America, the power surrendered by the people is first divided between two distinct governments, and then the portion allotted to each subdivided among distinct and separate departments. Hence a double security arises to the rights of the people. The different governments will control each other, at the same time that each will be controlled by itself.

Second. It is of great importance in a republic not only to guard the society against the oppression of its rulers, but to guard one part of the society against the injustice of the other part. Different interests necessarily exist in different classes of citizens. If a majority be united by a common interest, the rights of the minority will be insecure. There are but two methods of providing against this evil: the one by creating a will in the community independent of the majority—that is, of the society itself; the other, by comprehending in the society so many separate descriptions of citizens as will render an unjust combination of a majority of the whole very improbable, if not impracticable. The first method prevails in all governments possessing an hereditary or self-appointed authority. This, at best, is but a precarious security; because a power independent of the society may as well espouse the unjust views of the major as the rightful interests of the minor party, and may possibly be turned against both parties. The second method will be exemplified in the federal republic of the United States. Whilst all authority in it will be derived from and dependent on the society, society itself will be broken into so many parts, interests, and classes of citizens, that the rights of individuals, or of the minority, will be in little danger from interested combinations of the majority. In a free government the security for civil rights must be the same as that for religious rights. It consists in the one case in the multiplicity of interests, and in the other in the multiplicity of sects. The degree of security in both cases will depend on the number of interests and sects; and this may be presumed to depend on the extent of country and number of people comprehended under the same government. This view of the subject must particularly recommend a proper federal system to all the sincere and considerate friends of republican government, since it shows that in exact proportion as the territory of the Union may be formed into more circumscribed Confederacies, or States, oppressive combinations of a majority will be facilitated; the best security, under the republican forms, for the rights of every class of citizens, will be diminished; and consequently the stability and independence of some member of the government, the only other security, must be proportionately increased. Justice is the end of government. It is the end of civil society. It ever has been and ever will be pursued until it be obtained, or until liberty be lost in the pursuit. In a society under the forms of which the stronger faction can readily unite and oppress the weaker, anarchy may as truly be said to reign as in a state of nature, where the weaker individual is not secured against the violence of the stronger; and as, in the latter state, even the stronger individuals are prompted, by the uncertainty of their condition, to submit to a government which may protect the weak as well as themselves; so, in the former state, will the more powerful factions or parties be gradually induced, by a like motive, to wish for a government which will protect all parties, the weaker as well as the more powerful. It can be little doubted that if the State of Rhode Island was separated from the Confederacy and left to itself, the insecurity of rights under the popular form of government within such narrow limits would be displayed by such reiterated oppressions of factious majorities that some power altogether independent of the people would soon be called for by the voice of the very factions whose misrule had proved the necessity of it. In the extended republic of the United States, and among the great variety of interests, parties, and sects which it embraces, a coalition of a majority of the whole society could seldom take place on any other principles than those of justice and the general good; whilst there being thus less danger to a minor from the will of a major party, there must be less pretext, also, to provide for the security of the former, by introducing into the government a will not dependent on the latter, or, in other words, a will independent of the society itself. It is no less certain than it is important, notwithstanding the contrary opinions which have been entertained, that the larger the society, provided it lie within a practical sphere, the more duly capable it will be of self-government. And happily for the *republican cause*, the practicable sphere may be carried to a very great extent, by a judicious modification and mixture of the *federal principle.*

PUBLIUS

David Hume

An Enquiry Concerning the Principles of Morals

Appendix II. [1751]

Of Self-Love.

There is a principle, supposed to prevail among many, which is utterly incompatible with all virtue or moral sentiment; and as it can proceed from nothing but the most depraved disposition, so in its turn it tends still further to encourage that depravity. This principle is, that all benevolence is mere hypocrisy, friendship a cheat, public spirit a farce, fidelity a snare to procure trust and confidence, and that, while all of us, at bottom, pursue only our private interest, we wear these fair disguises, in order to put others off their guard, and expose them the more to our wiles and machinations. What heart one must be possessed of who professes such principles, and who feels no internal sentiment that belies so pernicious a theory, it is easy to imagine: And also, what degree of affection and benevolence he can bear to a species whom he represents under such odious colours, and supposes so little susceptible of gratitude or any return of affection. Or if we should not ascribe these principles wholly to a corrupted heart, we must, at least account for them from the most careless and precipitate examination. Superficial reasoners, indeed, observing many false pretences among mankind, and feeling, perhaps, no very strong restraint in their own disposition, might draw a general and a hasty conclusion that all is equally corrupted, and that men, different from all other animals, and indeed from all other species of existences, admit of no degrees of good or bad, but are, in every instance, the same creatures under different disguises and appearances.

There is another principle, somewhat resembling the former; which has been much insisted on by philosophers, and has been the foundation of many a system; that, whatever affection one may feel, or imagine he feels for others, no passion is, or can be disinterested; that the most generous friendship, however sincere, is a modification of self-love; and that, even unknown to ourselves, we seek only our own gratification, while we appear the most deeply engaged in schemes for the liberty and happiness of mankind. By a turn of imagination, by a refinement of reflection, by an enthusiasm of passion, we seem to take part in the interests of others, and imagine ourselves divested of all selfish considerations: but, at bottom, the most generous patriot and most niggardly miser, the bravest hero and most abject coward, have, in every action, an equal regard to their own happiness and welfare.

Whoever concludes from the seeming tendency of this opinion, that those, who make profession of it, cannot possibly feel the true sentiments of benevolence, or have any regard for genuine virtue, will often find himself, in practice, very much mistaken. Probity and honour were no strangers to Epicurus and his sect. Atticus and Horace seem to have enjoyed from nature, and cultivated by reflection, as generous and friendly dispositions as any disciple of the austerer schools. And among the moderns, Hobbes and Locke, who maintained the selfish system of morals, lived irreproachable lives; though the former lay not under any restraint of religion which might supply the defects of his philosophy.

An Epicurean or a Hobbist readily allows, that there is such a thing as friendship in the world, without hypocrisy or disguise; though he may attempt, by a philosophical chemistry, to resolve the elements of this passion, if I may so speak, into those of another, and explain every affection to be self-love, twisted and moulded, by a particular turn of imagination, into a variety of appearances. But as the same turn of imagination prevails not in every man, nor gives the same direction to the original passion; this is sufficient even according to the selfish system to make the widest difference in human characters, and denominate one man virtuous and humane, another vicious and meanly interested. I esteem the man whose self-love, by whatever means, is so directed as to give him a concern for others, and render him serviceable to society: As I hate or despise him, who has no regard to any thing beyond his own gratifications and enjoyments. In vain would you suggest that these characters, though seemingly opposite, are, at bottom, the same, and that a very inconsiderable turn of thought forms the whole difference between them. Each character, notwithstanding these inconsiderable differences, appears to me, in practice, pretty durable and untransmutable. And I find not in this more than in other subjects, that the natural sentiments arising from the general appearances of things are easily destroyed by subtile reflections concerning the minute origin of these appearances. Does not the lively, cheerful colour of a countenance inspire me with complacency and pleasure; even though I learn from philosophy that all difference of complexion arises from the most minute differences of thickness, in the most minute parts of the skin; by means of which a superficies is qualified to reflect one of the original colours of light, and absorb the others?

But though the question, concerning the universal or partial selfishness of man be not so material as is usually imagined to morality and practice, it is certainly of consequence in the speculative science of human nature, and is a proper object of curiosity and enquiry. It may not, therefore, be unsuitable, in this place, to bestow a few reflections upon it.[1]

The most obvious objection to the selfish hypothesis is, that, as it is contrary to common feeling and our most unprejudiced notions, there is required the highest stretch of philosophy to establish so extraordinary a paradox. To the most careless observer there appear to be such dispositions as benevolence and generosity; such affections as love, friendship, compassion, gratitude. These sentiments have their causes, effects, objects, and operations, marked by common language and observation, and plainly distinguished from those of the selfish passions. And as this is the obvious appearance of things, it must be admitted, till some hypothesis be discovered, which by penetrating deeper into human nature, may prove the former affections to be nothing but modifications of the latter. All attempts of this kind have hitherto proved fruitless, and seem to have proceeded entirely from that love of *simplicity*, which has been the source of much false reasoning in philosophy. I shall not here enter into any detail on the present subject. Many able philosophers have shown the insufficiency of these systems. And I shall take for granted what, I believe, the smallest reflection will make evident to every impartial enquirer.

But the nature of the subject furnishes the strongest presumption, that no better system will ever, for the future, be invented, in order to account for the origin of the benevolent from the selfish affections, and reduce all the various emotions of the human mind to a perfect simplicity. The case is not the same in this species of philosophy as in physics. Many an hypothesis in nature, contrary to first appearances, has been found, on more accurate scrutiny, solid and satisfactory. Instances of this kind are so frequent, that a judicious, as well as witty philosopher,[2] has ventured to affirm, if there be more than one way, in which any phenomenon may be produced, that there is a general presumption for its arising from the causes which are the least obvious and familiar. But the presumption always lies on the other side, in all enquiries concerning the origin of our passions, and of the internal operations of the human mind. The simplest and most obvious cause which can there be assigned for any phenomenon, is probably the true one. When a philosopher, in the explication of his system, is obliged to have recourse to some very intricate and refined reflections, and to suppose them essential to the production of any passion or emotion, we have reason to be extremely on our guard against so fallacious an hypothesis. The affections are not susceptible of any impression from the refinements of reason or imagination; and it is always found that a vigorous exertion of the latter faculties, necessarily, from the narrow capacity of the human mind, destroys all activity in the former. Our predominant motive or intention is, indeed, frequently concealed from ourselves when it is mingled and confounded with other motives which the mind, from vanity or self-conceit, is desirous of supposing more prevalent: But there is no instance that a concealment of this nature has ever arisen from the abstruseness and intricacy of the motive. A man that has lost a friend and patron may flatter himself that all his grief arises from generous sentiments, without any mixture of narrow or interested considerations: But a man that grieves for a valuable friend, who needed his patronage and protection; how can we suppose, that his passionate tenderness arises from some metaphysical regards to a self-interest, which has no foundation or reality? We may as well imagine, that minute wheels and springs, like those of a watch, give motion to a loaded wagon, as account for the origin of passion from such abstruse reflections.

Animals are found susceptible of kindness, both to their own species and to ours; nor is there, in this case, the least suspicion of disguise or artifice. Shall we account for all their sentiments, too, from refined deductions of self-interest? Or if we admit a disinterested benevolence in the inferior species, by what rule of analogy can we refuse it in the superior?

Love between the sexes begets a complacency and good-will, very distinct from the gratification of an appetite. Tenderness to their offspring, in all sensible beings, is commonly able alone to counter-balance the strongest motives of self-love, and has no manner of dependence on that affection. What interest can a fond mother have in view, who loses her health by assiduous attendance on her sick child, and afterwards languishes and dies of grief, when freed, by its death, from the slavery of that attendance?

Is gratitude no affection of the human breast, or is that a word merely, without any meaning or reality? Have we no satisfaction in one man's company above another's, and no desire of the welfare of our friend, even though absence or death should prevent us from all participation in it? Or what is it commonly, that gives us any participation in it, even while alive and present, but our affection and regard to him?

These and a thousand other instances are marks of a general benevolence in human nature where no real interest binds us to the object. And how an *imaginary* interest, known and avowed for such, can be the origin of any passion or emotion, seems difficult to explain. No satisfactory hypothesis of this kind has yet been discovered; nor is there the smallest probability that the future industry of men will ever be attended with more favourable success.

But farther, if we consider rightly of the matter, we shall find, that the hypothesis, which allows of a disinterested benevolence, distinct from self-love, has really more *simplicity* in it, and is more conformable to the analogy of nature, than that which pretends to resolve all friendship and humanity into this latter principle. There are bodily wants or appetites acknowledged by every one, which necessarily precede all sensual enjoyment, and carry us directly to seek possession of the object. Thus, hunger and thirst have eating and drinking for their end; and from the gratification of these primary appetites arises a pleasure, which may become the object of another species of desire or inclination that is secondary and interested. In the same manner there are mental passions by which we are impelled immediately to seek particular objects, such as fame, or power, or vengeance, without any regard to interest; and when these objects are attained a pleasing enjoyment ensues, as the consequence of our indulged affections. Nature must, by the internal frame and constitution of the mind, give an original propensity to fame, ere we can reap any pleasure from that acquisition, or pursue it from motives of self-love, and a desire of happiness. If I have no vanity, I take no delight in praise: if I be void of ambition, power gives me no enjoyment: if I be not angry, the punishment of an adversary is totally indifferent to me. In all these cases there is a passion which points immediately to the object, and constitutes it our good or happiness; as there are other secondary passions which afterwards arise and pursue it as a part of our happiness, when once it is constituted such by our original affections. Were there no appetite of any kind antecedent to self-love, that propensity could scarcely ever exert itself; because we should, in that case, have felt few and slender pains or pleasures, and have little misery or happiness to avoid or to pursue.

Now, where is the difficulty in conceiving, that this may likewise be the case with benevolence and friendship, and that, from the original frame of our temper, we may feel a desire of another's happiness or good, which, by means of that affection, becomes our own good, and is afterwards pursued, from the combined motives of benevolence and self-enjoyment? Who sees not that vengeance, from the force alone of passion, may be so eagerly pursued, as to make us knowingly neglect every consideration of ease, interest, or safety; and, like some vindictive animals, infuse our very souls into the wounds we give an enemy;[3] and what a malignant philosophy must it be, that will not allow, to humanity and friendship the same privileges which are indisputably granted to the darker passions of enmity and resentment; such a philosophy is more like a satyr than a true delineation or description of human nature; and may be a good foundation for paradoxical wit and raillery, but is a very bad one for any serious argument or reasoning.

Immanuel Kant

An Answer to the Question: "What is Enlightenment?"

Konigsberg in Prussia, 30th September, 1784.

Enlightenment is man's leaving self-caused immaturity. Immaturity is the incapacity to use one's intelligence without the guidance of another. Such immaturity is self-caused if it is not caused by lack of intelligence, but by lack of determination and courage to use one's intelligence without being guided by another. *Sapere aude!* Have the courage to use your own intelligence! is therefore the motto of the enlightenment.

Through laziness and cowardice a large part of mankind, even after nature has freed them from alien guidance, gladly remain immature. It is because of laziness and cowardice that it is easy for others to usurp the role of guardian. It is so comfortable to be a minor! If I have a book which provides meaning for me, a pastor who has conscience for me, a doctor who will judge my diet for me, and so on, then I do not need to exert myself. I do not have any need to think; if I can pay, others take over the tedious job for me. The guardians who have kindly undertaken the supervision will see to it that by far the largest part of mankind, including the entire "beautiful sex," should consider the step into maturity not only as difficult but as very dangerous.

After having made their domesticated animals dumb and having carefully prevented these quiet creatures from daring to take any step beyond the lead strings to which they have fastened them, these guardians then show them the danger which threatens them, should they attempt to walk alone. Now this danger is not really so very great; for they would presumably learn to walk after some stumbling. However an example of this kind intimidates frightens people out of all further attempts.

It is difficult for the isolated individual to work himself out of the immaturity which has become almost natural for him. He has even become fond of it and for the time being is incapable of employing his own intelligence, because he has never been allowed to make the attempt. Statutes and formulas, these mechanical tools of a serviceable use, or rather misuse, of his natural faculties, are the ankle-chains of a continuous immaturity. Whoever threw it off would make an uncertain jump over the smallest trench because he is not accustomed to such free movement. Therefore there are only a few who have pursued a firm path and have succeeded in escaping from immaturity by their own cultivation of the mind.

But it is more nearly possible for a public to enlighten itself: this is even inescapable if only the public concerned is left in freedom. For there will always be some people who think for themselves, even among the self-appointed guardians of the great mass who, after having thrown off the yoke of immaturity themselves, will spread about them the spirit of a reasonable estimate of their own value and of the need for every man to think for himself. It is strange that the very public, which had previously been put under this yoke by the guardians, forces the guardians thereafter to keep it there if it is stirred up by a few of its guardians who are themselves incapable of all enlightenment. It is thus very harmful to plant prejudices, because they come back to plague those very people who themselves (or whose predecessors) have been the originators of these prejudices. Therefore a public can only arrive at enlightenment slowly. Through revolution, the abandonment of personal despotism may be engendered and the end of profit-seeking and domineering oppression may occur, but never a true reform of the state of mind. Instead, new prejudices, just like the old ones, will serve as the great guiding reins of the great unthinking mass.

All that is required for this enlightenment is *freedom*; and particularly the least harmful of all that may be called freedom, namely, the freedom for man to make public use of his reason in all matters. But I hear people clamor on all side: Don't argue! The officer says: Don't argue drill! The tax collector: Don't argue, pay! The pastor: Don't argue, believe! (Only a single lord I the world says: *Argue*, as much as you want to and about what you please, *but obey!* on all sides the cry: Don't argue! The officer says: Don't argue, get on parade! The tax-official: Don't argue, pay! The clergyman: Don't argue, believe! (Only one ruler in the world says: Argue as much as you like and about whatever you like, but obey!) Here we have restrictions on freedom everywhere. Which restriction is hampering enlightenment, and which does not, or even promotes it? I answer: the *public* use of a man's reason must be free at all times, and this alone can bring enlightenment. Promote it? I reply: The public use of man's reason must always be free, and it alone can bring about enlightenment among men; while the private use of a man's reason may often be restricted rather narrowly without thereby unduly hampering the progress of enlightenment.

I mean by the public use of one's reason, the use which a scholar makes of it before the entire reading public. Private use I call the use which he may make of this reason in a civic post or office. For some affairs which are in the interest of commonwealth a certain mechanism is necessary though which some members of the commonwealth must remain purely passive in order that artificial agreement with the government for the public good be maintained or so that at least the destruction of he good be prevented. In such a situation it I not permitted to argue; one must obey. But in so far as this unit off the machine considers himself as a member of the entire commonwealth, in fact even of world society; in other words, he considers himself in the equality of a scholar who is addressing the true public through his writing, he may indeed argue without the affairs suffering for which he is employed partly as a passive member. Thus it would be very harmful if an officer who, given an order by his superior, should start, while I the service, to argue concerning the utility or appropriateness of hat command. He must obey, but he cannot equitably be prevented form making observations as a scholar concerning the mistakes in the military service nor from submitting these to the public for its judgment. The citizen cannot refuse to pay taxes imposed upon him. Indeed, a rash criticism of such taxes, if they are the ones to be paid by him, may be punished as a scandal which might cause general resistance. But the same man does not act contrary to the duty of a citizen if, as a scholar, he utters publicly this thoughts against the undesirability to even the injustice of such taxes. Likewise a clergyman is obliged to teach his pupils and his congregation according to the doctrine of the church which he serves, for he has been accepted on that condition. But as a scholar, he has full freedom, in fact, even the obligation, to communicate to the public all his diligently examined and well-intentioned thoughts concerning erroneous points in that doctrine and concerning proposals regarding the better institution of religious and ecclesiastical matters. There is nothing in this for which the conscience could be blamed. For what he teaches according to this office as one authorized by the church, he presents as something in regard to which he has no latitude to teach according to his own preference. . . . He will say: Our church teaches this or tat, these are the proofs which are employed for it. In this way he derives all possible practical benefit for his congregation from rules which he would not himself subscribe to with full conviction. But he may nevertheless undertake the presentation of these rules because it is not entirely inconceivable that truth may be contained I them. In any case, there is nothing directly contrary to inner religion to be found in such doctrines. For, should he believe that the latter was not the case he could not administer his force in good conscience he would have to resign it. Therefore the use which an employed teacher makes of his reason before his congregation is merely a private use since such a gathering is always only domestic, no matter how large. As a priest (a member of an organization) he is not free and ought not to be, since he is executing someone else's mandate. On the other hand, the scholar speaking through his writings to the true public which is the world, like the clergyman making public use of his reason, enjoys an unlimited freedom to employ his own reason and to speak in his own person. For to suggest that the guardians of the people in spiritual matters should always be immature minors is a non-sense which would mean perpetuating forever existing non-sense.

But should a society of clergymen, for instance an ecclesiastical assembly, be entitled to commit itself by oath to a certain unalterable doctrine in order to perpetuate an endless guardianship over each of its member and through them or the people? I answer that this is quite inconceivable. Such a contract which wood be concluded in order to keep humanity forever from all further enlightenment is absolutely impossible, even should it be confirmed by the highest authority through parliaments and the most solemn peace treaties. An age cannot conclude a pact and take an oath upon it to commit the succeeding age to a situation in which it would be impossible for the latter to enlarge even its most important knowledge, to eliminate error and altogether to progress in enlightenment. Such a thing would be a crime against human nature, the original destiny of which consists in such progress. Succeeding generations are entirely justified in discarding such decisions as unauthorized and criminal. The touchstone of all this to be agreed upon as a law for people is to be found in the question a people could impose such a law upon itself. Now it might be possible to introduce a certain order for a definite short period as if in anticipation of a better order. This would be true if one permitted at the same time each citizen and especially the clergyman to make his criticisms I his quality as a scholar. . . . In the meantime, the provisional order might continue until the insight into the particular matter in hand has publicly progressed to the point where through a combination of voices (although not, perhaps, of all) a proposal may be brought to the crown. Thus those congregations would be protected which had agreed to (a changed religious institution) according to their own ideas and better understanding, without hindering those who desired to allow the old institutions to continue.

A man may postpone for himself, but only for a short time, enlightening himself regarding what he ought to know. But to resign from such enlightenment altogether either for his own person or even more for his descendants means to violate and to trample underfoot the sacred rights of mankind. Whatever a people may not decide for themselves, a monarch may even less decide for the people, for his legislative reputation rests upon his uniting the entire people's will I his own. If the monarch will only see to it that every true or imagined reform (of religion) fits in with the civil order, he had best let his subjects do what they consider necessary for the sake of their salvation; that is not his affair. His only concern is to prevent one subject from hindering another by force, to work according to each subject's best ability to determine and to promote his salvation. In fact, it detracts from his majesty if he interferes in such matters and subjects to governmental supervision the writings by which his subjects seek to clarify their ideas (concerning religion). This is true whether he does it from his own highest insight, for in this case he exposes himself to the reproach: *Caesar non est supra grammaticos*; it is even more true when he debases his highest power to support the spiritual despotism of some tyrants in his state against the rest of his subjects.

The question may now be put: Do we live at present live in an enlightened age? The answer is: No, but in an age of enlightenment. Much still prevents men from being placed in a position or even being placed into position to use their own minds securely and well in matters of religion. But we do have very definite indications that this field of endeavor is being opened up for men to work freely and reduce gradually the hindrances preventing a general enlightenment and an escape from self-caused immaturity. In this sense, this age is the age of enlightenment and the age of Frederick (the Great).

A prince should not consider it beneath him to declare that he believes it to be his duty, not to prescribe anything to his subjects in matters of religion but to leave them complete freedom in such things. In other words, a prince who refuses the conceited title of being "tolerant," is himself enlightened. He deserves to be praised by his grateful contemporaries and descendants as the man who first freed humankind of immaturity, at least as far as the government is concerned and who permitted everyone to use his own reason in all matters of conscience. Under his rule, venerable clergymen could, regardless of their official duty, set forth their opinions and views even though they differ from the accepted doctrine here and there; they could do so in the quality of scholars, freely and publicly. The same holds even more true of every other person who is not thus restricted by official duty. This spirit of freedom is spreading even outside (the country of Frederick the Great) to places where it has to struggle with the external hindrances imposed by a government which misunderstands its own position. For an example is illuminating them which shows that such freedom (public discussion) need not cause the slightest worry regarding public security and unity of the commonwealth. Men raise themselves by and by out of backwardness if one does not purposely invent artifices to keep them down.

I have emphasized the main point of enlightenment, that is of man's release from his self-caused immaturity, primarily *in matters of religion.* I have done this because our rulers have no interest in playing the guardian of their subjects in matters of art and sciences. Furthermore immaturity in matters of religion is not only most noxious but also most dishonorable. But the point of view of a head of state who favors freedom in the arts and sciences goes eve further; for he understands that there is no danger in legislation permitting his subjects to make *public* use of their own reason and to submit *publicly* their thoughts regarding a better framing of such laws together with a frank criticism of existing *legislation.* We have a shining example of this; no prince excels him whom we admire. Only he who is himself enlightened does not rear specters when he at the same time has a well-disciplined army at his disposal as a guarantee of public peace. Only he can say what (the ruler of a) free state dare not say: *Argue as much as you want about whatever you want but obey!* Thus we see here as elsewhere an unexpected turn in human affairs just as we observe that almost everything therein is paradoxical. A great degree of civic freedom seems to be advantageous for the freedom of the *spirit* of the people and yet it established impassable limits. A lesser degree of such civic freedom provides additional space in which the spirit of a people can develop to its full capacity. Therefore nature has cherished, within its hard shell, the germ of the inclination and need for free *thought.* This free thought gradually acts upon the mind of the people and they gradually become more capable of acting in freedom. Eventually, the government is also influenced by this free thought and thereby it treats man, who is now more than a machine, according to his dignity.

Mary Wollstonecraft

A Vindication of the Rights of Women

Chapter II [1792]

The Prevailing Opinion of a Sexual Character Discussed

To account for, and excuse the tyranny of man, many ingenious arguments have been brought forward to prove, that the two sexes, in the acquirement of virtue, ought to aim at attaining a very different character; or, to speak explicitly, women are not allowed to have sufficient strength of mind to acquire what really deserves the name of virtue. Yet it should seem, allowing them to have souls, that there is but one way appointed by Providence to lead mankind to either virtue or happiness.

If then women are not a swarm of ephemeron triflers, why should they be kept in ignorance under the specious name of innocence? Men complain, and with reason, of the follies and caprices of our sex, when they do not keenly satirize our headstrong passions and groveling vices—Behold, I should answer, the natural effect of ignorance! The mind will ever be unstable that has only prejudices to rest on, and the current will run with destructive fury when there are no barriers to break its force. Women are told from their infancy, and taught by the example of their mothers, that a little knowledge of human weakness, justly termed cunning, softness of temper, *outward* obedience, and a scrupulous attention to a puerile kind of propriety, will obtain for them the protection of man; and should they be beautiful, everything else is needless, for at least twenty years of their lives.

Thus Milton describes our first frail mother; though when he tells us that women are formed for softness and sweet attractive grace, I cannot comprehend his meaning, unless, in the true Mahometan strain, he meant to deprive us of souls, and insinuate that we were beings only designed by sweet attractive grace, and docile blind obedience, to gratify the senses of man when he can no longer soar on the wing of contemplation.

How grossly do they insult us who thus advise us only to render ourselves gentle, domestic brutes! For instance, the winning softness so warmly and frequently recommended, that governs by obeying. What childish expressions, and how insignificant is the being—can it be an immortal one?—who will condescend to govern by such sinister methods! "Certainly," says Lord Bacon, "man is of kin to the beasts by his body; and if he be not of kin to God by his spirit, he is a base and ignoble creature!" Men, indeed, appear to me to act in a very unphilosophical manner, when they try to secure the good conduct of women by attempting to keep them always in a state of childhood. Rousseau was more consistent when he wished to stop the progress of reason in both sexes, for if men eat of the tree of knowledge, women will come in for a taste; but, from the imperfect cultivation which their understandings now receive, they only attain a knowledge of evil.

Children, I grant, should be innocent; but when the epithet is applied to men, or women, it is but a civil term for weakness. For if it be allowed that women were destined by Providence to acquire human virtues, and, by the exercise of their understandings, that stability of character which is the firmest ground to rest our future hopes upon, they must be permitted to turn to the fountain of light, and not forced to shape their course by the twinkling of a mere satellite. Milton, I grant, was of a very different opinion; for he only bends to the indefeasible right of beauty, though it would be difficult to render two passages which I now mean to contrast, consistent. But into similar inconsistencies are great men often led by their senses.

"To whom thus Eve with *perfect beauty* adorn'd
My author and disposer, what thou bid'st
Unargued I obey; so God ordains.
God is *thy law, thou mine*: to know no more
Is woman's *happiest* knowledge and her *praise*."

These are exactly the arguments that I have used to children; but I have added, your reason is now gaining strength, and, till it arrives at some degree of maturity, you must look up to me for advice—then you ought to *think*, and only rely on God.

Yet in the following lines Milton seems to coincide with me; when he makes Adam thus expostulate with his Maker.

"Hast Thou not made me here Thy substitute,
And these inferior far beneath me set?
Among *unequals* what society
Can sort, what harmony or true delight ?
Which must be mutual, in proportion due
Giv'n and received; but in *disparity*

The one intense, the other still remiss
Cannot well suit with either, but soon prove
Tedious alike: of *fellowship*
I speak Such as I seek fit to participate
All rational delight—"

In treating therefore of the manners of women, let us, disregarding sensual arguments, trace what we should endeavour to make them in order to co-operate, if the expression be not too bold, with the Supreme Being.

By individual education, I mean, for the sense of the word is not precisely defined, such an attention to a child as will slowly sharpen the senses, form the temper, regulate the passions as they begin to ferment, and set the understanding to work before the body arrives at maturity; so that the man may only have to proceed, not to begin, the important task of learning to think and reason.

To prevent any misconstruction, I must add, that I do not believe that a private education can work the wonders which some sanguine writers have attributed to it. Men and women must be educated, in a great degree, by the opinions and manners of the society they live in. In every age there has been a stream of popular opinion that has carried all before it, and given a family character, as it were, to the century. It may then fairly be inferred, that, till society be differently constituted, much cannot be expected from education. It is, however, sufficient for my present purpose to assert that, whatever effect circumstances have on the abilities, every being may become virtuous by the exercise of its own reason; for if but one being was created with vicious inclinations, that is positively bad, what can save us from atheism? or if we worship a God, is not that God a devil?

Consequently, the most perfect education, in my opinion, is such an exercise of the understanding as is best calculated to strengthen the body and form the heart. Or, in other words, to enable the individual to attain such habits of virtue as will render it independent. In fact, it is a farce to call any being virtuous whose virtues do not result from the exercise of its own reason. This was Rousseau's opinion respecting men; I extend it to women, and confidently assert that they have been drawn out of their sphere by false refinement, and not by an endeavour to acquire masculine qualities. Still the regal homage which they receive is so intoxicating, that until the manners of the times are changed, and formed on more reasonable principles, it may be impossible to convince them that the illegitimate power which they obtain by degrading themselves is a curse, and that they must return to nature and equality if they wish to secure the placid satisfaction that unsophisticated affections impart. But for this epoch we must wait—wait perhaps till kings and nobles, enlightened by reason, and, preferring the real dignity of man to childish state, throw off their gaudy hereditary trappings; and if then women do not resign the arbitrary power of beauty—they will prove that they have *less* mind than man.

I may be accused of arrogance; still I must declare what I firmly believe, that all the writers who have written on the subject of female education and manners, from Rousseau to Dr. Gregory, have contributed to render women more artificial, weak characters, than they would otherwise have been; and consequently, more useless members of society. I might have expressed this conviction in a lower key, but I am afraid it would have been the whine of affectation, and not the faithful expression of my feelings, of the clear result which experience and reflection have led me to draw. When I come to that division of the subject, I shall advert to the passages that I more particularly disapprove of, in the works of the authors I have just alluded to; but it is first necessary to observe that my objection extends to the whole purport of those books, which tend, in my opinion, to degrade one half of the human species, and render women pleasing at the expense of every solid virtue.

Though, to reason on Rousseau's ground, if man did attain a degree of perfection of mind when his body arrived at maturity, it might be proper, in order to make a man and his wife one, that she should rely entirely on his understanding; and the graceful ivy, clasping the oak that supported it, would form a whole in which strength and beauty would be equally conspicuous. But, alas! husbands, as well as their helpmates, are often only overgrown children; nay, thanks to early debauchery, scarcely men in their outward form—and if the blind lead the blind, one need not come from heaven to tell us the consequence.

Many are the causes that, in the present corrupt state of society, contribute to enslave women by cramping their understandings and sharpening their senses. One, perhaps, that silently does more mischief than all the rest, is their disregard of order.

To do everything in an orderly manner is a most important precept, which women, who, generally speaking, receive only a disorderly kind of education, seldom attend to with that degree of exactness that men, who from their infancy are broken into method, observe. This negligent kind of guesswork—for what other epithet can be used to point out the random exertions of a sort of instinctive common sense never brought to the test of reason? prevents their generalising matters of fact—so they do to-day what they did yesterday, merely because they did it yesterday.

This contempt of the understanding in early life has more baneful consequences than is commonly supposed; for the little knowledge which women of strong minds attain is, from various circumstances, of a more desultory kind than the knowledge of men, and it is acquired more by sheer observations on real life than from comparing what has been individually observed with the results of experience generalized by speculation. Led by their dependent situation and domestic employments more into society, what they learn is rather by snatches; and as learning is with them in general only a secondary thing, they do not pursue any one branch with that persevering ardour necessary to give vigour to the faculties and clearness to the judgment. In the present state of society a little learning is required to support the character of a gentleman, and boys are obliged to submit to a few years of discipline. But in the education of women, the cultivation of the understanding is always subordinate to the acquirement of some corporeal accomplishment; even when enervated by confinement and false notions of modesty, the body is prevented from attaining that grace and beauty which relaxed half-formed limbs never exhibit. Besides, in youth their faculties are not brought forward by emulation; and having no serious scientific study, if they have natural sagacity, it is turned too soon on life and manners. They dwell on effects and modifications, without tracing them back to causes; and complicated rules to adjust behaviour are a weak substitute for simple principles.

As a proof that education gives this appearance of weakness to females, we may instance the example of military men, who are, like them, sent into the world before their minds have been stored with knowledge, or fortified by principles. The consequences are similar; soldiers acquire a little superficial knowledge, snatched from the muddy current of conversation, and from continually mixing with society, they gain what is termed a knowledge of the world; and this acquaintance with manners and customs has frequently been confounded with a knowledge of the human heart. But can the crude fruit of casual observation, never brought to the test of judgment, formed by comparing speculation and experience, deserve such a distinction? Soldiers, as well as women, practise the minor virtues with punctilious politeness. Where is then the sexual difference, when the education has been the same? All the difference that I can discern arises from the superior advantage of liberty which enables the former to see more of life.

It is wandering from my present subject, perhaps, to make a political remark; but, as it was produced naturally by the train of my reflections, I shall not pass it silently over.

Standing armies can never consist of resolute robust men; they may be well-disciplined machines, but they will seldom contain men under the influence of strong passions, or with very vigorous faculties; and as for any depth of understanding, I will venture to affirm that it is as rarely to be found in the army as amongst women; and the cause, I maintain, is the same. It may be further observed, that officers are also particularly attentive to their persons, fond of dancing, crowded rooms, adventures, and ridicule.[1] Like the *fair* sex, the business of their lives is gallantry.—They were taught to please, and they only live to please. Yet they do not lose their rank in the distinction of sexes, for they are still reckoned superior to women, though in what their superiority consists, beyond what I have just mentioned, it is difficult to discover.

The great misfortune is this, that they both acquire manners before morals, and a knowledge of life before they have from reflection any acquaintance with the grand ideal outline of human nature. The consequence is natural; satisfied with common nature, they become a prey to prejudices, and taking all their opinions on credit, they blindly submit to authority. So that if they have any sense, it is a kind of instinctive glance, that catches proportions, and decides with respect to manners, but fails when arguments are to be pursued below the surface, or opinions analyzed.

May not the same remark be applied to women? Nay, the argument may be carried still further, for they are both thrown out of a useful station by the unnatural distinctions established in civilized life. Riches and hereditary honours have made cyphers of women to give consequence to the numerical figure; and idleness has produced a mixture of gallantry and despotism into society, which leads the very men who are the slaves of their mistresses to tyrannize over their sisters, wives, and daughters. This is only keeping them in rank and file, it is true. Strengthen the female mind by enlarging it, and there will be an end to blind obedience; but, as blind obedience is ever sought for by power, tyrants and sensualists are in the right when they to keep woman in the dark, because the former only want slaves, and the latter a plaything. The sensualist, indeed, has been the most dangerous of tyrants, and women have been duped by their lovers, as princes by their ministers, whilst dreaming that they reigned over them.

I now principally allude to Rousseau, for his character of Sophia is, undoubtedly, a captivating one, though it appears to me grossly unnatural; however, it is not the superstructure, but the foundation of her character, the principles on which her education was built, that I mean to attack; nay, warmly as I admire the genius of that able writer, whose opinions I shall often have occasion to cite, indignation always takes place of admiration, and the rigid frown of insulted virtue effaces the smile of complacency, which his eloquent periods are wont to raise, when I read his voluptuous reveries. Is this the man who, in his ardour for virtue, would banish all the soft arts of peace, and almost carry us back to Spartan discipline? Is this the man who delights to paint the useful struggles of passion, the triumphs of good dispositions, and the heroic flights which carry the glowing soul out of itself?—How are these mighty sentiments lowered when he describes the pretty foot and enticing airs of his little favourite! But for the present I waive the subject, and instead of severely reprehending the transient effusions of overweening sensibility, I shall only observe, that whoever has cast a benevolent eye on society must often have been gratified by the sight of humble mutual love, not dignified by sentiment, or strengthened by a union in intellectual pursuits. The domestic trifles of the day have afforded matters for cheerful converse, and innocent caresses have softened toils which did not require great exercise of mind or stretch of thought; yet, has not the sight of this moderate felicity excited more tenderness than respect? An emotion similar to what we feel when children are playing, or animals sporting,[2] whilst the contemplation of the noble struggles of suffering merit has raised admiration, and carried our thoughts to that world where sensation will give place to reason.

Women are therefore to be considered either as moral beings, or so weak that they must be entirely subjected to the superior faculties of men.

Let us examine this question. Rousseau declares that a woman should never for a moment feel herself independent, that she should be governed by fear to exercise her natural cunning, and made a coquettish slave in order to render her a more alluring object of desire, a sweeter companion to man, whenever he chooses to relax himself. He carries the arguments, which he pretends to draw from the indications of nature, still further, and insinuates that truth and fortitude, the cornerstones of all human virtue, should be cultivated with certain restrictions, because, with respect to the female character, obedience is the grand lesson which ought to be impressed with unrelenting rigour.

What nonsense! When will a great man arise with sufficient strength of mind to puff away the fumes which pride and sensuality have thus spread over the subject? If women are by nature inferior to men, their virtues must be the same in quality, if not in degree, or virtue is a relative idea; consequently their conduct should be founded on the same principles, and have the same aim.

Connected with man as daughters, wives, and mothers, their moral character may be estimated by their manner of fulfilling those simple duties; but the end, the grand end, of their exertions should be to unfold their own faculties and acquire the dignity of conscious virtue. They may try to render their road pleasant; but ought never to forget, in common with man, that life yields not the felicity which can satisfy an immortal soul. I do not mean to insinuate that either sex should be so lost in abstract reflections or distant views as to forget the affections and duties that lie before them, and are, in truth, the means appointed to produce the fruit of life; on the contrary, I would warmly recommend them, even while I assert, that they afford most satisfaction when they are considered in their true, sober light.

Probably the prevailing opinion that woman was created for man, may have taken its rise from Moses's poetical story; yet as very few, it is presumed, who have bestowed any serious thought on the subject ever supposed that Eve was, literally speaking, one of Adam's ribs, the deduction must be allowed to fall to the ground; or only be so far admitted as it proves that man, from the remotest antiquity, found it convenient to exert his strength to subjugate his companion, and his invention to show that she ought to have her neck bent under the yoke, because the whole creation was only created for his convenience or pleasure.

Let it not be concluded that I wish to invert the order of things; I have already granted, that, from the constitution of their bodies, men seemed to be designed by Providence to attain a greater degree of virtue. I speak collectively of the whole sex; but I see not the shadow of a reason to conclude that their virtues should differ in respect to their nature. In fact, how can they, if virtue has only one eternal standard? I must therefore, if I reason consequentially, as strenuously maintain that they have the same simple direction, as that there is a God.

It follows then that cunning should not be opposed to wisdom, little cares to great exertions, or insipid softness, varnished over with the name of gentleness, to that fortitude which grand views alone can inspire.

I shall be told that woman would then lose many of her peculiar graces, and the opinion of a well-known poet might be quoted to refute my unqualified assertion. For Pope has said in the name of the whole male sex:

> "Yet ne'er so sure our passion to create,
> As when she touch'd the brink of all we hate."

In what light this sally places men and women I shall leave to the judicious to determine. Meanwhile, I shall content myself with observing, that I cannot discover why, unless they are mortal, females should always be degraded by being made subservient to love or lust.

To speak disrespectfully of love is, I know, high treason against sentiment and fine feelings; but I wish to speak the simple language of truth, and rather to address the head than the heart. To endeavour to reason love out of the world would be to out Quixote Cervantes, and equally offend against common sense; but an endeavour to restrain this tumultuous passion, and to prove that it should not be allowed to dethrone superior powers, or to usurp the sceptre which the understanding should very coolly wield, appears less wild.

Youth is the season for love in both sexes; but in those days of thoughtless enjoyment provision should be made for the more important years of life, when reflection takes place of sensation. But Rousseau, and most of the male writers who have followed his steps, have warmly inculcated that the whole tendency of female education ought to be directed to one point:—to render them pleasing.

Let me reason with the supporters of this opinion who have any knowledge of human nature. Do they imagine that marriage can eradicate the habitude of life? The woman who has only been taught to please will soon find that her charms are oblique sunbeams, and that they cannot have much effect on her husband's heart when they are seen every day, when the summer is passed and gone. Will she then have sufficient native energy to look into herself for comfort, and cultivate her dormant faculties? or is it not more rational to expect that she will try to please other men; and, in the emotions raised by the expectation of new conquests, endeavour to forget the mortification her love or pride has received? When the husband ceases to be a lover—and the time will inevitably come, her desire of pleasing will then grow languid, or become a spring of bitterness; and love, perhaps, the most evanescent of all passions, gives place to jealousy or vanity.

I now speak of women who are restrained by principle or prejudice. Such women, though they would shrink from an intrigue with real abhorrence, yet, nevertheless, wish to be convinced by the homage of gallantry that they are cruelly neglected by their husbands; or, days and weeks are spent in dreaming of the happiness enjoyed by congenial souls till their health is undermined and their spirits broken by discontent. How then can the great art of pleasing be such a necessary study? it is only useful to a mistress; the chaste wife and serious mother should only consider her power to please as the polish of her virtues, and the affection of her husband as one of the comforts that render her task less difficult, and her life happier—But, whether she be loved or neglected, her first wish should be to make herself respectable, and not to rely for all her happiness on a being subject to like infirmities with herself.

The worthy Dr. Gregory fell into a similar error. I respect his heart; but entirely disapprove of his celebrated Legacy to his Daughters.

He advises them to cultivate a fondness for dress, because a fondness for dress, he asserts, is natural to them. I am unable to comprehend what either he or Rousseau mean when they frequently use this indefinite term. If they told us that in a pre-existent state the soul was fond of dress, and brought this inclination with it into a new body, I should listen to them with a halfsmile, as I often do when I hear a rant about innate elegance—But if he only meant to say that the exercise of the faculties will produce this fondness—I deny it. It is not natural; but arises, like false ambition in men, from a love of power.

Dr. Gregory goes much further; he actually recommends dissimulation, and advises an innocent girl to give the lie to her feelings, and not dance with spirit, when gaiety of heart would make her feet eloquent without making her gestures immodest. In the name of truth and common sense, why should not one woman acknowledge that she can take more exercise than another? or, in other words, that she has a sound constitution; and why, to damp innocent vivacity, is she darkly to be told that men will draw conclusions which she little thinks of?—Let the libertine draw what inference he pleases; but, I hope, that no sensible mother will restrain the natural frankness of youth by instilling such indecent cautions. Out of the abundance of the heart the mouth speaketh; and a wiser than Solomon hath said that the heart should be made clean, and not trivial ceremonies observed, which it is not very difficult to fulfill with scrupulous exactness when vice reigns in the heart.

Women ought to endeavour to purify their heart; but can they do so when their uncultivated understandings make them entirely dependent on their senses for employment and amusement, when no noble pursuits set them above the little vanities of the day, or enables them to curb the wild emotions that agitate a reed over which every passing breeze has power? To gain the affections of a virtuous man is affectation necessary? Nature has given woman a weaker frame than man; but, to ensure her husband's affections, must a wife, who, by the exercise of her mind and body whilst she was discharging the duties of a daughter, wife, and mother, has allowed her constitution to retain its natural strength, and her nerves a healthy tone, is she, I say, to condescend to use art and feign a sickly delicacy in order to secure her husband's affection? Weakness may excite tenderness, and gratify the arrogant pride of man; but the lordly caresses of a protector will not gratify a noble mind that pants for, and deserves to be respected. Fondness is a poor substitute for friendship!

In a seraglio, I grant, that all these arts are necessary; the epicure must have his palate tickled, or he will sink into apathy; but have women so little ambition as to be satisfied with such a condition? Can they supinely dream life away in the lap of pleasure, or the languor of weariness, rather than assert their claim to pursue reasonable pleasures and render themselves conspicuous by practising the virtues which dignify mankind? Surely she has not an immortal soul who can loiter life away merely employed to adorn her person, that she may amuse the languid hours, and soften the cares of a fellow-creature who is willing to be enlivened by her smiles and tricks, when the serious business of life is over.

Besides, the woman who strengthens her body and exercises her mind will, by managing her family and practising various virtues, become the friend, and not the humble dependent of her husband; and if she, by possessing such substantial qualities, merit his regard, she will not find it necessary to conceal her affection, nor to pretend to an unnatural coldness of constitution to excite her husband's passions. In fact, if we revert to history, we shall find that the women who have distinguished themselves have neither been the most beautiful nor the most gentle of their sex.

Nature, or, to speak with strict propriety, God, has made all things right; but man has sought him out many inventions to mar the work. I now allude to that part of Dr. Gregory's treatise, where he advises a wife never to let her husband know the extent of her sensibility or affection. Voluptuous precaution, and as ineffectual as absurd.—Love, from its very nature, must be transitory. To seek for a secret that would render it constant, would be as wild a search as for the philosopher's stone, or the grand panacea; and the discovery would be equally useless, or rather pernicious, to mankind. The most holy band of society is friendship. It has been well said, by a shrewd satirist, "that rare as true love is, true friendship is still rarer."

This is an obvious truth, and, the cause not lying deep, will not elude a slight glance of inquiry.

Love, the common passion, in which chance and sensation take place of choice and reason, is, in some degree, felt by the mass of mankind; for it is not necessary to speak, at present, of the emotions that rise above or sink below love. This passion, naturally increased by suspense and difficulties, draws the mind out of its accustomed state, and exalts the affections; but the security of marriage, allowing the fever of love to subside, a healthy temperature is thought insipid only by those who have not sufficient intellect to substitute the calm tenderness of friendship, the confidence of respect, instead of blind admiration, and the sensual emotions of fondness.

This is, must be, the course of nature—friendship or indifference inevitably succeeds love.—And this constitution seems perfectly to harmonize with the system of government which prevails in the moral world. Passions are spurs to action, and open the mind; but they sink into mere appetites, become a personal and momentary gratification when the object is gained, and the satisfied mind rests in enjoyment. The man who had some virtue whilst he was struggling for a crown, often becomes a voluptuous tyrant when it graces his brow; and, when the lover is not lost in the husband, the dotard, a prey to childish caprices and fond jealousies, neglects the serious duties of life, and the caresses which should excite confidence in his children are lavished on the overgrown child, his wife.

In order to fulfil the duties of life, and to be able to pursue with vigour the various employments which form the moral character, a master and mistress of a family ought not to continue to love each other with passion. I mean to say that they ought not to indulge those emotions which disturb the order of society, and engross the thoughts that should be otherwise employed. The mind that has never been engrossed by one object wants vigour—if it can long be so, it is weak.

A mistaken education, a narrow uncultivated mind, and many sexual prejudices, tend to make women more constant than men; but, for the present, I shall not touch on this branch of the subject. I will go still further, and advance, without dreaming of a paradox, that an unhappy marriage is often very advantageous to a family, and that the neglected wife is, in general, the best mother. And this would almost always be the consequence if the female mind were more enlarged; for, it seems to be the common dispensation of Providence, that what we gain in present enjoyment should be deducted from the treasure of life, experience; and that when we are gathering the flowers of the day, and revelling in pleasure, the solid fruit of toil and wisdom should not be caught at the same time. The way lies before us, we must turn to the right or left; and he who will pass life away in bounding from one pleasure to another, must not complain if he acquire neither wisdom nor respectability of character.

Supposing, for a moment, that the soul is not immortal, and that man was only created for the present scene,—I think we should have reason to complain that love, infantine fondness, ever grew insipid and palled upon the sense. Let us eat, drink, and love, for tomorrow we die, would be, in fact, the language of reason, the morality of life; and who but a fool would part with a reality for a fleeting shadow ? But, if awed by observing the improbable powers of the mind, we disdain to confine our wishes or thoughts to such a comparatively mean field of action; that only appears grand and important, as it is connected with a boundless prospect and sublime hopes, what necessity is there for falsehood in conduct, and why must the sacred majesty of truth be violated to detain a deceitful good that saps the very foundation of virtue? Why must the female mind be tainted by coquettish arts to gratify the sensualist, and prevent love from subsiding into friendship, or compassionate tenderness, when there are not qualities on which friendship can be built? Let the honest heart show itself, and *reason* teach passion to submit to necessity; or, let the dignified pursuit of virtue and knowledge raise the mind above those emotions which rather embitter than sweeten the cup of life, when they are not restrained within due bounds.

I do not mean to allude to the romantic passion, which is the concomitant of genius.—Who can clip its wing? But that grand passion not proportioned to the puny enjoyments of life, is only true to the sentiment, and feeds on itself. The passions which have been celebrated for their durability have always been unfortunate. They have acquired strength by absence and constitutional melancholy.—The fancy has hovered round a form of beauty dimly seen—but familiarity might have turned admiration into disgust, or, at least, into indifference, and allowed the imagination leisure to start fresh game. With perfect propriety, according to this view of things, does Rousseau make the mistress of his soul, Eloisa, love St. Preux, when life was fading before her; but this is no proof of the immortality of the passion.

Of the same complexion is Dr. Gregory's advice respecting delicacy of sentiment, which he advises a woman not to acquire, if she have determined to marry. This determination, however, perfectly consistent with his former advice, he calls *indelicate*, and earnestly persuades his daughters to conceal it, though it may govern their conduct:—as if it were indelicate to have the common appetites of human nature.

Noble morality! and consistent with the cautious prudence of a little soul that cannot extend its views beyond the present minute division of existence. If all the faculties of woman's mind are only to be cultivated as they respect her dependence on man; if, when a husband be obtained, she have arrived at her goal, and meanly proud rests satisfied with such a paltry crown, let her grovel contentedly, scarcely raised by her employments above the animal kingdom; but, if struggling for the prize of her high calling, she look beyond the present scene, let her cultivate her understanding without stopping to consider what character the husband may have whom she is destined to marry. Let her only determine, without being too anxious about present happiness, to acquire the qualities that ennoble a rational being, and a rough inelegant husband may shock her taste without destroying her peace of mind. She will not model her soul to suit the frailties of her companion, but to bear with them, his character may be a trial, but not an impediment to virtue.

If Dr. Gregory confined his remark to romantic.expectations of constant love and congenial feelings, he should have recollected that experience will banish what advice can never make us cease to wish for, when the imagination is kept alive at the expense of reason.

I own it frequently happens that women who have fostered a romantic unnatural delicacy of feeling, waste their[3] lives in *imagining* how happy they should have been with a husband who could love them with a fervid increasing affection every day, and all day. But they might as well pine married as single—and would not be a jot more unhappy with a bad husband than longing for a good one. That a proper education or, to speak with more precision, a well-stored mind, would enable a woman to support a single life with dignity, I grant; but that she should avoid cultivating her taste, lest her husband should occasionally shock it, is quitting a substance for a shadow. To say the truth, I do not know of what use is an improved taste, if the individual be not rendered more independent of the casualties of life; if new sources of enjoyment, only dependent on the solitary operations of the mind, are not opened. People of taste, married or single, without distinction, will ever be disgusted by various things that touch not less observing minds. On this conclusion the argument must not be allowed to hinge; but in the whole sum of enjoyment is taste to be denominated a blessing?

The question is, whether it procures most pain or pleasure? The answer will decide the propriety of Dr. Gregory's advice and show how absurd and tyrannic it is thus to lay down a system of slavery; or to attempt to educate moral beings by any other rules than those deduced from pure reason, which apply to the whole species.

Gentleness of manners, forbearance and long-suffering, are such amiable God-like qualities, that in sublime poetic strains the Deity has been invested with them; and, perhaps, no representation of His goodness so strongly fastens on the human affections as those that represent Him abundant in mercy and willing to pardon. Gentleness, considered in this point of view, bears on its front all the characteristics of grandeur, combined with the winning graces of condescension; but what a different aspect it assumes when it is the submissive demeanour of dependence, the support of weakness that loves, because it wants protection; and is forbearing, because it must silently endure injuries; smiling under the lash at which it dare not snarl. Abject as this picture appears, it is the portrait of an accomplished woman, according to the received opinion of female excellence, separated by specious reasoners from human excellence. Or, they[4] kindly restore the rib, and make one moral being of a man and woman; not forgetting to give her all the "submissive charms."

How women are to exist in that state where there is neither to be marrying nor giving in marriage, we are not told. For though moralists have agreed that the tenor of life seems to prove that *man* is prepared by various circumstances for a future state, they constantly concur in advising *woman* only to provide for the present. Gentleness, docility, and a spaniel-like affection are, on this ground, consistently recommended as the cardinal virtues of the sex; and, disregarding the arbitrary economy of nature, one writer has declared that it is masculine for a woman to be melancholy. She was created to be the toy of man, his rattle, and it must jingle in his ears whenever, dismissing reason, he chooses to be amused.

To recommend gentleness, indeed, on a broad basis is strictly philosophical. A frail being should labour to be gentle. But when forbearance confounds right and wrong, it ceases to be a virtue; and, however convenient it may be found in a companion—that companion will ever be considered as an inferior, and only inspire a vapid tenderness, which easily degenerates into contempt. Still, if advice could really make a being gentle, whose natural disposition admitted not of such a fine polish, something towards the advancement of order would be attained; but if, as might quickly be demonstrated, only affectation be produced by this indiscriminate counsel, which throws a stumbling-block in the way of gradual improvement, and true melioration of temper, the sex is not much benefited by sacrificing solid virtues to the attainment of superficial graces, though for a few years they may procure the individuals regal sway.

As a philosopher, I read with indignation the plausible epithets which men use to soften their insults; and, as a moralist, I ask what is meant by such heterogeneous associations, as fair defects, amiable weaknesses, etc.? If there be but one criterion of morals, but one archetype for man, women appear to be suspended by destiny, according to the vulgar tale of Mahomet's coffin; they have neither the unerring instinct of brutes, nor are allowed to fix the eye of reason on a perfect model. They were made to be loved, and must not aim at respect, lest they should be hunted out of society as masculine.

But to view the subject in another point of view. Do passive indolent women make the best wives? Confining our discussion to the present moment of existence, let us see how such weak creatures perform their part? Do the women who, by the attainment of a few superficial accomplishments, have strengthened the prevailing prejudice, merely contribute to the happiness of their husbands? Do they display their charms merely to amuse them? And have women who have early imbibed notions of passive obedience, sufficient character to manage a family or educate children? So far from it, that, after surveying the history of woman, I cannot help agreeing with the severest satirist, considering the sex as the weakest as well as the most oppressed half of the species. What does history disclose but marks of inferiority, and how few women have emancipated themselves from the galling yoke of sovereign man?—So few that the exceptions remind me of an ingenious conjecture respecting Newton: that he was probably a being of superior order accidentally caged in a human body. Following the same train of thinking, I have been led to imagine that the few extraordinary women who have rushed in eccentrical directions out of the orbit prescribed to their sex, were *male* spirits, confined by mistake in female frames. But if it be not philosophical to think of sex when the soul is mentioned, the inferiority must depend on the organs; or the heavenly fire, which is to ferment the clay, is not given in equal portions.

But avoiding, as I have hitherto done, any direct comparison of the two sexes collectively, or frankly acknowledging the inferiority of woman, according to the present appearance of things, I shall only insist that men have increased that inferiority till women are almost sunk below the standard of rational creatures. Let their faculties have room to unfold, and their virtues to gain strength, and then determine where the whole sex must stand in the intellectual scale. Yet let it be remembered, that for a small number of distinguished women I do not ask a place.

It is difficult for us purblind mortals to say to what height human discoveries and improvements may arrive when the gloom of despotism subsides, which makes us stumble at every step; but, when morality shall be settled on a more solid basis, then, without being gifted with a prophetic spirit, I will venture to predict that woman will be either the friend or slave of man. We shall not, as at present, doubt whether she is a moral agent, or the link which unites man with brutes. But should it then appear that like the brutes they were principally created for the use of man, he will let them patiently bite the bridle, and not mock them with empty praise; or, should their rationality be proved, he will not impede their improvement merely to gratify his sensual appetites. He will not, with all the graces of rhetoric, advise them to submit implicitly their understanding to the guidance of man. He will not, when he treats of the education of women, assert that they ought never to have the free use of reason, nor would he recommend cunning and dissimulation to beings who are acquiring, in like manner as himself, the virtues of humanity.

Surely there can be but one rule of right, if morality has an eternal foundation, and whoever sacrifices virtue, strictly so called, to present convenience, or whose duty it is to act in such a manner, lives only for the passing day, and cannot be an accountable creature.

The poet then should have dropped his sneer when he says:

"If weak women go astray,
The stars are more in fault than they."

For that they are bound by the adamantine chain of destiny is most certain, if it be proved that they are never to exercise their own reason, never to be independent, never to rise above opinion, or to feel the dignity of a rational will that only bows to God, and often forgets that the universe contains any being but itself and the model of perfection to which its ardent gaze is turned, to adore attributes that, softened into virtues, may be imitated in kind, though the degree overwhelms the enraptured mind.

If, I say, for I would not impress by declamation when Reason offers her sober light, if they be really capable of acting like rational creatures, let them not be treated like slaves; or, like the brutes who are dependent on the reason of man, when they associate with him; but cultivate their minds, give them the salutary, sublime curb of principle, and let them attain conscious dignity by feeling themselves only dependent on God. Teach them, in common with man, to submit to necessity, instead of giving, to render them more pleasing, a sex to morals.

Further, should experience prove that they cannot attain the same degree of strength of mind, perseverance, and fortitude, let their virtues be the same in kind, though they may vainly struggle for the same degree; and the superiority of man will be equally clear, if not clearer; and truth, as it is a simple principle, which admits of no modification, would be common to both. Nay, the order of society, as it is at present regulated would not be inverted, for woman would then only have the rank that reason assigned her, and arts could not be practised to bring the balance even, much less to turn it.

These may be termed Utopian dreams.—Thanks to that Being who impressed them on my soul, and gave me sufficient strength of mind to dare to exert my own reason, till, becoming dependent only on Him for the support of my virtue, I view, with indignation, the mistaken notions that enslave my sex.

I love man as my fellow; but his sceptre, real or usurped, extends not to me, unless the reason of an individual demands my homage; and even then the submission is to reason, and not to man. In fact, the conduct of an accountable being must be regulated by the operations of its own reason; or on what foundation rests the throne of God?

It appears to me necessary to dwell on these obvious truths, because females have been insulated, as it were; and while they have been stripped of the virtues that should clothe humanity, they have been decked with artificial graces that enable them to exercise a short-lived tyranny. Love, in their bosoms, taking place of every nobler passion, their sole ambition is to be fair, to raise emotion instead of inspiring respect; and this ignoble desire, like the servility in absolute monarchies, destroys all strength of character. Liberty is the mother of virtue, and if women be, by their very constitution, slaves, and not allowed to breathe the sharp invigorating air of freedom, they must ever languish like exotics, and be reckoned beautiful flaws in nature.

As to the argument respecting the subjection in which the sex has ever been held, it retorts on man. The many have always been enthralled by the few; and monsters, who scarcely have shown any discernment of human excellence, have tyrannized over thousands of their fellow-creatures. Why have men of superior endowments submitted to such degradation? For, is it not universally acknowledged that kings, viewed collectively, have ever been inferior, in abilities and virtue, to the same number of men taken from the common mass of mankind—yet, have they not, and are they not still treated with a degree of reverence that is an insult to reason? China is not the only country where a living man has been made a God. *Men* have submitted to superior strength to enjoy with impunity the pleasure of the moment: *women* have only done the same, and therefore till it is proved that the courtier, who servilely resigns the birthright of a man, is not a moral agent, it cannot be demonstrated that woman is essentially inferior to man because she has always been subjugated.

Brutal force has hitherto governed the world, and that the science of politics is in its infancy, is evident from philosophers scrupling to give the knowledge most useful to man that determinate distinction.

I shall not pursue this argument any further than to establish an obvious inference, that as sound politics diffuse liberty, mankind, including woman, will become more wise and virtuous.

Lucretia Mott and Elizabeth Cady Stanton

Declaration of Sentiments and Resolutions, Seneca Falls Convention, July 19–20, 1848

When, in the course of human events, it becomes necessary for one portion of the family of man to assume among the people of the earth a position different from that which they have hitherto occupied, but one to which the laws of nature and of nature's God entitle them, a decent respect to the opinions of mankind requires that they should declare the causes that impel them to such a course.

We hold these truths to be self-evident: that all men and women are created equal; that they are endowed by their Creator with certain inalienable rights; that among these are life, liberty, and the pursuit of happiness; that to secure these rights governments are instituted, deriving their just powers from the consent of the governed. Whenever any form of government becomes destructive of these ends, it is the right of those who suffer from it to refuse allegiance to it, and to insist upon the institution of a new government, laying its foundation on such principles and organizing its powers in such form, as to them shall seem most likely to effect their safety and happiness. Prudence, indeed, will dictate that governments long established should not be changed for light and transient causes; and accordingly all experience hath shown that mankind are more disposed to suffer, while evils are sufferable, than to right themselves by abolishing the forms to which they are accustomed. But when a long train of abuses and usurpations, pursuing invariably the same object evinces a design to reduce them under absolute despotism, it is their duty to throw off such government, and to provide new guards for their future security. Such has been the patient sufferance of the women under this government, and such is now the necessity which constrains them to demand the equal station to which they are entitled.

The history of mankind is a history of repeated injuries and usurpations on the part of man toward woman, having in direct object the establishment of an absolute tyranny over her. To prove this, let facts be submitted to a candid world.

He has never permitted her to exercise her inalienable right to the elective franchise.

He has compelled her to submit to laws, in the formation of which she had no voice.

He has withheld from her rights which are given to the most ignorant and degraded men—both natives and foreigners.

Having deprived her of this first right of a citizen, the elective franchise, thereby leaving her without representation in the halls of legislation, he has oppressed her on all sides.

He has made her, if married, in the eye of the law, civilly dead.

He has taken from her all right in property, even to the wages she earns.

He has made her, morally, an irresponsible being. as she can commit many crimes with impunity, provided they be done in the presence of her husband.

In the covenant of marriage, she is compelled to promise obedience to her husband, he becoming, to all intents and purposes, her master—the law giving him power to deprive her of her liberty. and to administer chastisement.

He has so framed the laws of divorce, as to what shall be the proper causes, and in case of separation, to whom the guardianship of the children shall be given, as to be wholly regardless of the happiness of women—the law, in all cases, going upon a false supposition of the supremacy of man, and giving all power into his hands.

After depriving her of all rights as a married woman, if single, and the owner of property, he has taxed her to support a government which recognizes her only when her property can be made profitable to it.

He has monopolized nearly all the profitable employments, and from those she is permitted to follow, she receives but a scanty remuneration. He closes against her all the avenues to wealth and distinction which he considers most honorable to himself. As a teacher of theology, medicine, or law, she is not known.

He has denied her the facilities for obtaining a thorough education, all colleges being closed against her.

He allows her in Church, as well as State, but a subordinate position, claiming Apostolic authority for her exclusion from the ministry, and, with some exceptions, from any public participation in the affairs of the Church.

He has created a false public sentiment by giving to the world a different code of morals for men and women, by which moral delinquencies which exclude women from society, are not only tolerated, but deemed of little account in man.

He has usurped the prerogative of Jehovah himself, claiming it as his right to assign for her a sphere of action, when that belongs to her conscience and to her God.

He has endeavored, in every way that he could, to destroy her confidence in her own powers to lessen her self-respect, and to make her willing to lead a dependent and abject life.

Now, in view of this entire disfranchisement of one-half the people of this country, their social and religious degradation—in view of the unjust laws above mentioned, and because women do feel themselves aggrieved, oppressed, and fraudulently deprived of their most sacred rights, we insist that they have immediate admission to all the rights and privileges which belong to them as citizens of the United States.

In entering upon the great work before us, we anticipate no small amount of misconception, misrepresentation, and ridicule; but we shall use every instrumentality within our power to effect our object. We shall employ agents, circulate tracts, petition the State and National legislatures, and endeavor to enlist the pulpit and the press in our behalf. We hope this Convention will be followed by a series of Conventions embracing every part of the country.

The following resolutions were discussed by Lucreatia Mott, Thomas and Mary Ann McClintock, Amy Post, Catharine A. F. Stebbins, and others, and were adopted:

WHEREAS, The great precept of nature is conceded to be, that "man shall pursue his own true and substantial happiness." Blackstone in his Commentaries remarks, that this law of Nature being coeval with mankind, and dictated by God himself, is of course superior in obligation to any other. It is binding over all the globe, in all countries and at all times; no human laws are of any validity if contrary to this. and such of them as are valid, derive all their force. and all their validity, and all their authority, mediately and immediately, from this original; therefore,

Resolved, that such laws as conflict, in any way with the true and substantial happiness of woman, are contrary to the great precept of nature and of no validity, for this is "superior in obligation to any other."

Resolved, that all laws which prevent woman from occupying such a station in society as her conscience shall dictate, or which place her in a position inferior to that of man, are contrary to the great precept of nature, and therefore of no force or authority.

Resolved, that woman is man's equal—was intended to be so by the Creator, and the highest good of the race demands that she should be recognized as such.

Resolved, that the women of this country ought to be enlightened in regard to the laws under which they live, that they may no longer publish their degradation by declaring themselves satisfied with their present position, nor their ignorance, by asserting that they have all the rights they want.

Resolved, that inasmuch as man, while claiming for himself intellectual superiority. does accord to woman moral superiority, it is pre-eminently his duty to encourage her to speak and teach. as she has an opportunity, in all religious assemblies.

Resolved, that the same amount of virtue, delicacy, and refinement of behavior that is required of woman in the social state, should also be required of man, and the same transgressions should be visited with equal severity on both man and woman.

Resolved, that the objection of indelicacy and impropriety, which is so often brought against woman when she addresses a public audience, comes with a very ill-grace from those who encourage, by their attendance, her appearance on the stage, in the concert, or in feats of the circus.

Resolved, that woman has too long rested satisfied in the circumscribed limits which corrupt customs and a perverted application of the Scriptures have marked out for her, and that it is time she should move in the enlarged sphere which her great Creator has assigned her.

Resolved, that it is the duty of the women of this country to secure to themselves their sacred right to the elective franchise.

Resolved, that the equality of human rights results necessarily from the fact of the identity of the race in capabilities and responsibilities.

Resolved, therefore, that being invested by the Creator with the same capabilities, and the same consciousness of responsibility for their exercise, it is demonstrably the right and duty of woman, equally with man, to promote every righteous cause by every righteous means; and especially in regard to the great subjects of morals and religion, it is self-evidently her right to participate with her brother in teaching them, both in private and in public, by writing and by speaking, by any instrumentalities proper to be used, and in any assemblies proper to be held; and this being a self-evident truth growing out of the divinely implanted principles of human nature, any custom or authority adverse to it, whether modern or wearing the hoary sanction of antiquity, is to be regarded as a self-evident falsehood, and at war with mankind.

Resolved, that the speedy success of our cause depends upon the zealous and untiring efforts of both men and women, for the overthrow of the monopoly of the pulpit, and for the securing to women an equal participation with men in the various trades, professions, and commerce.

Frederick Douglass

"What to the Slave is the Fourth of July?" (1852)

Mr. President, Friends and Fellow Citizens: He who could address this audience without a quailing sensation, has stronger nerves than I have. I do not remember ever to have appeared as a speaker before any assembly more shrinkingly, nor with greater distrust of my ability, than I do this day. A feeling has crept over me, quite unfavorable to the exercise of my limited powers of speech. The task before me is one which requires much previous thought and study for its proper performance. I know that apologies of this sort are generally considered flat and unmeaning. I trust, however, that mine will not be so considered. Should I seem at ease, my appearance would much misrepresent me. The little experience I have had in addressing public meetings, in country school houses, avails me nothing on the present occasion.

The papers and placards say, that I am to deliver a 4th [of] July oration. This certainly sounds large, and out of the common way, for it is true that I have often had the privilege to speak in this beautiful Hall, and to address many who now honor me with their presence. But neither their familiar faces, nor the perfect gage I think I have of Corinthian Hall, seems to free me from embarrassment.

The fact is, ladies and gentlemen, the distance between this platform and the slave plantation, from which I escaped, is considerable—and the difficulties to be overcome in getting from the latter to the former, are by no means slight. That I am here to-day is, to me, a matter of astonishment as well as of gratitude. You will not, therefore, be surprised, if in what I have to say. I evince no elaborate preparation, nor grace my speech with any high sounding exordium. With little experience and with less learning, I have been able to throw my thoughts hastily and imperfectly together; and trusting to your patient and generous indulgence, I will proceed to lay them before you.

This, for the purpose of this celebration, is the 4th of July. It is the birthday of your National Independence, and of your political freedom. This, to you, is what the Passover was to the emancipated people of God. It carries your minds back to the day, and to the act of your great deliverance; and to the signs, and to the wonders, associated with that act, and that day. This celebration also marks the beginning of another year of your national life; and reminds you that the Republic of America is now 76 years old. I am glad, fellow-citizens, that your nation is so young. Seventy-six years, though a good old age for a man, is but a mere speck in the life of a nation. Three score years and ten is the allotted time for individual men; but nations number their years by thousands. According to this fact, you are, even now, only in the beginning of your national career, still lingering in the period of childhood. I repeat, I am glad this is so. There is hope in the thought, and hope is much needed, under the dark clouds which lower above the horizon.

The eye of the reformer is met with angry flashes, portending disastrous times; but his heart may well beat lighter at the thought that America is young, and that she is still in the impressible stage of her existence. May he not hope that high lessons of wisdom, of justice and of truth, will yet give direction to her destiny? Were the nation older, the patriot's heart might be sadder, and the reformer's brow heavier. Its future might be shrouded in gloom, and the hope of its prophets go out in sorrow. There is consolation in the thought that America is young.—Great streams are not easily turned from channels, worn deep in the course of ages. They may sometimes rise in quiet and stately majesty, and inundate the land, refreshing and fertilizing the earth with their mysterious properties. They may also rise in wrath and fury, and bear away, on their angry waves, the accumulated wealth of years of toil and hardship. They, however, gradually flow back to the same old channel, and flow on as serenely as ever. But, while the river may not be turned aside, it may dry up, and leave nothing behind but the withered branch, and the unsightly rock, to howl in the abyss-sweeping wind, the sad tale of departed glory. As with rivers so with nations.

Fellow-citizens, I shall not presume to dwell at length on the associations that cluster about this day. The simple story of it is that, 76 years ago, the people of this country were British subjects. The style and title of your "sovereign people" (in which you now glory) was not then born. You were under the British Crown. Your fathers esteemed the English Government as the home government; and England as the fatherland. This home government, you know, although a considerable distance from your home, did, in the exercise of its parental prerogatives, impose upon its colonial children, such restraints, burdens and limitations, as, in its mature judgment, it deemed wise, right and proper.

But, your fathers, who had not adopted the fashionable idea of this day, of the infallibility of government, and the absolute character of its acts, presumed to differ from the home government in respect to the wisdom and the justice of some of those burdens and restraints. They went so far in their excitement as to pronounce the measures of government unjust, unreasonable, and oppressive, and altogether such as ought not to be quietly submitted to. I scarcely need say, fellow-citizens, that my opinion of those measures fully accords with that of your fathers. Such a declaration of agreement on my part would not be worth much to anybody. It would, certainly, prove nothing, as to what part I might have taken, had I lived during the great controversy of 1776. To say *now* that America was right, and England wrong, is exceedingly easy. Everybody can say it; the dastard, not less than the noble brave, can flippantly discant on the tyranny of England towards the American Colonies. It is fashionable to do so; but there was a time when to pronounce against England, and in favor of the cause of the colonies, tried men's souls. They who did so were accounted in their day, plotters of mischief, agitators and rebels, dangerous men. To side with the right, against the wrong, with the weak against the strong, and with the oppressed against the oppressor! *here* lies the merit, and the one which, of all others, seems unfashionable in our day. The cause of liberty may be stabbed by the men who glory in the deeds of your fathers. But, to proceed.

Feeling themselves harshly and unjustly treated by the home government, your fathers, like men of honesty, and men of spirit, earnestly sought redress. They petitioned and remonstrated; they did so in a decorous, respectful, and loyal manner. Their conduct was wholly unexceptionable. This, however, did not answer the purpose. They saw themselves treated with sovereign indifference, coldness and scorn. Yet they persevered. They were not the men to look back.

As the sheer anchor takes a firmer hold, when the ship is tossed by the storm, so did the cause of your fathers grow stronger, as it breasted the chilling blasts of kingly displeasure. The greatest and best of British statesmen admitted its justice, and the loftiest eloquence of the British Senate came to its support. But, with that blindness which seems to be the unvarying characteristic of tyrants, since Pharaoh and his hosts were drowned in the Red Sea, the British Government persisted in the exactions complained of.

The madness of this course, we believe, is admitted now, even by England; but we fear the lesson is wholly lost on our present rulers.

Oppression makes a wise man mad. Your fathers were wise men, and if they did not go mad, they became restive under this treatment. They felt themselves the victims of grievous wrongs, wholly incurable in their colonial capacity. With brave men there is always a remedy for oppression. Just here, the idea of a total separation of the colonies from the crown was born! It was a startling idea, much more so, than we, at this distance of time, regard it. The timid and the prudent (as has been intimated) of that day, were, of course, shocked and alarmed by it.

Such people lived then, had lived before, and will, probably, ever have a place on this planet; and their course, in respect to any great change (no matter how great the good to be attained, or the wrong to be redressed by it), may be calculated with as much precision as can be the course of the stars. They hate all changes, but silver, gold and copper change! Of this sort of change they are always strongly in favor.

These people were called Tories in the days of your fathers; and the appellation, probably, conveyed the same idea that is meant by a more modern, though a somewhat less euphonious term, which we often find in our papers, applied to some of our old politicians.

Their opposition to the then dangerous thought was earnest and powerful; but, amid all their terror and affrighted vociferations against it, the alarming and revolutionary idea moved on, and the country with it.

On the 2d of July, 1776, the old Continental Congress, to the dismay of the lovers of ease, and the worshipers of property, clothed that dreadful idea with all the authority of national sanction. They did so in the form of a resolution; and as we seldom hit upon resolutions, drawn up in our day, whose transparency is at all equal to this, it may refresh your minds and help my story if I read it.

"Resolved, That these united colonies *are*, and of right, ought to be free and Independent States; that they are absolved from all allegiance to the British Crown; and that all political connection between them and the State of Great Britain *is*, and ought to be, dissolved."

Citizens, your fathers made good that resolution. They succeeded; and to-day you reap the fruits of their success. The freedom gained is yours; and you, therefore, may properly celebrate this anniversary. The 4th of July is the first great fact in your nation's history—the very ring-bolt in the chain of your yet undeveloped destiny.

Pride and patriotism, not less than gratitude, prompt you to celebrate and to hold it in perpetual remembrance. I have said that the Declaration of Independence is the ring-bolt to the chain of your nation's destiny; so, indeed, I regard it. The principles contained in that instrument are saving principles. Stand by those principles, be true to them on all occasions, in all places, against all foes, and at whatever cost.

From the round top of your ship of state, dark and threatening clouds may be seen. Heavy billows, like mountains in the distance, disclose to the leeward huge forms of flinty rocks! That *bolt* drawn, that *chain* broken, and all is lost. *Cling to this day—cling to it*, and to its principles, with the grasp of a storm-tossed mariner to a spar at midnight.

The coming into being of a nation, in any circumstances, is an interesting event. But, besides general considerations, there were peculiar circumstances which make the advent of this republic an event of special attractiveness.

The whole scene, as I look back to it, was simple, dignified and sublime.

The population of the country, at the time, stood at the insignificant number of three millions. The country was poor in the munitions of war. The population was weak and scattered, and the country a wilderness unsubdued. There were then no means of concert and combination, such as exist now. Neither steam nor lightning had then been reduced to order and discipline. From the Potomac to the Delaware was a journey of many days. Under these, and innumerable other disadvantages, your fathers declared for liberty and independence and triumphed.

Fellow Citizens, I am not wanting in respect for the fathers of this republic. The signers of the Declaration of Independence were brave men. They were great men too—great enough to give fame to a great age. It does not often happen to a nation to raise, at one time, such a number of truly great men. The point from which I am compelled to view them is not, certainly, the most favorable; and yet I cannot contemplate their great deeds with less than admiration. They were statesmen, patriots and heroes, and for the good they did, and the principles they contended for, I will unite with you to honor their memory.

They loved their country better than their own private interests; and, though this is not the highest form of human excellence, all will concede that it is a rare virtue, and that when it is exhibited, it ought to command respect. He who will, intelligently, lay down his life for his country, is a man whom it is not in human nature to despise. Your fathers staked their lives, their fortunes, and their sacred honor, on the cause of their country. In their admiration of liberty, they lost sight of all other interests.

They were peace men; but they preferred revolution to peaceful submission to bondage. They were quiet men; but they did not shrink from agitating against oppression. They showed forbearance; but that they knew its limits. They believed in order; but not in the order of tyranny. With them, nothing was *settled* that was not right. With them, justice, liberty and humanity were *final;* not slavery and oppression. You may well cherish the memory of such men. They were great in their day and generation. Their solid manhood stands out the more as we contrast it with these degenerate times.

How circumspect, exact and proportionate were all their movements! How unlike the politicians of an hour! Their statesmanship looked beyond the passing moment, and stretched away in strength into the distant future. They seized upon eternal principles, and set a glorious example in their defense. Mark them!

Fully appreciating the hardship to be encountered, firmly believing in the right of their cause, honorably inviting the scrutiny of an on-looking world, reverently appealing to heaven to attest their sincerity, soundly comprehending the solemn responsibility they were about to assume, wisely measuring the terrible odds against them, your fathers, the fathers of this republic, did, most deliberately, under the inspiration of a glorious patriotism, and with a sublime faith in the great principles of justice and freedom, lay deep the corner-stone of the national superstructure, which has risen and still rises in grandeur around you.

Of this fundamental work, this day is the anniversary. Our eyes are met with demonstrations of joyous enthusiasm. Banners and pennants wave exultingly on the breeze. The din of business, too, is hushed. Even Mammon seems to have quitted his grasp on this day. The ear-piercing fife and the stirring drum unite their accents with the ascending peal of a thousand church bells. Prayers are made, hymns are sung, and sermons are preached in honor of this day; while the quick martial tramp of a great and multitudinous nation, echoed back by all the hills, valleys and mountains of a vast continent, bespeak the occasion one of thrilling and universal interests—a nation's jubilee.

Friends and citizens, I need not enter further into the causes which led to this anniversary. Many of you understand them better than I do. You could instruct me in regard to them. That is a branch of knowledge in which you feel, perhaps, a much deeper interest than your speaker. The causes which led to the separation of the colonies from the British crown have never lacked for a tongue. They have all been taught in your common schools, narrated at your firesides, unfolded from your pulpits, and thundered from your legislative halls, and are as familiar to you as household words. They form the staple of your national poetry and eloquence.

I remember, also, that, as a people, Americans are remarkably familiar with all facts which make in their own favor. This is esteemed by some as a national trait—perhaps a national weakness. It is a fact, that whatever makes for the wealth or for the reputation of Americans, and can be had *cheap*! will be found by Americans. I shall not be charged with slandering Americans, if I say I think the American side of any question may be safely left in American hands.

I leave, therefore, the great deeds of your fathers to other gentlemen whose claim to have been regularly descended will be less likely to be disputed than mine!

The Present

My business, if I have any here to-day, is with the present. The accepted time with God and his cause is the ever-living now.

"Trust no future, however pleasant,
  Let the dead past bury its dead;
Act, act in the living present,
  Heart within, and God overhead."

We have to do with the past only as we can make it useful to the present and to the future. To all inspiring motives, to noble deeds which can be gained from the past, we are welcome. But now is the time, the important time. Your fathers have lived, died, and have done their work, and have done much of it well. You live and must die, and you must do your work. You have no right to enjoy a child's share in the labor of your fathers, unless your children are to be blest by your labors. You have no right to wear out and waste the hard-earned fame of your fathers to cover your indolence. Sydney Smith tells us that men seldom eulogize the wisdom and virtues of their fathers, but to excuse some folly or wickedness of their own. This truth is not a doubtful one.

There are illustrations of it near and remote, ancient and modern. It was fashionable, hundreds of years ago, for the children of Jacob to boast, we have "Abraham to our father," when they had long lost Abraham's faith and spirit. That people contented themselves under the shadow of Abraham's great name, while they repudiated the deeds which made his name great. Need I remind you that a similar thing is being done all over this country to-day? Need I tell you that the Jews are not the only people who built the tombs of the prophets, and garnished the sepulchres of the righteous? Washington could not die till he had broken the chains of his slaves. Yet his monument is built up by the price of human blood, and the traders in the bodies and souls of men, shout—"We have Washington to *our father*." Alas! that it should be so; yet so it is.

"The evil that men do, lives after them,
The good is oft' interred with their bones."

Fellow-citizens, pardon me, allow me to ask, why am I called upon to speak here to-day? What have I, or those I represent, to do with your national independence? Are the great principles of political freedom and of natural justice, embodied in that Declaration of Independence, extended to us? and am I, therefore, called upon to bring our humble offering to the national altar, and to confess the benefits and express devout gratitude for the blessings resulting from your independence to us?

Would to God, both for your sakes and ours, that an affirmative answer could be truthfully returned to these questions! Then would my task be light, and my burden easy and delightful. For who is there so cold, that a nation's sympathy could not warm him? Who so obdurate and dead to the claims of gratitude, that would not thankfully acknowledge such priceless benefits? Who so stolid and selfish, that would not give his voice to swell the hallelujahs of a nation's jubilee, when the chains of servitude had been tom from his limbs? I am not that man. In a case like that, the dumb might eloquently speak, and the "lame man leap as an hart."

But, such is not the state of the case. I say it with a sad sense of the disparity between us. I am not included within the pale of this glorious anniversary! Your high independence only reveals the immeasurable distance between us. The blessings in which you, this day, rejoice, are not enjoyed in common.—The rich inheritance of justice, liberty, prosperity and independence, bequeathed by your fathers, is shared by you, not by me. The sunlight that brought life and healing to you, has brought stripes and death to me. This Fourth [of] July is *yours*, not *mine. You* may rejoice, I must mourn. To drag a man in fetters into the grand illuminated temple of liberty, and call upon him to join you in joyous anthems, were inhuman mockery and sacrilegious irony. Do you mean, citizens, to mock me, by asking me to speak to-day? If so, there is a parallel to your conduct. And let me warn you that it is dangerous to copy the example of a nation whose crimes, lowering up to heaven, were thrown down by the breath of the Almighty, burying that nation in irrecoverable ruin! I can to-day take up the plaintive lament of a peeled and woe-smitten people!

"By the rivers of Babylon, there we sat down. Yea! we wept when we remembered Zion. We hanged our harps upon the willows in the midst thereof. For there, they that carried us away captive, required of us a song; and they who wasted us required of us mirth, saying, Sing us one of the songs of Zion. How can we sing the Lord's song in a strange land? If I forget thee, O Jerusalem, let my right hand forget her cunning. If I do not remember thee, let my tongue cleave to the roof of my mouth."

Fellow-citizens; above your national, tumultuous joy, I hear the mournful wail of millions! whose chains, heavy and grievous yesterday, are, to-day, rendered more intolerable by the jubilee shouts that reach them. If I do forget, if I do not faithfully remember those bleeding children of sorrow this day, "may my right hand forget her cunning, and may my tongue cleave to the roof of my mouth!" To forget them, to pass lightly over their wrongs, and to chime in with the popular theme, would be treason most scandalous and shocking, and would make me a reproach before God and the world. My subject, then fellow-citizens, is AMERICAN SLAVERY. I shall see, this day, and its popular characteristics, from the slave's point of view. Standing, there, identified with the American bondman, making his wrongs mine, I do not hesitate to declare, with all my soul, that the character and conduct of this nation never looked blacker to me than on this 4th of July! Whether we turn to the declarations of the past, or to the professions of the present, the conduct of the nation seems equally hideous and revolting. America is false to the past, false to the present, and solemnly binds herself to be false to the future. Standing with God and the crushed and bleeding slave on this occasion, I will, in the name of humanity which is outraged, in the name of liberty which is fettered, in the name of the constitution and the Bible, which are disregarded and trampled upon, dare to call in question and to denounce, with all the emphasis I can command, everything that serves to perpetuate slavery—the great sin and shame of America! "I will not equivocate; I will not excuse;" I will use the severest language I can command; and yet not one word shall escape me that any man, whose judgment is not blinded by prejudice, or who is not at heart a slaveholder, shall not confess to be fight and just.

But I fancy I hear some one of my audience say, it is just in this circumstance that you and your brother abolitionists fail to make a favorable impression on the public mind. Would you argue more, and denounce less, would you persuade more, and rebuke less, your cause would be much more likely to succeed.

But, I submit, where all is plain there is nothing to be argued. What point in the anti-slavery creed would you have me argue? On what branch of the subject do the people of this country need light? Must I undertake to prove that the slave is a man? That point is conceded already. Nobody doubts it. The slaveholders themselves acknowledge it in the enactment of laws for their government. They acknowledge it when they punish disobedience on the part of the slave. There are seventy-two crimes in the State of Virginia, which, if committed by a black man (no matter how ignorant he be), subject him to the punishment of death; while only two of the same crimes will subject a white man to the like punishment.—What is this but the acknowledgement that the slave is a moral, intellectual and responsible being? The manhood of the slave is conceded. It is admitted in the fact that Southern statute books are covered with enactments forbidding, under severe fines and penalties, the teaching of the slave to read or to write.—When you can point to any such laws, in reference to the beasts of the field, then I may consent to argue the manhood of the slave. When the dogs in your streets, when the fowls of the air, when the cattle on your hills, when the fish of the sea, and the reptiles that crawl, shall be unable to distinguish the slave from a brute, then will I argue with you that the slave is a man!

For the present, it is enough to affirm the equal manhood of the Negro race. Is it not astonishing that, while we are ploughing, planting and reaping, using all kinds of mechanical tools, erecting houses, constructing bridges, building ships, working in metals of brass, iron, copper, silver and gold; that, while we are reading, writing and cyphering, acting as clerks, merchants and secretaries, having among us lawyers, doctors, ministers, poets, authors, editors, orators and teachers; that, while we are engaged in all manner of enterprises common to other men, digging gold in California, capturing the whale in the Pacific, feeding sheep and cattle on the hill-side, living, moving, acting, thinking, planning, living in families as husbands, wives and children, and, above all, confessing and worshipping the Christian's God, and looking hopefully for life and immortality beyond the grave, we are called upon to prove that we are men!

Would you have me argue that man is entitled to liberty? that he is the rightful owner of his own body? You have already declared it. Must I argue the wrongfulness of slavery?

Is that a question for Republicans? Is it to be settled by the rules of logic and argumentation, as a matter beset with great difficulty, involving a doubtful application of the principle of justice, hard to be understood? How should I look to-day, in the presence of Americans, dividing, and subdividing a discourse, to show that men have a natural right to freedom? speaking of it relatively, and positively, negatively, and affirmatively. To do so, would be to make myself ridiculous, and lo offer an insult to your understanding.—There is not a man beneath the canopy of heaven, that does not know that slavery is wrong *for him.*

What, am I to argue that it is wrong to make men brutes, to rob them of their liberty, to work them without wages, to keep them ignorant of their relations to their fellow men, to beat them with sticks, to flay their flesh with the lash, to load their limbs with irons, to hunt them with dogs, to sell them at auction, to sunder their families, to knock out their teeth, to burn their flesh, to starve them into obedience and submission to their masters? Must I argue that a system thus marked with blood, and stained with pollution, is *wrong*? No! I will not. I have better employments for my time and strength, than such arguments would imply.

What, then, remains to be argued? Is it that slavery is not divine; that God did not establish it; that our doctors of divinity are mistaken? There is blasphemy in the thought. That which is inhuman, cannot be divine! *Who* can reason on such a proposition? They that can, may; I cannot. The time for such argument is past.

At a time like this, scorching irony, not convincing argument, is needed.

O! had I the ability, and could I reach the nation's ear, I would, to-day, pour out a fiery stream of biting ridicule, blasting reproach, withering sarcasm, and stern rebuke. For it is not light that is needed, but fire; it is not the gentle shower, but thunder. We need the storm, the whirlwind, and the earthquake. The feeling of the nation must be quickened; the conscience of the nation must be roused; the propriety of the nation must be startled; the hypocrisy of the nation must be exposed; and its crimes against God and man must be proclaimed and denounced.

What, to the American slave, is your 4th of July? I answer: a day that reveals to him, more than all other days in the year, the gross injustice and cruelly to which he is the constant victim. To him, your celebration is a sham; your boasted liberty, an unholy license; your national greatness, swelling vanity; your sounds of rejoicing are empty and heartless; your denunciations of tyrants, brass-fronted impudence; your shouts of liberty and equality, hollow mockery; your prayers and hymns, your sermons and thanksgivings, with all your religious parade, and solemnity, are, to him, mere bombast, fraud, deception, impiety, and hypocrisy—a thin veil to cover up crimes which would disgrace a nation of savages.

There is not a nation on the earth guilty of practices more shocking and bloody, than are the people of these United States, at this very hour.

Go where you may, search where you will, roam through all the monarchies and despotisms of the old world, travel through South America, search out every abuse, and when you have found the last, lay your facts by the side of the everyday practices of this nation, and you will say with me, that, for revolting barbarity and shameless hypocrisy, America reigns without a rival.

The Internal Slave Trade

Take the American slave-trade, which, we are told by the papers, is especially prosperous just now. Ex-Senator Benton tells us that the price of men was never higher than now. He mentions the fact to show that slavery is in no danger. This trade is one of the peculiarities of American institutions. It is carried on in all the large towns and cities in one-half of this confederacy; and millions are pocketed every year, by dealers in this horrid traffic. In several states, this trade is a chief source of wealth. It is called (in contradistinction to the foreign slave-trade) "*the internal slave trade.*" It is, probably, called so, too, in order to divert from it the horror with which the foreign slave-trade is contemplated. That trade has long since been denounced by this government, as piracy. It has been denounced with burning words, from the high places of the nation, as an execrable traffic. To arrest it, to put an end to it, this nation keeps a squadron, at immense cost, on the coast of Africa. Everywhere, in this country, it is safe to speak of this foreign slave-trade, as a most inhuman traffic, opposed alike to the laws of God and of man. The duty to extirpate and destroy it, is admitted even by our DOCTORS OF DIVINITY. In order to put an end to it, some of these last have consented that their colored brethren (nominally free) should leave this country, and establish themselves on the western coast of Africa! It is, however, a notable fact that, while so much execration is poured out by Americans upon those engaged in the foreign slave-trade, the men engaged in the slave-trade between the states pass without condemnation, and their business is deemed honorable.

Behold the practical operation of this internal slave-trade, the American slave-trade, sustained by American politics and American religion. Here you will see men and women reared like swine for the market. You know what is a swine-drover? I will show you a man-drover. They inhabit all our Southern States. They perambulate the country, and crowd the highways of the nation, with droves of human stock. You will see one of these human flesh-jobbers, armed with pistol, whip and bowie-knife, driving a company of a hundred men, women, and children, from the Potomac to the slave market at New Orleans. These wretched people are to be sold singly, or in lots, to suit purchasers. They are food for the cotton-field, and the deadly sugar-mill. Mark the sad procession, as it moves wearily along, and the inhuman wretch who drives them. Hear his savage yells and his blood-chilling oaths, as he hurries on his affrighted captives! There, see the old man, with locks thinned and gray. Cast one glance, if you please, upon that young mother, whose shoulders are bare to the scorching sun, her briny tears falling on the brow of the babe in her arms. See, too, that girl of thirteen, weeping, *yes*! weeping, as she thinks of the mother from whom she has been torn! The drove moves tardily. Heat and sorrow have nearly consumed their strength; suddenly you hear a quick snap, like the discharge of a rifle; the fetters clank, and the chain rattles simultaneously; your ears are saluted with a scream, that seems to have torn its way to the centre of your soul! The crack you heard, was the sound of the slave-whip; the scream you heard, was from the woman you saw with the babe. Her speed had faltered under the weight of her child and her chains! that gash on her shoulder tells her to move on. Follow this drove to New Orleans. Attend the auction; see men examined like horses; see the forms of women rudely and brutally exposed to the shocking gaze of American slave-buyers. See this drove sold and separated forever; and never forget the deep, sad sobs that arose from that scattered multitude. Tell me citizens, WHERE, under the sun, you can witness a spectacle more fiendish and shocking. Yet this is but a glance at the American slave-trade, as it exists, at this moment, in the ruling part of the United States.

I was born amid such sights and scenes. To me the American slave-trade is a terrible reality. When a child, my soul was often pierced with a sense of its horrors. I lived on Philpot Street, Fell's Point, Baltimore, and have watched from the wharves, the slave ships in the Basin, anchored from the shore, with their cargoes of human flesh, waiting for favorable winds to waft them down the Chesapeake. There was, at that time, a grand slave mart kept at the head of Pratt Street, by Austin Woldfolk. His agents were sent into every town and county in Maryland, announcing their arrival, through the papers, and on flaming "*hand-bills*," headed CASH FOR NEGROES. These men were generally well-dressed men, and very captivating in their manners. Ever ready to drink, to treat, and to gamble. The fate of many a slave has depended upon the turn of a single card; and many a child has been snatched from the arms of its mother by bargains arranged in a state of brutal drunkenness.

The flesh-mongers gather up their victims by dozens, and drive them, chained, to the general depot at Baltimore. When a sufficient number have been collected here, a ship is chartered, for the purpose of conveying the forlorn crew to Mobile, or to New Orleans. From the slave prison to the ship, they are usually driven in the darkness of night; for since the antislavery agitation, a certain caution is observed.

In the deep still darkness of midnight, I have been often aroused by the dead heavy footsteps, and the piteous cries of the chained gangs that passed our door. The anguish of my boyish heart was intense; and I was often consoled, when speaking to my mistress in the morning, to hear her say that the custom was very wicked; that she hated to hear the rattle of the chains, and the heart-rending cries. I was glad to find one who sympathised with me in my horror.

Fellow-citizens, this murderous traffic is, to-day, in active operation in this boasted republic. In the solitude of my spirit, I see clouds of dust raised on the highways of the South; I see the bleeding footsteps; I hear the doleful wail of fettered humanity, on the way to the slave-markets, where the victims are to be sold like *horses*, *sheep*, and *swine*, knocked off to the highest bidder. There I see the tenderest ties ruthlessly broken, to gratify the lust, caprice and rapacity of the buyers and sellers of men. My soul sickens at the sight.

"Is this the land your Fathers loved,
  The freedom which they toiled to win?
Is this the earth whereon they moved?
  Are these the graves they slumber in?"

But a still more inhuman, disgraceful, and scandalous state of things remains to be presented.

By an act of the American Congress, not yet two years old, slavery has been nationalized in its most horrible and revolting form. By that act, Mason & Dixon's line has been obliterated; New York has become as Virginia; and the power to hold, hunt, and sell men, women, and children as slaves remains no longer a mere state institution, but is now an institution of the whole United States. The power is co-extensive with the star-spangled banner and American Christianity. Where these go, may also go the merciless slave-hunter. Where these are, man is not sacred. He is a bird for the sportsman's gun. By that most foul and fiendish of all human decrees, the liberty and person of every man are put in peril. Your broad republican domain is hunting ground for *men. Not* for thieves and robbers, enemies of society, merely, but for men guilty of no crime. Your lawmakers have commanded all good citizens to engage in this hellish sport. Your President, your Secretary of State, your *lords, nobles,* and ecclesiastics, enforce, as a duty you owe to your free and glorious country, and to your God, that you do this accursed thing. Not fewer than forty Americans have, within the past two years, been hunted down and, without a moment's warning, hurried away in chains, and consigned to slavery and excruciating torture. Some of these have had wives and children, dependent on them for bread; but of this, no account was made. The right of the hunter to his prey stands superior to the right of marriage, and to all rights in this republic, the rights of God included! For black men there are neither law, justice, humanity, not religion. The Fugitive Slave Law makes MERCY TO THEM, A CRIME; and bribes the judge who tries them. An American JUDGE GETS TEN DOLLARS FOR EVERY VICTIM HE CONSIGNS to slavery, and five, when he fails to do so. The oath of any two villains is sufficient, under this hell-black enactment, to send the most pious and exemplary black man into the remorseless jaws of slavery! His own testimony is nothing. He can bring no witnesses for himself. The minister of American justice is bound by the law to hear but *one* side; and *that* side, is the side of the oppressor. Let this damning fact be perpetually told. Let it be thundered around the world, that, in tyrant-killing, king-hating, people-loving, democratic, Christian America, the seats of justice are filled with judges, who hold their offices under an open and palpable *bribe*, and are bound, in deciding in the case of a man's liberty, *to hear only his accusers!*

In glaring violation of justice, in shameless disregard of the forms of administering law, in cunning arrangement to entrap the defenceless, and in diabolical intent, this Fugitive Slave Law stands alone in the annals of tyrannical legislation. I doubt if there be another nation on the globe, having the brass and the baseness to put such a law on the statute-book. If any man in this assembly thinks differently from me in this matter, and feels able to disprove my statements, I will gladly confront him at any suitable time and place he may select.

Religious Liberty

I take this law to be one of the grossest infringements of Christian Liberty, and, if the churches and ministers of our country were not stupidly blind, or most wickedly indifferent, they, too, would so regard it.

At the very moment that they are thanking God for the enjoyment of civil and religious liberty, and for the right to worship God according to the dictates of their own consciences, they are utterly silent in respect to a law which robs religion of its chief significance, and makes it utterly worthless to a world lying in wickedness. Did this law concern the *"mint, anise and cumin"*—abridge the right to sing psalms, to partake of the sacrament, or to engage in any of the ceremonies of religion, it would be smitten by the thunder of a thousand pulpits. A general shout would go up from the church, demanding *repeal, repeal, instant repeal!*—And it would go hard with that politician who presumed to solicit the votes of the people without inscribing this motto on his banner. Further, if this demand were not complied with, another Scotland would be added to the history of religious liberty, and the stern old Covenanters would be thrown into the shade. A John Knox would be seen at every church door, and heard from every pulpit, and Fillmore would have no more quarter than was shown by Knox, to the beautiful, but treacherous Queen Mary of Scotland.—The fact that the church of our country, (with fractional exceptions), does not esteem "the Fugitive Slave Law" as a declaration of war against religious liberty, implies that that church regards religion simply as a form of worship, an empty ceremony, and not a vital principle, requiring active benevolence, justice, love and good will towards man. It esteems sacrifice above mercy; psalm-singing above right doing; solemn meetings above practical righteousness. A worship that can be conducted by persons who refuse to give shelter to the houseless, to give bread to the hungry, clothing to the naked, and who enjoin obedience to a law forbidding these acts of mercy, is a curse, not a blessing to mankind. The Bible addresses all such persons as "scribes, Pharisees, hypocrites, who pay tithe of *mint, anise*, and *cumin*, and have omitted the weightier matters of the law, judgement, mercy and faith."

The Church Responsible

But the church of this country is not only indifferent to the wrongs of the slave, it actually takes sides with the oppressors. It has made itself the bulwark of American slavery, and the shield of American slave-hunters. Many of its most eloquent Divines. who stand as the very lights of the church, have shamelessly given the sanction of religion and the Bible to the whole slave system.—They have taught that man may, properly, be a slave; that the relation of master and slave is ordained of God; that to send back an escaped bondman to his master is clearly the duty of all the followers of the Lord Jesus Christ; and this horrible blasphemy is palmed off upon the world for Christianity.

For my part, I would say, welcome infidelity! welcome atheism! Welcome anything! In preference to the gospel, as *preached by those Divines!* They convert the very name of religion into an engine of tyranny, and barbarous cruelty, and serve to confirm more infidels, in this age, than all the infidel writings of Thomas Paine, Voltaire, and Bolingbroke, put together, have done! These ministers make religion a cold and flinty-hearted thing, having neither principles of right action, nor bowels of compassion. They strip the love of God of its beauty, and leave the throne of religion a huge, horrible, repulsive form. It is a religion for oppressors, tyrants, man-stealers, and *thugs.* It is not that *"pure and undefiled religion"* which is from above, and which is *"first pure, then peaceable, easy to be entreated, full of mercy and good fruits, without partiality, and without hypocrisy."* But a religion which favors the rich against the poor; which exalts the proud above the humble; which divides mankind into two classes, tyrants and slaves; which says to the man in chains, *stay there*; and to the oppressor, *oppress on*; it is a religion which may be professed and enjoyed by all the robbers and enslavers of mankind; it makes God a respecter of persons, denies his fatherhood of the race, and tramples in the dust the great truth of the brotherhood of man. All this we affirm to be true of the popular church, and the popular worship of our land and nation—a religion, a church, and a worship which, on the authority of inspired wisdom, we pronounce to be an abomination in the sight of God. In the language of Isaiah, the American church might be well addressed, "Bring no more vain ablations; incense is an abomination unto me: the new moons and Sabbaths, the calling of assemblies, I cannot away with; it is iniquity, even the solemn meeting. Your new moons and your appointed feasts my soul hateth. They are a trouble to me; I am weary to bear them; and when ye spread forth your hands I will hide mine eyes from you. Yea! when ye make many prayers, I will not hear. YOUR HANDS ARE FULL OF BLOOD; cease to do evil, learn to do well; seek judgment; relieve the oppressed; judge for the fatherless; plead for the widow."

The American church is guilty, when viewed in connection with what it is doing to uphold slavery; but it is superlatively guilty when viewed in connection with its ability to abolish slavery.

The sin of which it is guilty is one of omission as well as of commission. Albert Barnes but uttered what the common sense of every man at all observant of the actual state of the case will receive as truth, when he declared that "There is no power out of the church that could sustain slavery an hour, if it were not sustained in it."

Let the religious press, the pulpit, the Sunday school, the conference meeting, the great ecclesiastical, missionary, Bible and tract associations of the land array their immense powers against slavery and slave-holding; and the whole system of crime and blood would be scattered to the winds; and that they do not do this involves them in the most awful responsibility of which the mind can conceive.

In prosecuting the anti-slavery enterprise, we have been asked to spare the church, to spare the ministry; but *how*, we ask, could such a thing be done? We are met on the threshold of our efforts for the redemption of the slave, by the church and ministry of the country, in battle arrayed against us; and we are compelled to fight or flee. From *what* quarter, I beg to know, has proceeded a fire so deadly upon our ranks, during the last two years, as from the Northern pulpit? As the champions of oppressors, the chosen men of American theology have appeared—men, honored for their so-called piety, and their real learning. The LORDS of Buffalo, the SPRINGS of New York, the LATHROPS of Auburn, the COXES and SPENCERS of Brooklyn, the GANNETS and SHARPS of Boston, the DEWEYS of Washington, and other great religious lights of the land, have, in utter denial of the authority of *Him*, by whom they professed to he called to the ministry, deliberately taught us, against the example or the Hebrews and against the remonstrance of the Apostles, they teach *"that we ought to obey man's law before the law of God."*

My spirit wearies of such blasphemy; and how such men can be supported, as the "standing types and representatives of Jesus Christ," is a mystery which I leave others to penetrate. In speaking of the American church, however, let it be distinctly understood that I mean the *great mass* of the religious organizations of our land. There are exceptions, and I thank God that there are. Noble men may be found, scattered all over these Northern States, of whom Henry Ward Beecher of Brooklyn, Samuel J. May of Syracuse, and my esteemed friend* on the platform, are shining examples; and let me say further, that upon these men lies the duty to inspire our ranks with high religious faith and zeal, and to cheer us on in the great mission of the slave's redemption from his chains. [*Rev. R. R. Raymond]

Religion in England and Religion in America

One is struck with the difference between the attitude of the American church towards the anti-slavery movement, and that occupied by the churches in England towards a similar movement in that country. There, the church, true to its mission of ameliorating, elevating, and improving the condition of mankind, came forward promptly, bound up the wounds of the West Indian slave, and restored him to his liberty. There, the question of emancipation was a high[ly] religious question. It was demanded, in the name of humanity, and according to the law of the living God. The Sharps, the Clarksons, the Wilberforces, the Buxtons, and Burchells and the Knibbs, were alike famous for their piety, and for their philanthropy. The anti-slavery movement *there* was not an anti-church movement, for the reason that the church took its full share in prosecuting that movement: and the anti-slavery movement in this country will cease to be an anti-church movement, when the church of this country shall assume a favorable, instead or a hostile position towards that movement.

Americans! your republican politics, not less than your republican religion, are flagrantly inconsistent. You boast of your love of liberty, your superior civilization, and your pure Christianity, while the whole political power of the nation (as embodied in the two great political parties), is solemnly pledged to support and perpetuate the enslavement of three millions of your countrymen. You hurl your anathemas at the crowned headed tyrants of Russia and Austria, and pride yourselves on your Democratic institutions, while you yourselves consent to be the mere *tools* and *bodyguards* of the tyrants of Virginia and Carolina. You invite to your shores fugitives of oppression from abroad, honor them with banquets, greet them with ovations, cheer them, toast them, salute them, protect them, and pour out your money to them like water; but the fugitives from your own land you advertise, hunt, arrest, shoot and kill. You glory in your refinement and your universal education; yet you maintain a system as barbarous and dreadful as ever stained the character of a nation—a system begun in avarice, supported in pride, and perpetuated in cruelty.

You shed tears over fallen Hungary, and make the sad story of her wrongs the theme of your poets, statesmen and orators, till your gallant sons are ready to fly to arms to vindicate her cause against her oppressors; but, in regard to the ten thousand wrongs of the American slave, you would enforce the strictest silence, and would hail him as an enemy of the nation who dares to make those wrongs the subject of public discourse! You are all on fire at the mention of liberty for France or for Ireland; but are as cold as an iceberg at the thought of liberty for the enslaved of America.—You discourse eloquently on the dignity of labor; yet, you sustain a system which, in its very essence, casts a stigma upon labor. You can bare your bosom to the storm of British artillery to throw off a three-penny tax on tea; and yet wring the last hard-earned farthing from the grasp of the black laborers of your country. You profess to believe "that, of one blood, God made all nations of men to dwell on the face of all the earth," and hath commanded all men, everywhere to love one another; yet you notoriously hate, (and glory in your hatred), all men whose skins are not colored like your own. You declare, before the world, and are understood by the world to declare, that you *"hold these truths to be self evident, that all men are created equal; and are endowed by their Creator with certain inalienable rights; and that, among these are, life, liberty, and the pursuit of happiness;"* and yet, you hold securely, in a bondage which, according to your own Thomas Jefferson, *"is worse than ages of that which your fathers rose in rebellion to oppose,"* a seventh part of the inhabitants of your country.

Fellow-citizens! I will not enlarge further on your national inconsistencies. The existence of slavery in this country brands your republicanism as a sham, your humanity as a base pretence, and your Christianity as a lie. It destroys your moral power abroad; it corrupts your politicians at home. It saps the foundation of religion; it makes your name a hissing, and a by-word to a mocking earth. It is the antagonistic force in your government, the only thing that seriously disturbs and endangers your *Union.* It fetters your progress; it is the enemy of improvement, the deadly foe of education; it fosters pride; it breeds insolence; it promotes vice; it shelters crime; it is a curse to the earth that supports it; and yet, you cling to it, as if it were the sheer anchor of all your hopes. Oh! be warned! be warned! a horrible reptile is coiled up in your nation's bosom; the venomous creature is nursing at the tender breast of your youthful republic; *for the love of God, tear away,* and fling from you the hideous monster, and *let the weight of twenty millions crush and destroy it forever!*

The Constitution

But it is answered in reply to all this, that precisely what I have now denounced is, in fact, guaranteed and sanctioned by the Constitution of the United States; that the right to hold and to hunt slaves is a part of that Constitution framed by the illustrious Fathers of this Republic.

Then, I dare to affirm, notwithstanding all I have said before, your fathers stooped, basely stooped

"To palter with us in a double sense:
And keep the word of promise to the ear,
But break it to the heart."

And instead of being the honest men I have before declared them to be, they were the veriest imposters that ever practised on mankind. *This* is the inevitable conclusion, and from it there is no escape. But I differ from those who charge this baseness on the framers of the Constitution of the United States. *It is a slander upon their memory*, at least, so I believe.

There is not time now to argue the constitutional question at length; nor have I the ability to discuss it as it ought to be discussed. The subject has been handled with masterly power by Lysander Spooner, Esq., by William Goodell, by Samuel E. Sewall, Esq., and last, though not least, by Gerritt Smith, Esq. These gentlemen have, as I think, fully and clearly vindicated the Constitution from any design to support slavery for an hour.

Fellow-citizens! there is no matter in respect to which, the people of the North have allowed themselves to be so ruinously imposed upon, as that of the pro-slavery character of the Constitution. In *that* instrument I hold there is neither warrant, license, nor sanction of the hateful thing; but, interpreted as it *ought* to be interpreted, the Constitution is a Glorious Liberty Document. Read its preamble, consider its purposes. Is slavery among them? Is it at the gateway? or is it in the temple? it is neither. While I do not intend to argue this question on the present occasion, let me ask, if it be not somewhat singular that, if the Constitution were intended to be, by its framers and adopters, a slave-holding instrument, why neither *slavery, slaveholding*, nor *slave* can anywhere be found in it. What would be thought of an instrument, drawn up, *legally* drawn up, for the purpose of entitling the city of Rochester to a track of land, in which no mention of land was made? Now, there are certain rules of interpretation, for the proper understanding of all legal instruments. These rules are well established. They are plain, common-sense rules, such as you and I, and all of us, can understand and apply, without having passed years in the study of law. I scout the idea that the question of the constitutionality or unconstitutionality of slavery is not a question for the people. I hold that every American citizen has a fight to form an opinion of the Constitution, and to propagate that opinion, and to use all honorable means to make his opinion the prevailing one. Without this fight, the liberty of an American citizen would be as insecure as that of a Frenchman. Ex-Vice-President Dallas tells us that the Constitution is an object to which no American mind can be too attentive, and no American heart too devoted. He further says, the Constitution, in its words, is plain and intelligible, and is meant for the home-bred, unsophisticated understandings of our fellow-citizens. Senator Berrien tell us that the Constitution is the fundamental law, that which controls all others. The charter of our liberties, which every citizen has a personal interest in understanding thoroughly. The testimony of Senator Breese, Lewis Cass, and many others that might be named, who are everywhere esteemed as sound lawyers, so regard the constitution. I take it, therefore, that it is not presumption in a private citizen to form an opinion of that instrument.

Now, take the constitution according to its plain reading, and I defy the presentation of a single pro-slavery clause in it. On the other hand it will be found to contain principles and purposes, entirely hostile to the existence of slavery.

I have detained my audience entirely too long already. At some future period I will gladly avail myself of an opportunity to give this subject a full and fair discussion.

Allow me to say, in conclusion, notwithstanding the dark picture I have this day presented of the state of the nation, I do not despair of this country. There are forces in operation, which must inevitably work The downfall of slavery. "*The arm of the Lord is not shortened,*" and the doom of slavery is certain. I, therefore, leave off where I began, with *hope.* While drawing encouragement from the Declaration of Independence, the great principles it contains, and the genius of American Institutions, my spirit is also cheered by the obvious tendencies of the age. Nations do not now stand in the same relation to each other that they did ages ago. No nation can now shut itself up from the surrounding world, and trot round in the same old path of its fathers without interference. The time *was* when such could be done. Long established customs of hurtful character could formerly fence themselves in, and do their evil work with social impunity. Knowledge was then confined and enjoyed by the privileged few, and the multitude walked on in mental darkness. But a change has now come over the affairs of mankind. Walled cities and empires have become unfashionable. The arm of commerce has borne away the gates of the strong city. Intelligence is penetrating the darkest corners of the globe. It makes its pathway over and under the sea, as well as on the earth. Wind, steam, and lightning are its chartered agents. Oceans no longer divide, but link nations together. From Boston to London is now a holiday excursion. Space is comparatively annihilated.—Thoughts expressed on one side of the Atlantic are distinctly heard on the other.

The far off and almost fabulous Pacific rolls in grandeur at our feet. The Celestial Empire, the mystery of ages, is being solved. The fiat of the Almighty, "*Let there be Light,*" has not yet spent its force. No abuse, no outrage whether in taste, sport or avarice, can now hide itself from the all-pervading light. The iron shoe, and crippled foot of China must be seen, in contrast with nature. *Africa must rise and put on her yet unwoven garment. "Ethiopia shall stretch out her hand unto God."* In the fervent aspirations of William Lloyd Garrison, I say, and let every heart join in saying it:

God speed the year of jubilee
  The wide world o'er!
When from their galling chains set free,
Th' oppress'd shall vilely bend the knee,
And wear the yoke of tyranny
  Like brutes no more.
That year will come, and freedom's reign,
To man his plundered fights again
  Restore.
God speed the day when human blood

Shall cease to flow!
In every clime be understood,
The claims of human brotherhood,
And each return for evil, good,
Not blow for blow;
That day will come all feuds to end
And change into a faithful friend
Each foe.

God speed the hour, the glorious hour,
When none on earth
Shall exercise a lordly power,
Nor in a tyrant's presence cower;
But all to manhood's stature tower,
By equal birth!
THAT HOUR WILL COME, to each, to all,
And from his prison-house, the thrall
Go forth.

Until that year, day, hour, arrive,
With head, and heart, and hand I'll strive,
To break the rod, and rend the gyve,
The spoiler of his prey deprive—
So witness Heaven!
And never from my chosen post,
Whate'er the peril or the cost,
Be driven.

Abraham Lincoln

Speech at Springfield, Illinois June 26, 1857

. . . I have said, in substance, that the Dred Scott decision was, in part, based on assumed historical facts which were not really true; and I ought not to leave the subject without giving some reasons for saying this; I therefore give an instance or two, which I think fully sustain me. Chief Justice Taney, in delivering the opinion of the majority of the Court, insists at great length that negroes were no part of the people who made, or for whom was made, the Declaration of Independence, or the Constitution of the United States.

On the contrary, Judge Curtis, in his dissenting opinion, shows that in five of the then thirteen states, to wit, New Hampshire, Massachusetts, New York, New Jersey and North Carolina, free negroes were voters, and, in proportion to their numbers, had the same part in making the Constitution that the white people had.

Again, Chief Justice Taney says:

> *"It is difficult at this day to realize the state of public opinion in relation to that unfortunate race, which prevailed in the civilized and enlightened portions of the world at the time of the Declaration of Independence, and when the Constitution of the United States was framed and adopted."*

And again, after quoting from the Declaration, he says:

"The general words above quoted would seem to include the whole human family, and if they were used in a similar instrument at this day, would be so understood."

In these the Chief Justice does not directly assert, but plainly assumes, as a fact, that the public estimate of the black man is more favorable now than it was in the days of the Revolution. This assumption is a mistake. In some trifling particulars, the condition of that race has been ameliorated; but, as a whole, in this country, the change between then and now is decidedly the other way; and their ultimate destiny has never appeared so hopeless as in the last three or four years. In two of the five States—New Jersey and North Carolina—that then gave the free negro the right of voting, the right has since been taken away; and in a third—New York—it has been greatly abridged; while it has not been extended, so far as I know, to a single additional State, though the number of the States has more than doubled. In those days, as I understand, masters could, at their own pleasure, emancipate their slaves; but since then such legal restraints have been made upon emancipation as to amount almost to prohibition. In those days, legislatures held the unquestioned power to abolish slavery in their respective States; but now it is becoming quite fashionable for State Constitutions to withhold that power from the Legislatures. In those days, by common consent, the spread of the black man's bondage to new countries was prohibited; but now, Congress decides that it will not continue the prohibition, and the Supreme Court decides that it could not if it would. In those days, our Declaration of Independence was held sacred by all, and thought to include all; but now, to aid in making the bondage of the negro universal and eternal, it is assailed and sneered at and construed, and hawked at and torn, till, if its framers could rise from their graves, they could not at all recognize it. All the powers of earth seem rapidly combining against him. Mammon is after him; ambition follows, and philosophy follows, and the theology of the day is fast joining the cry. They have him in his prison house; they have searched his person, and left no prying instrument with him. One after another they have closed the heavy iron doors upon him, and now they have him, as it were, bolted in with a lock of a hundred keys, which can never be unlocked without the concurrence of every key; the keys in the hands of a hundred different men, and they scattered to a hundred different and distant places; and they stand musing as to what invention, in all the dominions of mind and matter, can be produced to make the impossibility of his escape more complete than it is.

It is grossly incorrect to say or assume, that the public estimate of the negro is more favorable now than it was at the origin of the government.

There is a natural disgust in the minds of nearly all white people, to the idea of an indiscriminate amalgamation of the white and black races; and Judge Douglas evidently is basing his chief hope, upon the chances of being able to appropriate the benefit of this disgust to himself. If he can, by much drumming and repeating, fasten the odium of that idea upon his adversaries, he thinks he can struggle through the storm. He therefore clings to this hope, as a drowning man to the last plank. He makes an occasion for lugging it in from the opposition to the Dred Scott decision. He finds the Republicans insisting that the Declaration of Independence includes all men, black as well as white; and forthwith he boldly denies that it includes negroes at all, and proceeds to argue gravely that all who contend it does, do so only because they want to vote, and eat, and sleep, and marry with negroes! He will have it that they cannot be consistent else. Now I protest against that counterfeit logic which concludes that, because I do not want a black woman for a slave I must necessarily want her for a wife. I need not have her for either, I can just leave her alone. In some respects she certainly is not my equal; but in her natural right to eat the bread she earns with her own hands without asking leave of any one else, she is my equal, and the equal of all others.

Chief Justice Taney, in his opinion in the Dred Scott case, admits that the language of the Declaration is broad enough to include the whole human family, but he and Judge Douglas argue that the authors of that instrument did not intend to include negroes, by the fact that they did not at once, actually place them on an equality with whites. Now this grave argument comes to just nothing at all, by the other fact, that they did not at once, or ever afterwards, actually place all white people on an equality with one or another. And this is the staple argument of both the Chief Justice and the Senator for doing this obvious violence to the plain unmistakable language of the Declaration.

I think the authors of that notable instrument intended to include all men, but they did not intend to declare all men equal in all respects. They did not mean to say all were equal in color, size, intellect, moral developments, or social capacity. They defined with tolerable distinctness, in what respects they did consider all men created equal—equal in "certain inalienable rights, among which are life, liberty, and the pursuit of happiness." This they said, and this they meant. They did not mean to assert the obvious untruth that all were then actually enjoying that equality, nor yet, that they were about to confer it immediately upon them. In fact they had no power to confer such a boon. They meant simply to declare the right, so that the enforcement of it might follow as fast as circumstances should permit.

They meant to set up a standard maxim for free society, which should be familiar to all, and revered by all; constantly looked to, constantly labored for, and even though never perfectly attained, constantly approximated, and thereby constantly spreading and deepening its influence, and augmenting the happiness and value of life to all people of all colors everywhere. The assertion that "all men are created equal" was of no practical use in effecting our separation from Great Britain; and it was placed in the Declaration, nor for that, but for future use. Its authors meant it to be,—as thank God, it is now proving itself,—a stumbling block to those who in after times might seek to turn a free people back into the hateful paths of despotism.

The Gettysburg Address, November 19, 1863

Four score and seven years ago our fathers brought forth, upon this continent, a new nation, conceived in Liberty, and dedicated to the proposition that all men are created equal.

Now we are engaged in a great civil war, testing whether that nation, or any nation so conceived, and so dedicated, can long endure. We are met here on a great battlefield of that war. We have come to dedicate a portion of it as a final resting place for those who here gave their lives that that nation might live. It is altogether fitting and proper that we should do this.

But in a larger sense we can not dedicate—we can not consecrate—we can not hallow—this ground. The brave men, living and dead, who struggled here, have consecrated it far above our poor power to add or detract. The world will little note, nor long remember what we say here, but it can never forget what they did here. It is for us, the living, rather to be dedicated here to the unfinished work which they have, thus far, so nobly advanced. It is rather for us to be here dedicated to the great task remaining before us—that from these honored dead we take increased devotion to that cause for which they here gave the last full measure of devotion—that we here highly resolve that these dead shall not have died in vain—that this nation, under God, shall have a new birth of freedom—and that this government of the people, by the people, for the people, shall not perish from the earth.

Second Inaugural Address, March 4, 1865

Fellow-Countrymen:

At this second appearing to take the oath of the Presidential office, there is less occasion for an extended address than there was at the first. Then a statement somewhat in detail of a course to be pursued seemed fitting and proper. Now, at the expiration of four years, during which public declarations have been constantly called forth on every point and phase of the great contest which still absorbs the attention and engrosses the energies of the nation, little that is new could be presented. The progress of our arms, upon which all else chiefly depends, is as well known to the public as to myself, and it is, I trust, reasonably satisfactory and encouraging to all. With high hope for the future, no prediction in regard to it is ventured.

On the occasion corresponding to this four years ago all thoughts were anxiously directed to an impending civil war. All dreaded it, all sought to avert it. While the inaugural address was being delivered from this place, devoted altogether to *saving* the Union without war, urgent agents were in the city seeking to *destroy* it without war—seeking to dissolve the Union and divide effects by negotiation. Both parties deprecated war, but one of them would *make* war rather than let the nation survive, and the other would *accept* war rather than let it perish. And the war came.

One-eighth of the whole population were colored slaves, not distributed generally over the Union, but localized in the southern part of it. These slaves constituted a peculiar and powerful interest. All knew that this interest was somehow the cause of the war. To strengthen, perpetuate, and extend this interest was the object for which the insurgents would rend the Union, even by war, while the Government claimed no right to do more than to restrict the territorial enlargement of it.

Neither party expected for the war the magnitude or the duration which it has already attained. Neither anticipated that the *cause* of the conflict might cease with, or even before the conflict itself should cease. Each looked for an easier triumph, and a result less fundamental and astounding. Both read the same Bible and pray to the same God, and each invokes His aid against the other. It may seem strange that any men should dare to ask a just God's assistance in wringing their bread from the sweat of other men's faces, but let us judge not, that we be not judged. The prayers of both could not be answered—that of neither has been answered fully.

The Almighty has His own purposes. "Woe unto the world because of offenses! For it must needs be that offenses come, but woe to that man by whom the offense cometh." If we shall suppose that American slavery is one of those offenses which, in the providence of God, must needs come, but which, having continued through His appointed time, He now wills to remove, and that He gives to both North and South this terrible war as the woe due to those by whom the offense came, shall we discern therein any departure from those divine attributes which the believers in a living God always ascribe to Him? Fondly do we hope—fervently do we pray—that this mighty scourge of war may speedily pass away. Yet, if God wills that it continue until all the wealth piled by the bondsman's two hundred and fifty years of unrequited toil shall be sunk, and until every drop of blood drawn with the lash shall be paid by another drawn with the sword, as was said three thousand years ago, so still it must be said "The judgments of the Lord are true and righteous altogether."

With malice toward none; with charity for all; with firmness in the right as God gives us to see the right, let us strive on to finish the work we are in; to bind up the nation's wounds; to care for him who shall have borne the battle and for his widow and his orphan—to do all which may achieve and cherish a just and lasting peace among ourselves, and with all nations.

PART II

The Romantic Rebellion

William Blake (1757–1827)

The Lamb (1789)

  Little Lamb, who made thee
  Dost thou know who made thee
Gave thee life & bid thee feed.
By the stream & o'er the mead;
Gave thee clothing of delight,
Softest clothing wooly bright;
Gave thee such a tender voice,
Making all the vales rejoice!
  Little Lamb who made thee
  Dost thou know who made thee

  Little Lamb I'll tell thee,
  Little Lamb I'll tell thee!
He is called by thy name,
For he calls himself a Lamb:
He is meek & he is mild,
He became a little child:
I a child & thou a lamb,
We are called by his name.
  Little Lamb God bless thee.
  Little Lamb God bless thee.

The Tyger (1794)

Tyger Tyger, burning bright,
In the forests of the night;
What immortal hand or eye,
Could frame thy fearful symmetry?

In what distant deeps or skies
Burnt the fire of thine eyes!
On what wings dare he aspire?
What the hand, dare seize the fire?

And what shoulder, & what art,
Could twist the sinews of thy heart?
And when thy heart began to beat,
What dread hand? & what dread feet?

What the hammer? what the chain,
In what furnace was thy brain?
What the anvil? what dread grasp,
Dare its deadly terrors clasp?

When the stars threw down their spears
And water'd heaven with their tears:
Did he smile his work to see?
Did he who made the Lamb make thee?

Tyger, Tyger burning bright,
In the forests of the night:
What immortal hand or eye,
Dare frame thy fearful symmetry?

The Chimney Sweeper (1789)

When my mother died I was very young,
And my father sold me while yet my tongue
Could scarcely cry "weep! 'weep! 'weep! 'weep!"
So your chimneys I sweep & in soot I sleep.
There's little Tom Dacre, who cried when his head
That curl'd like a lamb's back, was shav'd, so I said,

"Hush Tom never mind it, for when your head's bare,
You know that the soot cannot spoil your white hair."

And so he was quiet, & that very night,
As Tom was asleeping he had such a sight!
That thousands of sweepers Dick, Joe, Ned, & Jack,
Were all of them lock'd up in coffins of black;

And by came an Angel who had a bright key,
And he open'd the coffins & set them all free;
Then down a green plain leaping laughing they run,
And wash in a river and shine in the Sun.

Then naked & white, all their bags left behind,
They rise upon clouds, and sport in the wind.
And the Angel told Tom if he'd be a good boy,
He'd have God for his father & never want joy.

And so Tom awoke and we rose in the dark
And got with our bags & our brushes to work,
Tho' the morning was cold, Tom was happy & warm;
So if all do their duty, they need not fear harm.

The Chimney Sweeper (1794)

A little black thing in the snow:
Crying weep, weep, in notes of woe!
Where are thy father & mother? say?
They are both gone up to the church to pray.

Because I was happy upon the heath,
And smil'd among the winter's snow:
They clothed me in the clothes of death,
And taught me to sing the notes of woe;

And because I am happy & dance & sing,
They think they have done me no injury:
And are gone to praise God & his Priest & King
Who make up a heaven of our misery.

London (1794)

I wander thro' each charter'd street,
Near where the charter'd Thames does flow.
And mark in every face I meet
Marks of weakness, marks of woe.

In every cry of every Man,
In every Infant's cry of fear,
In every voice: in every ban,
The mind-forg'd manacles I hear

How the Chimney-sweeper's cry
Every blacking Church appalls,
And the hapless Soldiers sigh,
Runs in blood down Palace walls

But most thro' midnight streets I hear
How the youthful Harlots curse
Blasts the new-born Infants tear
And blights with plagues the Marriage hearse

from Auguries of Innocence (1801–03)

To see a World in a Grain of Sand
And Heaven in a Wild Flower
Hold Infinity in the palm of your hand
And Eternity in an hour
A Robin Red breast in a Cage
Puts all Heaven in a Rage
A dove house filld with doves & Pigeons
Shudders Hell thro' all its regions
A dog starvd at his Masters Gate
Predicts the ruin of the State

from The Everlasting Gospel

Was Jesus Humble? Or did he
Give any proofs of Humility?

When but a Child he ran away
And left his Parents in dismay.
When they had wonder'd three days long
These were the words upon his Tongue:
"No earthly Parents I confess:
I am doing my Father's business."
When the rich learned Pharisee
Came to consult him secretly,
Upon his heart with iron pen
He wrote, "Ye must be born again."
He was too Proud to take a bribe;
He spoke with authority, not like a Scribe.

If he had been Antichrist. Creeping Jesus,
He'd have done anything to please us:
Gone sneaking into the Synagogues
And not used the Elders & Priests like Dogs,
But humble as a Lamb or an Ass,
Obey himself to Caiaphas.
God wants not Man to humble himself: . . .

from The Prophetic Books

"I must Create a System or be enslav'd by another Man's.
I will not Reason & Compare: my business is to Create."

from The Marriage of Heaven and Hell (1790)

Without Contraries is no progression. Attraction and Repulsion.
Reason and Energy,
Love and Hate, are necessary to Human existence.
From these contraries spring what the religious call Good & Evil.
Good is the passive that
obeys Reason. Evil is the active springing from Energy.
Good is Heaven. Evil is Hell.

The Voice of the Devil

All Bibles or sacred codes have been the causes of the following errors:

1. That Man has two real existing principles: Viz: a Body & a Soul.

2. That Energy, call'd Evil, is alone from the Body; & that Reason, call'd Good, is alone from the Soul.

3. That God will torment Man in Eternity for following his Energies.

But the following Contraries to these are True:

1. Man has no Body distinct from his Soul; for that call'd Body is a portion of the Soul discern'd by the five Senses, the chief inlets of Soul in this age.

2. Energy is the only life, and is from the Body; and Reason is the bound or outward circumference of Energy.

3. Energy is Eternal Delight.

Those who restrain desire, do so because theirs is weak enough to be restrained: and the restrainer or reason usurps its place & governs the unwilling.
And being restrain'd, it by degrees becomes passive, till it is only the shadow of desire.

Mock On, Mock On (ca. 1800)

Mock on, mock on, Voltaire, Rousseau:
Mock on, mock on, 'tis all in vain!
You throw the sand against the wind,
And the wind blows it back again.

And every sand becomes a Gem
Reflected in the beams divine;
Blown back they blind the mocking eye,
But still in Israel's paths they shine.

The atoms of Democritus
And Newton's particles of light
Are sands upon the Red Sea shore,
Where Israel's tents do shine so bright.

William Wordsworth (1770–1850)

Selections from Preface to Lyrical Ballads (1802)

Low and rustic life was generally chosen, because in that condition, the essential passions of the heart find a better soil in which they can attain their maturity, are less under restraint, and speak a plainer and more emphatic language; because in that condition of life our elementary feelings coexist in a state of greater simplicity, and consequently, may be more accurately contemplated, and more forcibly communicated....

[Common people] being less under the influence of social vanity, they convey their feelings and notions in simple and unelaborated expressions. Accordingly, such a language, arising out of repeated experience and regular feelings, is a more permanent and far more philosophical language, than that which is frequently substituted for it by poets, who think they are conferring honor upon themselves and their art, in proportion as they separate themselves from the sympathies of men.

For all good poetry is the spontaneous overflow of powerful feelings .... recollected in tranquility.

What is a poet? ... He is a man speaking to men: a man, it is true, endued with more lively sensibility, more enthusiasm and tenderness, who has a greater knowledge of human nature, and a more comprehensive soul, than are supposed to be common among mankind; a man pleased with his own passions and volitions, and who rejoices more than other men in the spirit of life that is in him.

Poetry is a homage paid to the native and naked dignity of man, to the grand elementary principle of pleasure, by which he knows, and feels, and lives, and moves.

The Tables Turned: An Evening Scene on the Same Subject (1798)

Up! up! my Friend, and quit your books,
Or surely you'll grow double:
Up! up! my Friend, and clear your looks;
Why all this toil and trouble?

The sun, above the mountain's head,
A freshening lustre mellow
Through all the long green fields has spread,
His first sweet evening yellow.

Books! 'Tis a dull and endless strife:
Come, hear the woodland linnet,
How sweet his music! on my life,
There's more of wisdom in it.

And hark! how blithe the throstle sings!
He, too, is no mean preacher:
Come forth into the light of things,
Let Nature be your Teacher.

She has a world of ready wealth,
Our minds and hearts to bless—
Spontaneous wisdom breathed by health,
Truth breathed by cheerfulness.

One impulse from a vernal wood
May teach you more of man,
Of moral evil and of good,
Than all the sages can.

Sweet is the lore which Nature brings;
Our meddling intellect
Mis-shapes the beauteous forms of things:
—We murder to dissect.

Enough of Science and of Art;
Close up those barren leaves;
Come forth, and bring with you a heart
That watches and receives.

Lines Composed a Few Miles Above Tintern Abbey, on Revisiting the Banks of the Wye During a Tour, July 13, 1798

Five years have passed; five summers, with the length
Of five long winters! and again I hear
These waters, rolling from their mountain-springs
With a sweet inland murmur.—Once again
Do I behold these steep and lofty cliffs,
Which on a wild secluded scene impress
Thoughts of more deep seclusion; and connect
The landscape with the quiet of the sky.
The day is come when I again repose
Here, under this dark sycamore, and view
These plots of cottage-ground, these orchard-tufts,
Which, at this season, with their unripe fruits,
Among the woods and copses lose themselves,
Nor, with their green and simple hue, disturb
The wild green landscape. Once again I see
These hedge-rows, hardly hedge-rows, little lines
Of sportive wood run wild; these pastoral farms
Green to the very door; and wreathes of smoke
Sent up, in silence, from among the trees,
With some uncertain notice, as might seem,
Of vagrant dwellers in the houseless woods,
Or of some hermit's cave, where by his fire
The hermit sits alone.
                                        Though absent long,
These forms of beauty have not been to me,
As is a landscape to a blind man's eye:
But oft, in lonely rooms, and mid the din
Of towns and cities, I have owed to them,
In hours of weariness, sensations sweet,
Felt in the blood, and felt along the heart,
And passing even into my purer mind
With tranquil restoration: —feelings too
Of unremembered pleasure; such, perhaps,
As may have had no trivial influence
On that best portion of a good man's life;
His little, nameless, unremembered acts
Of kindness and of love. Nor less, I trust,

To them I may have owed another gift,
Of aspect more sublime; that blessed mood,
In which the burthen of the mystery,
In which the heavy and the weary weight
Of all this unintelligible world
Is lighten'd:—that serene and blessed mood,
In which the affections gently lead us on,
Until, the breath of this corporeal frame,
And even the motion of our human blood
Almost suspended, we are laid asleep
In body, and become a living soul:
While with an eye made quiet by the power
Of harmony, and the deep power of joy,
We see into the life of things.
If this
Be but a vain belief, yet, oh! how oft,
In darkness, and amid the many shapes
Of joyless day-light; when the fretful stir
Unprofitable, and the fever of the world,
Have hung upon the beatings of my heart,
How oft, in spirit, have I turned to thee
O sylvan Wye! Thou wanderer through the wood
How often has my spirit turned to thee!
And now, with gleams of half-extinguished thought,
With many recognitions dim and faint,
And somewhat of a sad perplexity,
The picture of the mind revives again:
While here I stand, not only with the sense
Of present pleasure, but with pleasing thoughts
That in this moment there is life and food
For future years. And so I dare to hope
Though changed, no doubt, from what I was, when first
I came among these hills; when like a roe
I bounded o'er the mountains, by the sides
Of the deep rivers, and the lonely streams,
Wherever nature led; more like a man
Flying from something that he dreads, than one
Who sought the thing he loved. For nature then
(The coarser pleasures of my boyish days,
And their glad animal movements all gone by,)
To me was all in all. —I cannot paint
What then I was. The sounding cataract

Haunted me like a passion: the tall rock,
The mountain, and the deep and gloomy wood,
Their colours and their forms, were then to me
An appetite: a feeling and a love,
That had no need of a remoter charm,
By thought supplied, or any interest
Unborrowed from the eye. —That time is past,
And all its aching joys are now no more,
And all its dizzy raptures. Not for this
Faint I, nor mourn nor murmur: other gifts
Have followed, for such loss, I would believe,
Abundant recompence. For I have learned
To look on nature, not as in the hour
Of thoughtless youth, but hearing oftentimes
The still, sad music of humanity,
Not harsh or grating, though of ample power
To chasten and subdue. And I have felt
A presence that disturbs me with the joy
Of elevated thoughts; a sense sublime
Of something far more deeply interfused,
Whose dwelling is the light of setting suns,
And the round ocean, and the living air,
And the blue sky, and in the mind of man,
A motion and a spirit, that impels
All thinking things, all objects of all thought,
And rolls through all things. Therefore am I still
A lover of the meadows and the woods,
And mountains; and of all that we behold
From this green earth; of all the mighty world
Of eye and ear, both what they half-create,
And what perceive; well pleased to recognize
In nature and the language of the sense,
The anchor of my purest thoughts, the nurse,
The guide, the guardian of my heart, and soul
Of all my moral being.

Nor, perchance,
If I were not thus taught, should I the more
Suffer my genial spirits to decay:
For thou art with me, here, upon the banks
Of this fair river; thou, my dearest Friend,
My dear, dear Friend, and in thy voice I catch
The language of my former heart, and read

My former pleasures in the shooting lights
Of thy wild eyes. Oh! yet a little while
May I behold in thee what I was once,
My dear, dear Sister! And this prayer I make,
Knowing that Nature never did betray
The heart that loved her; 'tis her privilege,
Through all the years of this our life, to lead
From joy to joy: for she can so inform
The mind that is within us, so impress
With quietness and beauty, and so feed
With lofty thoughts, that neither evil tongues,
Rash judgments, nor the sneers of selfish men,
Nor greetings where no kindness is, nor all
The dreary intercourse of daily life,
Shall e'er prevail against us, or disturb
Our chearful faith that all which we behold
Is full of blessings. Therefore let the moon
Shine on thee in thy solitary walk;
And let the misty mountain winds be free
To blow against thee: and in after years,
When these wild ecstasies shall be matured
Into a sober pleasure, when thy mind
Shall be a mansion for all lovely forms,
Thy memory be as a dwelling-place
For all sweet sounds and harmonies; Oh! then,
If solitude, or fear, or pain, or grief,
Should be thy portion, with what healing thoughts
Of tender joy wilt thou remember me,
And these my exhortations! Nor, perchance,
If I should be, where I no more can hear
Thy voice, nor catch from thy wild eyes these gleams
Of past existence, wilt thou then forget
That on the banks of this delightful stream
We stood together; And that I, so long
A worshipper of Nature, hither came,
Unwearied in that service: rather say
With warmer love, oh! with far deeper zeal
Of holier love. Now wilt thou then forget,
That after many wanderings, many years
Of absence, these steep woods and lofty cliffs,
And this green pastoral landscape, were to me
More dear, both for themselves, and for thy sake.

Ode: Intimations of Immortality From Recollections of Early Childhood (1807)

I

THERE was a time when meadow, grove, and stream,
The earth, and every common sight,
To me did seem
Apparelled in celestial light,
The glory and the freshness of a dream.
It is not now as it hath been of yore;—
Turn wheresoe'er I may,
By night or day,
The things which I have seen I now can see no more.

II

The Rainbow comes and goes,
And lovely is the Rose,
The Moon doth with delight
Look round her when the heavens are bare,
Waters on a starry night
Are beautiful and fair;
The sunshine is a glorious birth;
But yet I know, where'er I go,
That there hath past away a glory from the earth.

III

Now, while the birds thus sing a joyous song,
And while the young lambs bound
As to the tabor's sound,
To me alone there came a thought of grief:
A timely utterance gave that thought relief,
And I again am strong:
The cataracts blow their trumpets from the steep;
No more shall grief of mine the season wrong;
I hear the Echoes through the mountains throng,
The Winds come to me from the fields of sleep,
And all the earth is gay;
Land and sea
Give themselves up to jollity,

And with the heart of May
Doth every Beast keep holiday;—
Thou Child of Joy,
Shout round me, let me hear thy shouts, thou happy
Shepherd-boy!

IV

Ye blessed Creatures, I have heard the call
Ye to each other make; I see
The heavens laugh with you in your jubilee;
My heart is at your festival,
My head hath its coronal,
The fullness of your bliss, I feel—I feel it all.
Oh evil day! if I were sullen
While Earth herself is adorning,
This sweet May-morning,
And the Children are culling
On every side,
In a thousand valleys far and wide,
Fresh flowers; while the sun shines warm,
And the Babe leaps up on his Mother's arm:—
I hear, I hear, with joy I hear!
—But there's a Tree, of many, one,
A single Field which I have looked upon,
Both of them speak of something that is gone:
The Pansy at my feet
Doth the same tale repeat:
Whither is fled the visionary gleam?
Where is it now, the glory and the dream?

V

Our birth is but a sleep and a forgetting:
The Soul that rises with us, our life's Star,
Hath had elsewhere its setting,
And cometh from afar:
Not in entire forgetfulness,
And not in utter nakedness,
But trailing clouds of glory do we come
From God, who is our home:
Heaven lies about us in our infancy!

Shades of the prison-house begin to close
    Upon the growing Boy,
But He beholds the light, and whence it flows,
    He sees it in his joy;
The Youth, who daily farther from the east
    Must travel, still is Nature's Priest,
    And by the vision splendid
    Is on his way attended;
At length the Man perceives it die away,
And fade into the light of common day.

VI

Earth fills her lap with pleasures of her own;
Yearnings she hath in her own natural kind,
And, even with something of a Mother's mind,
    And no unworthy aim,
    The homely Nurse doth all she can
To make her Foster-child, her Inmate Man,
    Forget the glories he hath known,
And that imperial palace whence he came.

VII

Behold the Child among his new-born blisses,
A six years' Darling of a pigmy size!
See, where 'mid work of his own hand he lies,
Fretted by sallies of his mother's kisses,
With light upon him from his father's eyes!
See, at his feet, some little plan or chart,
Some fragment from his dream of human life,
Shaped by himself with newly-learnèd art;
    A wedding or a festival,
    A mourning or a funeral;
        And this hath now his heart,
    And unto this he frames his song:
        Then will he fit his tongue
To dialogues of business, love, or strife;
    But it will not be long
    Ere this be thrown aside,
    And with new joy and pride
The little Actor cons another part;

Filling from time to time his "humorous stage"
With all the Persons, down to palsied Age,
That Life brings with her in her equipage;
As if his whole vocation
Were endless imitation.

VIII

Thou, whose exterior semblance doth belie
Thy Soul's immensity;
Thou best Philosopher, who yet dost keep
Thy heritage, thou Eye among the blind,
That, deaf and silent, read'st the eternal deep,
Haunted for ever by the eternal mind,—
Mighty Prophet! Seer blest!
On whom those truths do rest,
Which we are toiling all our lives to find,
In darkness lost, the darkness of the grave;
Thou, over whom thy Immortality
Broods like the Day, a Master o'er a Slave,
A Presence which is not to be put by;
Thou little Child, yet glorious in the might
Of heaven-born freedom on thy being's height,
Why with such earnest pains dost thou provoke
The years to bring the inevitable yoke,
Thus blindly with thy blessedness at strife?
Full soon thy Soul shall have her earthly freight,
And custom lie upon thee with a weight
Heavy as frost, and deep almost as life!

IX

O joy! that in our embers
Is something that doth live,
That nature yet remembers
What was so fugitive!
The thought of our past years in me doth breed
Perpetual benediction: not indeed
For that which is most worthy to be blest—
Delight and liberty, the simple creed
Of Childhood, whether busy or at rest,
With new-fledged hope still fluttering in his breast:—

Not for these I raise
The song of thanks and praise;
But for those obstinate questionings
Of sense and outward things,
Fallings from us, vanishings;
Blank misgivings of a Creature
Moving about in worlds not realised,
High instincts before which our mortal Nature
Did tremble like a guilty Thing surprised:
But for those first affections,
Those shadowy recollections,
Which, be they what they may,
Are yet the fountain light of all our day,
Are yet a master light of all our seeing;
Uphold us, cherish, and have power to make
Our noisy years seem moments in the being
Of the eternal Silence: truths that wake,
To perish never;
Which neither listlessness, nor mad endeavour,
Nor Man nor Boy,
Nor all that is at enmity with joy,
Can utterly abolish or destroy!
Hence in a season of calm weather
Though inland far we be,
Our Souls have sight of that immortal sea
Which brought us hither,
Can in a moment travel thither,
And see the Children sport upon the shore,
And hear the mighty waters rolling evermore.

X

Then sing, ye Birds, sing, sing a joyous song!
And let the young Lambs bound
As to the tabor's sound!
We in thought will join your throng,
Ye that pipe and ye that play,
Ye that through your hearts to-day
Feel the gladness of the May!
What though the radiance which was once so bright
Be now for ever taken from my sight,
Though nothing can bring back the hour

Of splendour in the grass, of glory in the flower;
    We will grieve not, rather find
    Strength in what remains behind;
    In the primal sympathy
    Which having been must ever be;
    In the soothing thoughts that spring
    Out of human suffering;
    In the faith that looks through death,
In years that bring the philosophic mind.

XI

And O, ye Fountains, Meadows, Hills, and Groves,
Forebode not any severing of our loves!
Yet in my heart of hearts I feel your might;
I only have relinquished one delight
To live beneath your more habitual sway.
I love the Brooks which down their channels fret,
Even more than when I tripped lightly as they;
The innocent brightness of a new-born Day
    Is lovely yet;
The Clouds that gather round the setting sun
Do take a sober colouring from an eye
That hath kept watch o'er man's mortality;
Another race hath been, and other palms are won.
Thanks to the human heart by which we live,
Thanks to its tenderness, its joys, and fears,
To me the meanest flower that blows can give
Thoughts that do often lie too deep for tears.

Composed upon Westminster Bridge, September 3, 1803

Earth has not anything to show more fair:
Dull would he be of soul who could pass by
A sight so touching in its majesty:
This City now doth, like a garment, wear
The beauty of the morning; silent, bare,
Ships, towers, domes, theatres, and temples lie
Open unto the fields, and to the sky;

All bright and glittering in the smokeless air.
Never did sun more beautifully steep
In his first splendour, valley, rock, or hill;
Ne'er saw I, never felt, a calm so deep!
The river glideth at his own sweet will:
Dear God! the very houses seem asleep;
And all that mighty heart is lying still!

'The World Is Too Much With Us; Late and Soon' (1807)

The world is too much with us; late and soon,
Getting and spending, we lay waste our powers
Little we see in nature that is ours;
We have given our hearts away, a sordid boon!
This Sea that bares her bosom to the moon,
The winds that will be howling at all hours,
And are up-gathered now like sleeping flowers,
For this, for everything, we are out of tune;
It moves us not. Great God! I'd rather be
A Pagan suckled in a creed outworn;
So might I, standing on this pleasant lea,
Have glimpses that would make me less forlorn;
Have sight of Proteus rising from the sea;
Or hear old Triton blow his wreathed horn.

To My Sister (1798)

It is the first mild day of March:
Each minute sweeter than before,
The redbreast sings from the tall larch
That stands beside our door.

There is a blessing in the air,
Which seems a sense of joy to yield
To the bare trees, and the mountains bare,
And grass in the green field.

My Sister! ('Tis a wish of mine)
Now that our morning meal is done,

Make haste, your morning task resign;
Come forth and feel the sun.

Edward will come with you;—and pray,
Put on with speed your woodland dress:
And bring no book: for this one day
We'll give to idleness.

No joyless forms shall regulate
Our living calendar:
We from to-day, my friend, will date
The opening of the year.

Love, now a universal birth,
From heart to heart is stealing,
From earth to man, from man to earth:
—It is the hour of feeling.

One moment now may give us more
Than years of toiling reason:
Our minds shall drink at every pore
The spirit of the season.

Some silent laws our hearts will make,
Which they shall long obey:
We for the year to come may take
Our temper from to-day.

And from the blessed power that rolls
About, below, above,
We'll frame the measure of our souls:
They shall be tuned to love.

Then come, my Sister! come, I pray,
With speed put on your woodland dress;
And bring no book: for this one day
We'll give to idleness.

Samuel Taylor Coleridge (1772–1834)

Kubla Khan: or, a Vision in a Dream of the Fragment of Kubla Khan

The following fragment is here published at the request of a poet of great and deserved celebrity, and, as far as the Author's own opinions are concerned, rather as a psychological curiosity, than on the ground of any supposed poetic merits.

In the summer of the year 1797, the Author, then in ill health, had retired to a lonely farm-house between Porlock and Linton, on the Exmoor confines of Somerset and Devonshire. In consequence of a slight indisposition, an anodyne had been prescribed, from the effects of which he fell asleep in his chair at the moment that he was reading the following sentence, or words of the same substance, in *Purchas's Pilgrimage:* "Here the Khan Kubla commanded a palace to be built, and a stately garden thereunto. And thus ten miles of fertile ground were inclosed with a wall." The Author continued for about three hours in a profound sleep, at least of the external senses, during which time he has the most vivid confidence, that he could not have composed less than from two to three hundred lines; if that indeed can be called composition in which all the images rose up before him as *things*, with a parallel production of the correspondent expressions, without any sensation or consciousness of effort. On awakening he appeared to himself to have a distinct recollection of the whole, and taking his pen, ink, and paper, instantly and eagerly wrote down the lines that are here preserved. At this moment he was unfortunately called out by a person on business from Porlock, and detained by him above an hour, and on his return to his room, found, to his no small surprise and mortification, that though he still retained some vague and dim recollection of the general purport of the vision, yet, with the exception of some eight or ten scattered lines and images, all the rest had passed away like the images on the surface of a stream into which a stone has been cast, but, alas! without the after restoration of the latter!

Then all the charm
Is broken—all that phantom world so fair
Vanishes, and a thousand circlets spread,
And each misshape[s] the other. Stay awhile,
Poor youth! who scarcely dar'st lift up thine eyes—
The stream will soon renew its smoothness, soon
The visions will return! And lo, he stays,
And soon the fragments dim of lovely forms
Come trembling back, unite, and now once more
The pool becomes a mirror.

Yet from the still surviving recollections in his mind, the Author has frequently purposed to finish for himself what had been originally, as it were, given to him. "I shall sing a sweeter song today": but the tomorrow is yet to come.

As a contrast to this vision, I have annexed a fragment of a very different character, describing with equal fidelity the dream of pain and disease.

In Xanadu did Kubla Khan
A stately pleasure-dome decree:
Where Alph, the sacred river, ran
Through caverns measureless to man
Down to a sunless sea.
So twice five miles of fertile ground
With walls and towers were girdled round:
And there were gardens bright with sinuous rills,
Where blossomed many an incense-bearing tree;
And here were forests ancient as the hills,
And folding sunny spots of greenery.

But oh that deep romantic chasm which slanted
Down the green hill athwart a cedarn cover!
A savage place! as holy and enchanted
As e'er beneath a waning moon was haunted
By woman wailing for her demon-lover!
And from this chasm, with ceaseless turmoil seething,
As if this earth in fast thick pants were breathing,
A mighty fountain momently was forced:
Amid whose swift half-intermitted burst
Huge fragments vaulted like rebounding hail,

Or chaffy grain beneath the thresher's flail:
And 'mid these dancing rocks at once and ever
It flung up momently the sacred river.
Five miles meandering with a mazy motion
Through wood and dale the sacred river ran,
Then reached the caverns measureless to man,
And sank in tumult to a lifeless ocean:
And 'mid this tumult Kubla heard from far
Ancestral voices prophesying war!

The shadow of the dome of pleasure
Floated midway on the waves;
Where was heard the mingled measure
From the fountain and the caves.
It was a miracle of rare device,
A sunny pleasure-dome with caves of ice!

A damsel with a dulcimer
In a vision once I saw:
It was an Abyssinian maid,
And on her dulcimer she played,
Singing of Mount Abora.
Could I revive within me
Her symphony and song,
To such a deep delight 'twould win me,
That with music loud and long,
I would build that dome in air,
That sunny dome! those caves of ice!
And all who heard should see them there,
And all should cry, Beware! Beware!
His flashing eyes, his floating hair!
Weave a circle round him thrice,
And close your eyes with holy dread,
For he on honey-dew hath fed,
And drunk the milk of Paradise.

Percy Bysshe Shelley (1792–1822)

Ozymandias

I met a traveler from an antique land
Who said: Two vast and trunkless legs of stone
Stand in the desert. Near them, on the sand,
Half sunk, a shattered visage lies, whose frown,
And wrinkled lip, and sneer of cold command,
Tell that its sculptor well those passions read,
Which yet survive, stamped on these lifeless things,
The hand that mocked them, and the heart that fed,
And on the pedestal these words appear:
"My name is Ozymandias, King of Kings:
Look upon my works, ye Mighty, and despair!"
Nothing beside remains. Round the decay
Of that colossal wreck, boundless and bare
The lone and level sands stretch far away.

Sonnet: England in 1819

An old, mad, blind, despised, and dying king,—
Princes, the dregs of their dull race, who flow

Through public scorn,—mud from a muddy spring,—
Rulers who neither see, nor feel, nor know,
But leech-like to their fainting country cling,
Till they drop, blind in blood, without a blow,—
A people starved and stabbed in the untilled field,—
An army, which liberticide and prey
Makes as a two-edged sword to all who wield,—
Golden and sanguine laws which tempt and slay;
Religion Christless, Godless—a book sealed;
A Senate,—Time's worst statute unrepealed,—
Are graves, from which a glorious Phantom may
Burst, to illumine our tempestous day.

George Gordon, Lord Byron (1788–1824)

She Walks in Beauty (1815)

I

She walks in beauty, like the night
Of cloudless climes and starry skies;
And all that's best of dark and bright
Meets in her aspect and her eyes:
Thus mellow'd to that tender light
Which Heaven to gaudy day denies.

II

One shade the more, one ray the less,
Had half impair'd the nameless grace
Which waves in every raven tress,
Or softly lightens o'er her face;
Where thoughts serenely sweet express,
How pure, how dear their dwelling-place.

III

And on that cheek and o'er that brow,
So soft, so calm, yet eloquent,
The smiles that win, the tints that glow,
But tell of days in goodness spent,
A mind at peace with all below,
A heart whose love is innocent.

John Keats (1795–1821)

Ode to a Nightingale (1819)

1

My heart aches, and a drowsy numbness pains
   My sense, as though of hemlock I had drunk,
Or emptied some dull opiate to the drains
   One minute past, and Lethe-wards had sunk:
'Tis not through envy of thy happy lot,
   But being too happy in thine happiness,—
      That thou, light-winged Dryad of the trees,
         In some melodious plot
Of beechen green, and shadows numberless,
   Singest of summer in full-throated ease.

2

O for a draught of vintage! that hath been
   Cool'd a long age in the deep-delved earth,
Tasting of Flora and the country-green,
   Dance, and Provençal song, and sunburnt mirth!
O for a beaker full of the warm South!
   Full of the true, the blushful Hippocrene,

With beaded bubbles winking at the brim,
And purple-stained mouth;
That I might drink, and leave the world unseen,
And with thee fade away into the forest dim:

3

Fade far away, dissolve, and quite forget
What thou among the leaves hast never known,
The weariness, the fever, and the fret
Here, where men sit and hear each other groan;
Where palsy shakes a few, sad, last grey hairs,
Where youth grows pale, and spectre-thin, and dies;
Where but to think is to be full of sorrow
And leaden-eyed despairs;
Where Beauty cannot keep her lustrous eyes,
Or new Love pine at them beyond to-morrow.

4

Away! away! for I will fly to thee,
Not charioted by Bacchus and his pards,
But on the viewless wings of Poesy,
Though the dull brain perplexes and retards:
Already with thee! tender is the night,
And haply the Queen-Moon is on her throne,
Cluster'd around by all her starry Fays;
But here there is no light,
Save what from heaven is with the breezes blown
Through verdurous glooms and winding mossy ways.

5

I cannot see what flowers are at my feet,
Nor what soft incense hangs upon the boughs,
But, in embalmed darkness, guess each sweet
Wherewith the seasonable month endows
The grass, the thicket, and the fruit-tree wild;
White hawthorn, and the pastoral eglantine;
Fast-fading violets cover'd up in leaves;
And mid-May's eldest child,

The coming musk-rose, full of dewy wine,
   The murmurous haunt of flies on summer eves.

6

Darkling I listen; and, for many a time
   I have been half in love with easeful Death,
Call'd him soft names in many a mused rhyme,
   To take into the air my quiet breath;
Now more than ever seems it rich to die,
   To cease upon the midnight with no pain,
      While thou art pouring forth thy soul abroad
         In such an ecstasy!
Still wouldst thou sing, and I have ears in vain—
To thy high requiem become a sod.

7

Thou wast not born for death, immortal Bird!
   No hungry generations tread thee down;
The voice I hear this passing night was heard
   In ancient days by emperor and clown:
Perhaps the self-same song that found a path
   Through the sad heart of Ruth, when, sick for home,
      She stood in tears amid the alien corn;
         The same that oft-times hath
Charm'd magic casements, opening on the foam
   Of perilous seas, in faery lands forlorn.

8

Forlorn! the very word is like a bell
   To toll me back from thee to my sole self!
Adieu! the fancy cannot cheat so well
   As she is fam'd to do, deceiving elf.
Adieu! adieu! thy plaintive anthem fades
   Past the near meadows, over the still stream,
      Up the hill-side; and now 'tis buried deep
         In the next valley-glades:
Was it a vision, or a waking dream?
   Fled is that music:—do I wake or sleep?

Ode on a Grecian Urn (1820)

1

Thou still unravish'd bride of quietness,
Thou foster-child of Silence and slow Time,
Sylvan historian, who canst thus express
A flowery tale more sweetly than our rhyme:
What leaf-fring'd legend haunts about thy shape
Of deities or mortals, or of both,
In Tempe or the dales of Arcady?
What men or gods are these? What maidens loth?
What mad pursuit? What struggle to escape?
What pipes and timbrels? What wild ecstasy?

2

Heard melodies are sweet, but those unheard
Are sweeter; therefore, ye soft pipes, play on;
Not to the sensual ear, but, more endear'd,
Pipe to the spirit ditties of no tone:
Fair youth, beneath the trees, thou canst not leave
Thy song, nor ever can those trees be bare;
Bold Lover, never, never canst thou kiss,
Though winning near the goal—yet, do not grieve;
She cannot fade, though thou hast not thy bliss,
For ever wilt thou love, and she be fair!

3

Ah, happy, happy boughs! that cannot shed
Your leaves, nor ever bid the Spring adieu;
And, happy melodist, unwearied,
For ever piping songs for ever new;
More happy love! more happy, happy love!
For ever warm and still to be enjoy'd,
For ever panting, and for ever young;
All breathing human passion far above,
That leaves a heart high-sorrowful and cloy'd,
A burning forehead, and a parching tongue.

4

Who are these coming to the sacrifice?
To what green altar, O mysterious priest,
Lead'st thou that heifer lowing at the skies,
And all her silken flanks with garlands drest?
What little town by river or sea-shore,
Or mountain-built with peaceful citadel,
Is emptied of its folk, this pious morn?
And, little town, thy streets for evermore
Will silent be; and not a soul, to tell
Why thou art desolate, can e'er return.

5

O Attic shape! fair attitude! with brede
Of marble men and maidens overwrought,
With forest branches and the trodden weed;
Thou, silent form! dost tease us out of thought
As doth eternity: Cold Pastoral!
When old age shall this generation waste,
Thou shalt remain, in midst of other woe
Than ours, a friend to man, to whom thou say'st,
"Beauty is truth, truth beauty,"—that is all
Ye know on earth, and all ye need to know.

Ode on Melancholy (1820)

1

No, no! go not to Lethe, neither twist
Wolf's-bane, tight-rooted, for its poisonous wine;
Nor suffer thy pale forehead to be kiss'd
By nightshade, ruby grape of Proserpine;
Make not your rosary of yew-berries,
Nor let the beetle, nor the death-moth be
Your mournful Psyche, nor the downy owl
A partner in your sorrow's mysteries;
For shade to shade will come too drowsily,
And drown the wakeful anguish of the soul.

2

But when the melancholy fit shall fall
   Sudden from heaven like a weeping cloud,
That fosters the droop-headed flowers all,
   And hides the green hill in an April shroud;
Then glut thy sorrow on a morning rose,
   Or on the rainbow of the salt sand-wave,
      Or on the wealth of globed peonies;
Or if thy mistress some rich anger shows,
   Emprison her soft hand, and let her rave,
      And feed deep, deep upon her peerless eyes.

3

She dwells with Beauty—Beauty that must die;
   And Joy, whose hand is ever at his lips
Bidding adieu; and aching Pleasure nigh,
   Turning to poison while the bee-mouth sips:
Ay, in the very temple of Delight
   Veil'd Melancholy has her sovran shrine,
      Though seen of none save him whose strenuous tongue
   Can burst Joy's grape against his palate fine;
His soul shall taste the sadness of her might,
   And be among her cloudy trophies hung.

Emily Dickinson (1830–1886)

238

How many times these low feet staggered—
Only the soldered mouth can tell—
Try—can you stir the awful rivet—
Try—can you lift the hasps of steel!

Stroke the cool forehead—hot so often—
Lift—if you care—the listless hair—
Handle the adamantine fingers
Never a thimble—more—shall wear—

Buzz the full flies—on the chamber window—
Brave—shines the sun through the freckled pane—
Fearless—the cobweb swings from the ceiling—
Indolent Housewife—in Daisies—lain!

207

I taste a liquor never brewed—
From Tankards scooped in Pearl—

Not all the Frankfort Berries
Yield such an Alcohol!

Inebriate of air—am I—
And Debauchee of Dew—
Reeling—thro' endless summer days—
From inns of molten Blue—

When "Landlords" turn the drunken Bee
Out of the Foxglove's door—
When Butterflies—renounce their "drams"—
I shall but drink the more!

Till Seraphs swing their snowy Hats—
And Saints—to windows run—
To see the little Tippler
Leaning against the—Sun!

269

Wild nights—Wild nights!
Were I with thee
Wild nights should be
Our luxury!

Futile—the winds—
To a Heart in port—
Done with the Compass—
Done with the Chart!

Rowing in Eden—
Ah—the Sea!
Might I but moor—tonight—
In thee!

314

"Hope" is the thing with feathers—
That perches in the soul—
And sings the tune without the words—

And never stops—at all—

And sweetest—in the Gale—is heard—
And sore must be the storm—
That could abash the little Bird
That kept so many warm—

I've heard it in the chillest land—
And on the strangest Sea—
Yet—never—in Extremity,
It asked a crumb—of me.

330

He put the Belt around my life—
I heard the Buckle snap—
And turned away, imperial,
My Lifetime folding up—
Deliberate, as a Duke would do
A Kingdom's Title Deed—
Henceforth—a Dedicated sort—
A Member of the Cloud—

Yet not too far to come at call—
And do the little Toils
That make the Circuit of the Rest—
And deal occasional smiles
To lives that stoop to notice mine—
And kindly ask it in—
Whose invitation, know you not
For Whom I must decline?

340

I felt a Funeral, in my Brain,
And Mourners to and fro
Kept treading—treading—till it seemed
That Sense was breaking through—

And when they all were seated,

A Service, like a Drum—
Kept beating—beating—till I thought
My mind was going numb—

And then I heard them lift a Box
And creak across my Soul
With those same Boots of Lead, again,
Then Space—began to toll,

As all the Heavens were a Bell,
And Being, but an Ear,
And I, and Silence, some strange Race
Wrecked, solitary, here—

And then a Plank in Reason, broke,
And I dropped down, and down—
And hit a World, at every plunge,
And Finished knowing—then—

409

The Soul selects her own Society—
Then—shuts the Door—
To her divine Majority—
Present no more—

Unmoved—she notes the Chariots—pausing—
At her low Gate—
Unmoved—an Emperor be kneeling
Opon her Mat—

I've known her—from an ample nation—
Choose One-
Then—close the Valves of her attention—
Like Stone—

620

Much Madness is divinest Sense—
To a discerning Eye—

Much Sense—the starkest Madness—
'Tis the Majority
In this, as all, prevail—
Assent—and you are sane—
Demur—you're straightway dangerous—
And handled with a Chain—

591

I heard a Fly buzz—when I died—
The Stillness in the Room
Was like the Stillness in the Air—
Between the Heaves of Storm—

The Eyes around—had wrung them dry—
And Breaths were gathering firm
For that last Onset—when the King
Be witnessed—in the Room—

I will my Keepsakes—Signed away
What portion of me be
Assignable—and then it was
There interposed a Fly—

With Blue—uncertain—stumbling Buzz—
Between the light—and me—
And then the Window failed—and then
I could not see to see—

588

The Heart asks Pleasure—first—
And then—excuse from Pain—
And then—those little Anodynes
That deaden suffering—

And then—to go to sleep—
And then—if it should be
The will of it's Inquisitor
The privilege to die—

439

I had been hungry, all the Years—
My Noon had Come—to dine—
I trembling drew the Table near—
And touched the Curious Wine—

'Twas this on Tables I had seen—
When turning, hungry, Home
I looked on Windows, for the Wealth
I could not hope—for Mine—

I did not know the ample Bread—
'Twas so unlike the Crumb
The Birds and I, had often shared
In Nature's—Dining Room—

The Plenty hurt me—'twas so new—
Myself felt ill—and odd—
As Berry—of a Mountain Bush—
Transplanted—to the Road—

Nor was I hungry—so I found
That Hunger—was a way
Of persons Outside Windows—
The entering—takes away—

383

I like to see it lap the Miles—
And lick the Valleys up—
And stop to feed itself at Tanks—
And then—prodigious step

Around a Pile of Mountains—
And supercilious peer
In Shanties—by the sides of Roads—
And then a Quarry pare

To fit it's sides

And crawl between
Complaining all the while
In horrid—hooting stanza—
Then chase itself down Hill—

And neigh like Boanerges—
Then—prompter than a Star
Stop—docile and omnipotent
At it's own stable door—

598

The Brain—is wider than the Sky—
For—put them side by side—
The one the other will contain
With ease—and You—beside—

The Brain is deeper than the sea—
For—hold them—Blue to Blue—
The one the other will absorb—
As Sponges—Buckets—do—

The Brain is just the weight of God—
For—Heft them—Pound for Pound—
And they will differ—if they do—
As Syllable from Sound—

704

My Portion is Defeat—today—
A paler luck than Victory—
Less Paeans—fewer Bells—
The Drums dont follow Me—with tunes—
Defeat—a somewhat slower—means—
More Arduous than Balls—

'Tis populous with Bone and stain—
And Men too straight to stoop again—
And Piles of solid Moan—
And Chips of Blank—in Boyish Eyes—

And scraps of Prayer—
And Death's surprise,
Stamped visible—in stone—

There's somewhat prouder, Over there—
The Trumpets tell it to the Air—
How different Victory
To Him who has it—and the One
Who to have had it, would have been
Contenteder—to die—

479

Because I could not stop for Death—
He kindly stopped for me—
The Carriage held but just Ourselves—
And Immortality.

We slowly drove—He knew no haste
And I had put away
My labor and my leisure too,
For His Civility—

We passed the School, where Children strove
At Recess—in the Ring—
We passed the Fields of Gazing Grain—
We passed the Setting Sun—

Or rather—He passed Us—
The Dews drew quivering and Chill—
For only Gossamer, my Gown—
My Tippet—only Tulle—

We paused before a House that seemed
A Swelling of the Ground—
The Roof was scarcely visible—
The Cornice—in the Ground—

Since then—'tis Centuries—and yet
Feels shorter than the Day
I first surmised the Horses' Heads
Were toward Eternity—

1263

Tell all the truth but tell it slant—
Success in Circuit lies
Too bright for our infirm Delight
The Truth's superb surprise
As Lightning to the Children eased
With explanation kind
The Truth must dazzle gradually
Or every man be blind—

1773

My life closed twice before it's close;
It yet remains to see
If Immortality unveil
A third event to me,

So huge, so hopeless to conceive,
As these that twice befell.
Parting is all we know of heaven,
And all we need of hell.

1590

Elysium is as far as to
The very nearest Room
If in that Room a Friend await
Felicity or Doom—

What fortitude the Soul contains,
That it can so endure
The accent of a coming Foot—
The opening of a Door—

Walt Whitman (1819–1892)

Song of the Open Road
(originally "Poem of the Road," 1856/1860)

1

Afoot and light-hearted I take to the open road,
Healthy, free, the world before me,
The long brown path before me leading wherever I choose.

Henceforth I ask not good-fortune, I myself am good-fortune,
Henceforth I whimper no more, postpone no more, need nothing,
Done with indoor complaints, libraries, querulous criticisms,
Strong and content I travel the open road.

The earth, that is sufficient,
I do not want the constellations any nearer,
I know they are very well where they are,
I know they suffice for those who belong to them.

(Still here I carry my old delicious burdens,
I carry them, men and women, I carry them with me wherever I go,
I swear it is impossible for me to get rid of them,
I am fill'd with them, and I will fill them in return.)

2

You road I enter upon and look around, I believe you are not all that is here,
I believe that much unseen is also here.

Here the profound lesson of reception, nor preference nor denial,
The black with his wooly head, the felon, the diseas'd, the illiterate person, are not denied;
The birth, the hasting after the physician, the beggar's tramp, the drunkard's stagger, the laughing party of mechanics,
The escaped youth, the rich person's carriage, the fop, the eloping couple,
The early market-man, the hearse, the moving of furniture into the town, the return back from the town,
They pass, I also pass, any thing passes, none can be interdicted,
None but are accepted, none but shall be dear to me.

3

You air that serves me with breath to speak!
You objects that call from diffusion my meanings and give them shape!
You light that wraps me and all things in delicate equable showers!
You paths worn in the irregular hollows by the roadsides!
I believe you are latent with unseen existences, you are so dear to me.

You flagg'd walks of the cities! you strong curbs at the edges!
You ferries! you planks and posts of wharves! you timber-lined sides! you distant ships!
You rows of houses! you window-pierc'd facades! you roofs!
You porches and entrances! you copings and iron guards!
You windows whose transparent shells might expose so much!
You doors and ascending steps! you arches!
You grey stones of interminable pavements! you trodden crossings!
From all that has touch'd you I believe you have imparted to yourselves, and now would impart the same secretly to me,
From the living and the dead you have peopled your impassive surfaces, and the spirits thereof would be evident and amicable with me.

4

The earth expanding right hand and left hand,
The picture alive, every part in its best light,
The music falling in where it is wanted, and stopping where it is not wanted,
The cheerful voice of the public road, the gay fresh sentiment of the road.

O highway I travel, do you say to me *Do not leave me?*

Do you say *Venture not—if you leave me you are lost?*
Do you say *I am already prepared, I am well-beaten and undenied, adhere to me?*

O public road, I say back I am not afraid to leave you, yet I love you,
You express me better than I can express myself,
You shall be more to me than my poem.

I think heroic deeds were all conceiv'd in the open air, and all free poems also,
I think I could stop here myself and do miracles,
I think whatever I shall meet on the road I shall like, and whoever beholds
    me shall like me,
I think whoever I see must be happy.

5

From this hour I ordain myself loos'd of limits and imaginary lines,
Going where I list, my own master total and absolute,
Listening to others, considering well what they say,
Pausing, searching, receiving, contemplating,
Gently, but with undeniable will, divesting myself of the holds that would hold me.

I inhale great draughts of space,
The east and the west are mine, and the north and the south are mine.

I am larger, better than I thought;
I did not know I held so much goodness.

All seems beautiful to me;
I can repeat over to men and women You have done such good to me,
    I would do the same to you.
I will recruit for myself and you as I go,
I will scatter myself among men and women as I go,
I will toss new gladness and roughness among them,
Whoever denies me it shall not trouble me,
Whoever accepts me he or she shall be blessed and shall bless me.

Once I Pass'd through a Populous City (1861)

Once I pass'd through a populous city imprinting my brain for future use
    with its shows, architecture, customs, traditions
Yet now of all that city I remember only a woman I casually met there
    who detain'd me for love of me,

Day by day and night by night we were together—all else has long
been forgotten by me,
I remember I say only that woman who passionately clung to me,
Again we wander, we love, we separate again,
Again she holds me by the hand, I must not go,
I see her close beside me with silent lips sad and tremulous.

Mannahatta (in *Leaves of Grass*, 1860)

I was asking for something specific and perfect for my city,
Whereupon lo! upsprang the aboriginal name.

Now I see what there is in a name, a word, liquid, sane, unruly,
musical, self-sufficient,
I see that the word of my city is that word from of old,
Because I see that word nested in nests of water-bays, superb,
Rich hemm'd thick all around with sailships and steamships, an island
sixteen miles long, solid-founded,
Numberless crowded streets, high growths of iron, slender, strong, light,
splendidly uprising toward the clear skies,
Tides swift and ample, well-loved by me, toward sundown,
The flowing sea-currents, the little islands, larger adjoining islands,
the heights, the villas,
The countless masts, the white shore-steamers, the lighters, the ferry-boats,
the black sea-steamers well-model'd,
The down-town streets, the jobbers' houses of business, the houses of
business of the ship-merchants and money-brokers, the river-streets,
Immigrants arriving, fifteen or twenty thousand in a week,
The carts hauling goods, the manly race of drivers of horses, the
brown-faced sailors,
The summer air, the bright sun shining, and the sailing clouds aloft,
The winter snows, the sleigh-bells, the broken ice in the river, passing
along up and down with the flood-tide or ebb-tide,
The mechanics of the city, the masters, well-form'd, beautiful-faced,
looking you straight in the eyes,
Trottoirs throng'd, vehicles, Broadway, the women, the shops and shows,
A million people—manners free and superb—open voices—hospitality—the
most courageous and friendly young men,
City of hurried and sparkling waters! city of spires and masts!
City nested in bays! my city!

I Hear It Was Charged against Me (revision, 1857)

I Hear it was charged against me that I sought to destroy institutions,
But really I am neither for nor against institutions,
(What indeed have I in common with them? or what with
the destruction of them?)
Only I will establish in the Mannahatta and in every city of these States
inland and seaboard,
And in the fields and woods, and above every keel little or large that
dents the water,
Without edifices or rules or trustees or any argument,
The institutions of the dear love of comrades.

I Sit and Look Out (in *Leaves of Grass*, 1860; retitled, 1871)

I sit and look out upon all the sorrows of the world, and upon all
oppression and shame,
I hear secret convulsive sobs from young men at anguish with
themselves, remorseful after deeds done,
I see in low life the mother misused by her children, dying, neglected,
gaunt, desperate,
I see the wife misused by her husband, I see the treacherous seducer
of young women,
I mark the ranklings of jealousy and unrequited love attempted to
be hid, I see these sights on the earth,
I see the workings of battle, pestilence, tyranny, I see martyrs and prisoners,
I observe a famine at sea, I observe the sailors casting lots
who shall be kill'd to preserve the lives of the rest,
I observe the slights and degradations cast by arrogant persons upon
laborers, the poor, and upon negroes, and the like;
All these—all the meanness and agony without end I sitting look out upon,
See, hear, and am silent.

I Hear America Singing (in *Leaves of Grass*, 1860)

I hear America singing, the varied carols I hear,
Those of mechanics, each one singing his as it should be blithe and strong,
The carpenter singing his as he measures his plank or beam,
The mason singing his as he makes ready for work, or leaves off work,

The boatman singing what belongs to him in his boat, the
 deckhand singing on the steamboat deck,
The shoemaker singing as he sits on his bench, the hatter singing as he stands,
The wood-cutter's song, the ploughboy's on his way in the morning, or
 at noon intermission or at sundown,
The delicious singing of the mother, or of the young wife at work, or
 of the girl sewing or washing,
Each singing what belongs to him or her and to none else,
The day what belongs to the day—at night the party of young
 fellows, robust, friendly,
Singing with open mouths their strong melodious songs.

I Sing the Body Electric
(originally, 1855; titled and revised 1867)

1

I Sing the body electric,
The armies of those I love engirth me and I engirth them,
They will not let me off till I go with them, respond to them,
And discorrupt them, and charge them full with the charge of the soul.
Was it doubted that those who corrupt their own bodies conceal themselves?
And if those who defile the living are as bad as they who defile the dead?
And if the body does not do fully as much as the soul?
And if the body were not the soul, what is the soul?

2

The love of the body of man or woman balks account, the body itself
 balks account,
That of the male is perfect, and that of the female is perfect.
The expression of the face balks account,
But the expression of a well-made man appears not only in his face,
It is in his limbs and joints also, it is curiously in the joints of his hips and wrists,
It is in his walk, the carriage of his neck, the flex of his waist and knees,
 dress does not hide him,
The strong sweet quality he has strikes through the cotton and broadcloth,
To see him pass conveys as much as the best poem, perhaps more,
You linger to see his back, the back of his neck and shoulder-side.

The sprawl and fulness of babes, the bosoms and heads of women, the
folds of their dress, their style as we pass in the street, the contour
of their shape downwards,
The swimmer naked in the swimming-bath, seen as he swims through
the transparent green-shine, or lies with his face up and rolls
silently to and fro in the heave of the water,
The bending forward and backward of rowers in row-boats, the horseman
in his saddle,
Girls, mothers, house-keepers, in all their performances,
The group of laborers seated at noon-time with their open dinner-kettles,
and their wives waiting,
The female soothing a child, the farmer's daughter in the garden or cow-yard,
The young fellow hoeing corn, the sleigh-driver driving his six horses
through the crowd,
The wrestle of wrestlers, two apprentice-boys, quite grown, lusty,
good-natured, native-born, out on the vacant lot at sundown after work,
The coats and caps thrown down, the embrace of love and resistance,
The upper-hold and under-hold, the hair rumpled over and blinding the eyes;
The march of firemen in their own costumes, the play of masculine muscle
through clean-setting trowsers and waist-straps,
The slow return from the fire, the pause when the bell strikes suddenly
again,and the listening on the alert,
The natural, perfect, varied attitudes, the bent head, the curv'd neck and
the counting;
Such-like I love—I loosen myself, pass freely, am at the mother's breast
with the little child,
Swim with the swimmers, wrestle with the wrestlers, march in line
with the firemen, and pause, listen, count.

3

I knew a man, a common farmer—the father of five sons;
And in them were the fathers of sons—and in them were the fathers of sons.
This man was of wonderful vigor, calmness, beauty of person,
The shape of his head, the pale yellow and white of his hair and beard,
the immeasurable meaning of his black eyes—the richness and
breadth of his manners,
These I used to go and visit him to see, he was wise also;
He was six feet tall, he was over eighty years old, his sons were massive,
clean, bearded, tan-faced, handsome,
They and his daughters loved him, all who saw him loved him,
They did not love him by allowance, they loved him with personal love,

He drank water only, the blood show'd like scarlet through the
clear-brown skin of his face,
He was a frequent gunner and fisher, he sail'd his boat himself, he had
a fine one presented to him by a ship-joiner, he had fowling-pieces,
presented to him by men that loved him,
When he went with his five sons and many grand-sons to hunt or fish,
you would pick him out as the most beautiful and vigorous of the gang.
You would wish long and long to be with him, you would wish to sit by him
in the boat, that you and he might touch each other.

4

I have perceiv'd that to be with those I like is enough,
To stop in company with the rest at evening is enough,
To be surrounded by beautiful, curious, breathing, laughing flesh is enough,
To pass among them, or touch any one, or rest my arm ever so lightly round his
or her neck for a moment—what is this, then?
I do not ask any more delight—I swim in it, as in a sea.

There is something in staying close to men and women, and looking on them,
and in the contact and odor of them, that pleases the soul well;
All things please the soul, but these please the soul well.

5

This is the female form,
A divine nimbus exhales from it from head to foot,
It attracts with fierce undeniable attraction,
I am drawn by its breath as if I were no more than a helpless vapor, all falls
aside but myself and it,
Books, art, religion, time, the visible and solid earth, and what was expected
of heaven or fear'd of hell, are now consumed,
Mad filaments, ungovernable shoots play out of it, the response likewise
ungovernable,
Hair, bosom, hips, bend of legs, negligent falling hands all diffused, mine
too diffused,
Ebb stung by the flow and flow stung by the ebb, love-flesh swelling and
deliciously aching,
Limitless limpid jets of love hot and enormous, quivering jelly of love,
white-blow and delirious juice,
Bridegroom night of love working surely and softly into the prostrate dawn,
Undulating into the willing and yielding day,

Lost in the cleave of the clasping and sweet-flesh'd day.

This is the nucleus—after the child is born of woman, man is born of woman,
This the bath of birth, this the merge of small and large, and the outlet again.

Be not ashamed women, your privilege encloses the rest, and is the exit
of the rest,
You are the gates of the body, and you are the gates of the soul.

The female contains all qualities and tempers them,
She is in her place and moves with perfect balance,
She is all things duly veil'd, she is both passive and active,
She is to conceive daughters as well as sons, and sons as well as daughters.

As I see my soul reflected in Nature,
As I see through a mist, One with inexpressible completeness, sanity, beauty,
See the bent head and arms folded over the breast, the Female I see.

6

The male is not less the soul, nor more, he too is in his place,
He too is all qualities, he is action and power,
The flush of the known universe is in him;
Scorn becomes him well, and appetite and defiance become him well;
The wildest largest passions, bliss that is utmost, sorrow that is utmost,
become him well, pride is for him;
The full-spread pride of man is calming and excellent to the soul;
Knowledge becomes him, he likes it always, he brings everything to the
test of himself,
Whatever the survey, whatever the sea and the sail, he strikes soundings
at last only here,
(Where else does he strike soundings, except here?)

The man's body is sacred, and the woman's body is sacred;
No matter who it is, it is sacred—is it the meanest one in the laborer's gang?
Is it one of the dull-faced immigrants just landed on the wharf?
Each belongs here or anywhere, just as much as the well-off, just as much as you,
Each has his or her place in the procession.

(All is a procession,
The universe is a procession, with measured and beautiful motion.)

Do you know so much yourself, that you call the meanest ignorant?
Do you suppose you have a right to a good sight, and he or she has no
right to a sight?
Do you think matter has cohered together from its diffuse float, and the
soil is on the surface, and water runs, and vegetation sprouts,
For you only, and not for him and her?

7 — about slave trade

A man's body at auction,
(For before the war I often go to the slave-mart and watch the sale,)
I help the auctioneer, the sloven does not half know his business.

Gentlemen look on this wonder,
Whatever the bids of the bidders they cannot be high enough for it,
For it the globe lay preparing, quintillions of years without one animal or plant,
For it the revolving cycles truly and steadily roll'd.

In this head the all-baffling brain,
In it and below it the makings of heroes.

Examine these limbs, red, black, or white, they are cunning in tendon and nerve,
They shall be stript that you may see them.
Exquisite senses, life-lit eyes, pluck, volition,
Flakes of breast-muscle, pliant backbone and neck, flesh not flabby,
good-sized arms and legs,
And wonders within there yet.

Within there runs blood,
The same old blood! the same red-running blood!
There swells and jets a heart, there all passions, desires, reachings, aspirations,
(Do you think they are not there because they are not express'd in parlors
and lecture-rooms?)

This is not only one man, this is the father of those who shall be fathers
in their turns,
In him the start of populous states and rich republics,
Of him countless immortal lives with countless embodiments and enjoyments.

How do you know who shall come from the offspring of his offspring
through the centuries?

(Who might you find you have come from yourself, if you could trace
back through the centuries?)

This Compost

1

Something startles me where I thought I was safest;
I withdraw from the still woods I loved;
I will not go now on the pastures to walk;
I will not strip the clothes from my body to meet my lover the sea;
I will not touch my flesh to the earth, as to other flesh, to renew me.

O how can it be that the ground does not sicken?
How can you be alive, you growths of spring?
How can you furnish health, you blood of herbs, roots, orchards, grain?
Are they not continually putting distemper'd corpses within you?
Is not every continent work'd over and over with sour dead?

Where have you disposed of their carcasses?
Those drunkards and gluttons of so many generations;
Where have you drawn off all the foul liquid and meat?
I do not see any of it upon you to-day—or perhaps I am deceiv'd;
I will run a furrow with my plough—I will press my spade through the sod,
and turn it up underneath;
I am sure I shall expose some of the foul meat.

2

Behold this compost! behold it well!
Perhaps every mite has once form'd part of a sick person—yet behold!
The grass of spring covers the prairies,
The bean bursts noiselessly through the mould in the garden,
The delicate spear of the onion pierces upward,
The apple-buds cluster together on the apple-branches,
The resurrection of the wheat appears with pale visage out of its graves,
The tinge awakes over the willow-tree and the mulberry-tree,
The he-birds carol mornings and evenings, while the she-birds sit on their nests,
The young of poultry break through the hatch'd eggs,
The new-born of animals appear—the calf is dropt from the cow, the colt
from the mare,
Out of its little hill faithfully rise the potato's dark green leaves,

Out of its hill rises the yellow maize-stalk—the lilacs bloom in the door-yards;
The summer growth is innocent and disdainful above all those strata of sour dead.

What chemistry!
That the winds are really not infectious,
That this is no cheat, this transparent green-wash of the sea, which is so amorous after me,
That it is safe to allow it to lick my naked body all over with its tongues,
That it will not endanger me with the fevers that have deposited themselves in it,
That all is clean forever and forever.
That the cool drink from the well tastes so good,
That blackberries are so flavorous and juicy,
That the fruits of the apple-orchard, and of the orange-orchard that melons, grapes, peaches, plums, will none of them poison me,
That when I recline on the grass I do not catch any disease,
Though probably every spear of grass rises out of what was once a catching disease.

3

Now I am terrified at the Earth! it is that calm and patient,
It grows such sweet things out of such corruptions,
It turns harmless and stainless on its axis, with such endless successions of diseas'd corpses,
It distils such exquisite winds out of such infused fetor,
It renews with such unwitting looks, its prodigal, annual, sumptuous crops,
It gives such divine materials to men, and accepts such leavings from them at last.

O Captain! My Captain!

O Captain! my Captain! our fearful trip is done,
The ship has weather'd every rack, the prize we sought is won,
The port is near, the bells I hear, the people all exulting,
While follow eyes the steady keel, the vessel grim and daring;
But O heart! heart! heart!
O the bleeding drops of red,
Where on the deck my Captain lies,
Fallen cold and dead.

O Captain! my Captain! rise up and hear the bells;
Rise up—for you the flag is flung—for you the bugle trills,
For you bouquets and ribbon'd wreaths—for you the shores a-crowding,
For you they call, the swaying mass, their eager faces turning;
Here Captain! dear father!
This arm beneath your head;
It is some dream that on the deck,
You've fallen cold and dead.

My Captain does not answer, his lips are pale and still,
My father does not feel my arm, he has no pulse nor will,
The ship is anchor'd safe and sound, its voyage closed and done,
From fearful trip, the victor ship, comes in with object won;
Exult, O shores, and ring, O bells!
But I, with mournful tread,
Walk the deck my Captain lies,
Fallen cold and dead.†

Memories of President Lincoln

When Lilacs Last in the Dooryard Bloom'd

1

When lilacs last in the dooryard bloom'd,
And the great star early droop'd in the western sky in the night,
I mourn'd, and yet shall mourn with ever-returning spring.

Ever-returning spring, trinity sure to me you bring,
Lilac blooming perennial and drooping star in the west,
And thought of him I love.

2

O powerful western fallen star!
O shades of night—O moody, tearful night!
O great star disappear'd—O the black murk that hides the star!
O cruel hands that hold me powerless—O helpless soul of me!
O harsh surrounding cloud that will not free my soul.

3

In the dooryard fronting an old farm-house near the white-wash'd palings,
Stands the lilac-bush tall-growing with heart-shaped leaves of rich green,

With many a pointed blossom rising delicate, with the perfume strong I love,
With every leaf a miracle—and from this bush in the dooryard,
With delicate-color'd blossoms and heart-shaped leaves of rich green,
A sprig with its flower I break.

4

In the swamp in secluded recesses,
A shy and hidden bird is warbling a song.

Solitary the thrush,
The hermit withdrawn to himself, avoiding the settlements,
Sings by himself a song.

Song of the bleeding throat,
Death's outlet song of life, (for well dear brother I know,
If thou wast not granted to sing thou would'st surely die.)

5

Over the breast of the spring, the land, amid cities,
Amid lanes and through old woods, where lately the violets peep'd from the ground, spotting the gray debris,
Amid the grass in the fields each side of the lanes, passing the endless grass,
Passing the yellow-spear'd wheat, every grain from its shroud in the dark-brown fields uprisen,
Passing the apple-tree blows of white and pink in the orchards,
Carrying a corpse to where it shall rest in the grave,
Night and day journeys a coffin.

6

Coffin that passes through lanes and streets,
Through day and night with the great cloud darkening the land,
With the pomp of the inloop'd flags with the cities draped in black,
With the show of the States themselves as of crape-veil'd women standing,
With processions long and winding and the flambeaus of the night,
With the countless torches lit, with the silent sea of faces and the unbared heads,
With the waiting depot, the arriving coffin, and the sombre faces,
With dirges through the night, with the thousand voices rising strong and solemn,
With all the mournful voices of the dirges pour'd around the coffin,
The dim-lit churches and the shuddering organs—where amid these you journey,
With the tolling tolling bells' perpetual clang,

Here, coffin that slowly passes,
I give you my sprig of lilac.

Passages from the "Preface" to *Leaves of Grass* (1855 edition)

On America: The Americans of all nations at any time upon the earth are probably the fullest poetical nature. The United States themselves are essentially the greatest poem. . . . Here is not merely a nation but a teeming nation of nations . . . moving in vast masses . . . the tremendous audacity of its crowds. . . . Here is the hospitality which forever indicates heroes.

On Common People: The genius of the United States is not best or most in its executives or legislatures, nor in the ambassadors or authors or colleges or churches or parlors, nor even in its newspapers or inventors . . . but always most in the common people. Their manners speech dress friendships—the freshness and candor of their physiognomy . . . their deathless attachment to freedom . . . who never know how it felt to stand in the presence of superiors.

On the Individual: The largeness of nature or the nation were monstrous without a corresponding largeness and generosity of the spirit of the citizen. . . . The pride of the U.S. leaves the wealth and finesse of the cities and all returns of commerce and agriculture and all the magnitude of geography or shows of exterior victory to enjoy the breed of full-sized men or one full-sized man unconquerable and simple.

On the Poet: Of them a bard is to be commensurate with a people. . . . His spirit responds to his country's spirit. . . . To him enter the essences of the real things and past and present events. . . . The fluid movement of the population.

The expression of the American poet is to be transcendent and new. It is to be indirect and not direct or descriptive or epic. . . . Let the age and wars of other nations be chanted and their eras and characters be illustrated and that finish the verse. Not so the great psalm of the republic. Here the theme is creative and has vista.

On Poetic Subject Matter: Great genius and the people of these states must never be demeaned to romances. As soon as histories are promptly told there is no more need and romances . . . [Poets] shall find their inspiration in real objects today, symptoms of the past and future.

On Meaning and Transcendence: People expect of the poet to indicate more than the beauty and dignity which always attach to dumb real objects . . . they expect him to indicate the path between reality and their souls. Men and women perceive the beauty well enough. . . . They can never be assisted by poets to perceive. . . . The poetic quality is not marshaled in rhyme or uniformity or abstract addresses to things nor in melancholy complaints or good precepts, but is the life of these [people] and much else and is in the soul.

On Reading Poetry: Read these leaves in the open air. . . . Dismiss whatever insults your own soul, and your very flesh shall be a great poem.

The great poem is no finish to a man or woman but rather a beginning. Has any one fancied he could sit at last under some due authority and rest satisfied with explanations and realize and be content and full? To no such terminus does the greatest poet bring.

On Poetic Style: The art of art, the glory of expression and the sunshine of the light of letters is simplicity. . . . The greatest poet has less a marked style and is more the channel of thoughts and things without increase or diminution, and is the free channel of himself. He swears to his art. . . . I will not have in my writing any elegance or effect or originality to hang in the way between me and the rest like curtains. . . . A heroic person walks at his ease through and out of that custom or precedent or authority that suits him not. Of the traits of the brotherhood of writers savants musicians artists nothing is finer than silent defiance advancing from new free forms. . . . Most works are most beautiful without ornament.

On Science and Technology: Exact science and its practical movements are no checks on the greatest poet but always his encouragement and support.

Langston Hughes (1902–1967)

I, Too

I, too, sing America.

I am the darker brother.
They send me to eat in the kitchen
When company comes,
But I laugh,
And eat well,
And grow strong.

Tomorrow,
I'll be at the table
When company comes.
Nobody'll dare
Say to me,
"Eat in the kitchen,"
Then.

Besides,
They'll see how beautiful I am
And be ashamed—

I, too, am America.

PART III

Revolutionary Thinkers

Charles Darwin

On the Origin of Species, *6th Edition*

Chapter I

Variation Under Domestication

Causes of Variability • Effects of Habit and the use and disuse of Parts • Correlated Variation • Inheritance • Character of Domestic Varieties • Difficulty of distinguishing between Varieties and Species • Origin of Domestic Varieties from one or more Species • Domestic Pigeons, their Differences and Origin • Principles of Selection, anciently followed, their Effects • Methodical and Unconscious Selection • Unknown Origin of our Domestic Productions • Circumstances favorable to Man's power of Selection.

Causes of Variability

When we compare the individuals of the same variety or sub-variety of our older cultivated plants and animals, one of the first points which strikes us is, that they generally differ more from each other than do the individuals of any one species or variety in a state of nature. And if we reflect on the vast diversity of the plants and animals which have been cultivated, and which have varied during all ages under the most different climates and treatment, we are driven to conclude that this great variability is due to our domestic productions having been raised under conditions of life not so uniform as, and somewhat different from, those to which the parent species had been exposed under nature. There is, also, some probability in the view propounded by Andrew Knight, that this variability may be partly connected with excess of food. It seems clear that organic beings must be exposed during several generations to new conditions to cause any great amount of variation; and that, when the organisation has once begun to vary, it generally continues varying for many generations. No case is on record of a variable organism ceasing to vary under cultivation. Our oldest cultivated plants, such as wheat, still yield new varieties: our oldest domesticated animals are still capable of rapid improvement or modification.

As far as I am able to judge, after long attending to the subject, the conditions of life appear to act in two ways,—directly on the whole organisation or on certain parts alone and in directly by affecting the reproductive system. With respect to the direct action, we must bear in mind that in every case, as Professor Weismann has lately insisted, and as I have incidently shown in my work on "Variation under Domestication," there are two factors: namely, the nature of the organism and the nature of the conditions. The former seems to be much the more important; for nearly similar variations sometimes arise under, as far as we can judge, dissimilar conditions; and, on the other hand, dissimilar variations arise under conditions which appear to be nearly uniform. The effects on the offspring are either definite or indefinite. They may be considered as definite when all or nearly all the offspring of individuals exposed to certain conditions during several generations are modified in the same manner. It is extremely difficult to come to any conclusion in regard to the extent of the changes which have been thus definitely induced. There can, however, be little doubt about many slight changes, such as size from the amount of food, colour from the nature of the food, thickness of the skin and hair from climate, etc. Each of the endless variations which we see in the plumage of our fowls must have had some efficient cause; and if the same cause were to act uniformly during a long series of generations on many individuals, all probably would be modified in the same manner.

Effects of Habit and of the Use or Disuse of Parts; Correlated Variation; Inheritance

Changed habits produce an inherited effect as in the period of the flowering of plants when transported from one climate to another. With animals the increased use or disuse of parts has had a more marked influence; thus I find in the domestic duck that the bones of the wing weigh less and the bones of the leg more, in proportion to the whole skeleton, than do the same bones in the wild duck; and this change may be safely attributed to the domestic duck flying much less, and walking more, than its wild parents. The great and inherited development of the udders in cows and goats in countries where they are habitually milked, in comparison with these organs in other countries, is probably another instance of the effects of use. Not one of our domestic animals can be named which has not in some country drooping ears; and the view which has been suggested that the drooping is due to disuse of the muscles of the ear, from the animals being seldom much alarmed, seems probable.

Many laws regulate variation, some few of which can be dimly seen, and will hereafter be briefly discussed. I will here only allude to what may be called correlated variation.

Hairless dogs have imperfect teeth; long-haired and coarse-haired animals are apt to have, as is asserted, long or many horns; pigeons with feathered feet have skin between their outer toes; pigeons with short beaks have small feet, and those with long beaks large feet. Hence if man goes on selecting, and thus augmenting, any peculiarity, he will almost certainly modify unintentionally other parts of the structure, owing to the mysterious laws of correlation.

* * *

Any variation which is not inherited is unimportant for us. But the number and diversity of inheritable deviations of structure, both those of slight and those of considerable physiological importance, are endless.

No breeder doubts how strong is the tendency to inheritance; that like produces like is his fundamental belief: doubts have been thrown on this principle only by theoretical writers.

Every one must have heard of cases of albinism, prickly skin, hairy bodies, etc., appearing in several members of the same family. If strange and rare deviations of structure are truly inherited, less strange and commoner deviations may be freely admitted to be inheritable. Perhaps the correct way of viewing the whole subject would be, to look at the inheritance of every character whatever as the rule, and non-inheritance as the anomaly.

The laws governing inheritance are for the most part unknown; no one can say why the same peculiarity in different individuals of the same species, or in different species, is sometimes inherited and sometimes not so; why the child often reverts in certain characteristics to its grandfather or grandmother or more remote ancestor; why a peculiarity is often transmitted from one sex to both sexes, or to one sex alone, more commonly but not exclusively to the like sex. It is a fact of some importance to us, that peculiarities appearing in the males of our domestic breeds are often transmitted, either exclusively or in a much greater degree, to the males alone. A much more important rule, which I think may be trusted, is that, at whatever period of life a peculiarity first appears, it tends to reappear in the offspring at a corresponding age, though sometimes earlier. In many cases this could not be otherwise; thus the inherited peculiarities in the horns of cattle could appear only in the offspring when nearly mature; peculiarities in the silk-worm are known to appear at the corresponding caterpillar or cocoon stage. But hereditary diseases and some other facts make me believe that the rule has a wider extension, and that, when there is no apparent reason why a peculiarity should appear at any particular age, yet that it does tend to appear in the offspring at the same period at which it first appeared in the parent. I believe this rule to be of the highest importance in explaining the laws of embryology.

Character of Domestic Varieties; Difficulty of Distinguishing Between Varieties and Species; Origin of Domestic Varieties From One or More Species

When we look to the hereditary varieties or races of our domestic animals and plants, and compare them with closely allied species, we generally perceive in each domestic race, as already remarked, less uniformity of character than in true species. Domestic races often have a somewhat monstrous character; by which I mean, that, although differing from each other and from other species of the same genus, in several trifling respects, they often differ in an extreme degree in some one part, both when compared one with another, and more especially when compared with the species under nature to which they are nearest allied. With these exceptions (and with that of the perfect fertility of varieties when crossed, a subject hereafter to be discussed), domestic races of the same species differ from each other in the same manner as do the closely allied species of the same genus in a state of nature, but the differences in most cases are less in degree. This must be admitted as true, for the domestic races of many animals and plants have been ranked by some competent judges as the descendants of aboriginally distinct species, and by other competent judges as mere varieties. If any well marked distinction existed between a domestic race and a species, this source of doubt would not so perpetually recur. It has often been stated that domestic races do not differ from each other in characters of generic value. It can be shown that this statement is not correct; but naturalists differ much in determining what characters are of generic value; all such valuations being at present empirical. When it is explained how genera originate under nature, it will be seen that we have no right to expect often to find a generic amount of difference in our domesticated races.

In attempting to estimate the amount of structural difference between allied domestic races, we are soon involved in doubt, from not knowing whether they are descended from one or several parent species. This point, if it could be cleared up, would be interesting; if, for instance, it could be shown that the greyhound, bloodhound, terrier, spaniel and bulldog, which we all know propagate their kind truly, were the offspring of any single species, then such facts would have great weight in making us doubt about the immutability of the many closely allied natural species—for instance, of the many foxes—inhabiting the different quarters of the world. I do not believe, as we shall presently see, that the whole amount of difference between the several breeds of the dog has been produced under domestication; I believe that a small part of the difference is due to their being descended from distinct species. In the case of strongly marked races of some other domesticated species, there is presumptive or even strong evidence that all are descended from a single wild stock.

In the case of most of our anciently domesticated animals and plants, it is not possible to come to any definite conclusion, whether they are descended from one or several wild species. The argument mainly relied on by those who believe in the multiple origin of our domestic animals is, that we find in the most ancient times, on the monuments of Egypt, and in the lake-habitations of Switzerland, much diversity in the breeds; and that some of these ancient breeds closely resemble, or are even identical with, those still existing. But this only throws far backward the history of civilisation, and shows that animals were domesticated at a much earlier period than has hitherto been supposed. The lake-inhabitants of Switzerland cultivated several kinds of wheat and barley, the pea, the poppy for oil and flax; and they possessed several domesticated animals. They also carried on commerce with other nations. All this clearly shows, as Heer has remarked, that they had at this early age progressed considerably in civilisation; and this again implies a long continued previous period of less advanced civilisation, during which the domesticated animals, kept by different tribes in different districts, might have varied and given rise to distinct races. Since the discovery of flint tools in the superficial formations of many parts of the world, all geologists believe that barbarian men existed at an enormously remote period; and we know that at the present day there is hardly a tribe so barbarous as not to have domesticated at least the dog.

The origin of most of our domestic animals will probably forever remain vague. But I may here state that, looking to the domestic dogs of the whole world, I have, after a laborious collection of all known facts, come to the conclusion that several wild species of Canidae have been tamed, and that their blood, in some cases mingled together, flows in the veins of our domestic breeds. In regard to sheep and goats I can form no decided opinion. From facts communicated to me by Mr. Blyth, on the habits, voice, constitution and structure of the humped Indian cattle, it is almost certain that they are descended from a different aboriginal stock from our European cattle; and some competent judges believe that these latter have had two or three wild progenitors,—whether or not these deserve to be called species. This conclusion, as well as that of the specific distinction between the humped and common cattle, may, indeed, be looked upon as established by the admirable researches of Professor R¸timeyer. With respect to horses, from reasons which I cannot here give, I am doubtfully inclined to believe, in opposition to several authors, that all the races belong to the same species. Having kept nearly all the English breeds of the fowl alive, having bred and crossed them, and examined their skeletons, it appears to me almost certain that all are the descendants of the wild Indian fowl, *Gallus Bankiva.*

Breeds of the Domestic Pigeon, Their Differences and Origin

Believing that it is always best to study some special group, I have, after deliberation, taken up domestic pigeons. I have kept every breed which I could purchase or obtain, and have been most kindly favoured with skins from several quarters of the world.

I have associated with several eminent fanciers, and have been permitted to join two of the London Pigeon Clubs. The diversity of the breeds is something astonishing. Compare the English carrier and the short-faced tumbler, and see the wonderful difference in their beaks, entailing corresponding differences in their skulls. The carrier, more especially the male bird, is also remarkable from the wonderful development of the carunculated skin about the head, and this is accompanied by greatly elongated eyelids, very large external orifices to the nostrils, and a wide gape of mouth. The short-faced tumbler has a beak in outline almost like that of a finch; and the common tumbler has the singular inherited habit of flying at a great height in a compact flock, and tumbling in the air head over heels. The runt is a bird of great size, with long, massive beak and large feet; some of the sub-breeds of runts have very long necks, others very long wings and tails, others singularly short tails. The barb is allied to the carrier, but, instead of a long beak, has a very short and broad one. The pouter has a much elongated body, wings, and legs; and its enormously developed crop, which it glories in inflating, may well excite astonishment and even laughter. The turbit has a short and conical beak, with a line of reversed feathers down the breast; and it has the habit of continually expanding, slightly, the upper part of the oesophagus. The Jacobin has the feathers so much reversed along the back of the neck that they form a hood, and it has, proportionally to its size, elongated wing and tail feathers. The trumpeter and laugher, as their names express, utter a very different coo from the other breeds. The fantail has thirty or even forty tail-feathers, instead of twelve or fourteen, the normal number in all the members of the great pigeon family: these feathers are kept expanded and are carried so erect that in good birds the head and tail touch: the oil-gland is quite aborted. Several other less distinct breeds might be specified.

In the skeletons of the several breeds, the development of the bones of the face, in length and breadth and curvature, differs enormously. The shape, as well as the breadth and length of the ramus of the lower jaw, varies in a highly remarkable manner. The caudal and sacral vertebrae vary in number; as does the number of the ribs, together with their relative breadth and the presence of processes. The size and shape of the apertures in the sternum are highly variable; so is the degree of divergence and relative size of the two arms of the furcula. The proportional width of the gape of mouth, the proportional length of the eyelids, of the orifice of the nostrils, of the tongue (not always in strict correlation with the length of beak), the size of the crop and of the upper part of the oesophagus; the development and abortion of the oil-gland; the number of the primary wing and caudal feathers; the relative length of the wing and tail to each other and to the body; the relative length of the leg and foot; the number of scutellae on the toes, the development of skin between the toes, are all points of structure which are variable. The period at which the perfect plumage is acquired varies, as does the state of the down with which the nestling birds are clothed when hatched. The shape and size of the eggs vary. The manner of flight, and in some breeds the voice and disposition, differ remarkably. Lastly, in certain breeds, the males and females have come to differ in a slight degree from each other.

Altogether at least a score of pigeons might be chosen, which, if shown to an ornithologist, and he were told that they were wild birds, would certainly be ranked by him as well-defined species. Moreover, I do not believe that any ornithologist would in this case place the English carrier, the short-faced tumbler, the runt, the barb, pouter, and fantail in the same genus; more especially as in each of these breeds several truly-inherited sub-breeds, or species, as he would call them, could be shown him.

Great as are the differences between the breeds of the pigeon, I am fully convinced that the common opinion of naturalists is correct, namely, that all are descended from the rock-pigeon (*Columba livia*), including under this term several geographical races or sub-species, which differ from each other in the most trifling respects.

An argument of great weight, and applicable in several other cases, is, that the above-specified breeds, though agreeing generally with the wild rock-pigeon in constitution, habits, voice, colouring, and in most parts of their structure, yet are certainly highly abnormal in other parts; we may look in vain through the whole great family of Columbidae for a beak like that of the English carrier, or that of the short-faced tumbler, or barb; for reversed feathers like those of the Jacobin; for a crop like that of the pouter; for tail-feathers like those of the fantail. Hence it must be assumed, not only that half-civilized man succeeded in thoroughly domesticating several species, but that he intentionally or by chance picked out extraordinarily abnormal species; and further, that these very species have since all become extinct or unknown. So many strange contingencies are improbable in the highest degree.

* * *

From these several reasons, namely,—the improbability of man having formerly made seven or eight supposed species of pigeons to breed freely under domestication;—these supposed species being quite unknown in a wild state, and their not having become anywhere feral;—these species presenting certain very abnormal characters, as compared with all other Columbidae, though so like the rock-pigeon in most other respects—the occasional reappearance of the blue colour and various black marks in all the breeds, both when kept pure and when crossed;—and lastly, the mongrel offspring being perfectly fertile;—from these several reasons, taken together, we may safely conclude that all our domestic breeds are descended from the rock-pigeon or Columba livia with its geographical sub-species.

In favour of this view, I may add, firstly, that the wild C. livia has been found capable of domestication in Europe and in India; and that it agrees in habits and in a great number of points of structure with all the domestic breeds. Secondly, that although an English carrier or a short-faced tumbler differs immensely in certain characters from the rock-pigeon, yet that by comparing the several sub-breeds of these two races, more especially those brought from distant countries, we can make, between them and the rock-pigeon, an almost perfect series; so we can in some other cases, but not with all the breeds. Thirdly, those characters which are mainly distinctive of each breed are in each eminently variable, for instance, the wattle and length of beak of the carrier, the shortness of that of the tumbler, and the number of tail-feathers in the fantail; and the explanation of this fact will be obvious when we treat of selection. Fourthly, pigeons have been watched and tended with the utmost care, and loved by many people.

They have been domesticated for thousands of years in several quarters of the world. . . . The paramount importance of these considerations in explaining the immense amount of variation which pigeons have undergone, will likewise be obvious when we treat of selection. We shall then, also, see how it is that the several breeds so often have a somewhat monstrous character. It is also a most favourable circumstance for the production of distinct breeds, that male and female pigeons can be easily mated for life; and thus different breeds can be kept together in the same aviary.

I have discussed the probable origin of domestic pigeons at some, yet quite insufficient, length; because when I first kept pigeons and watched the several kinds, well knowing how truly they breed, I felt fully as much difficulty in believing that since they had been domesticated they had all proceeded from a common parent, as any naturalist could in coming to a similar conclusion in regard to the many species of finches, or other groups of birds, in nature. One circumstance has struck me much; namely, that nearly all the breeders of the various domestic animals and the cultivators of plants, with whom I have conversed, or whose treatises I have read, are firmly convinced that the several breeds to which each has attended, are descended from so many aboriginally distinct species. Ask, as I have asked, a celebrated raiser of Hereford cattle, whether his cattle might not have descended from Long-horns, or both from a common parent-stock, and he will laugh you to scorn. I have never met a pigeon, or poultry, or duck, or rabbit fancier, who was not fully convinced that each main breed was descended from a distinct species. Van Mons, in his treatise on pears and apples, shows how utterly he disbelieves that the several sorts, for instance a Ribston-pippin or Codlin-apple, could ever have proceeded from the seeds of the same tree. Innumerable other examples could be given. The explanation, I think, is simple: from long-continued study they are strongly impressed with the differences between the several races; and though they well know that each race varies slightly, for they win their prizes by selecting such slight differences, yet they ignore all general arguments, and refuse to sum up in their minds slight differences accumulated during many successive generations. May not those naturalists who, knowing far less of the laws of inheritance than does the breeder, and knowing no more than he does of the intermediate links in the long lines of descent, yet admit that many of our domestic races are descended from the same parents—may they not learn a lesson of caution, when they deride the idea of species in a state of nature being lineal descendants of other species?

Principles of Selection Anciently Followed, and Their Effects

Let us now briefly consider the steps by which domestic races have been produced, either from one or from several allied species. Some effect may be attributed to the direct and definite action of the external conditions of life, and some to habit; but he would be a bold man who would account by such agencies for the differences between a dray- and race-horse, a greyhound and bloodhound, a carrier and tumbler pigeon. One of the most remarkable features in our domesticated races is that we see in them adaptation, not indeed to the animal's or plant's own good, but to man's use or fancy. Some variations useful to him have probably arisen suddenly, or by one step; many botanists, for instance, believe that the fuller's teasel, with its hooks, which can not be rivalled by any mechanical contrivance, is only a variety of the wild Dipsacus; and this amount of change may have suddenly arisen in a seedling. So it has probably been with the turnspit dog; and this is known to have been the case with the ancon sheep. But when we compare the dray-horse and race-horse, the dromedary and camel, the various breeds of sheep fitted either for cultivated land or mountain pasture, with the wool of one breed good for one purpose, and that of another breed for another purpose; when we compare the many breeds of dogs, each good for man in different ways; when we compare the game-cock, so pertinacious in battle, with other breeds so little quarrelsome, with "everlasting layers" which never desire to sit, and with the bantam so small and elegant; when we compare the host of agricultural, culinary, orchard, and flower-garden races of plants, most useful to man at different seasons and for different purposes, or so beautiful in his eyes, we must, I think, look further than to mere variability. We can not suppose that all the breeds were suddenly produced as perfect and as useful as we now see them; indeed, in many cases, we know that this has not been their history. The key is man's power of accumulative selection: nature gives successive variations; man adds them up in certain directions useful to him. In this sense he may be said to have made for himself useful breeds.

The great power of this principle of selection is not hypothetical. It is certain that several of our eminent breeders have, even within a single lifetime, modified to a large extent their breeds of cattle and sheep. In order fully to realise what they have done it is almost necessary to read several of the many treatises devoted to this subject, and to inspect the animals. Breeders habitually speak of an animal's organisation as something plastic, which they can model almost as they please. If I had space I could quote numerous passages to this effect from highly competent authorities. Youatt, who was probably better acquainted with the works of agriculturalists than almost any other individual, and who was himself a very good judge of animals, speaks of the principle of selection as "that which enables the agriculturist, not only to modify the character of his flock, but to change it altogether. It is the magician's wand, by means of which he may summon into life whatever form and mould he pleases." Lord Somerville, speaking of what breeders have done for sheep, says:—"It would seem as if they had chalked out upon a wall a form perfect in itself, and then had given it existence."

* * *

Unconscious Selection

At the present time, eminent breeders try by methodical selection, with a distinct object in view, to make a new strain or sub-breed, superior to anything of the kind in the country. But, for our purpose, a form of Selection, which may be called Unconscious, and which results from every one trying to possess and breed from the best individual animals, is more important. Thus, a man who intends keeping pointers naturally tries to get as good dogs as he can, and afterwards breeds from his own best dogs, but he has no wish or expectation of permanently altering the breed. Nevertheless we may infer that this process, continued during centuries, would improve and modify any breed, in the same way as Bakewell, Collins, etc., by this very same process, only carried on more methodically, did greatly modify, even during their lifetimes, the forms and qualities of their cattle. Slow and insensible changes of this kind could never be recognised unless actual measurements or careful drawings of the breeds in question have been made long ago, which may serve for comparison. In some cases, however, unchanged, or but little changed, individuals of the same breed exist in less civilised districts, where the breed has been less improved. There is reason to believe that King Charles' spaniel has been unconsciously modified to a large extent since the time of that monarch. Some highly competent authorities are convinced that the setter is directly derived from the spaniel, and has probably been slowly altered from it. It is known that the English pointer has been greatly changed within the last century, and in this case the change has, it is believed, been chiefly effected by crosses with the foxhound; but what concerns us is, that the change has been effected unconsciously and gradually, and yet so effectually that, though the old Spanish pointer certainly came from Spain, Mr. Borrow has not seen, as I am informed by him, any native dog in Spain like our pointer.

By a similar process of selection, and by careful training, English race-horses have come to surpass in fleetness and size the parent Arabs, so that the latter, by the regulations for the Goodwood Races, are favoured in the weights which they carry. Lord Spencer and others have shown how the cattle of England have increased in weight and in early maturity, compared with the stock formerly kept in this country. By comparing the accounts given in various old treatises of the former and present state of carrier and tumbler pigeons in Britain, India, and Persia, we can trace the stages through which they have insensibly passed, and come to differ so greatly from the rock-pigeon.

* * *

To sum up on the origin of our domestic races of animals and plants. Changed conditions of life are of the highest importance in causing variability, both by acting directly on the organisation, and indirectly by affecting the reproductive system. It is not probable that variability is an inherent and necessary contingent, under all circumstances. The greater or less force of inheritance and reversion determine whether variations shall endure. Variability is governed by many unknown laws, of which correlated growth is probably the most important. Something, but how much we do not know, may be attributed to the definite action of the conditions of life. Some, perhaps a great, effect may be attributed to the increased use or disuse of parts. The final result is thus rendered infinitely complex.

Over all these causes of change, the accumulative action of selection, whether applied methodically and quickly, or unconsciously and slowly, but more efficiently seems to have been the predominant power.

Chapter II

Variation Under Nature

Variability • Individual differences • Doubtful species • Wide ranging, much diffused, and common species, vary most • Species of the larger genera in each country vary more frequently than the species of the smaller genera • Many of the species of the larger genera resemble varieties in being very closely, but unequally, related to each other, and in having restricted ranges.

Before applying the principles arrived at in the last chapter to organic beings in a state of nature, we must briefly discuss whether these latter are subject to any variation. To treat this subject properly, a long catalogue of dry facts ought to be given; but these I shall reserve for a future work. Nor shall I here discuss the various definitions which have been given of the term species. No one definition has satisfied all naturalists; yet every naturalist knows vaguely what he means when he speaks of a species. Generally the term includes the unknown element of a distinct act of creation. The term "variety" is almost equally difficult to define; but here community of descent is almost universally implied, though it can rarely be proved.

* * *

Individual Differences

The many slight differences which appear in the offspring from the same parents, or which it may be presumed have thus arisen, from being observed in the individuals of the same species inhabiting the same confined locality, may be called individual differences. No one supposes that all the individuals of the same species are cast in the same actual mould. These individual differences are of the highest importance for us, for they are often inherited, as must be familiar to every one; and they thus afford materials for natural selection to act on and accumulate, in the same manner as man accumulates in any given direction individual differences in his domesticated production.

* * *

Doubtful Species

The forms which possess in some considerable degree the character of species, but which are so closely similar to other forms, or are so closely linked to them by intermediate gradations, that naturalists do not like to rank them as distinct species, are in several respects the most important for us. We have every reason to believe that many of these doubtful and closely allied forms have permanently retained their characters for a long time; for as long, as far as we know, as have good and true species. Practically, when a naturalist can unite by means of intermediate links any two forms, he treats the one as a variety of the other, ranking the most common, but sometimes the one first described as the species, and the other as the variety. But cases of great difficulty, which I will not here enumerate, sometimes arise in deciding whether or not to rank one form as a variety of another, even when they are closely connected by intermediate links; nor will the commonly assumed hybrid nature of the intermediate forms always remove the difficulty. In very many cases, however, one form is ranked as a variety of another, not because the intermediate links have actually been found, but because analogy leads the observer to suppose either that they do now somewhere exist, or may formerly have existed; and here a wide door for the entry of doubt and conjecture is opened.

Hence, in determining whether a form should be ranked as a species or a variety, the opinion of naturalists having sound judgment and wide experience seems the only guide to follow. We must, however, in many cases, decide by a majority of naturalists, for few well-marked and well-known varieties can be named which have not been ranked as species by at least some competent judges.

* * *

Many years ago, when comparing, and seeing others compare, the birds from the closely neighbouring islands of the Galapagos Archipelago, one with another, and with those from the American mainland, I was much struck how entirely vague and arbitrary is the distinction between species and varieties. On the islets of the little Madeira group there are many insects which are characterized as varieties in Mr. Wollaston's admirable work, but which would certainly be ranked as distinct species by many entomologists. Even Ireland has a few animals, now generally regarded as varieties, but which have been ranked as species by some zoologists. Several experienced ornithologists consider our British red grouse as only a strongly marked race of a Norwegian species, whereas the greater number rank it as an undoubted species peculiar to Great Britain. A wide distance between the homes of two doubtful forms leads many naturalists to rank them as distinct species; but what distance, it has been well asked, will suffice if that between America and Europe is ample, will that between Europe and the Azores, or Madeira, or the Canaries, or between the several islets of these small archipelagos, be sufficient?

* * *

When a young naturalist commences the study of a group of organisms quite unknown to him he is at first much perplexed in determining what differences to consider as specific and what as varietal; for he knows nothing of the amount and kind of variation to which the group is subject; and this shows, at least, how very generally there is some variation. But if he confine his attention to one class within one country he will soon make up his mind how to rank most of the doubtful forms. His general tendency will be to make many species, for he will become impressed, just like the pigeon or poultry fancier before alluded to, with the amount of difference in the forms which he is continually studying; and he has little general knowledge of analogical variation in other groups and in other countries by which to correct his first impressions. As he extends the range of his observations he will meet with more cases of difficulty; for he will encounter a greater number of closely-allied forms. But if his observations be widely extended he will in the end generally be able to make up his own mind; but he will succeed in this at the expense of admitting much variation, and the truth of this admission will often be disputed by other naturalists. When he comes to study allied forms brought from countries not now continuous, in which case he cannot hope to find intermediate links, he will be compelled to trust almost entirely to analogy, and his difficulties will rise to a climax.

Certainly no clear line of demarcation has as yet been drawn between species and sub-species—that is, the forms which in the opinion of some naturalists come very near to, but do not quite arrive at, the rank of species; or, again, between sub-species and well-marked varieties, or between lesser varieties and individual differences. These differences blend into each other by an insensible series; and a series impresses the mind with the idea of an actual passage.

Hence I look at individual differences, though of small interest to the systematist, as of the highest importance for us, as being the first step towards such slight varieties as are barely thought worth recording in works on natural history. And I look at varieties which are in any degree more distinct and permanent, as steps toward more strongly marked and permanent varieties; and at the latter, as leading to sub-species, and then to species. The passage from one stage of difference to another may, in many cases, be the simple result of the nature of the organism and of the different physical conditions to which it has long been exposed; but with respect to the more important and adaptive characters, the passage from one stage of difference to another may be safely attributed to the cumulative action of natural selection, hereafter to be explained, and to the effects of the increased use or disuse of parts. A well-marked variety may therefore be called an incipient species; but whether this belief is justifiable must be judged by the weight of the various facts and considerations to be given throughout this work.

It need not be supposed that all varieties or incipient species attain the rank of species. They may become extinct, or they may endure as varieties for very long periods, as has been shown to be the case by Mr. Wollaston with the varieties of certain fossil land-shells in Madeira, and with plants by Gaston de Saporta. If a variety were to flourish so as to exceed in numbers the parent species, it would then rank as the species, and the species as the variety; or it might come to supplant and exterminate the parent species; or both might co-exist, and both rank as independent species. But we shall hereafter return to this subject.

From these remarks it will be seen that I look at the term species as one arbitrarily given, for the sake of convenience, to a set of individuals closely resembling each other, and that it does not essentially differ from the term variety, which is given to less distinct and more fluctuating forms. The term variety, again, in comparison with mere individual differences, is also applied arbitrarily, for convenience sake.

Wide-Ranging, Much Diffused, and Common Species Vary Most

Alphonse de Candolle and others have shown that plants which have very wide ranges generally present varieties; and this might have been expected, as they are exposed to diverse physical conditions, and as they come into competition (which, as we shall hereafter see, is an equally or more important circumstance) with different sets of organic beings. But my tables further show that, in any limited country, the species which are the most common, that is abound most in individuals, and the species which are most widely diffused within their own country (and this is a different consideration from wide range, and to a certain extent from commonness), oftenest give rise to varieties sufficiently well-marked to have been recorded in botanical works. Hence it is the most flourishing, or, as they may be called, the dominant species—those which range widely, are the most diffused in their own country, and are the most numerous in individuals—which oftenest produce well-marked varieties, or, as I consider them, incipient species. And this, perhaps, might have been anticipated; for, as varieties, in order to become in any degree permanent, necessarily have to struggle with the other inhabitants of the country, the species which are already dominant will be the most likely to yield offspring, which, though in some slight degree modified, still inherit those advantages that enabled their parents to become dominant over their compatriots.

Summary

Finally, varieties cannot be distinguished from species—except, first, by the discovery of intermediate linking forms; and, secondly, by a certain indefinite amount of difference between them; for two forms, if differing very little, are generally ranked as varieties, notwithstanding that they cannot be closely connected; but the amount of difference considered necessary to give to any two forms the rank of species cannot be defined. In genera having more than the average number of species in any country, the species of these genera have more than the average number of varieties. In large genera the species are apt to be closely but unequally allied together, forming little clusters round other species. Species very closely allied to other species apparently have restricted ranges. In all these respects the species of large genera present a strong analogy with varieties. And we can clearly understand these analogies, if species once existed as varieties, and thus originated; whereas, these analogies are utterly inexplicable if species are independent creations.

We have also seen that it is the most flourishing or dominant species of the larger genera within each class which on an average yield the greatest number of varieties, and varieties, as we shall hereafter see, tend to become converted into new and distinct species. Thus the larger genera tend to become larger; and throughout nature the forms of life which are now dominant tend to become still more dominant by leaving many modified and dominant descendants. But, by steps hereafter to be explained, the larger genera also tend to break up into smaller genera. And thus, the forms of life throughout the universe become divided into groups subordinate to groups.

Chapter III

Struggle For Existence

Its bearing on natural selection • The term used in a wide sense • Geometrical ratio of increase • Rapid increase of naturalised animals and plants • Nature of the checks to increase • Competition universal • Effects of climate • Protection from the number of individuals—Complex relations of all animals and plants throughout nature • Struggle for life most severe between individuals and varieties of the same species: often severe between species of the same genus • The relation of organism to organism the most important of all relations.

Before entering on the subject of this chapter I must make a few preliminary remarks to show how the struggle for existence bears on natural selection. It has been seen in the last chapter that among organic beings in a state of nature there is some individual variability: indeed I am not aware that this has ever been disputed. It is immaterial for us whether a multitude of doubtful forms be called species or sub-species or varieties; what rank, for instance, the two or three hundred doubtful forms of British plants are entitled to hold, if the existence of any well-marked varieties be admitted. But the mere existence of individual variability and of some few well-marked varieties, though necessary as the foundation for the work, helps us but little in understanding how species arise in nature. How have all those exquisite adaptations of one part of the organisation to another part, and to the conditions of life and of one organic being to another being, been perfected? We see these beautiful co-adaptations most plainly in the woodpecker and the mistletoe; and only a little less plainly in the humblest parasite which clings to the hairs of a quadruped or feathers of a bird; in the structure of the beetle which dives through the water; in the plumed seed which is wafted by the gentlest breeze; in short, we see beautiful adaptations everywhere and in every part of the organic world.

Again, it may be asked, how is it that varieties, which I have called incipient species, become ultimately converted into good and distinct species, which in most cases obviously differ from each other far more than do the varieties of the same species? How do those groups of species, which constitute what are called distinct genera and which differ from each other more than do the species of the same genus, arise? All these results, as we shall more fully see in the next chapter, follow from the struggle for life. Owing to this struggle, variations, however slight and from whatever cause proceeding, if they be in any degree profitable to the individuals of a species, in their infinitely complex relations to other organic beings and to their physical conditions of life, will tend to the preservation of such individuals, and will generally be inherited by the offspring. The offspring, also, will thus have a better chance of surviving, for, of the many individuals of any species which are periodically born, but a small number can survive. I have called this principle, by which each slight variation, if useful, is preserved, by the term natural selection, in order to mark its relation to man's power of selection. But the expression often used by Mr. Herbert Spencer, of the Survival of the Fittest, is more accurate, and is sometimes equally convenient. We have seen that man by selection can certainly produce great results, and can adapt organic beings to his own uses, through the accumulation of slight but useful variations, given to him by the hand of Nature. But Natural Selection, we shall hereafter see, is a power incessantly ready for action, and is as immeasurably superior to man's feeble efforts, as the works of Nature are to those of Art.

We will now discuss in a little more detail the struggle for existence. In my future work this subject will be treated, as it well deserves, at greater length. The elder De Candolle and Lyell have largely and philosophically shown that all organic beings are exposed to severe competition. In regard to plants, no one has treated this subject with more spirit and ability than W. Herbert, Dean of Manchester, evidently the result of his great horticultural knowledge. Nothing is easier than to admit in words the truth of the universal struggle for life, or more difficult—at least I found it so—than constantly to bear this conclusion in mind. Yet unless it be thoroughly engrained in the mind, the whole economy of nature, with every fact on distribution, rarity, abundance, extinction, and variation, will be dimly seen or quite misunderstood. We behold the face of nature bright with gladness, we often see superabundance of food; we do not see or we forget that the birds which are idly singing round us mostly live on insects or seeds, and are thus constantly destroying life; or we forget how largely these songsters, or their eggs, or their nestlings, are destroyed by birds and beasts of prey; we do not always bear in mind, that, though food may be now superabundant, it is not so at all seasons of each recurring year.

The Term, **Struggle for Existence,** *Used in a Large Sense*

I should premise that I use this term in a large and metaphorical sense, including dependence of one being on another, and including (which is more important) not only the life of the individual, but success in leaving progeny. Two canine animals, in a time of dearth, may be truly said to struggle with each other which shall get food and live. But a plant on the edge of a desert is said to struggle for life against the drought, though more properly it should be said to be dependent on the moisture. A plant which annually produces a thousand seeds, of which only one of an average comes to maturity, may be more truly said to struggle with the plants of the same and other kinds which already clothe the ground. The mistletoe is dependent on the apple and a few other trees, but can only in a far-fetched sense be said to struggle with these trees, for, if too many of these parasites grow on the same tree, it languishes and dies. But several seedling mistletoes, growing close together on the same branch, may more truly be said to struggle with each other. As the mistletoe is disseminated by birds, its existence depends on them; and it may metaphorically be said to struggle with other fruit-bearing plants, in tempting the birds to devour and thus disseminate its seeds. In these several senses, which pass into each other, I use for convenience sake the general term of Struggle for Existence.

Geometrical Ratio of Increase

A struggle for existence inevitably follows from the high rate at which all organic beings tend to increase. Every being, which during its natural lifetime produces several eggs or seeds, must suffer destruction during some period of its life, and during some season or occasional year, otherwise, on the principle of geometrical increase, its numbers would quickly become so inordinately great that no country could support the product. Hence, as more individuals are produced than can possibly survive, there must in every case be a struggle for existence, either one individual with another of the same species, or with the individuals of distinct species, or with the physical conditions of life. It is the doctrine of Malthus applied with manifold force to the whole animal and vegetable kingdoms; for in this case there can be no artificial increase of food, and no prudential restraint from marriage. Although some species may be now increasing, more or less rapidly, in numbers, all cannot do so, for the world would not hold them.

There is no exception to the rule that every organic being naturally increases at so high a rate, that, if not destroyed, the earth would soon be covered by the progeny of a single pair. Even slow-breeding man has doubled in twenty-five years, and at this rate, in less than a thousand years, there would literally not be standing room for his progeny. Linnaeus has calculated that if an annual plant produced only two seeds—and there is no plant so unproductive as this—and their seedlings next year produced two, and so on, then in twenty years there would be a million plants. The elephant is reckoned the slowest breeder of all known animals, and I have taken some pains to estimate its probable minimum rate of natural increase; it will be safest to assume that it begins breeding when thirty years old, and goes on breeding till ninety years old, bringing forth six young in the interval, and surviving till one hundred years old; if this be so, after a period of from 740 to 750 years there would be nearly nineteen million elephants alive descended from the first pair.

But we have better evidence on this subject than mere theoretical calculations, namely, the numerous recorded cases of the astonishingly rapid increase of various animals in a state of nature, when circumstances have been favourable to them during two or three following seasons. Still more striking is the evidence from our domestic animals of many kinds which have run wild in several parts of the world; if the statements of the rate of increase of slow-breeding cattle and horses in South America, and latterly in Australia, had not been well authenticated, they would have been incredible. So it is with plants; cases could be given of introduced plants which have become common throughout whole islands in a period of less than ten years. Several of the plants, such as the cardoon and a tall thistle, which are now the commonest over the wide plains of La Plata, clothing square leagues of surface almost to the exclusion of every other plant, have been introduced from Europe; and there are plants which now range in India, as I hear from Dr. Falconer, from Cape Comorin to the Himalaya, which have been imported from America since its discovery. In such cases, and endless others could be given, no one supposes that the fertility of the animals or plants has been suddenly and temporarily increased in any sensible degree. The obvious explanation is that the conditions of life have been highly favourable, and that there has consequently been less destruction of the old and young and that nearly all the young have been enabled to breed. Their geometrical ratio of increase, the result of which never fails to be surprising, simply explains their extraordinarily rapid increase and wide diffusion in their new homes.

In a state of nature almost every full-grown plant annually produces seed, and among animals there are very few which do not annually pair. Hence we may confidently assert that all plants and animals are tending to increase at a geometrical ratio—that all would rapidly stock every station in which they could any how exist, and that this geometrical tendency to increase must be checked by destruction at some period of life. Our familiarity with the larger domestic animals tends, I think, to mislead us; we see no great destruction falling on them, and we do not keep in mind that thousands are annually slaughtered for food, and that in a state of nature an equal number would have somehow to be disposed of.

The only difference between organisms which annually produce eggs or seeds by the thousand, and those which produce extremely few, is, that the slow breeders would require a few more years to people, under favourable conditions, a whole district, let it be ever so large. The condor lays a couple of eggs and the ostrich a score, and yet in the same country the condor may be the more numerous of the two. The Fulmar petrel lays but one egg, yet it is believed to be the most numerous bird in the world. One fly deposits hundreds of eggs, and another, like the hippobosca, a single one. But this difference does not determine how many individuals of the two species can be supported in a district. A large number of eggs is of some importance to those species which depend on a fluctuating amount of food, for it allows them rapidly to increase in number. But the real importance of a large number of eggs or seeds is to make up for much destruction at some period of life; and this period in the great majority of cases is an early one. If an animal can in any way protect its own eggs or young, a small number may be produced, and yet the average stock be fully kept up; but if many eggs or young are destroyed, many must be produced or the species will become extinct. It would suffice to keep up the full number of a tree, which lived on an average for a thousand years, if a single seed were produced once in a thousand years, supposing that this seed were never destroyed and could be ensured to germinate in a fitting place; so that, in all cases, the average number of any animal or plant depends only indirectly on the number of its eggs or seeds.

In looking at Nature, it is most necessary to keep the foregoing considerations always in mind—never to forget that every single organic being may be said to be striving to the utmost to increase in numbers; that each lives by a struggle at some period of its life; that heavy destruction inevitably falls either on the young or old during each generation or at recurrent intervals. Lighten any check, mitigate the destruction ever so little, and the number of the species will almost instantaneously increase to any amount.

Nature of the Checks to Increase

The causes which check the natural tendency of each species to increase are most obscure. Look at the most vigorous species; by as much as it swarms in numbers, by so much will it tend to increase still further. We know not exactly what the checks are even in a single instance. Nor will this surprise any one who reflects how ignorant we are on this head, even in regard to mankind, although so incomparably better known than any other animal. This subject of the checks to increase has been ably treated by several authors, and I hope in a future work to discuss it at considerable length, more especially in regard to the feral animals of South America. Here I will make only a few remarks, just to recall to the reader's mind some of the chief points. Eggs or very young animals seem generally to suffer most, but this is not invariably the case. With plants there is a vast destruction of seeds, but from some observations which I have made it appears that the seedlings suffer most from germinating in ground already thickly stocked with other plants. Seedlings, also, are destroyed in vast numbers by various enemies; for instance, on a piece of ground three feet long and two wide, dug and cleared, and where there could be no choking from other plants, I marked all the seedlings of our native weeds as they came up, and out of 357 no less than 295 were destroyed, chiefly by slugs and insects. If turf which has long been mown, and the case would be the same with turf closely browsed by quadrupeds, be let to grow, the more vigorous plants gradually kill the less vigorous, though fully grown plants; thus out of twenty species grown on a little plot of mown turf (three feet by four) nine species perished, from the other species being allowed to grow up freely.

The amount of food for each species, of course, gives the extreme limit to which each can increase; but very frequently it is not the obtaining food, but the serving as prey to other animals, which determines the average number of a species. Thus, there seems to be little doubt that the stock of partridges, grouse, and hares on any large estate depends chiefly on the destruction of vermin. If not one head of game were shot during the next twenty years in England, and, at the same time, if no vermin were destroyed, there would, in all probability, be less game than at present, although hundreds of thousands of game animals are now annually shot. On the other hand, in some cases, as with the elephant, none are destroyed by beasts of prey; for even the tiger in India most rarely dares to attack a young elephant protected by its dam.

Climate plays an important part in determining the average numbers of a species, and periodical seasons of extreme cold or drought seem to be the most effective of all checks. I estimated (chiefly from the greatly reduced numbers of nests in the spring) that the winter of 1854-5 destroyed four-fifths of the birds in my own grounds; and this is a tremendous destruction, when we remember that ten per cent. is an extraordinarily severe mortality from epidemics with man. The action of climate seems at first sight to be quite independent of the struggle for existence; but in so far as climate chiefly acts in reducing food, it brings on the most severe struggle between the individuals, whether of the same or of distinct species, which subsist on the same kind of food. Even when climate, for instance, extreme cold, acts directly, it will be the least vigorous individuals, or those which have got least food through the advancing winter, which will suffer the most.

* * *

Complex Relations of All Animals and Plants to Each Other in the Struggle for Existence

Many cases are on record showing how complex and unexpected are the checks and relations between organic beings, which have to struggle together in the same country. I will give only a single instance, which, though a simple one, interested me. In Staffordshire, on the estate of a relation, where I had ample means of investigation, there was a large and extremely barren heath, which had never been touched by the hand of man; but several hundred acres of exactly the same nature had been enclosed twenty-five years previously and planted with Scotch fir. The change in the native vegetation of the planted part of the heath was most remarkable, more than is generally seen in passing from one quite different soil to another: not only the proportional numbers of the heath-plants were wholly changed, but twelve species of plants (not counting grasses and carices) flourished in the plantations, which could not be found on the heath. The effect on the insects must have been still greater, for six insectivorous birds were very common in the plantations, which were not to be seen on the heath; and the heath was frequented by two or three distinct insectivorous birds. Here we see how potent has been the effect of the introduction of a single tree, nothing whatever else having been done, with the exception of the land having been enclosed, so that cattle could not enter. But how important an element enclosure is, I plainly saw near Farnham, in Surrey. Here there are extensive heaths, with a few clumps of old Scotch firs on the distant hill-tops: within the last ten years large spaces have been enclosed, and self-sown firs are now springing up in multitudes, so close together that all cannot live. When I ascertained that these young trees had not been sown or planted I was so much surprised at their numbers that I went to several points of view, whence I could examine hundreds of acres of the unenclosed heath, and literally I could not see a single Scotch fir, except the old planted clumps. But on looking closely between the stems of the heath, I found a multitude of seedlings and little trees, which had been perpetually browsed down by the cattle. In one square yard, at a point some hundred yards distant from one of the old clumps, I counted thirty-two little trees; and one of them, with twenty-six rings of growth, had, during many years tried to raise its head above the stems of the heath, and had failed. No wonder that, as soon as the land was enclosed, it became thickly clothed with vigorously growing young firs. Yet the heath was so extremely barren and so extensive that no one would ever have imagined that cattle would have so closely and effectually searched it for food.

* * *

In the case of every species, many different checks, acting at different periods of life, and during different seasons or years, probably come into play; some one check or some few being generally the most potent, but all will concur in determining the average number, or even the existence of the species. In some cases it can be shown that widely-different checks act on the same species in different districts. When we look at the plants and bushes clothing an entangled bank, we are tempted to attribute their proportional numbers and kinds to what we call chance. But how false a view is this! Every one has heard that when an American forest is cut down, a very different vegetation springs up; but it has been observed that ancient Indian ruins in the Southern United States, which must formerly have been cleared of trees, now display the same beautiful diversity and proportion of kinds as in the surrounding virgin forests. What a struggle must have gone on during long centuries between the several kinds of trees, each annually scattering its seeds by the thousand; what war between insect and insect—between insects, snails, and other animals with birds and beasts of prey—all striving to increase, all feeding on each other, or on the trees, their seeds and seedlings, or on the other plants which first clothed the ground and thus checked the growth of the trees. Throw up a handful of feathers, and all fall to the ground according to definite laws; but how simple is the problem where each shall fall compared to that of the action and reaction of the innumerable plants and animals which have determined, in the course of centuries, the proportional numbers and kinds of trees now growing on the old Indian ruins!

The dependency of one organic being on another, as of a parasite on its prey, lies generally between beings remote in the scale of nature. This is likewise sometimes the case with those which may strictly be said to struggle with each other for existence, as in the case of locusts and grass-feeding quadrupeds. But the struggle will almost invariably be most severe between the individuals of the same species, for they frequent the same districts, require the same food, and are exposed to the same dangers. In the case of varieties of the same species, the struggle will generally be almost equally severe, and we sometimes see the contest soon decided: for instance, if several varieties of wheat be sown together, and the mixed seed be resown, some of the varieties which best suit the soil or climate, or are naturally the most fertile, will beat the others and so yield more seed, and will consequently in a few years supplant the other varieties. To keep up a mixed stock of even such extremely close varieties as the variously coloured sweet-peas, they must be each year harvested separately, and the seed then mixed in due proportion, otherwise the weaker kinds will steadily decrease in number and disappear. So again with the varieties of sheep: it has been asserted that certain mountain-varieties will starve out other mountain-varieties, so that they cannot be kept together. The same result has followed from keeping together different varieties of the medicinal leech. It may even be doubted whether the varieties of any of our domestic plants or animals have so exactly the same strength, habits, and constitution, that the original proportions of a mixed stock (crossing being prevented) could be kept up for half-a-dozen generations, if they were allowed to struggle together, in the same manner as beings in a state of nature, and if the seed or young were not annually preserved in due proportion.

* * *

Chapter IV

Natural Selection; or the Survival of the Fittest

Natural Selection • its power compared with man's selection • its power on characters of trifling importance • its power at all ages and on both sexes • Sexual Selection • On the generality of intercrosses between individuals of the same species • Circumstances favourable and unfavourable to the results of Natural Selection, namely, intercrossing, isolation, number of individuals • Slow action • Extinction caused by Natural Selection • Divergence of Character, related to the diversity of inhabitants of any small area and to naturalisation • Action of Natural Selection, through Divergence of Character and Extinction, on the descendants from a common parent • Explains the Grouping of all organic beings • Advance in organisation • Low forms preserved • Convergence of character • Indefinite multiplication of species • Summary.

How will the struggle for existence, briefly discussed in the last chapter, act in regard to variation? Can the principle of selection, which we have seen is so potent in the hands of man, apply under nature? I think we shall see that it can act most efficiently. Let the endless number of slight variations and individual differences occurring in our domestic productions, and, in a lesser degree, in those under nature, be borne in mind; as well as the strength of the hereditary tendency. Under domestication, it may truly be said that the whole organisation becomes in some degree plastic. But the variability, which we almost universally meet with in our domestic productions is not directly produced, as Hooker and Asa Gray have well remarked, by man; he can neither originate varieties nor prevent their occurrence; he can only preserve and accumulate such as do occur. Unintentionally he exposes organic beings to new and changing conditions of life, and variability ensues; but similar changes of conditions might and do occur under nature. Let it also be borne in mind how infinitely complex and close-fitting are the mutual relations of all organic beings to each other and to their physical conditions of life; and consequently what infinitely varied diversities of structure might be of use to each being under changing conditions of life. Can it then be thought improbable, seeing that variations useful to man have undoubtedly occurred, that other variations useful in some way to each being in the great and complex battle of life, should occur in the course of many successive generations? If such do occur, can we doubt (remembering that many more individuals are born than can possibly survive) that individuals having any advantage, however slight, over others, would have the best chance of surviving and procreating their kind? On the other hand, we may feel sure that any variation in the least degree injurious would be rigidly destroyed. This preservation of favourable individual differences and variations, and the destruction of those which are injurious, I have called Natural Selection, or the Survival of the Fittest. Variations neither useful nor injurious would not be affected by natural selection, and would be left either a fluctuating element, as perhaps we see in certain polymorphic species, or would ultimately become fixed, owing to the nature of the organism and the nature of the conditions.

Several writers have misapprehended or objected to the term Natural Selection. Some have even imagined that natural selection induces variability, whereas it implies only the preservation of such variations as arise and are beneficial to the being under its conditions of life. No one objects to agriculturists speaking of the potent effects of man's selection; and in this case the individual differences given by nature, which man for some object selects, must of necessity first occur. Others have objected that the term selection implies conscious choice in the animals which become modified; and it has even been urged that, as plants have no volition, natural selection is not applicable to them! In the literal sense of the word, no doubt, natural selection is a false term; but who ever objected to chemists speaking of the elective affinities of the various elements?—and yet an acid cannot strictly be said to elect the base with which it in preference combines. It has been said that I speak of natural selection as an active power or Deity; but who objects to an author speaking of the attraction of gravity as ruling the movements of the planets? Every one knows what is meant and is implied by such metaphorical expressions; and they are almost necessary for brevity. So again it is difficult to avoid personifying the word Nature; but I mean by nature, only the aggregate action and product of many natural laws, and by laws the sequence of events as ascertained by us. With a little familiarity such superficial objections will be forgotten.

We shall best understand the probable course of natural selection by taking the case of a country undergoing some slight physical change, for instance, of climate. The proportional numbers of its inhabitants will almost immediately undergo a change, and some species will probably become extinct. We may conclude, from what we have seen of the intimate and complex manner in which the inhabitants of each country are bound together, that any change in the numerical proportions of the inhabitants, independently of the change of climate itself, would seriously affect the others. If the country were open on its borders, new forms would certainly immigrate, and this would likewise seriously disturb the relations of some of the former inhabitants. Let it be remembered how powerful the influence of a single introduced tree or mammal has been shown to be. But in the case of an island, or of a country partly surrounded by barriers, into which new and better adapted forms could not freely enter, we should then have places in the economy of nature which would assuredly be better filled up if some of the original inhabitants were in some manner modified; for, had the area been open to immigration, these same places would have been seized on by intruders. In such cases, slight modifications, which in any way favoured the individuals of any species, by better adapting them to their altered conditions, would tend to be preserved; and natural selection would have free scope for the work of improvement.

We have good reason to believe, as shown in the first chapter, that changes in the conditions of life give a tendency to increased variability; and in the foregoing cases the conditions have changed, and this would manifestly be favourable to natural selection, by affording a better chance of the occurrence of profitable variations. Unless such occur, natural selection can do nothing. Under the term of "variations," it must never be forgotten that mere individual differences are included. As man can produce a great result with his domestic animals and plants by adding up in any given direction individual differences, so could natural selection, but far more easily from having incomparably longer time for action. Nor do I believe that any great physical change, as of climate, or any unusual degree of isolation, to check immigration, is necessary in order that new and unoccupied places should be left for natural selection to fill up by improving some of the varying inhabitants. For as all the inhabitants of each country are struggling together with nicely balanced forces, extremely slight modifications in the structure or habits of one species would often give it an advantage over others; and still further modifications of the same kind would often still further increase the advantage, as long as the species continued under the same conditions of life and profited by similar means of subsistence and defence. No country can be named in which all the native inhabitants are now so perfectly adapted to each other and to the physical conditions under which they live, that none of them could be still better adapted or improved; for in all countries, the natives have been so far conquered by naturalised productions that they have allowed some foreigners to take firm possession of the land. And as foreigners have thus in every country beaten some of the natives, we may safely conclude that the natives might have been modified with advantage, so as to have better resisted the intruders.

As man can produce, and certainly has produced, a great result by his methodical and unconscious means of selection, what may not natural selection effect? Man can act only on external and visible characters: Nature, if I may be allowed to personify the natural preservation or survival of the fittest, cares nothing for appearances, except in so far as they are useful to any being. She can act on every internal organ, on every shade of constitutional difference, on the whole machinery of life. Man selects only for his own good; Nature only for that of the being which she tends. Every selected character is fully exercised by her, as is implied by the fact of their selection. Man keeps the natives of many climates in the same country. He seldom exercises each selected character in some peculiar and fitting manner; he feeds a long and a short-beaked pigeon on the same food; he does not exercise a long-backed or long-legged quadruped in any peculiar manner; he exposes sheep with long and short wool to the same climate; does not allow the most vigorous males to struggle for the females; he does not rigidly destroy all inferior animals, but protects during each varying season, as far as lies in his power, all his productions. He often begins his selection by some half-monstrous form, or at least by some modification prominent enough to catch the eye or to be plainly useful to him. Under nature, the slightest differences of structure or constitution may well turn the nicely-balanced scale in the struggle for life, and so be preserved. How fleeting are the wishes and efforts of man! How short his time, and consequently how poor will be his results, compared with those accumulated by Nature during whole geological periods! Can we wonder, then, that Nature's productions should be far "truer" in character than man's productions; that they should be infinitely better adapted to the most complex conditions of life, and should plainly bear the stamp of far higher workmanship?

It may metaphorically be said that natural selection is daily and hourly scrutinising, throughout the world, the slightest variations; rejecting those that are bad, preserving and adding up all that are good; silently and insensibly working, *Whenever and Wherever Opportunity Offers*, at the improvement of each organic being in relation to its organic and inorganic conditions of life. We see nothing of these slow changes in progress, until the hand of time has marked the long lapse of ages, and then so imperfect is our view into long-past geological ages that we see only that the forms of life are now different from what they formerly were.

In order that any great amount of modification should be effected in a species, a variety, when once formed must again, perhaps after a long interval of time, vary or present individual differences of the same favourable nature as before; and these must again be preserved, and so onward, step by step. Seeing that individual differences of the same kind perpetually recur, this can hardly be considered as an unwarrantable assumption. But whether it is true, we can judge only by seeing how far the hypothesis accords with and explains the general phenomena of nature. On the other hand, the ordinary belief that the amount of possible variation is a strictly limited quantity, is likewise a simple assumption.

Although natural selection can act only through and for the good of each being, yet characters and structures, which we are apt to consider as of very trifling importance, may thus be acted on. When we see leaf-eating insects green, and bark-feeders mottled-grey; the alpine ptarmigan white in winter, the red-grouse the colour of heather, we must believe that these tints are of service to these birds and insects in preserving them from danger. Grouse, if not destroyed at some period of their lives, would increase in countless numbers; they are known to suffer largely from birds of prey; and hawks are guided by eyesight to their prey,—so much so that on parts of the continent persons are warned not to keep white pigeons, as being the most liable to destruction. Hence natural selection might be effective in giving the proper colour to each kind of grouse, and in keeping that colour, when once acquired, true and constant. Nor ought we to think that the occasional destruction of an animal of any particular colour would produce little effect; we should remember how essential it is in a flock of white sheep to destroy a lamb with the faintest trace of black. We have seen how the colour of hogs, which feed on the "paint-root" in Virginia, determines whether they shall live or die. In plants, the down on the fruit and the colour of the flesh are considered by botanists as characters of the most trifling importance; yet we hear from an excellent horticulturist, Downing, that in the United States smooth-skinned fruits suffer far more from a beetle, a Curculio, than those with down; that purple plums suffer far more from a certain disease than yellow plums; whereas another disease attacks yellow-fleshed peaches far more than those with other coloured flesh. If, with all the aids of art, these slight differences make a great difference in cultivating the several varieties, assuredly, in a state of nature, where the trees would have to struggle with other trees and with a host of enemies, such differences would effectually settle which variety, whether a smooth or downy, a yellow- or a purple-fleshed fruit, should succeed.

In looking at many small points of difference between species, which, as far as our ignorance permits us to judge, seem quite unimportant, we must not forget that climate, food, etc., have no doubt produced some direct effect. It is also necessary to bear in mind that, owing to the law of correlation, when one part varies and the variations are accumulated through natural selection, other modifications, often of the most unexpected nature, will ensue.

As we see that those variations which, under domestication, appear at any particular period of life, tend to reappear in the offspring at the same period; for instance, in the shape, size and flavour of the seeds of the many varieties of our culinary and agricultural plants; in the caterpillar and cocoon stages of the varieties of the silkworm; in the eggs of poultry, and in the colour of the down of their chickens; in the horns of our sheep and cattle when nearly adult; so in a state of nature natural selection will be enabled to act on and modify organic beings at any age, by the accumulation of variations profitable at that age, and by their inheritance at a corresponding age. If it profit a plant to have its seeds more and more widely disseminated by the wind, I can see no greater difficulty in this being effected through natural selection, than in the cotton-planter increasing and improving by selection the down in the pods on his cotton-trees. Natural selection may modify and adapt the larva of an insect to a score of contingencies, wholly different from those which concern the mature insect; and these modifications may affect, through correlation, the structure of the adult. So, conversely, modifications in the adult may affect the structure of the larva; but in all cases natural selection will ensure that they shall not be injurious: for if they were so, the species would become extinct.

* * *

It may be well here to remark that with all beings there must be much fortuitous destruction, which can have little or no influence on the course of natural selection. For instance, a vast number of eggs or seeds are annually devoured, and these could be modified through natural selection only if they varied in some manner which protected them from their enemies. Yet many of these eggs or seeds would perhaps, if not destroyed, have yielded individuals better adapted to their conditions of life than any of those which happened to survive. So again a vast number of mature animals and plants, whether or not they be the best adapted to their conditions, must be annually destroyed by accidental causes, which would not be in the least degree mitigated by certain changes of structure or constitution which would in other ways be beneficial to the species. But let the destruction of the adults be ever so heavy, if the number which can exist in any district be not wholly kept down by such causes,—or again let the destruction of eggs or seeds be so great that only a hundredth or a thousandth part are developed, yet of those which do survive, the best adapted individuals, supposing that there is any variability in a favourable direction, will tend to propagate their kind in larger numbers than the less well adapted. If the numbers be wholly kept down by the causes just indicated, as will often have been the case, natural selection will be powerless in certain beneficial directions; but this is no valid objection to its efficiency at other times and in other ways; for we are far from having any reason to suppose that many species ever undergo modification and improvement at the same time in the same area.

Sexual Selection

Inasmuch as peculiarities often appear under domestication in one sex and become hereditarily attached to that sex, so no doubt it will be under nature. Thus it is rendered possible for the two sexes to be modified through natural selection in relation to different habits of life, as is sometimes the case; or for one sex to be modified in relation to the other sex, as commonly occurs. This leads me to say a few words on what I have called sexual selection. This form of selection depends, not on a struggle for existence in relation to other organic beings or to external conditions, but on a struggle between the individuals of one sex, generally the males, for the possession of the other sex. The result is not death to the unsuccessful competitor, but few or no offspring. Sexual selection is, therefore, less rigorous than natural selection. Generally, the most vigorous males, those which are best fitted for their places in nature, will leave most progeny. But in many cases victory depends not so much on general vigour, but on having special weapons, confined to the male sex. A hornless stag or spurless cock would have a poor chance of leaving numerous offspring. Sexual selection, by always allowing the victor to breed, might surely give indomitable courage, length of spur, and strength to the wing to strike in the spurred leg, in nearly the same manner as does the brutal cockfighter by the careful selection of his best cocks. How low in the scale of nature the law of battle descends I know not; male alligators have been described as fighting, bellowing, and whirling round, like Indians in a war-dance, for the possession of the females; male salmons have been observed fighting all day long; male stag-beetles sometimes bear wounds from the huge mandibles of other males; the males of certain hymenopterous insects have been frequently seen by that inimitable observer M. Fabre, fighting for a particular female who sits by, an apparently unconcerned beholder of the struggle, and then retires with the conqueror. The war is, perhaps, severest between the males of polygamous animals, and these seem oftenest provided with special weapons. The males of carnivorous animals are already well armed; though to them and to others, special means of defence may be given through means of sexual selection, as the mane of the lion, and the hooked jaw to the male salmon; for the shield may be as important for victory as the sword or spear.

Among birds, the contest is often of a more peaceful character. All those who have attended to the subject, believe that there is the severest rivalry between the males of many species to attract, by singing, the females. The rock-thrush of Guiana, birds of paradise, and some others, congregate, and successive males display with the most elaborate care, and show off in the best manner, their gorgeous plumage; they likewise perform strange antics before the females, which, standing by as spectators, at last choose the most attractive partner. Those who have closely attended to birds in confinement well know that they often take individual preferences and dislikes: thus Sir R. Heron has described how a pied peacock was eminently attractive to all his hen birds. I cannot here enter on the necessary details; but if man can in a short time give beauty and an elegant carriage to his bantams, according to his standard of beauty, I can see no good reason to doubt that female birds, by selecting, during thousands of generations, the most melodious or beautiful males, according to their standard of beauty, might produce a marked effect. Some well-known laws, with respect to the plumage of male and female birds, in comparison with the plumage of the young, can partly be explained through the action of sexual selection on variations occurring at different ages, and transmitted to the males alone or to both sexes at corresponding ages; but I have not space here to enter on this subject.

Thus it is, as I believe, that when the males and females of any animal have the same general habits of life, but differ in structure, colour, or ornament, such differences have been mainly caused by sexual selection: that is, by individual males having had, in successive generations, some slight advantage over other males, in their weapons, means of defence, or charms; which they have transmitted to their male offspring alone. Yet, I would not wish to attribute all sexual differences to this agency: for we see in our domestic animals peculiarities arising and becoming attached to the male sex, which apparently have not been augmented through selection by man. The tuft of hair on the breast of the wild turkey-cock cannot be of any use, and it is doubtful whether it can be ornamental in the eyes of the female bird; indeed, had the tuft appeared under domestication it would have been called a monstrosity.

Illustrations of the Action of Natural Selection, or the Survival of the Fittest

In order to make it clear how, as I believe, natural selection acts, I must beg permission to give one or two imaginary illustrations. Let us take the case of a wolf, which preys on various animals, securing some by craft, some by strength, and some by fleetness; and let us suppose that the fleetest prey, a deer for instance, had from any change in the country increased in numbers, or that other prey had decreased in numbers, during that season of the year when the wolf was hardest pressed for food. Under such circumstances the swiftest and slimmest wolves have the best chance of surviving, and so be preserved or selected, provided always that they retained strength to master their prey at this or some other period of the year, when they were compelled to prey on other animals. I can see no more reason to doubt that this would be the result, than that man should be able to improve the fleetness of his greyhounds by careful and methodical selection, or by that kind of unconscious selection which follows from each man trying to keep the best dogs without any thought of modifying the breed. I may add that, according to Mr. Pierce, there are two varieties of the wolf inhabiting the Catskill Mountains, in the United States, one with a light greyhound-like form, which pursues deer, and the other more bulky, with shorter legs, which more frequently attacks the shepherd's flocks.

* * *

It should not, however, be overlooked that certain rather strongly marked variations, which no one would rank as mere individual differences, frequently recur owing to a similar organisation being similarly acted on—of which fact numerous instances could be given with our domestic productions. In such cases, if the varying individual did not actually transmit to its offspring its newly-acquired character, it would undoubtedly transmit to them, as long as the existing conditions remained the same, a still stronger tendency to vary in the same manner. There can also be little doubt that the tendency to vary in the same manner has often been so strong that all the individuals of the same species have been similarly modified without the aid of any form of selection. Or only a third, fifth, or tenth part of the individuals may have been thus affected, of which fact several instances could be given. Thus Graba estimates that about one-fifth of the guillemots in the Faroe Islands consist of a variety so well marked, that it was formerly ranked as a distinct species under the name of Uria lacrymans. In cases of this kind, if the variation were of a beneficial nature, the original form would soon be supplanted by the modified form, through the survival of the fittest.

To the effects of intercrossing in eliminating variations of all kinds, I shall have to recur; but it may be here remarked that most animals and plants keep to their proper homes, and do not needlessly wander about; we see this even with migratory birds, which almost always return to the same spot. Consequently each newly-formed variety would generally be at first local, as seems to be the common rule with varieties in a state of nature; so that similarly modified individuals would soon exist in a small body together, and would often breed together. If the new variety were successful in its battle for life, it would slowly spread from a central district, competing with and conquering the unchanged individuals on the margins of an ever-increasing circle.

It may be worth while to give another and more complex illustration of the action of natural selection. Certain plants excrete sweet juice, apparently for the sake of eliminating something injurious from the sap: this is effected, for instance, by glands at the base of the stipules in some Leguminosae, and at the backs of the leaves of the common laurel. This juice, though small in quantity, is greedily sought by insects; but their visits do not in any way benefit the plant. Now, let us suppose that the juice or nectar was excreted from the inside of the flowers of a certain number of plants of any species. Insects in seeking the nectar would get dusted with pollen, and would often transport it from one flower to another. The flowers of two distinct individuals of the same species would thus get crossed; and the act of crossing, as can be fully proved, gives rise to vigorous seedlings, which consequently would have the best chance of flourishing and surviving. The plants which produced flowers with the largest glands or nectaries, excreting most nectar, would oftenest be visited by insects, and would oftenest be crossed; and so in the long-run would gain the upper hand and form a local variety. The flowers, also, which had their stamens and pistils placed, in relation to the size and habits of the particular insect which visited them, so as to favour in any degree the transportal of the pollen, would likewise be favoured. We might have taken the case of insects visiting flowers for the sake of collecting pollen instead of nectar; and as pollen is formed for the sole purpose of fertilisation, its destruction appears to be a simple loss to the plant; yet if a little pollen were carried, at first occasionally and then habitually, by the pollen-devouring insects from flower to flower, and a cross thus effected, although nine-tenths of the pollen were destroyed it might still be a great gain to the plant to be thus robbed; and the individuals which produced more and more pollen, and had larger anthers, would be selected.

When our plant, by the above process long continued, had been rendered highly attractive to insects, they would, unintentionally on their part, regularly carry pollen from flower to flower; and that they do this effectually I could easily show by many striking facts.

I will give only one, as likewise illustrating one step in the separation of the sexes of plants. Some holly-trees bear only male flowers, which have four stamens producing a rather small quantity of pollen, and a rudimentary pistil; other holly-trees bear only female flowers; these have a full-sized pistil, and four stamens with shrivelled anthers, in which not a grain of pollen can be detected. Having found a female tree exactly sixty yards from a male tree, I put the stigmas of twenty flowers, taken from different branches, under the microscope, and on all, without exception, there were a few pollen-grains, and on some a profusion. As the wind had set for several days from the female to the male tree, the pollen could not thus have been carried. The weather had been cold and boisterous and therefore not favourable to bees, nevertheless every female flower which I examined had been effectually fertilised by the bees, which had flown from tree to tree in search of nectar. But to return to our imaginary case; as soon as the plant had been rendered so highly attractive to insects that pollen was regularly carried from flower to flower, another process might commence. No naturalist doubts the advantage of what has been called the "physiological division of labour;" hence we may believe that it would be advantageous to a plant to produce stamens alone in one flower or on one whole plant, and pistils alone in another flower or on another plant. In plants under culture and placed under new conditions of life, sometimes the male organs and sometimes the female organs become more or less impotent; now if we suppose this to occur in ever so slight a degree under nature, then, as pollen is already carried regularly from flower to flower, and as a more complete separation of the sexes of our plant would be advantageous on the principle of the division of labour, individuals with this tendency more and more increased, would be continually favoured or selected, until at last a complete separation of the sexes might be effected. It would take up too much space to show the various steps, through dimorphism and other means, by which the separation of the sexes in plants of various kinds is apparently now in progress; but I may add that some of the species of holly in North America are, according to Asa Gray, in an exactly intermediate condition, or, as he expresses it, are more or less dioeciously polygamous.

Let us now turn to the nectar-feeding insects; we may suppose the plant of which we have been slowly increasing the nectar by continued selection, to be a common plant; and that certain insects depended in main part on its nectar for food. I could give many facts showing how anxious bees are to save time: for instance, their habit of cutting holes and sucking the nectar at the bases of certain flowers, which with a very little more trouble they can enter by the mouth. Bearing such facts in mind, it may be believed that under certain circumstances individual differences in the curvature or length of the proboscis, etc., too slight to be appreciated by us, might profit a bee or other insect, so that certain individuals would be able to obtain their food more quickly than others; and thus the communities to which they belonged would flourish and throw off many swarms inheriting the same peculiarities. The tubes of the corolla of the common red or incarnate clovers (Trifolium pratense and incarnatum) do not on a hasty glance appear to differ in length; yet the hive-bee can easily suck the nectar out of the incarnate clover, but not out of the common red clover, which is visited by humble-bees alone; so that whole fields of the red clover offer in vain an abundant supply of precious nectar to the hive-bee. That this nectar is much liked by the hive-bee is certain; for I have repeatedly seen, but only in the autumn, many hive-bees sucking the flowers through holes bitten in the base of the tube by humble-bees. The difference in the length of the corolla in the two kinds of clover, which determines the visits of the hive-bee, must be very trifling; for I have been assured that when red clover has been mown, the flowers of the second crop are somewhat smaller, and that these are visited by many hive-bees. I do not know whether this statement is accurate; nor whether another published statement can be trusted, namely, that the Ligurian bee, which is generally considered a mere variety of the common hive-bee, and which freely crosses with it, is able to reach and suck the nectar of the red clover. Thus, in a country where this kind of clover abounded, it might be a great advantage to the hive-bee to have a slightly longer or differently constructed proboscis. On the other hand, as the fertility of this clover absolutely depends on bees visiting the flowers, if humble-bees were to become rare in any country, it might be a great advantage to the plant to have a shorter or more deeply divided corolla, so that the hive-bees should be enabled to suck its flowers. Thus I can understand how a flower and a bee might slowly become, either simultaneously or one after the other, modified and adapted to each other in the most perfect manner, by the continued preservation of all the individuals which presented slight deviations of structure mutually favourable to each other.

I am well aware that this doctrine of natural selection, exemplified in the above imaginary instances, is open to the same objections which were first urged against Sir Charles Lyell's noble views on "the modern changes of the earth, as illustrative of geology;" but we now seldom hear the agencies which we see still at work, spoken of as trifling and insignificant, when used in explaining the excavation of the deepest valleys or the formation of long lines of inland cliffs. Natural selection acts only by the preservation and accumulation of small inherited modifications, each profitable to the preserved being; and as modern geology has almost banished such views as the excavation of a great valley by a single diluvial wave, so will natural selection banish the belief of the continued creation of new organic beings, or of any great and sudden modification in their structure.

* * *

Circumstances Favourable for the Production of New Forms Through Natural Selection

This is an extremely intricate subject. A great amount of variability, under which term individual differences are always included, will evidently be favourable. A large number of individuals, by giving a better chance within any given period for the appearance of profitable variations, will compensate for a lesser amount of variability in each individual, and is, I believe, a highly important element of success. Though nature grants long periods of time for the work of natural selection, she does not grant an indefinite period; for as all organic beings are striving to seize on each place in the economy of nature, if any one species does not become modified and improved in a corresponding degree with its competitors it will be exterminated. Unless favourable variations be inherited by some at least of the offspring, nothing can be effected by natural selection. The tendency to reversion may often check or prevent the work; but as this tendency has not prevented man from forming by selection numerous domestic races, why should it prevail against natural selection?

In the case of methodical selection, a breeder selects for some definite object, and if the individuals be allowed freely to intercross, his work will completely fail. But when many men, without intending to alter the breed, have a nearly common standard of perfection, and all try to procure and breed from the best animals, improvement surely but slowly follows from this unconscious process of selection, notwithstanding that there is no separation of selected individuals. Thus it will be under nature; for within a confined area, with some place in the natural polity not perfectly occupied, all the individuals varying in the right direction, though in different degrees, will tend to be preserved. But if the area be large, its several districts will almost certainly present different conditions of life; and then, if the same species undergoes modification in different districts, the newly formed varieties will intercross on the confines of each. But we shall see in the sixth chapter that intermediate varieties, inhabiting intermediate districts, will in the long run generally be supplanted by one of the adjoining varieties. Intercrossing will chiefly affect those animals which unite for each birth and wander much, and which do not breed at a very quick rate. Hence with animals of this nature, for instance birds, varieties will generally be confined to separated countries; and this I find to be the case. With hermaphrodite organisms which cross only occasionally, and likewise with animals which unite for each birth, but which wander little and can increase at a rapid rate, a new and improved variety might be quickly formed on any one spot, and might there maintain itself in a body and afterward spread, so that the individuals of the new variety would chiefly cross together. On this principle nurserymen always prefer saving seed from a large body of plants, as the chance of intercrossing is thus lessened.

Even with animals which unite for each birth, and which do not propagate rapidly, we must not assume that free intercrossing would always eliminate the effects of natural selection; for I can bring forward a considerable body of facts showing that within the same area two varieties of the same animal may long remain distinct, from haunting different stations, from breeding at slightly different seasons, or from the individuals of each variety preferring to pair together.

Intercrossing plays a very important part in nature by keeping the individuals of the same species, or of the same variety, true and uniform in character. It will obviously thus act far more efficiently with those animals which unite for each birth; but, as already stated, we have reason to believe that occasional intercrosses take place with all animals and plants. Even if these take place only at long intervals of time, the young thus produced will gain so much in vigour and fertility over the offspring from long-continued self-fertilisation, that they will have a better chance of surviving and propagating their kind; and thus in the long run the influence of crosses, even at rare intervals, will be great. With respect to organic beings extremely low in the scale, which do not propagate sexually, nor conjugate, and which cannot possibly intercross, uniformity of character can be retained by them under the same conditions of life, only through the principle of inheritance, and through natural selection which will destroy any individuals departing from the proper type. If the conditions of life change and the form undergoes modification, uniformity of character can be given to the modified offspring, solely by natural selection preserving similar favourable variations.

Isolation also is an important element in the modification of species through natural selection. In a confined or isolated area, if not very large, the organic and inorganic conditions of life will generally be almost uniform; so that natural selection will tend to modify all the varying individuals of the same species in the same manner. Intercrossing with the inhabitants of the surrounding districts, will also be thus prevented. Moritz Wagner has lately published an interesting essay on this subject, and has shown that the service rendered by isolation in preventing crosses between newly-formed varieties is probably greater even than I supposed. But from reasons already assigned I can by no means agree with this naturalist, that migration and isolation are necessary elements for the formation of new species. The importance of isolation is likewise great in preventing, after any physical change in the conditions, such as of climate, elevation of the land, etc., the immigration of better adapted organisms; and thus new places in the natural economy of the district will be left open to be filled up by the modification of the old inhabitants. Lastly, isolation will give time for a new variety to be improved at a slow rate; and this may sometimes be of much importance. If, however, an isolated area be very small, either from being surrounded by barriers, or from having very peculiar physical conditions, the total number of the inhabitants will be small; and this will retard the production of new species through natural selection, by decreasing the chances of favourable variations arising.

The mere lapse of time by itself does nothing, either for or against natural selection. I state this because it has been erroneously asserted that the element of time has been assumed by me to play an all-important part in modifying species, as if all the forms of life were necessarily undergoing change through some innate law. Lapse of time is only so far important, and its importance in this respect is great, that it gives a better chance of beneficial variations arising and of their being selected, accumulated, and fixed. It likewise tends to increase the direct action of the physical conditions of life, in relation to the constitution of each organism.

If we turn to nature to test the truth of these remarks, and look at any small isolated area, such as an oceanic island, although the number of the species inhabiting it is small, as we shall see in our chapter on Geographical Distribution; yet of these species a very large proportion are endemic,—that is, have been produced there and nowhere else in the world. Hence an oceanic island at first sight seems to have been highly favourable for the production of new species. But we may thus deceive ourselves, for to ascertain whether a small isolated area, or a large open area like a continent, has been most favourable for the production of new organic forms, we ought to make the comparison within equal times; and this we are incapable of doing.

Although isolation is of great importance in the production of new species, on the whole I am inclined to believe that largeness of area is still more important, especially for the production of species which shall prove capable of enduring for a long period, and of spreading widely. Throughout a great and open area, not only will there be a better chance of favourable variations, arising from the large number of individuals of the same species there supported, but the conditions of life are much more complex from the large number of already existing species; and if some of these many species become modified and improved, others will have to be improved in a corresponding degree, or they will be exterminated. Each new form, also, as soon as it has been much improved, will be able to spread over the open and continuous area, and will thus come into competition with many other forms. Moreover, great areas, though now continuous, will often, owing to former oscillations of level, have existed in a broken condition, so that the good effects of isolation will generally, to a certain extent, have concurred. Finally, I conclude that, although small isolated areas have been in some respects highly favourable for the production of new species, yet that the course of modification will generally have been more rapid on large areas; and what is more important, that the new forms produced on large areas, which already have been victorious over many competitors, will be those that will spread most widely, and will give rise to the greatest number of new varieties and species. They will thus play a more important part in the changing history of the organic world.

* * *

To sum up, as far as the extreme intricacy of the subject permits, the circumstances favourable and unfavourable for the production of new species through natural selection. I conclude that for terrestrial productions a large continental area, which has undergone many oscillations of level, will have been the most favourable for the production of many new forms of life, fitted to endure for a long time and to spread widely. While the area existed as a continent the inhabitants will have been numerous in individuals and kinds, and will have been subjected to severe competition. When converted by subsidence into large separate islands there will still have existed many individuals of the same species on each island: intercrossing on the confines of the range of each new species will have been checked: after physical changes of any kind immigration will have been prevented, so that new places in the polity of each island will have had to be filled up by the modification of the old inhabitants; and time will have been allowed for the varieties in each to become well modified and perfected. When, by renewed elevation, the islands were reconverted into a continental area, there will again have been very severe competition; the most favoured or improved varieties will have been enabled to spread; there will have been much extinction of the less improved forms, and the relative proportional numbers of the various inhabitants of the reunited continent will again have been changed; and again there will have been a fair field for natural selection to improve still further the inhabitants, and thus to produce new species.

That natural selection generally acts with extreme slowness I fully admit. It can act only when there are places in the natural polity of a district which can be better occupied by the modification of some of its existing inhabitants. The occurrence of such places will often depend on physical changes, which generally take place very slowly, and on the immigration of better adapted forms being prevented. As some few of the old inhabitants become modified the mutual relations of others will often be disturbed; and this will create new places, ready to be filled up by better adapted forms; but all this will take place very slowly. Although all the individuals of the same species differ in some slight degree from each other, it would often be long before differences of the right nature in various parts of the organisation might occur. The result would often be greatly retarded by free intercrossing. Many will exclaim that these several causes are amply sufficient to neutralise the power of natural selection. I do not believe so. But I do believe that natural selection will generally act very slowly, only at long intervals of time, and only on a few of the inhabitants of the same region. I further believe that these slow, intermittent results accord well with what geology tells us of the rate and manner at which the inhabitants of the world have changed.

Slow though the process of selection may be, if feeble man can do much by artificial selection, I can see no limit to the amount of change, to the beauty and complexity of the coadaptations between all organic beings, one with another and with their physical conditions of life, which may have been effected in the long course of time through nature's power of selection, that is by the survival of the fittest.

Extinction Caused By Natural Selection

This subject will be more fully discussed in our chapter on Geology; but it must here be alluded to from being intimately connected with natural selection. Natural selection acts solely through the preservation of variations in some way advantageous, which consequently endure. Owing to the high geometrical rate of increase of all organic beings, each area is already fully stocked with inhabitants, and it follows from this, that as the favoured forms increase in number, so, generally, will the less favoured decrease and become rare. Rarity, as geology tells us, is the precursor to extinction. We can see that any form which is represented by few individuals will run a good chance of utter extinction, during great fluctuations in the nature or the seasons, or from a temporary increase in the number of its enemies. But we may go further than this; for as new forms are produced, unless we admit that specific forms can go on indefinitely increasing in number, many old forms must become extinct. That the number of specific forms has not indefinitely increased, geology plainly tells us; and we shall presently attempt to show why it is that the number of species throughout the world has not become immeasurably great.

We have seen that the species which are most numerous in individuals have the best chance of producing favourable variations within any given period. We have evidence of this, in the facts stated in the second chapter, showing that it is the common and diffused or dominant species which offer the greatest number of recorded varieties. Hence, rare species will be less quickly modified or improved within any given period; they will consequently be beaten in the race for life by the modified and improved descendants of the commoner species.

From these several considerations I think it inevitably follows, that as new species in the course of time are formed through natural selection, others will become rarer and rarer, and finally extinct. The forms which stand in closest competition with those undergoing modification and improvement, will naturally suffer most. And we have seen in the chapter on the Struggle for Existence that it is the most closely-allied forms,—varieties of the same species, and species of the same genus or related genera,—which, from having nearly the same structure, constitution and habits, generally come into the severest competition with each other. Consequently, each new variety or species, during the progress of its formation, will generally press hardest on its nearest kindred, and tend to exterminate them. We see the same process of extermination among our domesticated productions, through the selection of improved forms by man. Many curious instances could be given showing how quickly new breeds of cattle, sheep and other animals, and varieties of flowers, take the place of older and inferior kinds. In Yorkshire, it is historically known that the ancient black cattle were displaced by the long-horns, and that these "were swept away by the short-horns" (I quote the words of an agricultural writer) "as if by some murderous pestilence."

Divergence of Character

The principle, which I have designated by this term, is of high importance, and explains, as I believe, several important facts. In the first place, varieties, even strongly-marked ones, though having somewhat of the character of species—as is shown by the hopeless doubts in many cases how to rank them—yet certainly differ far less from each other than do good and distinct species. Nevertheless according to my view, varieties are species in the process of formation, or are, as I have called them, incipient species. How, then, does the lesser difference between varieties become augmented into the greater difference between species? That this does habitually happen, we must infer from most of the innumerable species throughout nature presenting well-marked differences; whereas varieties, the supposed prototypes and parents of future well-marked species, present slight and ill-defined differences. Mere chance, as we may call it, might cause one variety to differ in some character from its parents, and the offspring of this variety again to differ from its parent in the very same character and in a greater degree; but this alone would never account for so habitual and large a degree of difference as that between the species of the same genus.

As has always been my practice, I have sought light on this head from our domestic productions. We shall here find something analogous. It will be admitted that the production of races so different as short-horn and Hereford cattle, race and cart horses, the several breeds of pigeons, etc., could never have been effected by the mere chance accumulation of similar variations during many successive generations. In practice, a fancier is, for instance, struck by a pigeon having a slightly shorter beak; another fancier is struck by a pigeon having a rather longer beak; and on the acknowledged principle that "fanciers do not and will not admire a medium standard, but like extremes," they both go on (as has actually occurred with the sub-breeds of the tumbler-pigeon) choosing and breeding from birds with longer and longer beaks, or with shorter and shorter beaks. Again, we may suppose that at an early period of history, the men of one nation or district required swifter horses, while those of another required stronger and bulkier horses. The early differences would be very slight; but, in the course of time, from the continued selection of swifter horses in the one case, and of stronger ones in the other, the differences would become greater, and would be noted as forming two sub-breeds. Ultimately after the lapse of centuries, these sub-breeds would become converted into two well-established and distinct breeds. As the differences became greater, the inferior animals with intermediate characters, being neither very swift nor very strong, would not have been used for breeding, and will thus have tended to disappear. Here, then, we see in man's productions the action of what may be called the principle of divergence, causing differences, at first barely appreciable, steadily to increase, and the breeds to diverge in character, both from each other and from their common parent.

But how, it may be asked, can any analogous principle apply in nature? I believe it can and does apply most efficiently (though it was a long time before I saw how), from the simple circumstance that the more diversified the descendants from any one species become in structure, constitution, and habits, by so much will they be better enabled to seize on many and widely diversified places in the polity of nature, and so be enabled to increase in numbers.

We can clearly discern this in the case of animals with simple habits. Take the case of a carnivorous quadruped, of which the number that can be supported in any country has long ago arrived at its full average. If its natural power of increase be allowed to act, it can succeed in increasing (the country not undergoing any change in conditions) only by its varying descendants seizing on places at present occupied by other animals: some of them, for instance, being enabled to feed on new kinds of prey, either dead or alive; some inhabiting new stations, climbing trees, frequenting water, and some perhaps becoming less carnivorous. The more diversified in habits and structure the descendants of our carnivorous animals become, the more places they will be enabled to occupy. What applies to one animal will apply throughout all time to all animals—that is, if they vary—for otherwise natural selection can effect nothing. So it will be with plants. It has been experimentally proved, that if a plot of ground be sown with one species of grass, and a similar plot be sown with several distinct genera of grasses, a greater number of plants and a greater weight of dry herbage can be raised in the latter than in the former case. The same has been found to hold good when one variety and several mixed varieties of wheat have been sown on equal spaces of ground. Hence, if any one species of grass were to go on varying, and the varieties were continually selected which differed from each other in the same manner, though in a very slight degree, as do the distinct species and genera of grasses, a greater number of individual plants of this species, including its modified descendants, would succeed in living on the same piece of ground. And we know that each species and each variety of grass is annually sowing almost countless seeds; and is thus striving, as it may be said, to the utmost to increase in number. Consequently, in the course of many thousand generations, the most distinct varieties of any one species of grass would have the best chance of succeeding and of increasing in numbers, and thus of supplanting the less distinct varieties; and varieties, when rendered very distinct from each other, take the rank of species.

The truth of the principle that the greatest amount of life can be supported by great diversification of structure, is seen under many natural circumstances. In an extremely small area, especially if freely open to immigration, and where the contest between individual and individual must be very severe, we always find great diversity in its inhabitants. For instance, I found that a piece of turf, three feet by four in size, which had been exposed for many years to exactly the same conditions, supported twenty species of plants, and these belonged to eighteen genera and to eight orders, which shows how much these plants differed from each other. So it is with the plants and insects on small and uniform islets: also in small ponds of fresh water. Farmers find that they can raise more food by a rotation of plants belonging to the most different orders: nature follows what may be called a simultaneous rotation. Most of the animals and plants which live close round any small piece of ground, could live on it (supposing its nature not to be in any way peculiar), and may be said to be striving to the utmost to live there; but, it is seen, that where they come into the closest competition, the advantages of diversification of structure, with the accompanying differences of habit and constitution, determine that the inhabitants, which thus jostle each other most closely, shall, as a general rule, belong to what we call different genera and orders.

The same principle is seen in the naturalisation of plants through man's agency in foreign lands. It might have been expected that the plants which would succeed in becoming naturalised in any land would generally have been closely allied to the indigenes; for these are commonly looked at as specially created and adapted for their own country. It might also, perhaps, have been expected that naturalised plants would have belonged to a few groups more especially adapted to certain stations in their new homes. But the case is very different; and Alph. de Candolle has well remarked, in his great and admirable work, that floras gain by naturalisation, proportionally with the number of the native genera and species, far more in new genera than in new species. To give a single instance: in the last edition of Dr. Asa Gray's "Manual of the Flora of the Northern United States," 260 naturalised plants are enumerated, and these belong to 162 genera. We thus see that these naturalised plants are of a highly diversified nature. They differ, moreover, to a large extent, from the indigenes, for out of the 162 naturalised genera, no less than 100 genera are not there indigenous, and thus a large proportional addition is made to the genera now living in the United States.

By considering the nature of the plants or animals which have in any country struggled successfully with the indigenes, and have there become naturalised, we may gain some crude idea in what manner some of the natives would have had to be modified in order to gain an advantage over their compatriots; and we may at least infer that diversification of structure, amounting to new generic differences, would be profitable to them.

The advantage of diversification of structure in the inhabitants of the same region is, in fact, the same as that of the physiological division of labour in the organs of the same individual body—a subject so well elucidated by Milne Edwards. No physiologist doubts that a stomach by being adapted to digest vegetable matter alone, or flesh alone, draws most nutriment from these substances. So in the general economy of any land, the more widely and perfectly the animals and plants are diversified for different habits of life, so will a greater number of individuals be capable of there supporting themselves. A set of animals, with their organisation but little diversified, could hardly compete with a set more perfectly diversified in structure. It may be doubted, for instance, whether the Australian marsupials, which are divided into groups differing but little from each other, and feebly representing, as Mr. Waterhouse and others have remarked, our carnivorous, ruminant, and rodent mammals, could successfully compete with these well-developed orders. In the Australian mammals, we see the process of diversification in an early and incomplete stage of development.

The Probable Effects of the Action of Natural Selection Through Divergence of Character and Extinction, On the Descendants of a Common Ancestor

After the foregoing discussion, which has been much compressed, we may assume that the modified descendants of any one species will succeed so much the better as they become more diversified in structure, and are thus enabled to encroach on places occupied by other beings. Now let us see how this principle of benefit being derived from divergence of character, combined with the principles of natural selection and of extinction, tends to act.

The accompanying diagram will aid us in understanding this rather perplexing subject. Let A to L represent the species of a genus large in its own country; these species are supposed to resemble each other in unequal degrees, as is so generally the case in nature, and as is represented in the diagram by the letters standing at unequal distances. I have said a large genus, because as we saw in the second chapter, on an average more species vary in large genera than in small genera; and the varying species of the large genera pre-

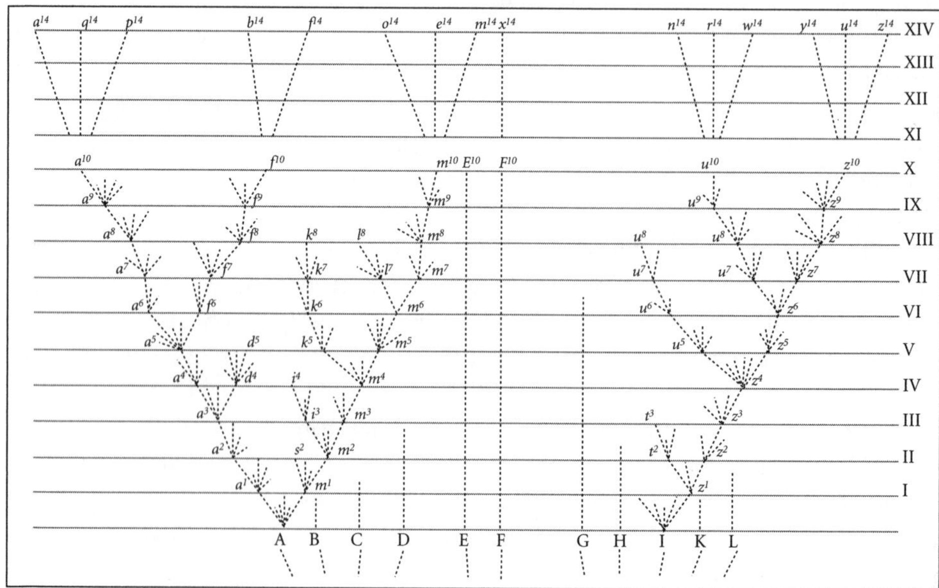

sent a greater number of varieties. We have, also, seen that the species, which are the commonest and most widely-diffused, vary more than do the rare and restricted species. Let (A) be a common, widely-diffused, and varying species, belonging to a genus large in its own country. The branching and diverging dotted lines of unequal lengths proceeding from (A), may represent its varying offspring. The variations are supposed to be extremely slight, but of the most diversified nature; they are not supposed all to appear simultaneously, but often after long intervals of time; nor are they all supposed to endure for equal periods. Only those variations which are in some way profitable will be preserved or naturally selected. And here the importance of the principle of benefit derived from divergence of character comes in; for this will generally lead to the most different or divergent variations (represented by the outer dotted lines) being preserved and accumulated by natural selection. When a dotted line reaches one of the horizontal lines, and is there marked by a small numbered letter, a sufficient amount of variation is supposed to have been accumulated to form it into a fairly well-marked variety, such as would be thought worthy of record in a systematic work.

The intervals between the horizontal lines in the diagram, may represent each a thousand or more generations. After a thousand generations, species (A) is supposed to have produced two fairly well-marked varieties, namely a^1 and m^1. These two varieties will generally still be exposed to the same conditions which made their parents variable, and the tendency to variability is in itself hereditary; consequently they will likewise tend to vary, and commonly in nearly the same manner as did their parents. Moreover, these two varieties, being only slightly modified forms, will tend to inherit those advantages which made their parent (A) more numerous than most of the other inhabitants of the same country; they will also partake of those more general advantages which made the genus to which the parent-species belonged, a large genus in its own country. And all these circumstances are favourable to the production of new varieties.

If, then, these two varieties be variable, the most divergent of their variations will generally be preserved during the next thousand generations. And after this interval, variety a^1 is supposed in the diagram to have produced variety a^2, which will, owing to the principle of divergence, differ more from (A) than did variety a^1. Variety m^1 is supposed to have produced two varieties, namely m^2 and s^2, differing from each other, and more considerably from their common parent (A). We may continue the process by similar steps for any length of time; some of the varieties, after each thousand generations, producing only a single variety, but in a more and more modified condition, some producing two or three varieties, and some failing to produce any. Thus the varieties or modified descendants of the common parent (A), will generally go on increasing in number and diverging in character. In the diagram the process is represented up to the ten-thousandth generation, and under a condensed and simplified form up to the fourteen-thousandth generation.

But I must here remark that I do not suppose that the process ever goes on so regularly as is represented in the diagram, though in itself made somewhat irregular, nor that it goes on continuously; it is far more probable that each form remains for long periods unaltered, and then again undergoes modification. Nor do I suppose that the most divergent varieties are invariably preserved: a medium form may often long endure, and may or may not produce more than one modified descendant; for natural selection will always act according to the nature of the places which are either unoccupied or not perfectly occupied by other beings; and this will depend on infinitely complex relations. But as a general rule, the more diversified in structure the descendants from any one species can be rendered, the more places they will be enabled to seize on, and the more their modified progeny will increase. In our diagram the line of succession is broken at regular intervals by small numbered letters marking the successive forms which have become sufficiently distinct to be recorded as varieties. But these breaks are imaginary, and might have been inserted anywhere, after intervals long enough to allow the accumulation of a considerable amount of divergent variation.

As all the modified descendants from a common and widely-diffused species, belonging to a large genus, will tend to partake of the same advantages which made their parent successful in life, they will generally go on multiplying in number as well as diverging in character: this is represented in the diagram by the several divergent branches proceeding from (A). The modified offspring from the later and more highly improved branches in the lines of descent, will, it is probable, often take the place of, and so destroy, the earlier and less improved branches: this is represented in the diagram by some of the lower branches not reaching to the upper horizontal lines. In some cases no doubt the process of modification will be confined to a single line of descent, and the number of modified descendants will not be increased; although the amount of divergent modification may have been augmented. This case would be represented in the diagram, if all the lines proceeding from (A) were removed, excepting that from a^1 to a^{10}. In the same way the English racehorse and English pointer have apparently both gone on slowly diverging in character from their original stocks, without either having given off any fresh branches or races.

After ten thousand generations, species (A) is supposed to have produced three forms, a^{10}, f^{10}, and m^{10}, which, from having diverged in character during the successive generations, will have come to differ largely, but perhaps unequally, from each other and from their common parent. If we suppose the amount of change between each horizontal line in our diagram to be excessively small, these three forms may still be only well-marked varieties; but we have only to suppose the steps in the process of modification to be more numerous or greater in amount, to convert these three forms into doubtful or at least into well-defined species: thus the diagram illustrates the steps by which the small differences distinguishing varieties are increased into the larger differences distinguishing species. By continuing the same process for a greater number of generations (as shown in the diagram in a condensed and simplified manner), we get eight species, marked by the letters between a^{14} and m^{14}, all descended from (A). Thus, as I believe, species are multiplied and genera are formed.

In a large genus it is probable that more than one species would vary. In the diagram I have assumed that a second species (I) has produced, by analogous steps, after ten thousand generations, either two well-marked varieties (w^{10} and z^{10}) or two species, according to the amount of change supposed to be represented between the horizontal lines. After fourteen thousand generations, six new species, marked by the letters n^{14} to z^{14}, are supposed to have been produced. In any genus, the species which are already very different in character from each other, will generally tend to produce the greatest number of modified descendants; for these will have the best chance of seizing on new and widely different places in the polity of nature: hence in the diagram I have chosen the extreme species (A), and the nearly extreme species (I), as those which have largely varied, and have given rise to new varieties and species. The other nine species (marked by capital letters) of our original genus, may for long but unequal periods continue to transmit unaltered descendants; and this is shown in the diagram by the dotted lines unequally prolonged upwards.

But during the process of modification, represented in the diagram, another of our principles, namely that of extinction, will have played an important part. As in each fully stocked country natural selection necessarily acts by the selected form having some advantage in the struggle for life over other forms, there will be a constant tendency in the improved descendants of any one species to supplant and exterminate in each stage of descent their predecessors and their original progenitor. For it should be remembered that the competition will generally be most severe between those forms which are most nearly related to each other in habits, constitution and structure. Hence all the intermediate forms between the earlier and later states, that is between the less and more improved states of a the same species, as well as the original parent-species itself, will generally tend to become extinct. So it probably will be with many whole collateral lines of descent, which will be conquered by later and improved lines. If, however, the modified offspring of a species get into some distinct country, or become quickly adapted to some quite new station, in which offspring and progenitor do not come into competition, both may continue to exist.

If, then, our diagram be assumed to represent a considerable amount of modification, species (A) and all the earlier varieties will have become extinct, being replaced by eight new species (a^{14} to m^{14}); and species (I) will be replaced by six (n^{14} to z^{14}) new species.

But we may go further than this. The original species of our genus were supposed to resemble each other in unequal degrees, as is so generally the case in nature; species (A) being more nearly related to B, C, and D than to the other species; and species (I) more to G, H, K, L, than to the others. These two species (A and I), were also supposed to be very common and widely diffused species, so that they must originally have had some advantage over most of the other species of the genus. Their modified descendants, fourteen in number at the fourteen-thousandth generation, will probably have inherited some of the same advantages: they have also been modified and improved in a diversified manner at each stage of descent, so as to have become adapted to many related places in the natural economy of their country. It seems, therefore, extremely probable that they will have taken the places of, and thus exterminated, not only their parents (A) and (I), but likewise some of the original species which were most nearly related to their parents. Hence very few of the original species will have transmitted offspring to the fourteen-thousandth generation. We may suppose that only one (F) of the two species (E and F) which were least closely related to the other nine original species, has transmitted descendants to this late stage of descent.

The new species in our diagram, descended from the original eleven species, will now be fifteen in number. Owing to the divergent tendency of natural selection, the extreme amount of difference in character between species a^{14} and z^{14} will be much greater than that between the most distinct of the original eleven species. The new species, moreover, will be allied to each other in a widely different manner. Of the eight descendants from (A) the three marked a^{14}, q^{14}, p^{14}, will be nearly related from having recently branched off from a^{10}, b^{14} and f^{14}, from having diverged at an earlier period from a^5, will be in some degree distinct from the three first-named species; and lastly, o^{14}, e^{14}, and m^{14}, will be nearly related one to the other, but, from having diverged at the first commencement of the process of modification, will be widely different from the other five species, and may constitute a sub-genus or a distinct genus.

The six descendants from (I) will form two sub-genera or genera. But as the original species (I) differed largely from (A), standing nearly at the extreme end of the original genus, the six descendants from (I) will, owing to inheritance alone, differ considerably from the eight descendants from (A); the two groups, moreover, are supposed to have gone on diverging in different directions. The intermediate species, also (and this is a very important consideration), which connected the original species (A) and (I), have all become, except (F), extinct, and have left no descendants. Hence the six new species descended from (I), and the eight descendants from (A), will have to be ranked as very distinct genera, or even as distinct sub-families.

Thus it is, as I believe, that two or more genera are produced by descent with modification, from two or more species of the same genus. And the two or more parent-species are supposed to be descended from some one species of an earlier genus. In our diagram this is indicated by the broken lines beneath the capital letters, converging in sub-branches downwards towards a single point; this point represents a species, the supposed progenitor of our several new sub-genera and genera.

It is worthwhile to reflect for a moment on the character of the new species F^{14}, which is supposed not to have diverged much in character, but to have retained the form of (F), either unaltered or altered only in a slight degree. In this case its affinities to the other fourteen new species will be of a curious and circuitous nature. Being descended from a form that stood between the parent-species (A) and (I), now supposed to be extinct and unknown, it will be in some degree intermediate in character between the two groups descended from these two species. But as these two groups have gone on diverging in character from the type of their parents, the new species (F^{14}) will not be directly intermediate between them, but rather between types of the two groups; and every naturalist will be able to call such cases before his mind.

In the diagram each horizontal line has hitherto been supposed to represent a thousand generations, but each may represent a million or more generations; it may also represent a section of the successive strata of the earth's crust including extinct remains. We shall, when we come to our chapter on geology, have to refer again to this subject, and I think we shall then see that the diagram throws light on the affinities of extinct beings, which, though generally belonging to the same orders, families, or genera, with those now living, yet are often, in some degree, intermediate in character between existing groups; and we can understand this fact, for the extinct species lived at various remote epochs when the branching lines of descent had diverged less.

I see no reason to limit the process of modification, as now explained, to the formation of genera alone. If, in the diagram, we suppose the amount of change represented by each successive group of diverging dotted lines to be great, the forms marked a^{14} to p^{14}, those marked b^{14} and f^{14}, and those marked o^{14} to m^{14}, will form three very distinct genera. We shall also have two very distinct genera descended from (I), differing widely from the descendants of (A). These two groups of genera will thus form two distinct families, or orders, according to the amount of divergent modification supposed to be represented in the diagram. And the two new families, or orders, are descended from two species of the original genus; and these are supposed to be descended from some still more ancient and unknown form.

We have seen that in each country it is the species belonging to the larger genera which oftenest present varieties or incipient species. This, indeed, might have been expected; for as natural selection acts through one form having some advantage over other forms in the struggle for existence, it will chiefly act on those which already have some advantage; and the largeness of any group shows that its species have inherited from a common ancestor some advantage in common. Hence, the struggle for the production of new and modified descendants will mainly lie between the larger groups, which are all trying to increase in number. One large group will slowly conquer another large group, reduce its number, and thus lessen its chance of further variation and improvement. Within the same large group, the later and more highly perfected sub-groups, from branching out and seizing on many new places in the polity of nature, will constantly tend to supplant and destroy the earlier and less improved sub-groups. Small and broken groups and sub-groups will finally disappear. Looking to the future, we can predict that the groups of organic beings which are now large and triumphant, and which are least broken up, that is, which have as yet suffered least extinction, will, for a long period, continue to increase. But which groups will ultimately prevail, no man can predict; for we know that many groups, formerly most extensively developed, have now become extinct. Looking still more remotely to the future, we may predict that, owing to the continued and steady increase of the larger groups, a multitude of smaller groups will become utterly extinct, and leave no modified descendants; and consequently that, of the species living at any one period, extremely few will transmit descendants to a remote futurity. I shall have to return to this subject in the chapter on Classification, but I may add that as, according to this view, extremely few of the more ancient species have transmitted descendants to the present day, and, as all the descendants of the same species form a class, we can understand how it is that there exist so few classes in each main division of the animal and vegetable kingdoms. Although few of the most ancient species have left modified descendants, yet, at remote geological periods, the earth may have been almost as well peopled with species of many genera, families, orders and classes, as at the present day.

On the Degree to Which Organisation Tends to Advance

Natural selection acts exclusively by the preservation and accumulation of variations, which are beneficial under the organic and inorganic conditions to which each creature is exposed at all periods of life. The ultimate result is that each creature tends to become more and more improved in relation to its conditions. This improvement inevitably leads to the gradual advancement of the organisation of the greater number of living beings throughout the world. But here we enter on a very intricate subject, for naturalists have not defined to each other's satisfaction what is meant by an advance in organisation. Among the vertebrata the degree of intellect and an approach in structure to man clearly come into play. It might be thought that the amount of change which the various parts and organs pass through in their development from embryo to maturity would suffice as a standard of comparison; but there are cases, as with certain parasitic crustaceans, in which several parts of the structure become less perfect, so that the mature animal cannot be called higher than its larva. Von Baer's standard seems the most widely applicable and the best, namely, the amount of differentiation of the parts of the same organic being, in the adult state, as I should be inclined to add, and their specialisation for different functions; or, as Milne Edwards would express it, the completeness of the division of physiological labour. But we shall see how obscure this subject is if we look, for instance, to fishes, among which some naturalists rank those as highest which, like the sharks, approach nearest to amphibians; while other naturalists rank the common bony or teleostean fishes as the highest, inasmuch as they are most strictly fish-like, and differ most from the other vertebrate classes. We see still more plainly the obscurity of the subject by turning to plants, among which the standard of intellect is of course quite excluded; and here some botanists rank those plants as highest which have every organ, as sepals, petals, stamens and pistils, fully developed in each flower; whereas other botanists, probably with more truth, look at the plants which have their several organs much modified and reduced in number as the highest.

If we take as the standard of high organisation, the amount of differentiation and specialisation of the several organs in each being when adult (and this will include the advancement of the brain for intellectual purposes), natural selection clearly leads towards this standard: for all physiologists admit that the specialisation of organs, inasmuch as in this state they perform their functions better, is an advantage to each being; and hence the accumulation of variations tending towards specialisation is within the scope of natural selection. On the other hand, we can see, bearing in mind that all organic beings are striving to increase at a high ratio and to seize on every unoccupied or less well occupied place in the economy of nature, that it is quite possible for natural selection gradually to fit a being to a situation in which several organs would be superfluous or useless: in such cases there would be retrogression in the scale of organisation. Whether organisation on the whole has actually advanced from the remotest geological periods to the present day will be more conveniently discussed in our chapter on Geological Succession.

But it may be objected that if all organic beings thus tend to rise in the scale, how is it that throughout the world a multitude of the lowest forms still exist; and how is it that in each great class some forms are far more highly developed than others? Why have not the more highly developed forms every where supplanted and exterminated the lower? Lamarck, who believed in an innate and inevitable tendency towards perfection in all organic beings, seems to have felt this difficulty so strongly that he was led to suppose that new and simple forms are continually being produced by spontaneous generation. Science has not as yet proved the truth of this belief, whatever the future may reveal. On our theory the continued existence of lowly organisms offers no difficulty; for natural selection, or the survival of the fittest, does not necessarily include progressive development—it only takes advantage of such variations as arise and are beneficial to each creature under its complex relations of life. And it may be asked what advantage, as far as we can see, would it be to an infusorian animalcule—to an intestinal worm—or even to an earthworm, to be highly organised. If it were no advantage, these forms would be left, by natural selection, unimproved or but little improved, and might remain for indefinite ages in their present lowly condition. And geology tells us that some of the lowest forms, as the infusoria and rhizopods, have remained for an enormous period in nearly their present state. But to suppose that most of the many now existing low forms have not in the least advanced since the first dawn of life would be extremely rash; for every naturalist who has dissected some of the beings now ranked as very low in the scale, must have been struck with their really wondrous and beautiful organisation.

Nearly the same remarks are applicable, if we look to the different grades of organisation within the same great group; for instance, in the vertebrata, to the co-existence of mammals and fish—among mammalia, to the coexistence of man and the ornithorhynchus—among fishes, to the co-existence of the shark and the lancelet (Amphioxus), which latter fish in the extreme simplicity of its structure approaches the invertebrate classes. But mammals and fish hardly come into competition with each other; the advancement of the whole class of mammals, or of certain members in this class, to the highest grade would not lead to their taking the place of fishes. Physiologists believe that the brain must be bathed by warm blood to be highly active, and this requires aerial respiration; so that warm-blooded mammals when inhabiting the water lie under a disadvantage in having to come continually to the surface to breathe. With fishes, members of the shark family would not tend to supplant the lancelet; for the lancelet, as I hear from Fritz Muller, has as sole companion and competitor on the barren sandy shore of South Brazil, an anomalous annelid. The three lowest orders of mammals, namely, marsupials, edentata, and rodents, co-exist in South America in the same region with numerous monkeys, and probably interfere little with each other. Although organisation, on the whole, may have advanced and be still advancing throughout the world, yet the scale will always present many degrees of perfection; for the high advancement of certain whole classes, or of certain members of each class, does not at all necessarily lead to the extinction of those groups with which they do not enter into close competition. In some cases, as we shall hereafter see, lowly organised forms appear to have been preserved to the present day, from inhabiting confined or peculiar stations, where they have been subjected to less severe competition, and where their scanty numbers have retarded the chance of favourable variations arising.

Finally, I believe that many lowly organised forms now exist throughout the world, from various causes. In some cases variations or individual differences of a favourable nature may never have arisen for natural selection to act on and accumulate. In no case, probably, has time sufficed for the utmost possible amount of development. In some few cases there has been what we must call retrogression or organisation. But the main cause lies in the fact that under very simple conditions of life a high organisation would be of no service—possibly would be of actual disservice, as being of a more delicate nature, and more liable to be put out of order and injured.

Looking to the first dawn of life, when all organic beings, as we may believe, presented the simplest structure, how, it has been asked, could the first step in the advancement or differentiation of parts have arisen? Mr. Herbert Spencer would probably answer that, as soon as simple unicellular organisms came by growth or division to be compounded of several cells, or became attached to any supporting surface, his law "that homologous units of any order become differentiated in proportion as their relations to incident forces become different" would come into action. But as we have no facts to guide us, speculation on the subject is almost useless. It is, however, an error to suppose that there would be no struggle for existence, and, consequently, no natural selection, until many forms had been produced: variations in a single species inhabiting an isolated station might be beneficial, and thus the whole mass of individuals might be modified, or two distinct forms might arise. But, as I remarked towards the close of the introduction, no one ought to feel surprise at much remaining as yet unexplained on the origin of species, if we make due allowance for our profound ignorance on the mutual relations of the inhabitants of the world at the present time, and still more so during past ages.

* * *

Summary of Chapter

If under changing conditions of life organic beings present individual differences in almost every part of their structure, and this cannot be disputed; if there be, owing to their geometrical rate of increase, a severe struggle for life at some age, season or year, and this certainly cannot be disputed; then, considering the infinite complexity of the relations of all organic beings to each other and to their conditions of life, causing an infinite diversity in structure, constitution, and habits, to be advantageous to them, it would be a most extraordinary fact if no variations had ever occurred useful to each being's own welfare, in the same manner as so many variations have occurred useful to man. But if variations useful to any organic being ever do occur, assuredly individuals thus characterised will have the best chance of being preserved in the struggle for life; and from the strong principle of inheritance, these will tend to produce offspring similarly characterised. This principle of preservation, or the survival of the fittest, I have called natural selection. It leads to the improvement of each creature in relation to its organic and inorganic conditions of life; and consequently, in most cases, to what must be regarded as an advance in organisation. Nevertheless, low and simple forms will long endure if well fitted for their simple conditions of life.

Natural selection, on the principle of qualities being inherited at corresponding ages, can modify the egg, seed, or young as easily as the adult. Among many animals sexual selection will have given its aid to ordinary selection by assuring to the most vigorous and best adapted males the greatest number of offspring. Sexual selection will also give characters useful to the males alone in their struggles or rivalry with other males; and these characters will be transmitted to one sex or to both sexes, according to the form of inheritance which prevails.

Whether natural selection has really thus acted in adapting the various forms of life to their several conditions and stations, must be judged by the general tenor and balance of evidence given in the following chapters. But we have already seen how it entails extinction; and how largely extinction has acted in the world's history, geology plainly declares. Natural selection, also, leads to divergence of character; for the more organic beings diverge in structure, habits and constitution, by so much the more can a large number be supported on the area, of which we see proof by looking to the inhabitants of any small spot, and to the productions naturalised in foreign lands. Therefore, during the modification of the descendants of any one species, and during the incessant struggle of all species to increase in numbers, the more diversified the descendants become, the better will be their chance of success in the battle for life. Thus the small differences distinguishing varieties of the same species, steadily tend to increase, till they equal the greater differences between species of the same genus, or even of distinct genera.

We have seen that it is the common, the widely diffused, and widely ranging species, belonging to the larger genera within each class, which vary most; and these tend to transmit to their modified offspring that superiority which now makes them dominant in their own countries. Natural selection, as has just been remarked, leads to divergence of character and to much extinction of the less improved and intermediate forms of life. On these principles, the nature of the affinities, and the generally well defined distinctions between the innumerable organic beings in each class throughout the world, may be explained. It is a truly wonderful fact—the wonder of which we are apt to overlook from familiarity—that all animals and all plants throughout all time and space should be related to each other in groups, subordinate to groups, in the manner which we everywhere behold—namely, varieties of the same species most closely related, species of the same genus less closely and unequally related, forming sections and sub-genera, species of distinct genera much less closely related, and genera related in different degrees, forming sub-families, families, orders, sub-classes, and classes. The several subordinate groups in any class cannot be ranked in a single file, but seem clustered round points, and these round other points, and so on in almost endless cycles. If species had been independently created, no explanation would have been possible of this kind of classification; but it is explained through inheritance and the complex action of natural selection, entailing extinction and divergence of character, as we have seen illustrated in the diagram.

The affinities of all the beings of the same class have sometimes been represented by a great tree. I believe this simile largely speaks the truth. The green and budding twigs may represent existing species; and those produced during former years may represent the long succession of extinct species. At each period of growth all the growing twigs have tried to branch out on all sides, and to overtop and kill the surrounding twigs and branches, in the same manner as species and groups of species have at all times overmastered other species in the great battle for life. The limbs divided into great branches, and these into lesser and lesser branches, were themselves once, when the tree was young, budding twigs; and this connexion of the former and present buds by ramifying branches may well represent the classification of all extinct and living species in groups subordinate to groups. Of the many twigs which flourished when the tree was a mere bush, only two or three, now grown into great branches, yet survive and bear the other branches; so with the species which lived during long-past geological periods, very few have left living and modified descendants. From the first growth of the tree, many a limb and branch has decayed and dropped off; and these fallen branches of various sizes may represent those whole orders, families, and genera which have now no living representatives, and which are known to us only in a fossil state. As we here and there see a thin, straggling branch springing from a fork low down in a tree, and which by some chance has been favoured and is still alive on its summit, so we occasionally see an animal like the Ornithorhynchus or Lepidosiren, which in some small degree connects by its affinities two large branches of life, and which has apparently been saved from fatal competition by having inhabited a protected station. As buds give rise by growth to fresh buds, and these, if vigorous, branch out and overtop on all sides many a feebler branch, so by generation I believe it has been with the great Tree of Life, which fills with its dead and broken branches the crust of the earth, and covers the surface with its ever-branching and beautiful ramifications.

Chapter VI

Difficulties of the Theory

Difficulties of the theory of descent with modification • Absence or rarity of transitional varieties • Transitions in habits of life • Diversified habits in the same species • Species with habits widely different from those of their allies • Organs of extreme perfection • Modes of transition • Cases of difficulty • Natura non facit saltum • Organs of small importance • Organs not in all cases absolutely perfect • The law of Unity of Type and of the Conditions of Existence embraced by the theory of Natural Selection.

Long before the reader has arrived at this part of my work, a crowd of difficulties will have occurred to him. Some of them are so serious that to this day I can hardly reflect on them without being in some degree staggered; but, to the best of my judgment, the greater number are only apparent, and those that are real are not, I think, fatal to the theory.

* * *

Organs of Extreme Perfection and Complication

To suppose that the eye with all its inimitable contrivances for adjusting the focus to different distances, for admitting different amounts of light, and for the correction of spherical and chromatic aberration, could have been formed by natural selection, seems, I freely confess, absurd in the highest degree. When it was first said that the sun stood still and the world turned round, the common sense of mankind declared the doctrine false; but the old saying of *Vox populi, vox Dei*, as every philosopher knows, cannot be trusted in science. Reason tells me, that if numerous gradations from a simple and imperfect eye to one complex and perfect can be shown to exist, each grade being useful to its possessor, as is certainly the case; if further, the eye ever varies and the variations be inherited, as is likewise certainly the case; and if such variations should be useful to any animal under changing conditions of life, then the difficulty of believing that a perfect and complex eye could be formed by natural selection, though insuperable by our imagination, should not be considered as subversive of the theory. How a nerve comes to be sensitive to light, hardly concerns us more than how life itself originated; but I may remark that, as some of the lowest organisms in which nerves cannot be detected, are capable of perceiving light, it does not seem impossible that certain sensitive elements in their sarcode should become aggregated and developed into nerves, endowed with this special sensibility.

In searching for the gradations through which an organ in any species has been perfected, we ought to look exclusively to its lineal progenitors; but this is scarcely ever possible, and we are forced to look to other species and genera of the same group, that is to the collateral descendants from the same parent-form, in order to see what gradations are possible, and for the chance of some gradations having been transmitted in an unaltered or little altered condition. But the state of the same organ in distinct classes may incidentally throw light on the steps by which it has been perfected.

The simplest organ which can be called an eye consists of an optic nerve, surrounded by pigment-cells and covered by translucent skin, but without any lens or other refractive body. We may, however, according to M. Jourdain, descend even a step lower and find aggregates of pigment-cells, apparently serving as organs of vision, without any nerves, and resting merely on sarcodic tissue. Eyes of the above simple nature are not capable of distinct vision, and serve only to distinguish light from darkness. In certain star-fishes, small depressions in the layer of pigment which surrounds the nerve are filled, as described by the author just quoted, with transparent gelatinous matter, projecting with a convex surface, like the cornea in the higher animals. He suggests that this serves not to form an image, but only to concentrate the luminous rays and render their perception more easy. In this concentration of the rays we gain the first and by far the most important step towards the formation of a true, picture-forming eye; for we have only to place the naked extremity of the optic nerve, which in some of the lower animals lies deeply buried in the body, and in some near the surface, at the right distance from the concentrating apparatus, and an image will be formed on it.

In the great class of the Articulata, we may start from an optic nerve simply coated with pigment, the latter sometimes forming a sort of pupil, but destitute of lens or other optical contrivance. With insects it is now known that the numerous facets on the cornea of their great compound eyes form true lenses, and that the cones include curiously modified nervous filaments. But these organs in the Articulata are so much diversified that Muller formerly made three main classes with seven subdivisions, besides a fourth main class of aggregated simple eyes.

When we reflect on these facts, here given much too briefly, with respect to the wide, diversified, and graduated range of structure in the eyes of the lower animals; and when we bear in mind how small the number of all living forms must be in comparison with those which have become extinct, the difficulty ceases to be very great in believing that natural selection may have converted the simple apparatus of an optic nerve, coated with pigment and invested by transparent membrane, into an optical instrument as perfect as is possessed by any member of the Articulata class.

He who will go thus far, ought not to hesitate to go one step further, if he finds on finishing this volume that large bodies of facts, otherwise inexplicable, can be explained by the theory of modification through natural selection; he ought to admit that a structure even as perfect as an eagle's eye might thus be formed, although in this case he does not know the transitional states. It has been objected that in order to modify the eye and still preserve it as a perfect instrument, many changes would have to be effected simultaneously, which, it is assumed, could not be done through natural selection; but as I have attempted to show in my work on the variation of domestic animals, it is not necessary to suppose that the modifications were all simultaneous, if they were extremely slight and gradual. Different kinds of modification would, also, serve for the same general purpose: as Mr. Wallace has remarked, "If a lens has too short or too long a focus, it may be amended either by an alteration of curvature, or an alteration of density; if the curvature be irregular, and the rays do not converge to a point, then any increased regularity of curvature will be an improvement. So the contraction of the iris and the muscular movements of the eye are neither of them essential to vision, but only improvements which might have been added and perfected at any stage of the construction of the instrument." Within the highest division of the animal kingdom, namely, the Vertebrata, we can start from an eye so simple, that it consists, as in the lancelet, of a little sack of transparent skin, furnished with a nerve and lined with pigment, but destitute of any other apparatus. In fishes and reptiles, as Owen has remarked, "The range of gradation of dioptric structures is very great." It is a significant fact that even in man, according to the high authority of Virchow, the beautiful crystalline lens is formed in the embryo by an accumulation of epidermic cells, lying in a sack-like fold of the skin; and the vitreous body is formed from embryonic subcutaneous tissue. To arrive, however, at a just conclusion regarding the formation of the eye, with all its marvellous yet not absolutely perfect characters, it is indispensable that the reason should conquer the imagination; but I have felt the difficulty far to keenly to be surprised at others hesitating to extend the principle of natural selection to so startling a length.

The Descent of Man

Chapter 21

General Summary and Conclusion

A brief summary will be sufficient to recall to the reader's mind the more salient points in this work. Many of the views which have been advanced are highly speculative, and some no doubt will prove erroneous; but I have in every case given the reasons which have led me to one view rather than to another. It seemed worth while to try how far the principle of evolution would throw light on some of the more complex problems in the natural history of man. False facts are highly injurious to the progress of science, for they often endure long; but false views, if supported by some evidence, do little harm, for every one takes a salutary pleasure in proving their falseness: and when this is done, one path towards error is closed and the road to truth is often at the same time opened.

The main conclusion here arrived at, and now held by many naturalists who are well competent to form a sound judgment is that man is descended from some less highly organised form. The grounds upon which this conclusion rests will never be shaken, for the close similarity between man and the lower animals in embryonic development, as well as in innumerable points of structure and constitution, both of high and of the most trifling importance,—the rudiments which he retains, and the abnormal reversions to which he is occasionally liable,—are facts which cannot be disputed. They have long been known, but until recently they told us nothing with respect to the origin of man. Now when viewed by the light of our knowledge of the whole organic world, their meaning is unmistakable. The great principle of evolution stands up clear and firm, when these groups or facts are considered in connection with others, such as the mutual affinities of the members of the same group, their geographical distribution in past and present times, and their geological succession. It is incredible that all these facts should speak falsely. He who is not content to look, like a savage, at the phenomena of nature as disconnected, cannot any longer believe that man is the work of a separate act of creation. He will be forced to admit that the close resemblance of the embryo of man to that, for instance, of a dog—the construction of his skull, limbs and whole frame on the same plan with that of other mammals, independently of the uses to which the parts may be put—the occasional re-appearance of various structures, for instance of several muscles, which man does not normally possess, but which are common to the Quadrumana—and a crowd of analogous facts—all point in the plainest manner to the conclusion that man is the co-descendant with other mammals of a common progenitor.

We have seen that man incessantly presents individual differences in all parts of his body and in his mental faculties. These differences or variations seem to be induced by the same general causes, and to obey the same laws as with the lower animals. In both cases similar laws of inheritance prevail. Man tends to increase at a greater rate than his means of subsistence; consequently he is occasionally subjected to a severe struggle for existence, and natural selection will have effected whatever lies within its scope. A succession of strongly-marked variations of a similar nature is by no means requisite; slight fluctuating differences in the individual suffice for the work of natural selection; not that we have any reason to suppose that in the same species, all parts of the organisation tend to vary to the same degree. We may feel assured that the inherited effects of the long-continued use or disuse of parts will have done much in the same direction with natural selection. Modifications formerly of importance, though no longer of any special use, are long-inherited. When one part is modified, other parts change through the principle of correlation, of which we have instances in many curious cases of correlated monstrosities. Something may be attributed to the direct and definite action of the surrounding conditions of life, such as abundant food, heat or moisture; and lastly, many characters of slight physiological importance, some indeed of considerable importance, have been gained through sexual selection.

No doubt man, as well as every other animal, presents structures, which seem to our limited knowledge, not to be now of any service to him, nor to have been so formerly, either for the general conditions of life, or in the relations of one sex to the other. Such structures cannot be accounted for by any form of selection, or by the inherited effects of the use and disuse of parts. We know, however, that many strange and strongly-marked peculiarities of structure occasionally appear in our domesticated productions, and if their unknown causes were to act more uniformly, they would probably become common to all the individuals of the species. We may hope hereafter to understand something about the causes of such occasional modifications, especially through the study of monstrosities: hence the labours of experimentalists such as those of M. Camille Dareste, are full of promise for the future. In general we can only say that the cause of each slight variation and of each monstrosity lies much more in the constitution of the organism, than in the nature of the surrounding conditions; though new and changed conditions certainly play an important part in exciting organic changes of many kinds.

Through the means just specified, aided perhaps by others as yet undiscovered, man has been raised to his present state. But since he attained to the rank of manhood, he has diverged into distinct races, or as they may be more fitly called, sub-species. Some of these, such as the Negro and European, are so distinct that, if specimens had been brought to a naturalist without any further information, they would undoubtedly have been considered by him as good and true species. Nevertheless all the races agree in so many unimportant details of structure and in so many mental peculiarities that these can be accounted for only by inheritance from a common progenitor; and a progenitor thus characterised would probably deserve to rank as man.

It must not be supposed that the divergence of each race from the other races, and of all from a common stock, can be traced back to any one pair of progenitors. On the contrary, at every stage in the process of modification, all the individuals which were in any way better fitted for their conditions of life, though in different degrees, would have survived in greater numbers than the less well-fitted. The process would have been like that followed by man, when he does not intentionally select particular individuals, but breeds from all the superior individuals, and neglects the inferior. He thus slowly but surely modifies his stock, and unconsciously forms a new strain. So with respect to modifications acquired independently of selection, and due to variations arising from the nature of the organism and the action of the surrounding conditions, or from changed habits of life, no single pair will have been modified much more than the other pairs inhabiting the same country, for all will have been continually blended through free intercrossing.

By considering the embryological structure of man,—the homologies which he presents with the lower animals,—the rudiments which he retains,—and the reversions to which he is liable, we can partly recall in imagination the former condition of our early progenitors; and can approximately place them in their proper place in the zoological series. We thus learn that man is descended from a hairy, tailed quadruped, probably arboreal in its habits, and an inhabitant of the Old World. This creature, if its whole structure had been examined by a naturalist, would have been classed amongst the Quadrumana, as surely as the still more ancient progenitor of the Old and New World monkeys. The Quadrumana and all the higher mammals are probably derived from an ancient marsupial animal, and this through a long series of diversified forms, from some amphibian-like creature, and this again from some fish-like animal. In the dim obscurity of the past we can see that the early progenitor of all the Vertebrata must have been an aquatic animal provided with branchiae, with the two sexes united in the same individual, and with the most important organs of the body (such as the brain and heart) imperfectly or not at all developed. This animal seems to have been more like the larvae of the existing marine ascidians than any other known form.

The high standard of our intellectual powers and moral disposition is the greatest difficulty which presents itself, after we have been driven to this conclusion on the origin of man. But every one who admits the principle of evolution, must see that the mental powers of the higher animals, which are the same in kind with those of man, though so different in degree, are capable of advancement. Thus the interval between the mental powers of one of the higher apes and of a fish, or between those of an ant and scale-insect, is immense; yet their development does not offer any special difficulty; for with our domesticated animals, the mental faculties are certainly variable, and the variations are inherited. No one doubts that they are of the utmost importance to animals in a state of nature. Therefore the conditions are favourable for their development through natural selection. The same conclusion may be extended to man; the intellect must have been all-important to him, even at a very remote period, as enabling him to invent and use language, to make weapons, tools, traps, etc., whereby with the aid of his social habits, he long ago became the most dominant of all living creatures.

A great stride in the development of the intellect will have followed, as soon as the half-art and half-instinct of language came into use; for the continued use of language will have reacted on the brain and produced an inherited effect; and this again will have reacted on the improvement of language. As Mr. Chauncey Wright[1] has well remarked, the largeness of the brain in man relatively to his body, compared with the lower animals, may be attributed in chief part to the early use of some simple form of language,—that wonderful engine which affixes signs to all sorts of objects and qualities, and excites trains of thought which would never arise from the mere impression of the senses, or if they did arise could not be followed out. The higher intellectual powers of man, such as those of ratiocination, abstraction, self-consciousness, etc., probably follow from the continued improvement and exercise of the other mental faculties.

The development of the moral qualities is a more interesting problem. The foundation lies in the social instincts, including under this term the family ties. These instincts are highly complex, and in the case of the lower animals give special tendencies towards certain definite actions; but the more important elements are love, and the distinct emotion of sympathy. Animals endowed with the social instincts take pleasure in one another's company, warn one another of danger, defend and aid one another in many ways. These instincts do not extend to all the individuals of the species, but only to those of the same community. As they are highly beneficial to the species, they have in all probability been acquired through natural selection.

A moral being is one who is capable of reflecting on his past actions and their motives—of approving of some and disapproving of others; and the fact that man is the one being who certainly deserves this designation, is the greatest of all distinctions between him and the lower animals. But in the fourth chapter I have endeavoured to shew that the moral sense follows, firstly, from the enduring and ever-present nature of the social instincts; secondly, from man's appreciation of the approbation and disapprobation of his fellows; and thirdly, from the high activity of his mental faculties, with past impressions extremely vivid; and in these latter respects he differs from the lower animals. Owing to this condition of mind, man cannot avoid looking both backwards and forwards, and comparing past impressions. Hence after some temporary desire or passion has mastered his social instincts, he reflects and compares the now weakened impression of such past impulses with the ever-present social instincts; and he then feels that sense of dissatisfaction which all unsatisfied instincts leave behind them, he therefore resolves to act differently for the future,—and this is conscience. Any instinct, permanently stronger or more enduring than another, gives rise to a feeling which we express by saying that it ought to be obeyed. A pointer dog, if able to reflect on his past conduct, would say to himself, I ought (as indeed we say of him) to have pointed at that hare and not have yielded to the passing temptation of hunting it.

Social animals are impelled partly by a wish to aid the members of their community in a general manner, but more commonly to perform certain definite actions. Man is impelled by the same general wish to aid his fellows; but has few or no special instincts. He differs also from the lower animals in the power of expressing his desires by words, which thus become a guide to the aid required and bestowed. The motive to give aid is likewise much modified in man: it no longer consists solely of a blind instinctive impulse, but is much influenced by the praise or blame of his fellows. The appreciation and the bestowal of praise and blame both rest on sympathy; and this emotion, as we have seen, is one of the most important elements of the social instincts. Sympathy, though gained as an instinct, is also much strengthened by exercise or habit. As all men desire their own happiness, praise or blame is bestowed on actions and motives, according as they lead to this end; and as happiness is an essential part of the general good, the greatest-happiness principle indirectly serves as a nearly safe standard of right and wrong. As the reasoning powers advance and experience is gained, the remoter effects of certain lines of conduct on the character of the individual, and on the general good, are perceived; and then the self-regarding virtues come within the scope of public opinion, and receive praise, and their opposites blame. But with the less civilised nations reason often errs, and many bad customs and base superstitions come within the same scope, and are then esteemed as high virtues, and their breach as heavy crimes.

The moral faculties are generally and justly esteemed as of higher value than the intellectual powers. But we should bear in mind that the activity of the mind in vividly recalling past impressions is one of the fundamental though secondary bases of conscience. This affords the strongest argument for educating and stimulating in all possible ways the intellectual faculties of every human being. No doubt a man with a torpid mind, if his social affections and sympathies are well developed, will be led to good actions, and may have a fairly sensitive conscience. But whatever renders the imagination more vivid and strengthens the habit of recalling and comparing past impressions, will make the conscience more sensitive, and may even somewhat compensate for weak social affections and sympathies.

The moral nature of man has reached its present standard, partly through the advancement of his reasoning powers and consequently of a just public opinion, but especially from his sympathies having been rendered more tender and widely diffused through the effects of habit, example, instruction, and reflection. It is not improbable that after long practice virtuous tendencies may be inherited. With the more civilised races, the conviction of the existence of an all-seeing Deity has had a potent influence on the advance of morality. Ultimately man does not accept the praise or blame of his fellows as his sole guide, though few escape this influence, but his habitual convictions, controlled by reason, afford him the safest rule. His conscience then becomes the supreme judge and monitor. Nevertheless the first foundation or origin of the moral sense lies in the social instincts, including sympathy; and these instincts no doubt were primarily gained, as in the case of the lower animals, through natural selection.

The belief in God has often been advanced as not only the greatest, but the most complete of all the distinctions between man and the lower animals. It is however impossible, as we have seen, to maintain that this belief is innate or instinctive in man. On the other hand a belief in all-pervading spiritual agencies seems to be universal; and apparently follows from a considerable advance in man's reason, and from a still greater advance in his faculties of imagination, curiosity and wonder. I am aware that the assumed instinctive belief in God has been used by many persons as an argument for His existence. But this is a rash argument, as we should thus be compelled to believe in the existence of many cruel and malignant spirits, only a little more powerful than man; for the belief in them is far more general than in a beneficent Deity. The idea of a universal and beneficent

Creator does not seem to arise in the mind of man, until he has been elevated by long-continued culture.

He who believes in the advancement of man from some low organised form, will naturally ask how does this bear on the belief in the immortality of the soul. The barbarous races of man, as Sir J. Lubbock has shewn, possess no clear belief of this kind; but arguments derived from the primeval beliefs of savages are, as we have just seen, of little or no avail. Few persons feel any anxiety from the impossibility of determining at what precise period in the development of the individual, from the first trace of a minute germinal vesicle, man becomes an immortal being; and there is no greater cause for anxiety because the period cannot possibly be determined in the gradually ascending organic scale.[2]

I am aware that the conclusions arrived at in this work will be denounced by some as highly irreligious; but he who denounces them is bound to shew why it is more irreligious to explain the origin of man as a distinct species by descent from some lower form, through the laws of variation and natural selection, than to explain the birth of the individual through the laws of ordinary reproduction. The birth both of the species and of the individual are equally parts of that grand sequence of events, which our minds refuse to accept as the result of blind chance. The understanding revolts at such a conclusion, whether or not we are able to believe that every slight variation of structure,—the union of each pair in marriage, the dissemination of each seed,—and other such events, have all been ordained for some special purpose.

Sexual selection has been treated at great length in this work; for, as I have attempted to shew, it has played an important part in the history of the organic world. I am aware that much remains doubtful, but I have endeavoured to give a fair view of the whole case. In the lower divisions of the animal kingdom, sexual selection seems to have done nothing: such animals are often affixed for life to the same spot, or have the sexes combined in the same individual, or what is still more important, their perceptive and intellectual faculties are not sufficiently advanced to allow of the feelings of love and jealousy, or of the exertion of choice. When, however, we come to the Arthropoda and Vertebrata, even to the lowest classes in these two great sub-kingdoms, sexual selection has effected much.

In the several great classes of the animal kingdom,—in mammals, birds, reptiles, fishes, insects, and even crustaceans,—the differences between the sexes follow nearly the same rules. The males are almost always the wooers; and they alone are armed with special weapons for fighting with their rivals. They are generally stronger and larger than the females, and are endowed with the requisite qualities of courage and pugnacity. They are provided, either exclusively or in a much higher degree than the females, with organs for vocal or instrumental music, and with odoriferous glands. They are ornamental with infinitely diversified appendages, and with the most brilliant or conspicuous colours, often arranged in elegant patterns, whilst the females are unadorned. When the sexes differ in more important structures, it is the male which is provided with special sense-organs for discovering the female, with locomotive organs for reaching her, and often with prehensile organs for holding her. These various structures for charming or securing the female are often developed in the male during only part of the year, namely the breeding-season. They have in many cases been more or less transferred to the females; and in the latter case they often appear in her as mere rudiments. They are lost or never gained by the males after emasculation. Generally they are not developed in the male during early youth, but appear a short time before the age for reproduction. Hence in most cases the young of both sexes resemble each other; and the female somewhat resembles her young offspring throughout life. In almost every great class a few anomalous cases occur, where there has been an almost complete transposition of the characters proper to the two sexes; the females assuming characters which properly belong to the males. This surprising uniformity in the laws regulating the differences between the sexes in so many and such widely separated classes, is intelligible if we admit the action of one common cause, namely sexual selection.

Sexual selection depends on the success of certain individuals over others of the same sex, in relation to the propagation of the species; whilst natural selection depends on the success of both sexes, at all ages, in relation to the general conditions of life. The sexual struggle is of two kinds; in the one it is between individuals of the same sex, generally the males, in order to drive away or kill their rivals, the females remaining passive; whilst in the other, the struggle is likewise between the individuals of the same sex, in order to excite or charm those of the opposite sex, generally the females, which no longer remain passive, but select the more agreeable partners. This latter kind of selection is closely analogous to that which man unintentionally, yet effectually, brings to bear on his domesticated productions, when he preserves during a long period the most pleasing or useful individuals, without any wish to modify the breed.

The laws of inheritance determine whether characters gained through sexual selection by either sex shall be transmitted to the same sex, or to both; as well as the age at which they shall be developed. It appears that variations arising late in life are commonly transmitted to one and the same sex. Variability is the necessary basis for the action of selection, and is wholly independent of it. It follows from this, that variations of the same general nature have often been taken advantage of and accumulated through sexual selection in relation to the propagation of the species, as well as through natural selection in relation to the general purposes of life. Hence secondary sexual characters, when equally transmitted to both sexes can be distinguished from ordinary specific characters only by the light of analogy. The modifications acquired through sexual selection are often so strongly pronounced that the two sexes have frequently been ranked as distinct species, or even as distinct genera. Such strongly-marked differences must be in some manner highly important; and we know that they have been acquired in some instances at the cost not only of inconvenience, but of exposure to actual danger.

The belief in the power of sexual selection rests chiefly on the following considerations. Certain characters are confined to one sex; and this alone renders it probable that in most cases they are connected with the act of reproduction. In innumerable instances these characters are fully developed only at maturity, and often during only a part of the year, which is always the breeding-season. The males (passing over a few exceptional cases) are the more active in courtship; they are the better armed, and are rendered the more attractive in various ways. It is to be especially observed that the males display their attractions with elaborate care in the presence of the females; and that they rarely or never display them excepting during the season of love. It is incredible that all this should be purposeless. Lastly we have distinct evidence with some quadrupeds and birds, that the individuals of one sex are capable of feeling a strong antipathy or preference for certain individuals of the other sex.

Bearing in mind these facts, and the marked results of man's unconscious selection, when applied to domesticated animals and cultivated plants, it seems to me almost certain that if the individuals of one sex were during a long series of generations to prefer pairing with certain individuals of the other sex, characterised in some peculiar manner, the offspring would slowly but surely become modified in this same manner. I have not attempted to conceal that, excepting when the males are more numerous than the females, or when polygamy prevails, it is doubtful how the more attractive males succeed in leaving a large number of offspring to inherit their superiority in ornaments or other charms than the less attractive males; but I have shewn that this would probably follow from the females,—especially the more vigorous ones, which would be the first to breed,—preferring not only the more attractive but at the same time the more vigorous and victorious males.

Although we have some positive evidence that birds appreciate bright and beautiful objects, as with the bower-birds of Australia, and although they certainly appreciate the power of song, yet I fully admit that it is astonishing that the females of many birds and some mammals should be endowed with sufficient taste to appreciate ornaments, which we have reason to attribute to sexual selection; and this is even more astonishing in the case of reptiles, fish, and insects. But we really know little about the minds of the lower animals. It cannot be supposed, for instance, that male birds of paradise or peacocks should take such pains in erecting, spreading, and vibrating their beautiful plumes before the females for no purpose. We should remember the fact given on excellent authority in a former chapter, that several peahens, when debarred from an admired male, remained widows during a whole season rather than pair with another bird.

Nevertheless I know of no fact in natural history more wonderful than that the female Argus pheasant should appreciate the exquisite shading of the ball-and-socket ornaments and the elegant patterns on the wing-feather of the male. He who thinks that the male was created as he now exists must admit that the great plumes, which prevent the wings from being used for flight, and which are displayed during courtship and at no other time in a manner quite peculiar to this one species, were given to him as an ornament. If so, he must likewise admit that the female was created and endowed with the capacity of appreciating such ornaments. I differ only in the conviction that the male Argus pheasant acquired his beauty gradually, through the preference of the females during many generations for the more highly ornamented males; the aesthetic capacity of the females having been advanced through exercise or habit, just as our own taste is gradually improved. In the male through the fortunate chance of a few feathers being left unchanged, we can distinctly trace how simple spots with a little fulvous shading on one side may have been developed by small steps into the wonderful ball-and-socket ornaments; and it is probable that they were actually thus developed.

Everyone who admits the principle of evolution, and yet feels great difficulty in admitting that female mammals, birds, reptiles, and fish, could have acquired the high taste implied by the beauty of the males, and which generally coincides with our own standard, should reflect that the nerve-cells of the brain in the highest as well as in the lowest members of the Vertebrate series, are derived from those of the common progenitor of this great Kingdom. For we can thus see how it has come to pass that certain mental faculties, in various and widely distinct groups of animals, have been developed in nearly the same manner and to nearly the same degree.

The reader who has taken the trouble to go through the several chapters devoted to sexual selection, will be able to judge how far the conclusions at which I have arrived are supported by sufficient evidence. If he accepts these conclusions he may, I think, safely extend them to mankind; but it would be superfluous here to repeat what I have so lately said on the manner in which sexual selection apparently has acted on man, both on the male and female side, causing the two sexes to differ in body and mind, and the several races to differ from each other in various characters, as well as from their ancient and lowly-organised progenitors.

He who admits the principle of sexual selection will be led to the remarkable conclusion that the nervous system not only regulates most of the existing functions of the body, but has indirectly influenced the progressive development of various bodily structures and of certain mental qualities. Courage, pugnacity, perseverance, strength and size of body, weapons of all kinds, musical organs, both vocal and instrumental, bright colours and ornamental appendages, have all been indirectly gained by the one sex or the other, through the exertion of choice, the influence of love and jealousy, and the appreciation of the beautiful in sound, colour or form; and these powers of the mind manifestly depend on the development of the brain.

Man scans with scrupulous care the character and pedigree of his horses, cattle, and dogs before he matches them; but when he comes to his own marriage he rarely, or never, takes any such care. He is impelled by nearly the same motives as the lower animals, when they are left to their own free choice, though he is in so far superior to them that he highly values mental charms and virtues. On the other hand he is strongly attracted by mere wealth or rank. Yet he might by selection do something not only for the bodily constitution and frame of his offspring, but for their intellectual and moral qualities. Both sexes ought to refrain from marriage if they are in any marked degree inferior in body or mind; but such hopes are Utopian and will never be even partially realised until the laws of inheritance are thoroughly known. Everyone does good service, who aids towards this end. When the principles of breeding and inheritance are better understood, we shall not hear ignorant members of our legislature rejecting with scorn a plan for ascertaining whether or not consanguineous marriages are injurious to man.

The advancement of the welfare of mankind is a most intricate problem: all ought to refrain from marriage who cannot avoid abject poverty for their children; for poverty is not only a great evil, but tends to its own increase by leading to recklessness in marriage. On the other hand, as Mr. Galton has remarked, if the prudent avoid marriage, whilst the reckless marry, the inferior members tend to supplant the better members of society. Man, like every other animal, has no doubt advanced to his present high condition through a struggle for existence consequent on his rapid multiplication; and if he is to advance still higher, it is to be feared that he must remain subject to a severe struggle. Otherwise he would sink into indolence, and the more gifted men would not be more successful in the battle of life than the less gifted. Hence our natural rate of increase, though leading to many and obvious evils, must not be greatly diminished by any means. There should be open competition for all men; and the most able should not be prevented by laws or customs from succeeding best and rearing the largest number of offspring. Important as the struggle for existence has been and even still is, yet as far as the highest part of man's nature is concerned there are other agencies more important. For the moral qualities are advanced, either directly or indirectly, much more through the effects of habit, the reasoning powers, instruction, religion, etc., than through natural selection; though to this latter agency may be safely attributed the social instincts, which afforded the basis for the development of the moral sense.

The main conclusion arrived at in this work, namely, that man is descended from some lowly organised form, will, I regret to think, be highly distasteful to many. But there can hardly be a doubt that we are descended from barbarians. The astonishment which I felt on first seeing a party of Fuegians on a wild and broken shore will never be forgotten by me, for the reflection at once rushed into my mind—such were our ancestors. These men were absolutely naked and bedaubed with paint, their long hair was tangled, their mouths frothed with excitement, and their expression was wild, startled, and distrustful. They possessed hardly any arts, and like wild animals lived on what they could catch; they had no government, and were merciless to every one not of their own small tribe. He who has seen a savage in his native land will not feel much shame, if forced to acknowledge that the blood of some more humble creature flows in his veins. For my own part I would as soon be descended from that heroic little monkey, who braved his dreaded enemy in order to save the life of his keeper, or from that old baboon, who descending from the mountains, carried away in triumph his young comrade from a crowd of astonished dogs—as from a savage who delights to torture his enemies, offers up bloody sacrifices, practices infanticide without remorse, treats his wives like slaves, knows no decency, and is haunted by the grossest superstitions.

Man may be excused for feeling some pride at having risen, though not through his own exertions, to the very summit of the organic scale; and the fact of his having thus risen, instead of having been aboriginally placed there, may give him hope for a still higher destiny in the distant future. But we are not here concerned with hopes or fears, only with the truth as far as our reason permits us to discover it; and I have given the evidence to the best of my ability. We must, however, acknowledge, as it seems to me, that man with all his noble qualities, with sympathy which feels for the most debased, with benevolence which extends not only to other men but to the humblest living creature, with his god-like intellect which has penetrated into the movements and constitution of the solar system—with all these exalted powers—Man still bears in his bodily frame the indelible stamp of his lowly origin.

Evolution and Human Culture

4,000,000	Aushralopithecines emerge in East Africa "Lucy" (Australopithecus afarensis), small brain, walked upright; Apelike head on humanoid body
2,500,000	Homo habilis (handy man) emerged in East Africa; First humans, with larger brain, upright, flint tools
2,000,000	Homo erectus (e.g., Peking Man); Spread from Africa to Middle East, Europe, and Asia Larger brain; eventually used fire and improved tools
300,000	
230,000	Neanderthal man (Homo sapiens neanderthalensis) Europe and Near East; better tools and ritual burial of the dead
200,000	Archaic sapiens evolved in Africa, spread to Near East, Asia, Europe
40,000	Homo sapiens now found in most of Old World (Europe, Asia, Africa) Hunting groups, advanced tools, stone sculpture, language
30,000	End of last ice age; cave paintings in France
21,000	By now or earlier, humans migrate from Asia to the Americas
9,000	Glaciers receding; farming groups in Middle East and Europe; domesticated plants and animals
6,500	Farming, villages, pottery from Africa to Asia and the Americas
3,500	Mesopotamian civilization, Tigris and Euphrates, with cities, writing, temples, irrigation
3,000	Egyptian civilization, Nile River Chinese civilization, Yellow River
2,500	Harappan civilization, Indus River in India
2,000	Additional Mediterranean civilizations, including Minoan and other early Greek cultures
1,500	Aryans begin invasions of Indian subcontinent
1200–1000	Period of the Judges as the Israelite tribes settle in the Promised Land
1,000	Rise of Olmec civilization in Central America
600	Buddha preaches in N. India; spread of Persian empire
500	Rise of the classic Greek polis; Confucius teaches in China
200	Spread of Roman empire
0	Jesus preaches the gospel
312 AD	Under Constantine, Christianity official religion of the Roman empire
620 AD	Mohammed initiates Islam's growth
1776 AD	American revolution
1945 AD	Atom Bombs dropped on Nagasaki and Hiroshima
?	

Evolutionary History: An Overview

13/15 Billion Years Ago:	THE BIG BANG: Beginning of the universe
4.5 Billion:	Planet earth formed
4.0 Billion:	End of asteroid collision: Origin of primate cells without nuclei
1.0 Billion:	Evolution of nucleated cells
600 Million:	CAMBRIAN EXPLOSION: Most phyla of invertebrate, multicelled life appeared within 20-million-year period
225 Million:	END OF THE PERMIAN ERA: Extinction of 90% of species of marine organisms; Land plants and vertebrates little disturbed
	Possible periods of extinction every 26.5 million years thereafter
65 Million:	Extinction of over 50% of species (including dinosaurs), followed by mammalian explosion

Evolution of Humankind

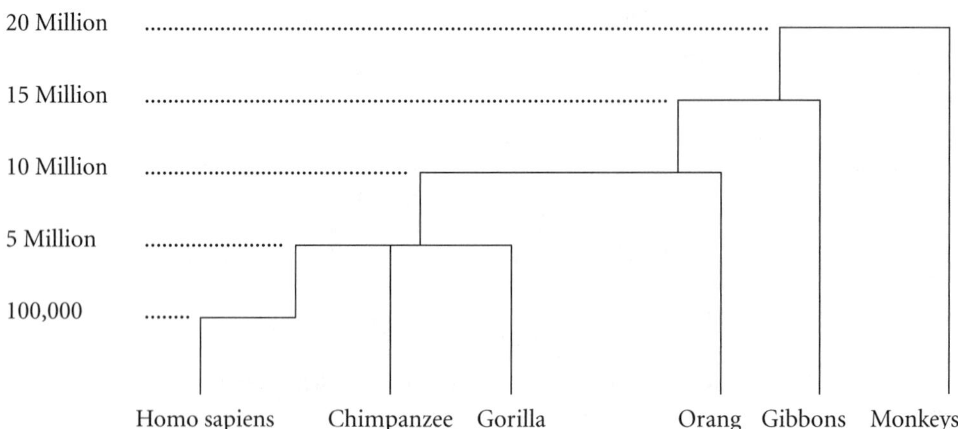

Frederick Engels

From Socialism: Utopian and Scientific [1880]

The materialist conception of history starts from the proposition that the production of the means to support human life and, next to production, the exchange of things produced, is the basis of all social structure; that in every society that has appeared in history, the manner in which wealth is distributed and society divided into classes or orders is dependent upon what is produced, how it is produced, and how the products are exchanged. From this point of view, the final causes of all social changes and political revolutions are to be sought, not in men's brains, not in men's better insights into eternal truth and justice, but in changes in the modes of production and exchange. They are to be sought, not in the *philosophy*, but in the *economics* of each particular epoch. The growing perception that existing social institutions are unreasonable and unjust, that reason has become unreason, and right wrong, is only proof that in the modes of production and exchange changes have silently taken place with which the social order, adapted to earlier economic conditions, is no longer in keeping. From this it also follows that the means of getting rid of the incongruities that have been brought to light must also be present, in a more or less developed condition, within the changed modes of production themselves. These means are not to be invented by deduction from fundamental principles, but are to be discovered in the stubborn facts of the existing system of production.

What is, then, the position of modern Socialism in this connection?

The present situation of society—this is now pretty generally conceded—is the creation of the ruling class of today, of the bourgeoisie. The mode of production peculiar to the bourgeoisie, known, since Marx, as the capitalist mode of production, was incompatible with the feudal system, with the privileges it conferred upon individuals, entire social ranks and local corporations, as well as with the hereditary ties of subordination which constituted the framework of its social organization. The bourgeoisie broke up the feudal system and built upon its ruins the capitalist order of society, the kingdom of free competition, of personal liberty, of the equality, before the law, of all commodity owners, of all the rest of the capitalist blessings. Thenceforward, the capitalist mode of production could develop in freedom. Since steam, machinery, and the making of machines by machinery transformed the older manufacture into modern industry, the productive forces, evolved under the guidance of the bourgeoisie, developed with a rapidity and in a degree unheard of before. But just as the older manufacture, in its time, and handicraft, becoming more developed under its influence, had come into collision with the feudal trammels of the guilds, so now modern industry, in its complete development, comes into collision with the bounds within which the capitalist mode of production holds it confined. The new productive forces have already outgrown the capitalistic mode of using them. And this conflict between productive forces and modes of production is not a conflict engendered in the mind of man, like that between original sin and divine justice. It exists, in fact, objectively, outside us, independently of the will and actions even of the men that have brought it on. Modern Socialism is nothing but the reflex, in thought, of this conflict in fact; its ideal reflection in the minds, first, of the class directly suffering under it, the working class.

Now, in what does this conflict consist?

Before capitalist production, i.e., in the Middle Ages, the system of petty industry obtained generally, based upon the private property of the laborers in their means of production; in the country, the agriculture of the small peasant, freeman, or serf; in the towns, the handicrafts organized in guilds. The instruments of labor—land, agricultural implements, the workshop, the tool—were the instruments of labor of single individuals, adapted for the use of one worker, and, therefore, of necessity, small, dwarfish, circumscribed. But, for this very reason, they belonged as a rule to the producer himself. To concentrate these scattered, limited means of production, to enlarge them, to turn them into the powerful levers of production of the present day—this was precisely the historic role of capitalist production and of its upholder, the bourgeoisie. In the fourth section of *Capital*, Marx has explained in detail how since the 15th century this has been historically worked out through the three phases of simple co-operation, manufacture, and modern industry. But the bourgeoisie, as is shown there, could not transform these puny means of production into mighty productive forces without transforming them, at the same time, from means of production of the individual into *social* means of production only workable by a collectivity of men. The spinning wheel, the handloom, the blacksmith's hammer, were replaced by the spinning-machine, the power-loom, the steam-hammer; the individual workshop, by the factory implying the co-operation of hundreds and thousands of workmen. In like manner, production itself changed from a series of individual into a series of social acts, and the production from individual to social products. The yarn, the cloth, the metal articles that now come out of the factory were the joint product of many workers, through whose hands they had successively to pass before they were ready. No one person could say of them: "I made that; this is *my* product."

But where, in a given society, the fundamental form of production is that spontaneous division of labor which creeps in gradually and not upon any preconceived plan, there the products take on the form of commodities, whose mutual exchange, buying and selling, enable the individual producers to satisfy their manifold wants. And this was the case in the Middle Ages. The peasant, e.g., sold to the artisan agricultural products and bought from him the products of handicraft. Into this society of individual producers, of commodity producers, the new mode of production thrust itself. In the midst of the old division of labor, grown up spontaneously and upon no definite plan, which had governed the whole of society, now arose division of labor upon a definite plan, as organized in the factory; side by side with individual production appeared social production. The products of both were sold in the same market, and, therefore, at prices at least approximately equal. But organization upon a definite plan was stronger than spontaneous division of labor. The factories working with the combined social forces of a collectivity of individuals produced their commodities far more cheaply than the individual small producers. Individual producers succumbed in one department after another. Socialized production revolutionized all the old methods of production. But its revolutionary character was, at the same time, so little recognized that it was, on the contrary, introduced as a means of increasing and developing the production of commodities. When it arose, it found ready-made, and made liberal use of, certain machinery for the production and exchange of commodities: merchants' capital, handicraft, wage labor. Socialized production thus introducing itself as a new form of the production of commodities, it was a matter of course that under it the old forms of appropriation remained in full swing, and were applied to its products as well.

In the medieval stage of evolution of the production of commodities, the question as to the owner of the product of labor could not arise. The individual producer, as a rule, had, from raw material belonging to himself, and generally his own handiwork, produced it with his own tools, by the labor of his own hands or of his family. There was no need for him to appropriate the new product. It belonged wholly to him, as a matter of course. His property in the product was, therefore, based upon his own labor. Even where external help was used, this was, as a rule, of little importance, and very generally was compensated by something other than wages. The apprentices and journeymen of the guilds worked less for board and wages than for education, in order that they might become master craftsmen themselves.

Then came the concentration of the means of production and of the producers in large workshops and manufactories, their transformation into actual socialized means of production and socialized producers. But the socialized producers and means of production and their products were still treated, after this change, just as they had been before, i.e., as the means of production and the products of individuals. Hitherto, the owner of the instruments of labor had himself appropriated the product, because, as a rule, it was his own product and the assistance of others was the exception. Now, the owner of the instruments of labor always appropriated to himself the product, although it was no longer his product but exclusively the product of the labor of others. Thus, the products now produced socially were not appropriated by those who had actually set in motion the means of production and actually produced the commodities, but by the capitalists. The means of production, and production itself, had become in essence socialized. But they were subjected to a form of appropriation which presupposes the private production of individuals, under which, therefore, every one owns his own product and brings it to market. The mode of production is subjected to this form of appropriation, although it abolishes the conditions upon which the latter rests.[1]

This contradiction, which gives to the new mode of production its capitalistic character, contains the germ of the whole of the social antagonisms of today. The greater the mastery obtained by the new mode of production over all important fields of production and in all manufacturing countries, the more it reduced individual production to an insignificant residuum, the more clearly was brought out the incompatibility of socialized production with capitalistic appropriation.

The first capitalists found, as we have said, alongside of other forms of labor, wage labor ready-made for them on the market. But it was exceptional, complementary, accessory, transitory wage labor. The agricultural laborer, though, upon occasion, he hired himself out by the day, had a few acres of his own land on which he could at all events live at a pinch. The guilds were so organized that the journeyman to today became the master of tomorrow. But all this changed, as soon as the means of production became socialized and concentrated in the hands of capitalists. The means of production, as well as the product, of the individual producer became more and more worthless; there was nothing left for him but to turn wage worker under the capitalist. Wage-labor, aforetime the exception and accessory, now became the rule and basis of all production; aforetime complementary, it now became the sole remaining function of the worker. The wage-worker for a time became a wage worker for life. The number of these permanent was further enormously increased by the breaking-up of the feudal system that occurred at the same time, by the disbanding of the retainers of the feudal lords, the eviction of the peasants from their homesteads, etc. The separation was made complete between the means of production concentrated in the hands of the capitalists, on the one side, and the producers, possessing nothing but their labor-power, on the other. The contradiction between socialized production and capitalistic appropriation manifested itself as the antagonism of proletariat and bourgeoisie.

Friedrich Nietzsche

On The Genealogy of Morals

A Polemic

Originally published 1887.
Selected, Translated, and Annotated by Robert Guay
Department of Philosophy, Temple University

Omissions in the text are indicated by [. . .] where internal to a passage and not, for example, at the beginning and end of a section. Ellipses not in square brackets and all italics are Nietzsche's own.

Preface

1. We are unknown to ourselves, we knowing ones, we to our own selves, and for a good reason. We have never sought ourselves—how could it happen, that one day we would *find* ourselves? Someone once correctly said: "where your treasure is, there your heart will be also";[1] *our* treasure is where the beehives of our knowledge are. We are always on the way to finding it; as winged creatures and honey-gatherers of the spirit, we truly care for only one thing from the heart: to "bring something home." Whatever else concerns life, the so-called "experiences"—who among us has enough seriousness for them? Or enough time? In these matters we have been, I fear, somewhat distracted: our hearts have not quite been in it, and not even our ears! More often, like some divine scatter-brain absorbed-in-himself into whose ear the bell has tolled at full power the twelve strikes of noon, who then suddenly wakes and asks himself, "What was really just struck?",

just like that we rub our ears *afterwards* and ask, completely amazed, completely embarrassed, "what did we really experience?" and further, "who *are* we really?" and afterwards, as said, count the twelve trembling bell-strikes of our experience, our life, our *being*—ugh! and miscount them . . . We necessarily remain strangers to ourselves, we do not understand ourselves, we *must* get ourselves wrong, for us the saying "Each is furthest from himself" holds for all eternity—we are not "knowing ones" with respect to ourselves.

2. —My thoughts on the *origin* of our moral prejudices—that is what this polemic is about—have their first spare and provisional expression in that collection of aphorisms that carried the title *Human, All-too-human. A book for free spirits.* [. . .] *That* I still hold fast to these ideas today, that in the intervening time they have become ever more bound to one another, that they have grown alongside and into each other, this strengthens in me the glad confidence that from the very beginning they have not arisen in me out of anything isolated, gratuitous, or sporadic, but from a common root, from of an ever more definitely speaking, ever more definitely demanding *fundamental will* of knowledge that commands from the depths. Only this is fitting for a philosopher. For we have no right to be *isolated* in any way: we may not make isolated mistakes, nor come across isolated truths. Rather, our thoughts, our values, our yes's and no's and if's and whether's grow out of us with the necessity with which a tree bears its fruit—all these things are related and interconnected as the testimony to One Will, One Health, One Soil, One Sun.—Whether these fruits of ours taste good to you?—But what do the trees care! What do we care, we philosophers!

3. Fortunately I learned a long time ago to detach the theological prejudice from the moral prejudice, and to stop looking for the origin of evil *behind* the world. A bit of historical and philological schooling, together with some innate fastidiousness concerning psychological questions in general, and my problem was quickly transformed into another one: under what conditions did humankind invent the value judgments good and evil? And *what value do those values themselves possess?* Have they inhibited or promoted human flourishing so far? Are they a sign of crisis, of impoverishment, of the degeneration of life? Or, on the contrary, do they betray the fullness, the force, the will of life, its courage, its confidence, its future?

6. This problem of the *value* of pity and of pity-morality (—I am opposed to the disgraceful modern mushiness of feeling—) appears at first to be something unconnected, a question mark standing all by itself. But anyone who hangs on to this problem and *learns* to ask questions will have the same experience as me: a tremendous new outlook opens itself up to him, a possibility takes hold of him like a dizzy spell, every kind of mistrust, suspicion, and fear leaps forth, and the belief in morality—in all morality—totters. Finally a new demand is heard. Let us proclaim this *new demand:* we need a *critique* of moral values, *the value of these values themselves must first be called into question*—and for this end we need a knowledge of the conditions and circumstances out of which they grew, under which they developed and shifted (morality as result, as symptom, as mask, as tartuffery,[2] as disease, as misunderstanding; but also morality as cause, as remedy, as stimulant, as inhibition, as poison), a knowledge the likes of which has never been seen, nor even desired. The *value* of these "values" has been taken as given, as a matter of fact, as be-

yond all putting-into-question; up to now no one has had the remotest doubt or hesitation in supposing that the "good man" is more valuable than the "evil man," more valuable with regard to the fostering, utility, and prosperity of *humanity* in general (the future of humanity included). What if just the opposite were true? What if the "good man" also comprised a symptom of decline, and likewise a danger, a seduction, a poison, a narcotic through which the present might be living *at the expense of the future?* Perhaps more comfortable and more secure, but also in a lowlier style, pettier? So that precisely morality would be to blame if the highest power and magnificence possible for the type human were never attained? So that precisely morality were the danger of dangers?

First Treatise: "Good and Bad," "Good and Evil."

1. These English psychologists—the ones whom we must thank for producing the only attempts at a history of the origin of morality up to now—they present us no small puzzle with their own selves. As incarnate puzzles they even have an essential advantage, I confess, over their books: *they themselves are interesting!* These English psychologists—what do they really want? One finds them, whether voluntarily or involuntarily, always at the same work: dragging the shameful parts of our inner world out into the open and looking just there for that which actually effects and governs, looking for that which is decisive in development exactly where the intellectual pride of humanity least *wished* to find it (for example, in the inertial force of habit or in forgetfulness or in a blind, random, and mechanical hooking-together of ideas, or in something purely passive, automatic, reflexive, molecular, and fundamentally stupid). What drove these psychologists in always just *this* direction? Is it a secret, malicious, base, perhaps yet unacknowledged instinct for the belittlement of the human? Or maybe a pessimistic suspicion, the mistrust that idealists possess after becoming disappointed, gloomy, poisonous, and envious? Or a petty subterranean enmity and rancor against Christianity (and Plato) that perhaps has not reached over the threshold of consciousness? Or even a lascivious taste for the strange, the painfully paradoxical, the questionable and senseless in existence? Or finally, something of everything—a little vulgarity, a little gloominess, a little anti-Christianity, a bit of an urge and need for spice? . . . But I have heard that they are merely old, cold, and tedious frogs who creep and hop around humanity and into humanity as if they were in exactly their proper element, namely, in a *swamp.* I resist that thought; I even refuse to believe it. And if one may wish where one cannot know,[3] then I wish from the heart that it's the other way around with them—that these researchers and microscopers of the soul are fundamentally brave, magnanimous, and proud animals who know how to bridle their hearts as well as their pain and have trained themselves to sacrifice all desirability to truth, *every* truth, even the plain, bitter, hateful, unfavorable, unchristian, immoral truth . . . For there are such truths . . .

2. [. . .] Now it is obvious to me, first, that, following this theory, the true original source of the concept "good" has been sought and presupposed in the wrong place: the judgment "good" did *not* come from those to whom "goodness" was shown! On the con-

trary it was "the good" themselves, that is, the noble, powerful, high-stationed, and high-minded who felt and posited themselves and their activity as good, that is, of the first rank, in contradistinction to all that is low, low-minded, common, and vulgar. It was out of this *pathos of distance*[4] that they first took the right to create value and to coin names for values. What does utility have to do with them! The viewpoint of utility is, with regards to such a fiery eruption of the highest rank-ordering, rank-distinguishing value-judgments, precisely as alien and inappropriate as possible: here the feeling has attained just the opposite, the tepid warmth that every calculating cleverness, every utility calculus requires—and not just once, not for one exceptional hour, but for the long term. The pathos of nobility and distance, as I said, the enduring and dominating complete and fundamental feeling of a higher ruling type in relation to a lower type, to a "below"—*that* is the origin of the opposition "good" and "bad." (The lordly right of giving names extends so far that we should allow ourselves to conceive the origin of language itself as power-expression of those ruling: they say "that *is* that and that," they stamp every thing and event with a sound and thereby, as it were, take possession of it.) In light of this origin, the word "good" is *not* from the outset bound up necessarily with "unegoistic" actions, as is the superstition of every genealogist of morality. Instead, only with the *decline* of aristocratic value-judgments did it come to pass that the entire opposition of "egoistic" and "unegoistic" could not help but insert itself more and more into human conscience. It is, to make use of my language, the *herd instinct* that with this antithesis finally gets its word (and also its *words*) in.

10. The slave revolt in morality begins when *ressentiment*[5] itself becomes creative and gives birth to values—the *ressentiment* of those beings to whom the genuine reaction, that of the deed, is denied, and whose only remedy is an imaginary revenge. While every noble morality grows forth from a triumphant Yes-saying to itself, from the very beginning the slave morality says "No" to some "outside," to some "other," to some "not itself"; and *this* "No" is its creative deed. This inversion of the value-positing eye—this *necessary* direction outwards rather than back to itself—belongs precisely to *ressentiment.* Slave morality, in order to arise, first requires a hostile and external world; it requires, physiologically speaking, external stimuli, in order to act at all—its action is fundamentally reaction. [. . .] While the noble person lives in trust and openness with himself (the ancient Greek word *gennaios*, "of noble birth," underscores the nuance "upright" and probably also "naïve"), the person of *ressentiment* is neither upright nor naïve, nor even honest and direct with himself. His soul *squints*; his spirit loves hiding places, secret paths, and back doors, everything concealed feels to him like his world, his safety, his refreshment; he knows what he is doing when it comes to keeping quiet, to not forgetting, to waiting, to provisionally demeaning and humbling himself. In the long run a race of such persons of *ressentiment* will necessarily be *more clever* than any noble race. They will honor cleverness in a wholly different measure: namely, as a condition of existence of the first rank, while among noble persons cleverness can easily take on a subtle flavoring of luxury and refinement—for here cleverness is not as essential as the perfected operational safety of the regulating *unconscious* instincts or even a certain uncleverness, maybe a kind of brave dynamism no matter whether facing danger or the enemy, or that fervent suddenness of anger, love, rev-

erence, gratitude, and revenge by which noble souls have at all times recognized each other.[. . .] To be incapable of taking one's enemies, one's mishaps, even one's *misdeeds* seriously for very long—that is the sign of strong, full natures in whom there is an excess of the force that shapes, replicates, heals, and even causes to forget . . . Such a person, with one shake, scatters away from him the maggots that burrow deeply into others; here alone, if anywhere on earth, the genuine "love of one's enemies" is possible. How much reverence for his enemies does the noble person have!—and such reverence is even a bridge to love . . . He desires his enemy for himself, as his mark of distinction, he cannot stand any enemy other than such a one in whom there is nothing to despise and *very much* to honor! Against this one may imagine "the enemy" as the person of *ressentiment* conceives of him—and exactly here is his deed, his creation: he has conceived of "the evil enemy," "the *evil one*," and this is indeed his fundamental concept, from which he then devises as replica and counterpart a "good one"—himself!

11. So this is just the opposite of what the noble person does, the one who conceives of his fundamental concept "good" straight away and spontaneously, that is, conceiving of it out of himself and only afterward bothering himself with the idea of "bad." This "bad" of noble origin and that "evil" out of the cauldron of unsatiated hate—the first an after-creation, a "by the way," a complementary color, the second, by contrast, the archetype, the beginning, the actual *deed* in the conception of a slave-morality—how different these words are, both apparently opposed to the same concept "good." But it is *not* the same concept "good": on the contrary, one should ask just *who* is "evil" in the sense of the *ressentiment*-morality. To answer in all strictness: *precisely* the "good" person of the other morality, precisely the noble, the powerful, the masterful—only dyed in another color, interpreted in another manner, seen in another way through the poisonous eye of *ressentiment.* [. . .] It may be quite right not to give up the fear of the blond beast that is at the bottom of all noble races, and to guard against it. But who would not prefer a hundred times more to fear when he may at the same time admire, than *not* to fear when he can no longer be rid of the revolting sight of the botched, diminished, atrophied, and poisoned? And is that not *our* fate? What *our* aversion to "humanity" consists in?—For we *suffer* from humanity, that is doubtless. *Not* fear; rather, that we have nothing more to fear in humanity; that the maggot "human" swarms in the foreground; that the "tame human," the hopelessly mediocre and unpleasant human has already learned how to feel himself as goal and summit, as meaning of history, as "higher human"; that he even has a certain right to feel that way, insofar as he feels superior to the glut of botched, sickly, tired, exhausted of which Europe is today beginning to stink, and thus he turned out at least relatively well, he is at least still capable of living, at least still says Yes to life . . .

16. Let us conclude. The two *opposite* values "good and bad," "good and evil" have been on earth for millennia, engaged in a terrible struggle; and although the latter value has been predominant for a long time, there do not yet lack places where the struggle rages on indecisively. One could even say that it has been brought ever higher, and precisely thereby become ever deeper, ever more spiritual: so that today there is no more decisive emblem of a "higher nature," of a more spiritual nature, than being conflicted in this sense

and really still a battlefield for those opposites. The symbol of this struggle, written in a script that remains legible across all human history so far, is "Rome against Judea, Judea against Rome":—there has so far been no greater event than *this* struggle, *this* putting into question, *this* mortally adversarial contradiction. Rome sensed in the Jew something like anti-nature itself, as it were his antipodal monster; in Rome the Jew was considered "*convicted* of hatred for the entire human race": and rightly, insofar as one has the right to fasten the well-being and the future of the human race to the unconditional rule of aristocratic values, of Roman values. [. . .] Which of them has meanwhile *won*? But there is absolutely no doubt; one may consider to whom one today bows down in Rome itself, as to the epitome of all the highest values—and not only in Rome, but over almost half the earth, everywhere the human being has become or wants to become tame: *three Jews*, as is known, and *one Jewess* (Jesus of Nazareth, the fisherman Peter, the carpet-knitter Paul, and the mother of the above-mentioned Jesus, named Mary). This is very remarkable: Rome is without any doubt defeated.

Second Treatise: "Guilt," "Bad Conscience," and So Forth

1. To breed an animal with *the prerogative of making promises*—is that not exactly the paradoxical task that Nature has set for itself with respect to humanity? Is it not the genuine problem *about* humanity? . . . That this problem has been for the most part solved must be all the more astounding for anyone who can fully appreciate the opposing force, that of *forgetfulness.* Forgetfulness is no mere "inertial force," as the superficial believe; rather, it is active, in the strictest sense a positive faculty of inhibition, through which one may explain that what we experience and encounter, all that we absorb, enters into consciousness during its digestion (one may call it "immentalization") just as little as does the entire thousand-fold process through which our bodily nourishment, so-called "incorporation," plays out. To close the doors and windows of consciousness for a while; to remain undisturbed by the noise and struggle with which our underworld of functioning organs operate for and against one another; a bit of quiet, a little bit of "blank slate" of consciousness, so that there can be room for something new, above all for the more refined functions and functionaries, for regulating, foreseeing, advance planning (for our organism is set up as an oligarchy)—that is the utility of, as said, active forgetfulness, a doorkeeper as it were, a bouncer for psychic order, repose, and etiquette: thereby one can anticipate the extent to which there would be no happiness, no cheerfulness, no pride, no *present* without forgetfulness. The person in whom this inhibiting-apparatus is damaged and no longer functioning may be compared to (and not merely compared to) a dyspeptic who is never "done" with anything . . . This necessarily forgetful animal, in whom forgetting exhibits a force, a form of *strong* health, has also cultivated an opposing faculty, a memory, with whose help forgetfulness can in certain cases be suspended—for the cases, namely, those in which a promise is made: this does not by any means involve a merely passive inability to get rid of a once-ingrained impression, nor merely the indigestion of

a once-pledged word which one cannot get "done" with, but an active not-*wanting*-to-get-rid-of, a further and longer wanting of what was once willed, a genuine *memory of the will:* so that between the original "I want," "I'll do it" and the actual discharge of the will, its *act,* a world of strange new things, circumstances, and even acts of will can be safely interposed without breaking this long chain of will. But how much all that presupposes! How much the human being must have already learned in order to decree the future: to separate necessary events from chance ones, to think causally, to see and anticipate what is distant as if it were present, to set out what is ends and what is means, in general to be able to reckon and calculate—how much the human being itself must have become *calculable, regular, necessary,* even for his own self-representation as able, like a promiser does, to vouch for himself *as future.*

2. Precisely this is the long history of the origin of *responsibility.* That task of breeding an animal with the prerogative of making promises, as we have already grasped, encompasses as its precondition and preparation the prior task of first *making* the human being to a certain degree necessary, uniform, equal among equals, regular, and consequently calculable. The tremendous labor involved, what I have previously called the "ethicality of custom"[6] (cf. *Daybreak* sections 9, 14, 16)—the actual labor of the human being on itself in the longest era of the human race, its whole prehistoric labor, has its meaning here, its great justification, disregarding all the harshness, tyranny, monotony, and idiocy it possesses: the human being, with the help of the ethicality of custom and the social strait-jacket was actually *made* calculable. Let us place ourselves, by contrast, at the end of this tremendous process, where the tree finally yielded its fruit, where society and the ethicality of custom finally brought to light that *to which* they were mere means: there we find as the tree's ripest fruit the *sovereign individual,* comparable to nothing but itself, setting itself free even from the ethicality of custom, the autonomous extra-ethical individual (as "autonomous" and "ethical" are mutually exclusive). [. . .] With him the proud knowledge of the extraordinary privilege of *responsibility,* the consciousness of this rare freedom, this power over oneself and fate has sunk to its lowest depths and turned into instinct, dominating instinct—what would he call this dominating instinct, assuming he feels a need to have a word for it? But there is no doubt: this sovereign human calls it his *conscience* . . .

3. His conscience? . . . It is easy to anticipate that the concept "conscience," which we encounter here in its highest, almost eerie manifestation, already has a long history and metamorphosis of form behind it. [. . .] The primeval problem, as one might expect, is not quite solved with tender answers and measures; in fact, there is perhaps nothing more frightful and uncanny in the entire prehistory of humankind than its *mnemotechnics.*[7] "One burns something in so that it stays in memory: only that which does not cease to *cause pain* stays in memory"—that is a basic principle of the most ancient (unfortunately also the most enduring) psychology on earth. One could even say that wherever on earth there is still solemnity, seriousness, mystery, and gloomy colors in the life of human being and people, something of the terror with which everything formerly promised, pledged, and vowed came to be *continues to operate*: the past, the longest, deepest, harshest past breathes on us and swells up in us whenever we become "serious." There was never any

lack of blood, martyrs, and sacrifices when a human being deemed it necessary to make a memory for himself; the most horrifying sacrifices and pledges (among them, sacrifices of the first-born), the most repulsive mutilations (for example, castrations), the cruelest forms of ritual of all the religious cults (and all religions are fundamentally systems of cruelty)—all that has its origin in the instinct that locates in pain its most powerful aid to mnemonics. In a certain sense the whole of asceticism belongs here: a few ideas are supposed to be made indelible, omnipresent, unforgettable, "fixed," with the aim of hypnotizing of the entire nervous and intellectual systems through these "fixed ideas"—and the ascetic procedures and forms of life are means to this, with the purpose of relieving those ideas from competition with any remaining ideas and making them "unforgettable." [...] Ah, reason, seriousness, mastery over the affects, this whole gloomy thing called reflection, all these privileges and showpieces of humanity: how dearly have they been bought! how much blood and cruelty is at the bottom of all "good things"! ...

4. But how then did that other "gloomy thing," the consciousness of guilt, the entire "bad conscience" come into the world?—And with this we turn back to our "genealogists of morals." To say it again—or have I not even said it yet?—they are completely useless. [...] Have these previous genealogists of morals even allowed themselves the remotest dream that, for example, the fundamental moral concept "guilt" (*Schuld*) has its origin in the very material concept of "debt" (*Schulden*)? Or that punishment as *retribution* developed in complete independence from any assumption about the freedom or unfreedom of the will?—and this to the degree that it in fact takes a *higher* level of humanization for the animal "human" to begin to make those much more primitive distinctions of "intentional," "negligent," "accidental," "accountable" and their opposites, and to take them into account in the allocation of punishment? That now so trite and seemingly so natural thought that "the criminal earns his punishment *because* he could have acted otherwise," which has had to suffice for the explanation of how the feeling of justice came into being on earth, is actually an extremely late achievement and refined form of human judgment and inference; whoever misattributes it to the beginnings coarsely mishandles the psychology of ancient humanity. Throughout the longest period of human history punishment did *not* take place *because* someone wanted to make the instigator responsible for his deed, and thus not with the assumption that only the culpable should be punished—instead, as parents still punish their children, it was out of an anger over some harm suffered that lashes out at the source of harm—this anger, but restrained and modified through the idea that every loss has its *equivalent* and can actually be paid back, even if through the *pain* of the malefactor. From where did this primeval, deep-rooted, perhaps no longer eradicable idea, that of an equivalence between harm and pain, take its power? I have already given it away: in the contractual relation between *creditor* and *debtor*, which is as old as that of "subjects of rights" in general and in turns points back to the fundamental forms of buying, selling, exchange, trade, and dealing.

6. To ask it again: to what extent can suffering compensate for "debts" or "guilt"? Insofar as *making* suffer is to the highest degree appealing, insofar as the one harmed accepts in exchange for the loss, including the displeasure over the loss, an extraordinary

counter-pleasure: *making* suffer,—a genuine *festival*, something that, as I said, was all the more valuable the more it contradicted the rank and social standing of the creditor. This is offered as speculation: for apart from it being uncomfortable, it is difficult to see such subterranean things in their foundations; and whoever plops down the concept of "revenge" here makes the insight darker and more mysterious rather than clearer (—revenge leads us back to the same problem: "how can making suffer serve as compensation?")

8. To take up the course of our investigation again, the feeling of guilt and personal obligation had, as we saw, its origin in the oldest and earliest personal relationship, that of the buyer and seller, creditor and debtor: this was the first manifestation of person coming against person, of one person *measuring himself* against another person. No one has yet discovered a degree of civilization so low that this relationship cannot be observed. Setting prices, measuring values, thinking out equivalents, exchanging—this preoccupied the oldest thoughts of humanity to such an extent that it constitutes, in a certain sense, what thinking is: here the oldest kind of astuteness was cultivated, and here, we may likewise surmise, are the first beginnings of human pride, humanity's feeling of superiority with respect to other animals.

12. Another word on the origin and purpose of punishment—two problems that are separate, or at least should be separate: unfortunately they are usually thrown together. How have the previous genealogists of morals pursued these questions? Naïvely, as they have in every pursuit—they discover some "purpose" in punishment, for example revenge or deterrence, then they guilelessly set this purpose at the beginning, as the cause of punishment coming into being, and then—they are done. The "purpose of laws" is absolutely the last thing that enters into the history of the origin of laws, however: on the contrary, there is for all kinds of history no more important proposition than this one, which was gained with a great deal of difficulty but really *should be* gained,—that, namely, the cause of the origin of a thing and its final utility, actual employment, and place in a system of purposes lie worlds apart; that something existing, having somehow come-into-being, is always again and again appropriated by a power superior to it and interpreted from new viewpoints, reorganized and redirected toward a new use; that everything that happens in the organic is an *overcoming*, a *becoming master*, and on the other hand that all overcoming and becoming master is a new-interpreting, a preparation in which the prior "meaning" and "purpose" must necessarily be obscured or entirely obliterated. [...] Thus has it been imagined that punishment was invented for the purpose of punishing. But all purposes, all utilities are only signs that a will to power has mastered something less powerful and stamped upon it the significance of a function; and the entire history of a "thing," of an organ, of a custom can in this way be a continuous sign-chain of ever newer interpretations and preparations whose very causes need not be connected to one another, but instead follow and take over from one another under chance circumstances. The "development" of a thing, a custom, an organ is accordingly by no means its progress toward a goal, still less a logical and direct progress, reached with the smallest possible outlay of force and expense—rather it is the succession of more or less far-reaching, more or less mutually independent processes of overcoming, adding in the resistances directed against

it, the attempted formal transformations with the purpose of reaction and defense, and even the results of successful counteractions. The form is fluid, the "meaning" even more so . . .

16. At this point a first, provisional form of my own hypothesis concerning the origin of the "bad conscience" can no longer be avoided: there are difficulties in giving voice to it, as it wants to be considered, guarded, and slept on for a while. I take the bad conscience to be the profound sickness that man was bound to contract under the pressure of the most fundamental of all changes that he ever experienced—that change which occurred when he found himself definitively closed up inside the confines of society and of peace. No less than what happened to the creatures of the sea when they were compelled to walk the land or die, so these half-animals who had adapted to wilderness, war, roaming, and adventure had all of their instincts devalued at one blow and became "unmoored." They had to travel by foot and "bear themselves," where they previously were borne along by water: a dreadful heaviness weighed on them. They felt ungainly in the smallest undertakings; in this new, unknown world they no longer had the old guide, the unconsciously regulating, securely governing instincts. These unfortunates were reduced to thinking, inferring, calculating, matching cause and effect, dependent on their "consciousness," on their poorest and most error-prone organ! I believe that nowhere on earth has there ever been such a feeling of misery, such a leaden discomfort,—and those old instincts did not suddenly cease to impose their demands in these circumstances! Only it was difficult and seldom feasible to do their bidding: for the most part they had to look for new and as it were subterranean satisfactions. All instincts that cannot be discharged externally *direct themselves back inward*—this is what I call the "*internalization*" of humankind: with this that which is later called its "soul" first arises. The entire inner world, originally as thin as if stretched between two skins, extended and enlarged itself, acquiring depth, breadth, and height to the extent that the human's outward discharge was *inhibited.* Those fearsome bulwarks with which political organization protects against the old instincts of freedom—punishments belong, above all, to these bulwarks—led to all those instincts of wildness, freedom, and roaming being directed backward, *against the human being itself.* Enmity, cruelty, joy in persecution, in aggression, in change, in destruction—all this directing itself against the possessor of such instincts—*that* is the origin of the "bad conscience." The human being who, from a lack of external enemies and resistances, was driven into the narrowness and regularity of custom, impatiently tearing himself apart, persecuting, gnawing at, tormenting, and abusing himself, this animal chafing at the bars of its cage during the struggle to "tame" it, deprived and consumed by longing for the desert, who must create an adventure, a torture chamber, and an uncertain and dangerous wilderness out of himself—this lunatic, this yearning and desperate prisoner was the inventor of the bad conscience. With him, however, the greatest and most uncanny sickness was instituted, one from which humankind has not yet recovered, humanity's suffering *of humanity, of itself*: as the result of a violent separation from its animal past, a leap and a plunge into new situations and conditions of existence, a declaration of war against the old instincts on which, until that point, its force, joy, and terribleness had rested.

21. The moralization of the concepts of guilt and duty, their push back into the *bad* conscience, represents an attempt to *turn around* the direction of the development just described, or at least to arrest its movement: now the very prospect of a final, once-and-for-all discharge is to be pessimistically closed off, now the gaze should be sent recoiling back inconsolably from an iron impossibility, now these concepts "guilt" and "duty" should be turned backwards—but back against *whom?* There can be no doubt: first against the "debtor," in whom the bad conscience is so firmly fixed, consuming, and expansive, that its tentacles find every breadth and depth, until finally the notion of the irredeemability of debt is conceptualized, along with the irredeemability of atonement, the thought of its incalculability (*eternal* punishment). But eventually guilt and duty are directed against the creditor, too, however one thinks of it: as the first cause of humanity, as the beginning of the human race, as its ancestor who is marked by a curse ("Adam," "original sin," "unfreedom of will"), as nature who gave birth to humankind but into which the principle of evil has been introduced ("devilization of nature"), or as existence in general, which is left over as *intrinsically worthless* (nihilistic turning away, longing for nothingness or longing for its opposite, some other way of being, as in Buddhism and so forth)—until suddenly we stand before the paradoxes and the horrifying explanatory expedient in which tormented humanity found a temporary relief, *Christianity*'s great stroke of genius, God sacrificing himself for the guilt of humankind, God himself making himself pay, God as the only one who can absolve humankind from what has become irredeemable for humankind—the creditor himself sacrificing himself for his debtors, out of *love* (was this credible?—), out of love for his debtors!

24. I conclude with three questions marks, so much is clear. Perhaps one asks me, "Is an ideal being constructed here, or one being demolished?" . . . But have you questioned yourselves adequately as to how costly the construction of *every* ideal on earth has been? How much reality had to be slandered and misjudged, how much lies had to be sanctified, how much conscience had to be distressed, how much God had to be sacrificed every time? So that a sanctuary could be constructed, *a sanctuary had to be destroyed:* that is the law—show me the case in which it is not fulfilled! . . . We moderns, we are the heirs of the conscience-vivisection and animal-self-cruelty of millennia: this is our longest practice, our artistry perhaps, or in any case our refinement, our discriminating palate. Humankind has treated its natural inclinations with an "evil eye" for so long that it has finally become inseparable from the "bad conscience." An attempt to reverse this would be *in itself* possible—but who is strong enough for it? To attach, that is, the bad conscience to all the *unnatural* inclinations, all those aspirations toward the Beyond, anti-sensual, anti-instinctual, anti-natural, anti-animal ideals, in short all the ideals there have ever been, all hostile-to-life and world-slandering ideals. [. . .] For such a goal a precisely *different* kind of spirit is required from the one likely in this age: spirits who are empowered by war and victory, for whom conquest, adventure, danger, and even pain have become necessities; this requires a habituation to biting, high air, to winter wanderings, to ice and mountains in every sense; it even requires a kind of sublime malice, an ultimate, self-confident wantonness in knowledge belonging to a great health, it requires, in brief and alas, precisely this *"great health"!*

Third Treatise: What Is the Meaning of Ascetic Ideals?

1. What do ascetic ideals mean? In the case of artists, nothing, or too many things; with philosophers and scholars something like a scent and instinct for the most favorable preconditions of a higher spirituality; among women, at best one *more* seductive appeal, a bit of softness on beautiful flesh, the angelic quality of a cute, plump animal; with the physiologically unfortunate and discordant (the *majority* of mortals), an attempt to feel "too good" for this world, a holy form of dissipation, their primary weapon in the struggle with dull pain and boredom; among priests they are the true priestly faith, their best tool for power, even the "almighty" permission for power; among saints, finally, a pretext for hibernation, their newest lust for glory, their repose in nothingness ("God"), their form of lunacy. But *that* the ascetic ideal has meant so many different things to humankind, therein the fundamental fact of human will expresses itself, its horror of a vacuum: *it requires a goal*—and it would much rather will *nothingness* than *not* will.

11. The idea being contested here is the *value* of our life according to the ascetic priests: this life (together with what belongs to it: "nature," "world," the entire sphere of becoming and transience) they only consider in relation to an entirely different kind of existence, which is its exclusively opposite counterpart, *unless* life somehow turns against itself, unless it *denies itself:* in this case, the case of ascetic life, this life counts as a bridge to that other existence. The ascetic treats life as a false turn that one must finally trace back, until one gets back to where one started; or like a mistake that one refutes through action—or *should* refute: then he demands that one go with him, he makes his own *evaluation* of existence, wherever he can, compulsory. What does that mean? Such a monstrous mode of evaluation does not stand inscribed as an exceptional case or a curiosity in the history of humankind: it is one of the most widespread and enduring facts. Read from a distant star, the upper-case script of our earthly existence would perhaps tempt one to the conclusion that the earth is actually the *ascetic star*, a little corner of ill-humored, arrogant, and adverse creatures who will not get rid of their profound annoyance at themselves, at the earth, and at all living, and who, out of pleasure in causing pain, hurt themselves as much as possible—as probably their only pleasure. Let us consider how regularly, how universally, how almost perpetually the ascetic priest makes an appearance; he does not belong to any isolated race; he thrives everywhere; he grows out of every class or rank. Not that he cultivated his mode of evaluation through heredity and then planted it further: the opposite is the case—a deeper instinct forbids him, by and large, from propagating. It must be a necessity of the first order which makes this *life-inimical* species always grow and thrive—it must be in the *interest of life itself* that such a type of self-contradiction does not die out.

13. The self-contradiction that seems to be manifest in ascetics, that of "life *against life*"—so much is obvious—is physiologically scrutinized, and not only physiologically scrutinized, simply nonsense. It can only be *apparent*; it must be a kind of provisional expression, an interpretation, a formula, a preparation, a psychological misunderstanding

of something whose true nature could not for a long time be understood, could not be depicted as it really is—a mere word, ensnared in an old *gap* in human knowledge. Against that I briefly set out the facts of the matter: *the ascetic ideal emerges out of the protective and healing instincts of a degenerating life* which seeks, by any means, to maintain itself, and which struggles for its existence; it points to a partial physiological inhibition and fatigue, against which the deepest instincts of life remain intact and fight relentlessly with new expedients and inventions. The ascetic ideal is one such expedient: it is therefore just the opposite of what those who revere this ideal suppose—in it and through it life grapples with death and *against* death, the ascetic ideal is a gambit for the *preservation* of life. [. . .] What does that kind of disease depend upon? Seeing that the human being is sicker, more insecure, more variable, and more indeterminate than any other animal, there can be no doubt—the human is *the* sick animal: where does that come from?

15. If one has deeply comprehended—and I demand that one grasp deeply, comprehend deeply right here—the extent to which it simply *cannot* be the task of the healthy to attend to the sick, to make the sick healthy, then one more necessity is thereby comprehended—the necessity of doctors and orderlies *who are themselves sick.* [. . .] If one wanted to express the value of the priestly existence in the shortest possible formula, so would one say straight away: the priest *changes the direction of ressentiment.* Every sufferer instinctively seeks a cause for his suffering: more precisely, a perpetrator, or rather, a guilty perpetrator who is susceptible to suffering—in short, some living thing against whom he can, on some pretext, discharge his emotions, either truly or in effigy. For this emotional discharge is the best way of providing relief—that is to say, it is the sufferer's attempt to provide himself *anaesthesia*, the narcotic against all kinds of anguish that he involuntarily desires. Here alone, according to my supposition, is the actual psychological causality of *ressentiment*, revenge, and associated phenomena to be found: in a longing for an *anaesthetic against pain through the emotions.* [. . .] "I suffer: someone must be to blame for it"—thus thinks every sickly sheep. But his shepherd, the ascetic priest, tells him: "Quite so, my sheep! someone must be to blame for it: but you yourself are this someone, you alone are to blame for it—*you alone are to blame for yourself!*"—This is bold and false enough, but one thing at least is achieved by it . . . the direction of *ressentiment* is *changed.*

20. The main hold that the ascetic priest takes the liberty of seizing in order to let that sort of disintegrating, ecstatic music resonate on the human soul was—as everyone knows—that he made use of the *feeling of guilt.* The previous treatise briefly indicated the origin of this feeling —as a piece of animal psychology, and nothing else: we encountered the feeling of guilt there in its raw state, as it were. Only in the hands of the priest, that true artist of guilty feelings, did it take shape—and oh what a shape! "Sin"—for that is the name of the priestly reinterpretation of the animal "bad conscience" (cruelty directed backwards)—has been the greatest event in the history of the sick soul so far. In it we have the most dangerous and most fateful artifice of religious interpretation. The human being, suffering from himself, somehow, in any case psychologically, almost like an animal trapped in a cage, wonders uncertainly, why? what for? Desirous of reasons—reasons relieve—also desirous of expedients and narcotics, finally gets advice from someone who knows hid-

den things—and voilá! He receives a hint, he receives the *first* hint from his magician, the ascetic priest, of the "cause" of his suffering: he should look for it *in himself*, in his *guilt*, in a bit of the past, he should understand his suffering itself as a *condition of punishment*...

21. With regard to *this* whole type of priestly medication, the "guilty" kind, any word of criticism is too much. [...] But when it comes to sick, peevish, depressed people, such a system, even granting that it makes them "better," whatever else happens, also makes them *sicker*. One only has to ask those who treat the insane what always follows from a methodical application of the anguish of atonement, remorse, and spasms of redemption. In the same way, one should inquire into history: wherever the ascetic priest has administered this treatment of the sick, disease has proliferated far and wide with amazing speed. What was the "success" every time? A shattered nervous system, in addition to whatever was afflicted before—and this happens among young and old alike, and as much among individuals as among the masses.

23. The ascetic ideal has not only ruined health and taste, it has also ruined a third, fourth, fifth and sixth thing. [...] What exactly does the *power* of that ideal mean, the *monstrosity* of its power? Why was so much space given to it? Why wasn't a better resistance raised? The ascetic ideal expresses one will: *where* is the opposing will, in which an *opposing ideal* expresses itself? The ascetic ideal has a *goal*—that goal is universal enough that all other interests of human existence appear narrow and petty when measured against it; it interprets times, peoples, persons inexorably in light of this One Goal; no other interpretation, no other goal counts; it rejects, denies, affirms, confirms according only to the meaning of *its* interpretation (—and has there ever been a more thoroughly thought out system of interpretation?); it submits to no power, rather it believes in its privilege before every power, in its unconditional *distance of rank* in relation to every power—it believes that there is no power on earth that does not receive its meaning, its right to exist, its value from it alone, as a tool for *its* work, as way and means to *its* goals, to One Goal... Where is the *counterpart* to this closed system of will, goal, and interpretation? Why is the counterpart *lacking*? ... Where is the *other* "One Goal"? ... But some say to me that it is *not* lacking, that not only has it been engaged in a long, favorable struggle with that ideal, it has in fact already mastered that ideal in all the big issues: our whole modern *science* is the testimony to that, this modern science which, as a genuine philosophy of reality, apparently believes only in itself, apparently possesses courage and will in itself, and has gotten along so far without God, the Beyond, or negating virtues. However, generating such noise and inflammatory prattle doesn't go very far with me: these reality-trumpeters are bad musicians. [...] The truth is exactly the opposite of what was claimed: today science simply has *no* faith in itself, let alone an ideal *over* itself—and where it is generally still passion, love, ardor, and *suffering*, it is not the contrary of that ascetic ideal, but rather its most recent and most distinguished form.

24. These negaters and outsiders of today, these absolutists in one point, in the demand for intellectual cleanliness, these tough, severe, abstemious, heroic spirits who constitute the honor of our age, all these pale atheists, antichrists, immoralists, nihilists. [.. .]—They are quite far from being *free* spirits: *for they still have faith in truth*... [...]—The

will to truth requires a critique—let us thus ordain our own task—the value of truth must be experimentally *called into question.*

27. The only thing that matters to me here is to have pointed this out: even in the most spiritual sphere, the ascetic ideal has at present only one kind of enemy who truly *harms* it: the comedians of this ideal, for they arouse mistrust in it. Everywhere else that the spirit is severe, powerful, and at work without counterfeiting today, it dispenses with ideals altogether—the popular expression for this abstinence is "atheism"—*not taking into account its will to truth.* But this will, this remains of an ideal, is, if anyone will believe me, that ideal itself in its more severe, most spiritual formulation, esoteric through and through, stripped of all external supports, thus not so much its remains as its *core.* Unconditional, honest atheism (—and we breathe only its air, we more spiritual persons of this age!) accordingly *does not* stand in opposition to that ideal, as it appeared, but is instead only its final phase of development, one of its conclusive forms and the consequence of its inner logic—it is the awe-inspiring *catastrophe* of two-thousand years of breeding for truth that in the end forbids itself the *lie in the belief in God.* [. . .] What, strictly speaking, actually *triumphed* over the Christian God? The answer can be found in my *The Gay Science,* section 357: "the Christian morality itself, the concept of truthfulness taken ever more strictly, the father-confessor's refinement of the Christian conscience, translated and sublimated into scientific conscience, to intellectual cleanliness at any price. To look upon nature as if it were proof of the goodness and providence of a God; to interpret history in honor of a divine reason, as perpetual testimony to a moral world order and ultimate moral intentions; to construe one's own experiences as pious persons have for long enough, as if everything were preordained, everything a hint, everything skillfully, lovingly arranged for the salvation of the soul: that is all gone now, that has conscience *against* it, that counts among all more subtle consciences as indecent, dishonest, mendacious, effeminate, weak, cowardly—by means of this severity, if by anything, we are *good Europeans* and heirs of Europe's longest and most courageous self-overcoming . . ." All great things perish through their own doing, through an act of self-sublimation: thus decrees the law of life, the law of the *necessary* "self-overcoming" in the essence of life—the call is always issued to the lawgiver himself: "submit to the law that you yourself proposed."[8] In such a way did Christianity *as a dogma* perish by its own morality; in just this way must Christianity as a *morality* now perish, too—we stand at the threshold of *this* event. After Christian truthfulness has drawn one conclusion after another, it will draw its *strongest conclusion,* its conclusion *against* itself; but this comes to pass when it poses the question, "What is the meaning of all will to truth?" . . . From the will to truth thus becoming self-conscious—there is no doubt—morality will henceforth perish: that great spectacle in a hundred acts, which is set in store for Europe's next two centuries, is the most terrible, most questionable, and perhaps even the most hopeful of all spectacles . . .

28. The human being, the most courageous animal and the one most accustomed to suffering, does *not* reject suffering as such: he *wants* it, he even seeks it out, provided he is shown a *meaning* for it, a *what for* of suffering. The meaninglessness of suffering, *not* suffering itself, was the curse that has extended over humankind so far—and *the ascetic*

ideal offered it a meaning! It has been the only meaning so far, any meaning is better than no meaning at all; the ascetic ideal was in every respect the *'faute de mieux' par excellence* that there has been so far. In it suffering was *interpreted*; the monstrous emptiness seemed to be filled up; the door closed itself on all suicidal nihilism. The interpretation—there is no doubt—brought new suffering with it, deeper, more interior, more poisonous, life-gnawing suffering: it brought all suffering under the perspective of *guilt* . . . But despite everything, the human being was thereby *saved*, he had a *meaning*, he was henceforth no longer like a leaf in the wind, a plaything of nonsense, of "without-meaning," he could now *will* something—no matter, at first, what, why, how he willed: *the will itself was saved*. What in fact that entire will expressed simply cannot be concealed, that from which the ascetic ideal acquired its direction: this hatred against the human, even stronger against the animal, even stronger against the corporeal, this repugnance of the senses and even of reason, this fear of happiness and beauty, this longing to get away from appearance, change, becoming, death, wish, even longing—all that means, let us dare to comprehend it, a *will to nothingness*, a counter-will against life, a rebellion against the most basic requirements of life, but it is and it remains *a will!* . . . And, to conclude by saying what I said at the beginning: the human being would rather will *nothingness* than *not* will . . .

PART IV

Nonviolent Struggle and Anticolonialism

W.E.B. Du Bois

From The Souls of Black Folks

Chapter I

Of Our Spiritual Strivings[1]

O water, voice of my heart, crying in the sand,
  All night long crying with a mournful cry,
As I lie and listen, and cannot understand
  The voice of my heart in my side or the voice of the sea,
O water, crying for rest, is it I, is it I?
  All night long the water is crying to me.

Unresting water, there shall never be rest
  Till the last moon droop and the last tide fail,
And the fire of the end begin to burn in the west;
  And the heart shall be weary and wonder and cry like the sea,
All life long crying without avail,
  As the water all night long is crying to me.

ARTHUR SYMONS.

Between me and the other world there is ever an unasked question: unasked by some through feelings of delicacy; by others through the difficulty of rightly framing it. All, nevertheless, flutter round it. They approach me in a half-hesitant sort of way, eye me curiously or compassionately, and then, instead of saying directly, How does it feel to be a problem? they say, I know an excellent colored man in my town; or, I fought at Mechanicsville;[2] or, Do not these Southern outrages make your blood boil? At these I smile, or am interested, or reduce the boiling to a simmer, as the occasion may require. To the real question, How does it feel to be a problem? I answer seldom a word.

And yet, being a problem is a strange experience,—peculiar even for one who has never been anything else, save perhaps in babyhood and in Europe. It is in the early days of rollicking boyhood that the revelation first bursts upon one, all in a day, as it were. I remember well when the shadow swept across me. I was a little thing, away up in the hills of New England, where the dark Housatonic[3] winds between Hoosac and Taghkanic to the sea. In a wee wooden schoolhouse, something put it into the boys' and girls' heads to buy gorgeous visiting-cards—ten cents a package—and exchange. The exchange was merry, till one girl, a tall newcomer, refused my card,—refused it peremptorily, with a glance.[4] Then it dawned upon me with a certain suddenness that I was different from the others; or like, mayhap, in heart and life and longing, but shut out from their world by a vast veil. I had thereafter no desire to tear down that veil, to creep through; I held all beyond it in common contempt, and lived above it in a region of blue sky and great wandering shadows. That sky was bluest when I could beat my mates at examination-time, or beat them at a foot-race, or even beat their stringy heads. Alas, with the years all this fine contempt began to fade; for the worlds I longed for, and all their dazzling opportunities, were theirs, not mine. But they should not keep these prizes, I said; some, all, I would wrest from them. Just how I would do it I could never decide: by reading law, by healing the sick, by telling the wonderful tales that swam in my head,—some way. With other black boys the strife was not so fiercely sunny: their youth shrunk into tasteless sycophancy, or into silent hatred of the pale world about them and mocking distrust of everything white; or wasted itself in a bitter cry, Why did God make me an outcast and a stranger in mine own house?[5] The shades of the prison-house closed round about us all:[6] walls strait and stubborn to the whitest, but relentlessly narrow, tall, and unscalable to sons of night who must plod darkly on in resignation, or beat unavailing palms against the stone, or steadily, half hopelessly, watch the streak of blue above.

After the Egyptian and Indian, the Greek and Roman, the Teuton and Mongolian, the Negro is a sort of seventh son, born with a veil, and gifted with second-sight in this American world,[7]—a world which yields him no true self-consciousness, but only lets him see himself through the revelation of the other world. It is a peculiar sensation, this double-consciousness,[8] this sense of always looking at one's self through the eyes of others, of measuring one's soul by the tape of a world that looks on in amused contempt and pity. One ever feels his two-ness,—an American, a Negro; two souls, two thoughts, two unreconciled strivings; two warring ideals in one dark body, whose dogged strength alone keeps it from being torn asunder.

The history of the American Negro is the history of this strife,—this longing to attain self-conscious manhood, to merge his double self into a better and truer self. In this merging he wishes neither of the older selves to be lost. He would not Africanize America, for America has too much to teach the world and Africa. He would not bleach his Negro soul in a flood of white Americanism, for he knows that Negro blood has a message for the world. He simply wishes to make it possible for a man to be both a Negro and an American, without being cursed and spit upon by his fellows, without having the doors of Opportunity closed roughly in his face.

This, then, is the end of his striving: to be a co-worker in the kingdom of culture, to escape both death and isolation, to husband and use his best powers and his latent genius. These powers of body and mind have in the past been strangely wasted, dispersed, or forgotten. The shadow of a mighty Negro past flits through the tale of Ethiopia the Shadowy and of Egypt the Sphinx. Throughout history, the powers of single black men flash here and there like falling stars, and die sometimes before the world has rightly gauged their brightness. Here in America, in the few days since Emancipation, the black man's turning hither and thither in hesitant and doubtful striving has often made his very strength to lose effectiveness, to seem like absence of power, like weakness. And yet it is not weakness,—it is the contradiction of double aims. The double-aimed struggle of the black artisan—on the one hand to escape white contempt for a nation of mere hewers of wood and drawers of water, and on the other hand to plough and nail and dig for a poverty-stricken horde—could only result in making him a poor craftsman, for he had but half a heart in either cause. By the poverty and ignorance of his people, the Negro minister or doctor was tempted toward quackery and demagogy; and by the criticism of the other world, toward ideals that made him ashamed of his lowly tasks. The would-be black *savant*[9] was confronted by the paradox that the knowledge his people needed was a twice-told tale to his white neighbors, while the knowledge which would teach the white world was Greek to his own flesh and blood. The innate love of harmony and beauty that set the ruder souls of his people a-dancing and a-singing raised but confusion and doubt in the soul of the black artist; for the beauty revealed to him was the soul-beauty of a race which his larger audience despised, and he could not articulate the message of another people. This waste of double aims, this seeking to satisfy two unreconciled ideals, has wrought sad havoc with the courage and faith and deeds of ten thousand thousand people,—has sent them often wooing false gods and invoking false means of salvation, and at times has even seemed about to make them ashamed of themselves.

Away back in the days of bondage they thought to see in one divine event the end of all doubt and disappointment; few men ever worshipped Freedom with half such unquestioning faith as did the American Negro for two centuries. To him, so far as he thought and dreamed, slavery was indeed the sum of all villainies, the cause of all sorrow, the root of all prejudice; Emancipation was the key to a promised land of sweeter beauty than ever stretched before the eyes of wearied Israelites.[10] In song and exhortation swelled one refrain—Liberty; in his tears and curses the God he implored had Freedom in his right hand. At last it came,—suddenly, fearfully, like a dream. With one wild carnival of blood and passion came the message in his own plaintive cadences:—

> "Shout, O children!
> Shout, you're free!
> For God has bought your liberty!"[11]

Years have passed away since then,—ten, twenty, forty; forty years of national life, forty years of renewal and development, and yet the swarthy spectre sits in its accustomed seat at the Nation's feast. In vain do we cry to this our vastest social problem:—

"Take any shape but that, and my firm nerves
Shall never tremble!"[12]

The Nation has not yet found peace from its sins; the freedman has not yet found in freedom his promised land. Whatever of good may have come in these years of change, the shadow of a deep disappointment rests upon the Negro people,—a disappointment all the more bitter because the unattained ideal was unbounded save by the simple ignorance of a lowly people.

The first decade was merely a prolongation of the vain search for freedom, the boon that seemed ever barely to elude their grasp,—like a tantalizing will-o'-the-wisp,[13] maddening and misleading the headless host. The holocaust of war, the terrors of the Ku-Klux-Klan,[14] the lies of carpet-baggers,[15] the disorganization of industry, and the contradictory advice of friends and foes, left the bewildered serf with no new watchword beyond the old cry for freedom. As the time flew, however, he began to grasp a new idea. The ideal of liberty demanded for its attainment powerful means, and these the Fifteenth Amendment gave him.[16] The ballot, which before he had looked upon as a visible sign of freedom, he now regarded as the chief means of gaining and perfecting the liberty with which war had partially endowed him. And why not? Had not votes made war and emancipated millions? Had not votes enfranchised the freedmen? Was anything impossible to a power that had done all this? A million black men started with renewed zeal to vote themselves into the kingdom. So the decade flew away, the revolution of 1876 came,[17] and left the half-free serf weary, wondering, but still inspired. Slowly but steadily, in the following years, a new vision began gradually to replace the dream of political power,—a powerful movement, the rise of another ideal to guide the unguided, another pillar of fire by night after a clouded day. It was the ideal of "book-learning"; the curiosity, born of compulsory ignorance, to know and test the power of the cabalistic[18] letters of the white man, the longing to know. Here at last seemed to have been discovered the mountain path to Canaan;[19] longer than the highway of Emancipation and law, steep and rugged, but straight, leading to heights high enough to overlook life.

Up the new path the advance guard toiled, slowly, heavily, doggedly; only those who have watched and guided the faltering feet, the misty minds, the dull understandings, of the dark pupils of these schools know how faithfully, how piteously, this people strove to learn. It was weary work. The cold statistician wrote down the inches of progress here and there, noted also where here and there a foot had slipped or some one had fallen. To the tired climbers, the horizon was ever dark, the mists were often cold, the Canaan was always dim and far away. If, however, the vistas disclosed as yet no goal, no resting-place, little but flattery and criticism, the journey at least gave leisure for reflection and self-examination; it changed the child of Emancipation to the youth with dawning self-consciousness, self-realization, self-respect. In those sombre forests of his striving his own soul rose before him, and he saw himself,—darkly as through a veil;[20] and yet he saw in himself some faint revelation of his power, of his mission. He began to have a dim feeling that, to attain his place in the world, he must be himself, and not another. For the first time he sought to analyze the burden he bore upon his back, that dead-weight of social degradation partially masked behind a half-named Negro problem. He felt his poverty; without a cent, without a home, without land, tools, or savings, he had entered into competition with rich, landed, skilled neighbors. To be a poor man is hard, but to be a poor race in a land of dollars is the very bottom of hardships. He felt the weight of his ignorance,—not simply of letters, but of life, of business, of the humanities; the accumulated sloth and shirking and awkwardness of decades and centuries shackled his hands and feet. Nor was his burden all poverty and ignorance. The red stain of bastardy, which two centuries of systematic legal defilement of Negro women had stamped upon his race, meant not only the loss of ancient African chastity, but also the hereditary weight of a mass of corruption from white adulterers, threatening almost the obliteration of the Negro home.

A people thus handicapped ought not to be asked to race with the world, but rather allowed to give all its time and thought to its own social problems. But alas! while sociologists gleefully count his bastards and his prostitutes, the very soul of the toiling, sweating black man is darkened by the shadow of a vast despair. Men call the shadow prejudice, and learnedly explain it as the natural defence of culture against barbarism, learning against ignorance, purity against crime, the "higher" against the "lower" races.[21] To which the Negro cries Amen! and swears that to so much of this strange prejudice as is founded on just homage to civilization, culture, righteousness, and progress, he humbly bows and meekly does obeisance.[22] But before that nameless prejudice that leaps beyond all this he stands helpless, dismayed, and well-nigh speechless; before that personal disrespect and mockery, the ridicule and systematic humiliation, the distortion of fact and wanton license of fancy, the cynical ignoring of the better and the boisterous welcoming of the worse, the all-pervading desire to inculcate disdain for everything black, from Toussaint[23] to the devil,—before this there rises a sickening despair that would disarm and discourage any nation save that black host to whom "discouragement" is an unwritten word.

But the facing of so vast a prejudice could not but bring the inevitable self-questioning, self-disparagement, and lowering of ideals which ever accompany repression and breed in an atmosphere of contempt and hate. Whisperings and portents came borne upon the four winds: Lo! we are diseased and dying, cried the dark hosts; we cannot write, our voting is vain; what need of education, since we must always cook and serve? And the Nation echoed and enforced this self-criticism, saying: Be content to be servants, and nothing more; what need of higher culture for half-men? Away with the black man's ballot, by force or fraud,—and behold the suicide of a race! Nevertheless, out of the evil came something of good,—the more careful adjustment of education to real life, the clearer perception of the Negroes' social responsibilities, and the sobering realization of the meaning of progress.

So dawned the time of *Sturm und Drang:*[24] storm and stress to-day rocks our little boat on the mad waters of the world-sea; there is within and without the sound of conflict, the burning of body and rending of soul; inspiration strives with doubt, and faith with vain questionings. The bright ideals of the past,—physical freedom, political power, the training of brains and the training of hands,—all these in turn have waxed and waned, until even the last grows dim and overcast. Are they all wrong,—all false? No, not that, but each alone was over-simple and incomplete,—the dreams of a credulous race-childhood, or the fond imaginings of the other world which does not know and does not want to know our power. To be really true, all these ideals must be melted and welded into one. The training of the schools we need to-day more than ever,—the training of deft hands, quick eyes and ears, and above all the broader, deeper, higher culture of gifted minds and pure hearts. The power of the ballot we need in sheer self-defence,—else what shall save us from a second slavery? Freedom, too, the long-sought, we still seek,—the freedom of life and limb, the freedom to work and think, the freedom to love and aspire. Work, culture, liberty,—all these we need, not singly but together, not successively but together, each growing and aiding each, and all striving toward that vaster ideal that swims before the Negro people, the ideal of human brotherhood, gained through the unifying ideal of Race; the ideal of fostering and developing the traits and talents of the Negro, not in opposition to or contempt for other races, but rather in large conformity to the greater ideals of the American Republic, in order that some day on American soil two world-races may give each to each those characteristics both so sadly lack. We the darker ones come even now not altogether empty-handed: there are to-day no truer exponents of the pure human spirit of the Declaration of Independence than the American Negroes; there is no true American music but the wild sweet melodies of the Negro slave; the American fairy tales and folk-lore are Indian and African; and, all in all, we black men seem the sole oasis of simple faith and reverence in a dusty desert of dollars and smartness. Will America be poorer if she replace her brutal dyspeptic blundering with light-hearted but determined Negro humility? or her coarse and cruel wit with loving jovial good-humor? or her vulgar music with the soul of the Sorrow Songs?

Merely a concrete test of the underlying principles of the great republic is the Negro Problem, and the spiritual striving of the freedmen's sons is the travail of souls whose burden is almost beyond the measure of their strength, but who bear it in the name of an historic race, in the name of this the land of their fathers' fathers, and in the name of human opportunity.

* * *

And now what I have briefly sketched in large outline let me on coming pages tell again in many ways, with loving emphasis and deeper detail, that men may listen to the striving in the souls of black folk.

Mahatma Gandhi

Untouchability

There is an ineffaceable blot that Hinduism today carries with it. I have declined to believe that it has been handed down to us from immemorial times. I think that this miserable, wretched, enslaving spirit of "untouchableness" must have come to us when we were at our lowest ebb. This evil has stuck to us and still remains with us.

Untouchability as it is practised in Hinduism today is, in my opinion, a sin against God and man and is therefore like a poison slowly eating into the very vitals of Hinduism. In my opinion, it has no sanction whatsoever in the Hindu *Shastras* [i.e., law books] taken as a whole. . . . It has degraded both the untouchables and the touchables. It has stunted the growth of nearly 40 million human beings. They are denied even the ordinary amenities of life. The sooner, therefore, it is ended, the better for Hinduism, the better for India, and perhaps the better for mankind in general.

So far as I am concerned with the untouchability question it is one of life and death for Hinduism. As I have said repeatedly, if untouchability lives, Hinduism perishes, and even India perishes; but if untouchability is eradicated from the Hindu heart, root and branch, then Hinduism has a definite message for the world. I have said the first thing to hundreds of audiences but not for the latter part. Now it is the utterance of a man who accepts Truth as God. It is therefore no exaggeration. If untouchability is an integral part of Hinduism, the latter is a spent bullet. But untouchability is a hideous untruth. My motive in launching the anti-untouchability campaign is clear. What I am aiming at is not every Hindu touching an "untouchable," but every touchable Hindu driving untouchability from his heart, going through a complete change of heart.

It is bad enough when dictated by selfish motives to considers ourselves high and other people low. But is not only worse but a double wrong when we tack religion to an evil like untouchability. It, therefore, grieves me when learned pundits come forward and invoke the authority of *Shastras* for a patent evil like untouchability. I have said, and I repeat today, that we, Hindus, are undergoing a period of probation. Whether we desire it or not, untouchability is going. But if during this period of probation we repent for the sin, if we reform and purify ourselves, history will record that one act as a supreme act of purification on the part of the Hindus. But if, through the working of the time spirit, we are compelled to do things against our will and Harijans come into their own, it will be no credit to the Hindus or to Hinduism. But I go a step further and say that if we fail in this trial, Hinduism and Hindus will perish.

Harijan means "a man of God." All the religions of the world describe God preeminently as the Friend of the friendless, Help of the helpless, and Protector of the weak. The rest of the world apart, in India who can be more friendless, helpless or weaker than the forty million or more Hindus of India who are classified as "untouchables"? If, therefore, any body of people can be fitly described as men of God, they are surely these helpless, friendless and despised people. Hence . . . I have always adopted Harijan as the name signifying "untouchables." Not that the change of name brings about any change of status but one may at least be spared the use of a term which is itself one of reproach. When caste Hindus have of their own inner conviction and, therefore, voluntarily, got rid of the present-day untouchability we shall all be called Harijans, for, according to my humble opinion, caste Hindus will then have found favour with God and may, therefore, be fitly described as his men.

Simone de Beauvoir

The Second Sex

Introduction

For a long time I have hesitated to write a book on woman. The subject is irritating, especially to women; and it is not new. Enough ink has been spilled in the quarreling over feminism, now practically over, and perhaps we should say no more about it. It is still talked about, however, for the voluminous nonsense uttered during the last century seems to have done little to illuminate the problem. After all, is there a problem? And if so, what is it? Are there women, really? Most assuredly the theory of the eternal feminine still has its adherents who will whisper in your car: "Even in Russia women still are women"; and other erudite persons—sometimes the very same—say with a sigh: "Woman is losing her way, woman is lost." One wonders if women still exist, if they will always exist, whether or not it is desirable that they should, what place they occupy in this world, what their place should be. "What has become of women?" was asked recently in an ephemeral magazine.[1]

But first we must ask: what is a woman? *"Tota mulier in utero,"* say one, "woman is a womb." But in speaking of certain women, connoisseurs declare that they are not women, although they are equipped with a uterus like the rest. All agree in recognizing the fact that females exist in the human species; today as always they make up about one half of humanity. And yet we are told that femininity is in danger; we are exhorted to be women, remain women, become women. It would appear, then, that every female human being is not necessarily a woman; to be so considered she must share in that mysterious and threatened reality known as femininity. Is this attribute something secreted by the ovaries? Or is it a Platonic essence, a product of the philosophic imagination? Is a rustling petticoat enough to bring it down to earth? Although some women try zealously to incarnate this essence, it is hardly patentable. It is frequently described in vague and dazzling terms that seem to have been borrowed from the vocabulary of the seers, and indeed in the times of St. Thomas it was considered an essence as certainly defined as the somniferous virtue of the poppy.

But conceptualism has lost ground. The biological and social sciences no longer admit the existence of unchangeably fixed entities that determine given characteristics, such as those ascribed to woman, the Jew, or the Negro. Science regards any characteristic as a reaction dependent in part upon a *situation.* If today femininity no longer exists, then it never existed. But does the word *woman,* then, have no specific content? This is stoutly affirmed by those who hold to the philosophy of the enlightenment, of rationalism, of nominalism; women, to them, are merely the human beings arbitrarily designated by the word *woman.* Many American women particularly are prepared to think that there is no longer any place for woman as such; if a backward individual still takes herself for a woman, her friends advise her to be psychoanalyzed and thus get rid of this obsession. In regard to a work, *Modern Woman: The Lost Sex,* which in other respects has its irritating features, Dorothy Parker has written: "I cannot be just to books which treat of woman as woman. . . . My idea is that all of us, men as well as women, should be regarded as human beings." But nominalism is a rather inadequate doctrine, and the antifeminists have had no trouble in showing that women simply *are not* men. Surely woman is, like man, a human being; but such a declaration is abstract. The fact is that every concrete human being is always a singular, separate individual. To decline to accept such notions as the eternal feminine, the black soul, the Jewish character, is not to deny that Jews, Negroes, women exist today—this denial does not represent a liberation for those concerned, but rather a flight from reality. Some years ago a well-known woman writer refused to permit her portrait to appear in a series of photographs especially devoted to women writers; she wished to be counted among the men. But in order to gain this privilege she made use of her husband's influence! Women who assert that they are men lay claim none the less to masculine consideration and respect. I recall also a young Trotskyite standing on a platform at a boisterous meeting and getting ready to use her fists, in spite of her evident fragility. She was denying her feminine weakness; but it was for love of a militant male whose equal she wished to be. The attitude of defiance of many American women proves that they are haunted by a sense of their femininity. In truth, to go for a walk with one's eyes open is enough to demonstrate that humanity is divided into two classes of individuals whose clothes, faces, bodies, smiles, gaits, interests, and occupations are manifestly different. Perhaps these differences are superficial, perhaps they are destined to disappear. What is certain is that right now they do most obviously exist.

If her functioning as a female is not enough to define woman, if we decline also to explain her through "the eternal feminine," and if nevertheless we admit, provisionally, that women do exist, then we must fact the question: what is a woman?

To state the question is, to me, to suggest, at once, a preliminary answer. The fact that I ask it is in itself significant. A man would never get the notion of writing a book on the peculiar situation of the human male.[2] But if I wish to define myself, I must first of all say: "I am a woman"; on this truth must be based all further discussion. A man never begins by presenting himself as an individual of a certain sex; it goes without saying that he is a man. The terms *masculine* and *feminine* are used symmetrically only as a matter of form, as on legal papers. In actuality the relation of the two sexes is not quite like that of two electrical poles, for man represents both the positive and the neutral, as is indicated by the common use of man to designate human beings in general; whereas woman represents only the negative, defined by limiting criteria, without reciprocity. In the midst of an abstract discussion it is vexing to hear a man say: "You think thus and so because you are a woman"; but I know that my only defense is to reply: "I think thus and so because it is true," thereby removing my subjective self from the argument. It would be out of the question to reply: "And you think the contrary because you are a man," for it is understood that the fact of being a man is no peculiarity. A man is in the right in being a man; it is the woman who is in the wrong. It amounts to this: just as for the ancients there was an absolute vertical with reference to which the oblique was defined, so there is an absolute human type, the masculine. Woman has ovaries, a uterus; these peculiarities imprison her in her subjectivity, circumscribe her within the limits of her own nature. It is often said that she thinks with her glands. Man superbly ignores the fact that his anatomy also includes glands, such as the testicles, and that they secrete hormones. He thinks of his body as a direct and normal connection with the world, which he believes he apprehends objectively, whereas he regards the body of woman as a hindrance, a prison, weighed down by everything peculiar to it. "The female is a female by virtue of a certain lack of qualities," said Aristotle; "we should regard the female nature as afflicted with a natural defectiveness." And St. Thomas for his part pronounced woman to be an "imperfect man," an "incidental" being. This is symbolized in Genesis where Eve is depicted as made from what Bossuet called "a supernumerary bone" of Adam.

Thus humanity is male and man defines woman not in herself but as relative to him; she is not regarded as an autonomous being. Michelet writes: "Woman, the relative being. . . ." And Benda is most positive in his *Rapport d'Uriel:* "The body of man makes sense in itself quite apart from that of woman, whereas the latter seems wanting in significance by itself. . . . Man can think of himself without woman. She cannot think of herself without man." And she is simply what man decrees; thus she is called "the sex," by which is meant that she appears essentially to the male as a sexual being. For him she is sex—absolute sex, no less. She is defined and differentiated with reference to man and not he with reference to her; she is the incidental, the inessential as opposed to the essential. He is the Subject, he is the Absolute—she is the Other.[3]

The category of the *Other* is as primordial as consciousness itself. In the most primitive societies, in the most ancient mythologies, one finds the expression of a duality—that of the Self and the Other. This duality was not originally attached to the division of the sexes; it was not dependent upon any empirical facts. It is revealed in such works as that of Granet on Chinese thought and those of Dumézil on the East Indies and Rome. The feminine element was at first no more involved in such pairs as Varuna-Mitra, Uranus-

Zeus, Sun-Moon, and Day-Night than it was in the contrasts between Good and Evil, lucky and unlucky auspices, right and left, God and Lucifer. Otherness is a fundamental category of human thought.

Thus it is that no group ever sets itself up as the One without at once setting up the Other over against itself. If three travelers chance to occupy the same compartment, that is enough to make vaguely hostile "others" out of all the rest of the passengers on the train. In small-town eyes all persons not belonging to the village are "strangers" and suspect; to the native of a country all who inhabit other countries are "foreigners"; Jews are "different" for the anti-Semite, Negroes are "inferior" for American racists, aborigines are "natives" for colonists, proletarians are the "lower class" for the privileged.

Lévi-Strauss, at the end of a profound work on the various forms of primitive societies, reaches the following conclusion: "Passage from the state of Nature to the state of Culture is marked by man's ability to view biological relations as a series of contrasts; duality, alternation, opposition, and symmetry, whether under definite or vague forms, constitute not so much phenomena to be explained as fundamental and immediately given data of social reality."[4] These phenomena would be incomprehensible if in fact human society were simply a *Mitsein* or fellowship based on solidarity and friendliness. Things become clear, on the contrary, if, following Hegel, we find in consciousness itself a fundamental hostility toward every other consciousness; the subject can be posed only in being opposed—he sets himself up as the essential, as opposed to the other, the inessential, the object.

But the other consciousness, the other ego, sets up a reciprocal claim. The native traveling abroad is shocked to find himself in turn regarded as a "stranger" by the natives of neighboring countries. As a matter of fact, wars, festivals, trading, treaties, and contests among tribes, nations, and classes tend to deprive the concept *Other* of its absolute sense and to make manifest its relativity; willy-nilly, individuals and groups are forced to realize the reciprocity of their relations. How is it, then, that this reciprocity has not been recognized between the sexes, that one of the contrasting terms is set up as the sole essential, denying any relativity in regard to its correlative and defining the latter as pure otherness? Why is it that women do not dispute male Sovereignty? No subject will readily volunteer to become the object, the inessential; it is not the Other who, in defining himself as the Other, establishes the One. The Other is posed as such by the One in defining himself as the One. But if the Other is not to regain the status of being the One, he must be submissive enough to accept this alien point of view. Whence comes this submission in the case of woman?

There are, to be sure, other cases in which a certain category has been able to dominate another completely for a time. Very often this privilege depends upon inequality of numbers—the majority imposes its rule upon the minority or persecutes it. But women are not a minority, like the American Negroes or the Jews; there are as many women as men on earth. Again, the two groups concerned have often been originally independent; they may have been formerly unaware of each other's existence, or perhaps they recognized each other's autonomy. But a historical even has resulted in the subjugation of the weaker by the stronger. The scattering of the Jews, the introduction of slavery into America, the conquests of imperialism are examples in point. In these cases the oppressed retained at least the memory of former days; they possessed in common a past, a tradition, sometimes a religion or a culture.

The parallel drawn by Bebel between women and the proletariat is valid in that neither ever formed a minority or a separate collective unit of mankind. And instead of a single historical event it is in both cases a historical development that explains their status as a class and accounts for the membership of *particular individuals* in that class. But proletarians have not always existed, whereas there have always been women. They are women in virtue of their anatomy and physiology. Throughout history they have always been subordinated to men,[5] and hence their dependency is not the result of a historical event or a social change—it was not something that *occurred.* The reason why otherness in this case seems to be an absolute is in part that it lacks the contingent or incidental nature of historical facts. A condition brought about at a certain time can be abolished at some other time, as the Negroes of Haiti and others have proved; but it might seem that a natural condition is beyond the possibility of change. In truth, however, the nature of things is no more immutably given, once for all, than is historical reality. If woman seems to be the inessential which never becomes the essential, it is because she herself fails to bring about this change. Proletarians say "We"; Negroes also. Regarding themselves as subjects, they transform the bourgeois, the whites, into "others." But women do not say "We," except at some congress of feminists or similar formal demonstration; men say "women," and women use the same word in referring to themselves. They do not authentically assume a subjective attitude. The proletarians have accomplished the revolution in Russia, the Negroes in Haiti, the Indo-Chinese are battling for it in Indo-China; but the women's effort has never been anything more than a symbolic agitation. They have gained only what men have been willing to grant; they have taken nothing, they have only received.[6]

The reason for this is that women lack concrete means for organizing themselves into a unit which can stand face to face with the correlative unit. They have no past, no history, no religion of their own; and they have no such solidarity of work and interest as that of the proletariat. They are not even promiscuously herded together in the way that creates community feeling among the American Negroes, the ghetto Jews, the workers of Saint-Denis, or the factory hands of Renault. They live dispersed among the males, attached through residence, housework, economic condition, and social standing to certain men—fathers or husbands—more firmly than they are to other women. If they belong to the bourgeoisie, they feel solidarity with men of that class, not with proletarian women; if they are white, their allegiance is to white men, not to Negro women. The proletariat can propose to massacre the ruling class, and a sufficiently fanatical Jew or Negro might dream of getting sole possession of the atomic bomb and making humanity wholly Jewish or black; but woman cannot even dream of exterminating the males. The bond that unites her to her oppressors is not comparable to any other. The division of the sexes is a biological fact, not an event in human history. Male and female stand opposed within a primordial *Mitsein,* and woman has not broken it. The couple is a fundamental unity with its two halves riveted together, and the cleavage of society along the line of sex is impossible. Here is to be found the basic trait of woman: she is the Other in a totality of which the two components are necessary to one another.

One could suppose that this reciprocity might have facilitated the liberation of woman. When Hercules sat at the feet of Omphale and helped with her spinning, his desire for her held him captive; but why did she fail to gain a lasting power? To revenge herself on Jason, Medea killed their children; and this grim legend would seem to suggest that she might have obtained a formidable influence over him through his, love for his offspring. In *Lysistrata* Aristophanes gaily depicts a band of women who joined forces to gain social ends through the sexual needs of their men; but this is only a play. In the legend of the Sabine women, the latter soon abandoned their plan of remaining sterile to punish their ravishers. In truth woman has not been socially emancipated through man's need—sexual desire and the desire for offspring—which makes the male dependent for satisfaction upon the female.

Master and slave, also, are united by a reciprocal need, in this case economic, which does not liberate the slave. In the relation of master to slave the master does not make a point of the need that he has for the other; he has in his grasp the power of satisfying this need through his own action; whereas the slave, in his dependent condition, his hope and fear, is quite conscious of the need he has for his master. Even if the need is at bottom equally urgent for both, it always works in favor of the oppressor and against the oppressed. That is why the liberation of the working class, for example, has been slow.

Now, woman has always been man's dependent, if not his slave; the two sexes have never shared the world in equality. And even today woman is heavily handicapped, though her situation is beginning to change. Almost nowhere is her legal status the same as man's,[7] and frequently it is much to her disadvantage. Even when her rights are legally recognized in the abstract, long-standing custom prevents their full expression in the mores. In the economic sphere men and women can almost be said to make up two castes; other things being equal, the former hold the better jobs, get higher wages, and have more opportunity for success than their new competitors. In industry and politics men have a great many more positions and they monopolize the most important posts. In addition to all this, they enjoy a traditional prestige that the education of children tends in every way to support, for the present enshrines the past-and in the past all history has been made by men. At the present time, when women are beginning to take part in the affairs of the world, it is still a world that belongs to men—they have no doubt of it at all and women have scarcely any. To decline to be the Other, to refuse to be a party to the deal—this would be for women to renounce all the advantages conferred upon them by their alliance with the superior caste. Man-the-sovereign will provide woman-the-liege with material protection and will undertake the moral justification of her existence; thus she can evade at once both economic risk and the metaphysical risk of a liberty in which ends and aims must be contrived without assistance. Indeed, along with the ethical urge of each individual to affirm his subjective existence, there is also the temptation to forgo liberty and become a thing. This is an inauspicious road, for he who takes it—passive, lost, ruined—becomes henceforth the creature of another's will, frustrated in his transcendence and deprived of every value. But it is an easy road; on it one avoids the strain involved in undertaking an authentic existence. When man makes of woman the *Other*, he may, then, expect her to manifest deep-seated tendencies toward complicity. Thus, woman may fail to lay claim to the status of subject because she lacks definite resources, because she feels the necessary bond that ties her to man regardless of reciprocity, and because she is often very well pleased with her role as the *Other*.

But it will be asked at once: how did all this begin? It is easy to see that the duality of the sexes, like any duality, gives rise to conflict. And doubtless the winner will assume the status of absolute. But why should man have won from the start? It seems possible that women could have won the victory; or that the outcome of the conflict might never have been decided. How is it that this world has always belonged to the men and that things have begun to change only recently? Is this change a good thing? Will it bring about an equal sharing of the world between men and women?

These questions are not new, and they have often been answered. But the very fact that woman *is the Other* tends to cast suspicion upon all the justifications that men have ever been able to provide for it. These have all too evidently been dictated by men's interest. A little-known feminist of the seventeenth century, Poulain de la Barre, put it this way: "All that has been written about women by men should be suspect, for the men are at once judge and party to the lawsuit." Everywhere, at all times, the males have displayed their satisfaction in feeling that they are the lords of creation. "Blessed be God . . . that He did not make me a woman," say the Jews in their morning prayers, while their wives pray on a note of resignation: "Blessed be the Lord, who created me according to His will." The first among the blessings for which Plato thanked the gods was that he had been created free, not enslaved; the second, a man, not a woman. But the males could not enjoy this privilege fully unless they believed it to be founded on the absolute and the eternal; they sought to make the fact of their supremacy into a right. "Being men, those who have made and compiled the laws have favored their own sex, and jurists have elevated these laws into principles," to quote Poulain de la Barre once more.

Legislators, priests, philosophers, writers, and scientists have striven to show that the subordinate position of woman is willed in heaven and advantageous on earth. The religions invented by men reflect this wish for domination. In the legends of Eve and Pandora men have taken up arms against women. They have made use of philosophy and theology, as the quotations from Aristotle and St. Thomas have shown. Since ancient times satirists and moralists have delighted in showing up the weaknesses of women. We are familiar with the savage indictments hurled against women throughout French literature. Montherlant, for example, follows the tradition of Jean de Meung, though with less gusto. This hostility may at times be well founded, often it is gratuitous; but in truth it more or less successfully conceals a desire for self-justification. As Montaigne says, "It is easier to accuse one sex than to excuse the other." Sometimes what is going on is clear enough. For instance, the Roman law limiting the rights of woman cited "the imbecility, the instability of the sex" just when the weakening of family ties seemed to threaten the interests of male heirs. And in the effort to keep the married woman under guardianship, appeal was made in the sixteenth century to the authority of St. Augustine, who declared that "woman is a creature neither decisive nor constant," at a time when the single woman was thought capable of managing her property. Montaigne understood clearly how arbitrary and unjust was woman's appointed lot: "Women are not in the wrong when they decline to accept the rules laid down for them, since the men make these rules without consulting them. No wonder intrigue and strife abound." But he did not go so far as to champion their cause.

It was only later, in the eighteenth century, that genuinely democratic men began to view the matter objectively. Diderot, among others, strove to show that woman is, like man, a human being. Later John Stuart Mill came fervently to her defense. But these philosophers displayed unusual impartiality. In the nineteenth century the feminist quarrel became again a quarrel of partisans. One of the consequences of the industrial revolution was the entrance of women into productive labor, and it was just here that the claims of the feminists emerged from the realm of theory and acquired an economic basis, while their opponents became the more aggressive. Although landed property lost power to some extent, the bourgeoisie clung to the old morality that found the guarantee of private property in the solidity of the family. Woman was ordered back into the home the more harshly as her emancipation became a real menace. Even within the working class the men endeavored to restrain woman's liberation, because they began to see the women as dangerous competitors—the more so because they were accustomed to work for lower wages.[8]

In proving woman's inferiority, the antifeminists then began to draw not only upon religion, philosophy, and theology, as before, but also upon science—biology, experimental psychology, etc. At most they were willing to grant "equality in difference" to the *other* sex. That profitable formula is most significant; it is precisely like the "equal but separate" formula of the Jim Crow laws aimed at the North American Negroes. As is well known, this so-called equalitarian segregation has resulted only in the most extreme discrimination. The similarity just noted is in no way due to chance, for whether it is a race, a caste, a class, or a sex that is reduced to a position of inferiority, the methods of justification are the same. "The eternal feminine" corresponds to "the black soul" and to "the Jewish character." True, the Jewish problem is on the whole very different from the other two—to the anti-Semite the Jew is not so much an inferior as he is an enemy for whom there is to be granted no place on earth, for whom annihilation is the fate desired. But there are deep similarities between the situation of woman and that of the Negro. Both are being emancipated today from a like paternalism, and the former master class wishes to "keep them in their place"—that is, the place chosen for them. In both cases the former masters lavish more or less sincere eulogies, either on the virtues of "the good Negro" with his dormant, childish, merry soul-the submissive Negro—or on the merits of the woman who is "truly feminine"—that is, frivolous, infantile, irresponsible—the submissive woman. In both cases the dominant class bases its argument on a state of affairs that it has itself created. As George Bernard Shaw puts it, in substance, "The American white relegates the black to the rank of shoeshine boy; and he concludes from this that the black is good for nothing but shining shoes." This vicious circle is met with in all analogous circumstances; when an individual (or a group of individuals) is kept in a situation of inferiority, the fact is that he is inferior. But the significance of the verb *to be* must be rightly understood here; it is in bad faith to give it a static value when it really has the dynamic Hegelian sense of "to have become." Yes, women on the whole *are* today inferior to men; that is, their situation affords them fewer possibilities. The question is: should that state of affairs continue?

Many men hope that it will continue; not all have given up the battle. The conservative bourgeoisie still see in the emancipation of women a menace to their morality and their interests. Some men dread feminine competition. Recently a male student wrote in the *Hebdo-Latin:* "Every woman student who goes into medicine or law robs us of a job." He never questioned his rights in this world. And economic interests are not the only ones concerned. One of the benefits that oppression confers upon the oppressors is that the most humble among them is made to *feel* superior; thus, a "poor white" in the South can console himself with the thought that he is not a "dirty nigger"—and the more prosperous whites cleverly exploit this pride.

Similarly, the most mediocre of males feels himself a demigod as compared with women. It was much easier for M. de Montherlant to think himself a hero when he faced women (and women chosen for his purpose) than when he was obliged to act the man among men—something many women have done better than he, for that matter. And in September 1948, in one of his articles in the *Figaro littéraire,* Claude Mauriac—whose great originality is admired by all—could[9] write regarding woman: "*We* listen on a tone (sic) of polite indifference . . . to the most brilliant among them, well knowing that her wit reflects more or less luminously ideas that come from us." Evidently the speaker referred to is not reflecting the ideas of Mauriac himself, for no one knows of his having any. It may be that she reflects ideas originating with men, but then, even among men there are those who have been known to appropriate ideas not their own; and one can well ask whether Claude Mauriac might not find more interesting a conversation reflecting Descartes, Marx, or Gide rather than himself. What is really remarkable is that by using the questionable *we* he identifies himself with St. Paul, Hegel, Lenin, and Nietzsche, and from the lofty eminence of their grandeur looks down disdainfully upon the bevy of women who make bold to converse with him on a footing of equality. In truth, I know of more than one woman who would refuse to suffer with patience Mauriac's "tone of polite indifference."

I have lingered on this example because the masculine attitude is here displayed with disarming ingenuousness. But men profit in many more subtle ways from the otherness, the alterity of woman. Here is miraculous balm for those afflicted with an inferiority complex, and indeed no one is more arrogant toward women, more aggressive or scornful, than the man who is anxious about his virility. Those who are not fear-ridden in the presence of their fellow men are much more disposed to recognize a fellow creature in woman; but even to these the myth of Woman, the Other, is precious for many reasons.[10] They cannot be blamed for not cheerfully relinquishing all the benefits they derive from the myth, for they realize what they would lose in relinquishing woman as they fancy her to be, while they fail to realize what they have to gain from the woman of tomorrow. Refusal to pose oneself as the Subject, unique and absolute, requires great self-denial. Furthermore, the vast majority of men make no such claim explicitly. They do not *postulate* woman as inferior, for today they are too thoroughly imbued with the ideal of democracy not to recognize all human beings as equals. In the bosom of the family, woman seems in the eyes of childhood and youth to be clothed in the same social dignity as the adult males. Later on, the young man, desiring and loving, experiences the resistance, the independence of the woman desired and loved; in marriage, he respects woman as wife and mother, and in the concrete events of conjugal life she stands there before him as a free being. He can therefore feel that social subordination as between the sexes no longer exists and that on the whole, in spite of differences, woman is an equal. As, however, he observes some points of inferiority—the most important being unfitness for the professions—he attributes these to natural causes. When he is in a co-operative and benevolent relation with woman, his theme is the principle of abstract equality, and he does not base his attitude upon such inequality as may exist. But when he is in conflict with her, the situation is reversed: his theme will be the existing inequality, and he will even take it as justification for denying abstract equality.[11]

So it is that many men will affirm as if in good faith that women *are* the equals of man and that they have nothing to clamor for, while *at the same time* they will say that women can never be the equals of man and that their demands are in vain. It is, in point of fact, a difficult matter for man to realize the extreme importance of social discriminations which seem outwardly insignificant but which produce in woman moral and intellectual effects so profound that they appear to spring from her original nature.[12] The most sympathetic of men never fully comprehend woman's concrete situation. And there is no reason to put much trust in the men when they rush to the defense of privileges whose full extent they can hardly measure. We shall not, then, permit ourselves to be intimidated by the number and violence of the attacks launched against women, nor to be entrapped by the self-seeking eulogies bestowed on the "true woman," nor to profit by the enthusiasm for woman's destiny manifested by men who would not for the world have any part of it.

We should consider the arguments of the feminists with no less suspicion, however, for very often their controversial aim deprives them of all real value. If the "woman question" seems trivial, it is because masculine arrogance has made of it a "quarrel" and when quarreling one no longer reasons well. People have tirelessly sought to prove that woman is superior, inferior, or equal to man. Some say that, having been created after Adam, she is evidently a secondary being; others say on the contrary that Adam was only a rough draft and that God succeeded in producing the human being in perfection when He created Eve. Woman's brain is smaller; yes, but it is relatively larger. Christ was made a man; yes, but perhaps for his greater humility. Each argument at once suggests its opposite, and both are often fallacious. If we are to gain understanding, we must get out of these ruts; we must discard the vague notions of superiority, inferiority, equality which have hitherto corrupted every discussion of the subject and start afresh.

Very well, but just how shall we pose the question? And, to begin with, who are we to propound it at all? Man is at once judge and party to the case; but so is woman. What we need is an angel—neither man nor woman—but where shall we find one? Still, the angel would be poorly qualified to speak, for an angel is ignorant of all the basic facts involved in the problem. With a hermaphrodite we should be no better off, for here the situation is most peculiar; the hermaphrodite is not really the combination of a whole man and a whole woman, but consists of parts of each and thus is neither. It looks to me as if there are, after all, certain women who are best qualified to elucidate the situation of woman. Let us not be misled by the sophism that because Epimenides was a Cretan he was necessarily a liar; it is not a mysterious essence that compels men and women to act in good or in bad faith, it is their situation that inclines them more or less toward the search for truth. Many of today's women, fortunate in the restoration of all the privileges pertaining to the estate of the human being, can afford the luxury of impartiality, we even recognize its necessity. We are no longer like our partisan elders; by and large we have won the game. In recent debates on the status of women the United Nations has persistently maintained that the equality of the sexes is now becoming a reality, and already some of us have never had to sense in our femininity an inconvenience or an obstacle. Many problems appear to us to be more pressing than those which concern us in particular, and this detachment even allows us to hope that our attitude will be objective. Still, we know the feminine world more intimately than do the men because we have our roots in it, we grasp more immediately than do men what it means to a human being to be feminine; and we are more concerned with such knowledge. I have said that there are more pressing problems, but this does not prevent us from seeing some importance in asking how the fact of being women will affect our lives. What opportunities precisely have been given us and what withheld? What fate awaits our younger sisters, and what directions should they take? It is significant that books by women on women are in general animated in our day less by a wish to demand our rights than by an effort toward clarity and understanding. As we emerge from an era of excessive controversy, this book is offered as one attempt among others to confirm that statement.

But it is doubtless impossible to approach any human problem with a mind free from bias. The way in which questions are put, the points of view assumed, presuppose a relativity of interest; all characteristics imply values, and every objective description, so called, implies an ethical background. Rather than attempt to conceal principles more or less definitely implied, it is better to state them openly at the beginning. This will make it unnecessary to specify on every page in just what sense one uses such words as *superior, inferior, better, worse, progress, reaction*, and the like. If we survey some of the works on woman, we note that one of the points of view most frequently adopted is that of the public good, the general interest; and one always means by this the benefit of society as one wishes it to be maintained or established. For our part, we hold that the only public good is that which assures the private good of the citizens; we shall pass judgment on institutions according to their effectiveness in giving concrete opportunities to individuals. But we do not confuse the idea of private interest with that of happiness, although that is another common point of view. Are not women of the harem more happy than women voters? Is not the housekeeper happier than the working-woman? It is not too clear just what the word *happy* really means and still less what true values it may mask. There is no possibility of measuring the happiness of others, and it is always easy to describe as happy the situation in which one wishes to place them.

In particular those who are condemned to stagnation are often pronounced happy on the pretext that happiness consists in being at rest. This notion we reject, for our perspective is that of existentialist ethics. Every subject plays his part as such specifically through exploits or projects that serve as a mode of transcendence; he achieves liberty only through a continual reaching out toward other liberties. There is no justification for present existence other than its expansion into an indefinitely open future. Every time transcendence falls back into immanence, stagnation, there is a degradation of existence into the *"en-soi"*—the brutish life of subjection to given conditions—and of liberty into constraint and contingence. This downfall represents a moral fault if the subject consents to it; if it is inflicted upon him, it spells frustration and oppression. In both cases it is an absolute evil. Every individual concerned to justify his existence feels that his existence involves an undefined need to transcend himself, to engage in freely chosen projects.

Now, what peculiarly signalizes the situation of woman is that she—a free and autonomous being like all human creatures—nevertheless finds herself living in a world where men compel her to assume the status of the Other. They propose to stabilize her as object and to doom her to immanence since her transcendence is to be overshadowed and forever transcended by another ego *(conscience)* which is essential and sovereign. The drama of woman lies in this conflict between the fundamental aspirations of every subject (ego)—who always regards the self as the essential—and the compulsions of a situation in which she is the inessential. How can a human being in woman's situation attain fulfillment? What roads are open to her? Which are blocked? How can independence be recovered in a state of dependency? What circumstances limit woman's liberty and how can they be overcome? These are the fundamental questions on which I would fain throw some light. This means that I am interested in the fortunes of the individual as defined not in terms of happiness but in terms of liberty.

Quite evidently this problem would be without significance if we were to believe that woman's destiny is inevitably determined by physiological, psychological, or economic forces. Hence I shall discuss first of all the light in which woman is viewed by biology, psychoanalysis, and historical materialism. Next I shall try to show exactly how the concept of the "truly feminine" has been fashioned—why woman has been defined as the Other—and what have been the consequences from man's point of view. Then from woman's point of view I shall describe the world in which women must live; and thus we shall be able to envisage the difficulties in their way as, endeavoring to make their escape from the sphere hitherto assigned them, they aspire to full membership in the human race.

Public Statement by Eight Alabama Clergymen, April 12, 1963

We the undersigned clergymen are among those who, in January, issued "An Appeal for Law and Order and Common Sense," in dealing with racial problems in Alabama. We expressed understanding that honest convictions in racial matters could properly be pursued in the courts, but urged that decisions of those courts should in the meantime be peacefully obeyed.

Since that time there had been some evidence of increased forbearance and a willingness to face facts. Responsible citizens have undertaken to work on various problems which cause racial friction and unrest. In Birmingham, recent public events have given indication that we all have opportunity for a new constructive and realistic approach to racial problems.

However, we are now confronted by a series of demonstrations by some of our Negro citizens, directed and led in part by outsiders. We recognize the natural impatience of people who feel that their hopes are slow in being realized. But we are convinced that these demonstrations are unwise and untimely.

We agree rather with certain local Negro leadership which has called for honest and open negotiation of racial issues in our area. And we believe this kind of facing of issues can best be accomplished by citizens of our own metropolitan area, white and Negro, meeting with their knowledge and experience of the local situation. All of us need to face that responsibility and find proper channels for its accomplishment.

Just as we formerly pointed out that "hatred and violence have no sanction in our religious and political traditions," we also point out that such actions as incite to hatred and violence, however technically peaceful those actions may be, have not contributed to the resolution of our local problems. We do not believe that these days of new hope are days when extreme measures are justified in Birmingham.

We commend the community as a whole, and the local news media and law enforcement in particular, on the calm manner in which these demonstrations have been handled. We urge the public to continue to show restraint should the demonstrations continue, and the law enforcement official to remain calm and continue to protect our city from violence.

We further strongly urge our own Negro community to withdraw support from these demonstrations, and to unite locally in working peacefully for a better Birmingham. When rights are consistently denied, a cause should be pressed in the courts and in negotiations among local leaders, and not in the streets. We appeal to both our white and Negro citizenry to observe the principles of law and order and common sense.

C.C.J. Carpenter, D.D., LL.D.,
Bishop of Alabama

Joseph A. Durick, D.D.,
Auxiliary Bishop, Diocese of Mobile, Birmingham

Rabbi Hilton L. Grafman
Temple Emanu-El, Birmingham, Alabama

Bishop Paul Hardin
Bishop of the Alabama-West Florida Conference

Bishop Holan B. Harmon
Bishop of the North Alabama Conference of the Methodist Church

George M. Murray, D.D., LL.D,
Bishop Coadjutor, Episcopal Diocese of Alabama

Edward V. Ramage
Moderator, Synod of the Alabama Presbyterian Church in the United States

Earl Stallings
Pastor, First Baptist Church, Birmingham, Alabama

Dr. Martin Luther King, Jr.

Letter from Birmingham Jail

N.B. All typographical errors are from the original source and therefore have not been corrected.

AUTHOR'S NOTE: This response to a published statement by eight fellow clergymen from Alabama (Bishop C.C.J. Carpenter, Bishop Joseph A. Durick, Rabbi Hilton L. Grafman, Bishop Paul Hardin, Bishop Holan B. Harmon, the Reverend George M. Murray. the Reverend Edward V. Ramage and the Reverend Earl Stallings) was composed under somewhat constricting circumstance. Begun on the margins of the newspaper in which the statement appeared while I was in jail, the letter was continued on scraps of writing paper supplied by a friendly Negro trusty, and concluded on a pad my attorneys were eventually permitted to leave me. Although the text remains in substance unaltered, I have indulged in the author's prerogative of polishing it for publication.

April 16, 1963

MY DEAR FELLOW CLERGYMEN:

While confined here in the Birmingham city jail, I came across your recent statement calling my present activities "unwise and untimely." Seldom do I pause to answer criticism of my work and ideas. If I sought to answer all the criticisms that cross my desk, my secretaries would have little time for anything other than such correspondence in the course of the day, and I would have no time for constructive work. But since I feel that you are men of genuine good will and that your criticisms are sincerely set forth, I want to try to answer your statements in what I hope will be patient and reasonable terms.

I think I should indicate why I am here In Birmingham, since you have been influenced by the view which argues against "outsiders coming in." I have the honor of serving as president of the Southern Christian Leadership Conference, an organization operating in every southern state, with headquarters in Atlanta, Georgia. We have some eighty-five affiliated organizations across the South, and one of them is the Alabama Christian Movement for Human Rights. Frequently we share staff, educational and financial resources with our affiliates. Several months ago the affiliate here in Birmingham asked us to be on call to engage in a nonviolent direct-action program if such were deemed necessary. We readily consented, and when the hour came we lived up to our promise. So I, along with several members of my staff, am here because I was invited here I am here because I have organizational ties here.

But more basically, I am in Birmingham because injustice is here. Just as the prophets of the eighth century B.C. left their villages and carried their "thus saith the Lord" far beyond the boundaries of their home towns, and just as the Apostle Paul left his village of Tarsus and carried the gospel of Jesus Christ to the far corners of the Greco-Roman world, so am I compelled to carry the gospel of freedom beyond my own home town. Like Paul, I must constantly respond to the Macedonian call for aid.

Moreover, I am cognizant of the interrelatedness of all communities and states. I cannot sit idly by in Atlanta and not be concerned about what happens in Birmingham. Injustice anywhere is a threat to justice everywhere. We are caught in an inescapable network of mutuality, tied in a single garment of destiny. Whatever affects one directly, affects all indirectly. Never again can we afford to live with the narrow, provincial "outside agitator" idea. Anyone who lives inside the United States can never be considered an outsider anywhere within its bounds.

You deplore the demonstrations taking place In Birmingham. But your statement, I am sorry to say, fails to express a similar concern for the conditions that brought about the demonstrations. I am sure that none of you would want to rest content with the superficial kind of social analysis that deals merely with effects and does not grapple with underlying causes. It is unfortunate that demonstrations are taking place in Birmingham, but it is even more unfortunate that the city's white power structure left the Negro community with no alternative.

In any nonviolent campaign there are four basic steps: collection of the facts to determine whether injustices exist; negotiation; self-purification; and direct action. We have gone through an these steps in Birmingham. There can be no gainsaying the fact that racial injustice engulfs this community. Birmingham is probably the most thoroughly segregated city in the United States. Its ugly record of brutality is widely known. Negroes have experienced grossly unjust treatment in the courts. There have been more unsolved bombings of Negro homes and churches in Birmingham than in any other city in the nation. These are the hard, brutal facts of the case. On the basis of these conditions, Negro leaders sought to negotiate with the city fathers. But the latter consistently refused to engage in good-faith negotiation.

Then, last September, came the opportunity to talk with leaders of Birmingham's economic community. In the course of the negotiations, certain promises were made by the merchants—for example, to remove the stores, humiliating racial signs. On the basis of these promises, the Reverend Fred Shuttlesworth and the leaders of the Alabama Christian Movement for Human Rights agreed to a moratorium on all demonstrations. As the weeks and months went by, we realized that we were the victims of a broken promise. A few signs, briefly removed, returned; the others remained.

As in so many past experiences, our hopes bad been blasted, and the shadow of deep disappointment settled upon us. We had no alternative except to prepare for direct action, whereby we would present our very bodies as a means of laying our case before the conscience of the local and the national community. Mindful of the difficulties involved, we decided to undertake a process of self-purification. We began a series of workshops on nonviolence, and we repeatedly asked ourselves : "Are you able to accept blows without retaliating?" "Are you able to endure the ordeal of jail?" We decided to schedule our direct-action program for the Easter season, realizing that except for Christmas, this is the main shopping period of the year. Knowing that a strong economic-withdrawal program would be the by-product of direct action, we felt that this would be the best time to bring pressure to bear on the merchants for the needed change.

Then it occurred to us that Birmingham's mayoral election was coming up in March, and we speedily decided to postpone action until after election day. When we discovered that the Commissioner of Public Safety, Eugene "Bull" Connor, had piled up enough votes to be in the run-off, we decided again to postpone action until the day after the run-off so that the demonstrations could not be used to cloud the issues. Like many others, we wanted to see Mr. Connor defeated, and to this end we endured postponement after postponement. Having aided in this community need, we felt that our direct-action program could be delayed no longer.

You may well ask: "Why direct action? Why sit-ins, marches and so forth? Isn't negotiation a better path?" You are quite right in calling, for negotiation. Indeed, this is the very purpose of direct action. Nonviolent direct action seeks to create such a crisis and foster such a tension that a community which has constantly refused to negotiate is forced to confront the issue. It seeks so to dramatize the issue that it can no longer be ignored. My citing the creation of tension as part of the work of the nonviolent-resister may sound rather shocking. But I must confess that I am not afraid of the word "tension." I have earnestly opposed violent tension, but there is a type of constructive, nonviolent tension which is necessary for growth. Just as Socrates felt that it was necessary to create a tension in the mind so that individuals could rise from the bondage of myths and half-truths to the unfettered realm of creative analysis and objective appraisal, we must we see the need for nonviolent gadflies to create the kind of tension in society that will help men rise from the dark depths of prejudice and racism to the majestic heights of understanding and brotherhood.

The purpose of our direct-action program is to create a situation so crisis-packed that it will inevitably open the door to negotiation. I therefore concur with you in your call for negotiation. Too long has our beloved Southland been bogged down in a tragic effort to live in monologue rather than dialogue.

One of the basic points in your statement is that the action that I and my associates have taken in Birmingham is untimely. Some have asked: "Why didn't you give the new city administration time to act?" The only answer that I can give to this query is that the new Birmingham administration must be prodded about as much as the outgoing one, before it will act. We are sadly mistaken if we feel that the election of Albert Boutwell as mayor will bring the millennium to Birmingham. While Mr. Boutwell is a much more gentle person than Mr. Connor, they are both segregationists, dedicated to maintenance of the status quo. I have hope that Mr. Boutwell will be reasonable enough to see the futility of massive resistance to desegregation. But he will not see this without pressure from devotees of civil rights. My friends, I must say to you that we have not made a single gain in civil rights without determined legal and nonviolent pressure. Lamentably, it is an historical fact that privileged groups seldom give up their privileges voluntarily. Individuals may see the moral light and voluntarily give up their unjust posture; but, as Reinhold Niebuhr has reminded us, groups tend to be more immoral than individuals.

We know through painful experience that freedom is never voluntarily given by the oppressor; it must be demanded by the oppressed. Frankly, I have yet to engage in a direct-action campaign that was "well timed" in the view of those who have not suffered unduly from the disease of segregation. For years now I have heard the word "Wait!" It rings in the ear of every Negro with piercing familiarity. This "Wait" has almost always meant "Never." We must come to see, with one of our distinguished jurists, that "justice too long delayed is justice denied."

We have waited for more than 340 years for our constitutional and God-given rights. The nations of Asia and Africa are moving with jetlike speed toward gaining political independence, but we still creep at horse-and-buggy pace toward gaining a cup of coffee at a lunch counter. Perhaps it is easy for those who have never felt the stinging dark of segregation to say, "Wait." But when you have seen vicious mobs lynch your mothers and fathers at will and drown your sisters and brothers at whim; when you have seen hate-filled policemen curse, kick and even kill your black brothers and sisters; when you see the vast majority of your twenty million Negro brothers smothering in an airtight cage of poverty in the midst of an affluent society; when you suddenly find your tongue twisted and your speech stammering as you seek to explain to your six-year-old daughter why she can't go to the public amusement park that has just been advertised on television, and see tears welling up in her eyes when she is told that Funtown is closed to colored children, and see ominous clouds of inferiority beginning to form in her little mental sky, and see her beginning to distort her personality by developing an unconscious bitterness toward white people; when you have to concoct an answer for a five-year-old son who is asking: "Daddy, why do white people treat colored people so mean?"; when you take a cross-county drive and find it necessary to sleep night after night in the uncomfortable corners of your automobile because no motel will accept you; when you are humiliated day in and day out by nagging signs reading "white" and "colored"; when your first name becomes "nigger," your middle name becomes "boy" (however old you are) and your last name becomes "John," and your wife and mother are never given the respected title "Mrs."; when you are harried by day and haunted by night by the fact that you are a Negro, living constantly at tiptoe stance, never quite knowing what to expect next, and are plagued with inner fears and outer resentments; when you no forever fighting a degenerating sense of "nobodiness"—then you will understand why we find it difficult to wait. There comes a time when the cup of endurance runs over, and men are no longer willing to be plunged into the abyss of despair. I hope, sirs, you can understand our legitimate and unavoidable impatience.

You express a great deal of anxiety over our willingness to break laws. This is certainly a legitimate concern. Since we so diligently urge people to obey the Supreme Court's decision of 1954 outlawing segregation in the public schools, at first glance it may seem rather paradoxical for us consciously to break laws. One may won ask: "How can you advocate breaking some laws and obeying others?" The answer lies in the fact that there are two types of laws: just and unjust. I would be the first to advocate obeying just laws. One has not only a legal but a moral responsibility to obey just laws. Conversely, one has a moral responsibility to disobey unjust laws. I would agree with St. Augustine that "an unjust law is no law at all."

Now, what is the difference between the two? How does one determine whether a law is just or unjust? A just law is a man-made code that squares with the moral law or the law of God. An unjust law is a code that is out of harmony with the moral law. To put it in the terms of St. Thomas Aquinas: An unjust law is a human law that is not rooted in eternal law and natural law. Any law that uplifts human personality is just. Any law that degrades human personality is unjust. All segregation statutes are unjust because segregation distort the soul and damages the personality. It gives the segregator a false sense of superiority and the segregated a false sense of inferiority. Segregation, to use the terminology of the Jewish philosopher Martin Buber, substitutes an "I-it" relationship for an "I-thou" relationship and ends up relegating persons to the status of things. Hence segregation is not only politically, economically and sociologically unsound, it is morally wrong and awful. Paul Tillich said that sin is separation. Is not segregation an existential expression of man's tragic separation, his awful estrangement, his terrible sinfulness? Thus it is that I can urge men to obey the 1954 decision of the Supreme Court, for it is morally right; and I can urge them to disobey segregation ordinances, for they are morally wrong.

Let us consider a more concrete example of just and unjust laws. An unjust law is a code that a numerical or power majority group compels a minority group to obey but does not make binding on itself. This is *difference* made legal. By the same token, a just law is a code that a majority compels a minority to follow and that it is willing to follow itself. This is *sameness* made legal.

Let me give another explanation. A law is unjust if it is inflicted on a minority that, as a result of being denied the right to vote, had no part in enacting or devising the law. Who can say that the legislature of Alabama which set up that state's segregation laws was democratically elected? Throughout Alabama all sorts of devious methods are used to prevent Negroes from becoming registered voters, and there are some counties in which, even though Negroes constitute a majority of the population, not a single Negro is registered. Can any law enacted under such circumstances be considered democratically structured?

Sometimes a law is just on its face and unjust in its application. For instance, I have been arrested on a charge of parading without a permit. Now, there is nothing wrong in having an ordinance which requires a permit for a parade. But such an ordinance becomes unjust when it is used to maintain segregation and to deny citizens the First Amendment privilege of peaceful assembly and protest.

I hope you are able to see the distinction I am trying to point out. In no sense do I advocate evading or defying the law, as would the rabid segregationist. That would lead to anarchy. One who breaks an unjust law must do so openly, lovingly, and with a willingness to accept the penalty. I submit that an individual who breaks a law that conscience tells him is unjust and who willingly accepts the penalty of imprisonment in order to arouse the conscience of the community over its injustice, is in reality expressing the highest respect for law.

Of course, there is nothing new about this kind of civil disobedience. It was evidenced sublimely in the refusal of Shadrach, Meshach and Abednego to obey the laws of Nebuchadnezzar, on the ground that a higher moral law was at stake. It was practiced superbly by the early Christians, who were willing to face hungry lions and the excruciating pain of chopping blocks rather than submit to certain unjust laws of the Roman Empire. To a degree, academic freedom is a reality today because Socrates practiced civil disobedience. In our own nation, the Boston Tea Party represented a massive act of civil disobedience.

We should never forget that everything Adolf Hitler did in Germany was "legal" and everything the Hungarian freedom fighters did in Hungary was "illegal." It was "illegal" to aid and comfort a Jew in Hitler's Germany. Even so, I am sure that, had I lived in Germany at the time, I would have aided and comforted my Jewish brothers. If today I lived in a Communist country where certain principles dear to the Christian faith are suppressed, I would openly advocate disobeying that country's antireligious laws.

I must make two honest confessions to you, my Christian and Jewish brothers. First, I must confess that over the past few years I have been gravely disappointed with the white moderate. I have almost reached the regrettable conclusion that the Negro's great stumbling block in his stride toward freedom is not the White Citizen's Counciler or the Ku Klux Klanner, but the white moderate, who is more devoted to "order" than to justice; who prefers a negative peace which is the absence of tension to a positive peace which is the presence of justice; who constantly says: "I agree with you in the goal you seek, but I cannot agree with your methods of direct action"; who paternalistically believes he can set the timetable for another man's freedom; who lives by a mythical concept of time and who constantly advises the Negro to wait for a "more convenient season." Shallow understanding from people of good will is more frustrating than absolute misunderstanding from people of ill will. Lukewarm acceptance is much more bewildering than outright rejection.

I had hoped that the white moderate would understand that law and order exist for the purpose of establishing justice and that when they fail in this purpose they become the dangerously structured dams that block the flow of social progress. I had hoped that the white moderate would understand that the present tension in the South is a necessary phase of the transition from an obnoxious negative peace, in which the Negro passively accepted his unjust plight, to a substantive and positive peace, in which all men will respect the dignity and worth of human personality. Actually, we who engage in nonviolent direct action are not the creators of tension. We merely bring to the surface the hidden tension that is already alive. We bring it out in the open, where it can be seen and dealt with. Like a boil that can never be cured so long as it is covered up but must be opened with an its ugliness to the natural medicines of air and light, injustice must be exposed, with all the tension its exposure creates, to the light of human conscience and the air of national opinion before it can be cured.

In your statement you assert that our actions, even though peaceful, must be condemned because they precipitate violence. But is this a logical assertion? Isn't this like condemning a robbed man because his possession of money precipitated the evil act of robbery? Isn't this like condemning Socrates because his unswerving commitment to truth and his philosophical inquiries precipitated the act by the misguided populace in which they made him drink hemlock? Isn't this like condemning Jesus because his unique God-consciousness and never-ceasing devotion to God's will precipitated the evil act of crucifixion? We must come to see that, as the federal courts have consistently affirmed, it is wrong to urge an individual to cease his efforts to gain his basic constitutional rights because the quest may precipitate violence. Society must protect the robbed and punish the robber.

I had also hoped that the white moderate would reject the myth concerning time in relation to the struggle for freedom. I have just received a letter from a white brother in Texas. He writes: "All Christians know that the colored people will receive equal rights eventually, but it is possible that you are in too great a religious hurry. It has taken Christianity almost two thousand years to accomplish what it has. The teachings of Christ take time to come to earth." Such an attitude stems from a tragic misconception of time, from the strangely rational notion that there is something in the very flow of time that will inevitably cure all ills. Actually, time itself is neutral; it can be used either destructively or constructively. More and more I feel that the people of ill will have used time much more effectively than have the people of good will. We will have to repent in this generation not merely for the hateful words and actions of the bad people but for the appalling silence of the good people. Human progress never rolls in on wheels of inevitability; it comes through the tireless efforts of men willing to be co-workers with God, and without this hard work, time itself becomes an ally of the forces of social stagnation. We must use time creatively, in the knowledge that the time is always ripe to do right. Now is the time to make real the promise of democracy and transform our pending national elegy into a creative psalm of brotherhood. Now is the time to lift our national policy from the quicksand of racial injustice to the solid rock of human dignity.

You speak of our activity in Birmingham as extreme. At first I was rather disappointed that fellow clergymen would see my nonviolent efforts as those of an extremist. I began thinking about the fact that I stand in the middle of two opposing forces in the Negro community. One is a force of complacency, made up in part of Negroes who, as a result of long years of oppression, are so drained of self-respect and a sense of "somebodiness" that they have adjusted to segregation; and in part of a few middle-class Negroes who, because of a degree of academic and economic security and because in some ways they profit by segregation, have become insensitive to the problems of the masses. The other force is one of bitterness and hatred, and it comes perilously close to advocating violence. It is expressed in the various black nationalist groups that are springing up across the nation, the largest and best-known being Elijah Muhammad's Muslim movement. Nourished by the Negro's frustration over the continued existence of racial discrimination, this movement is made up of people who have lost faith in America, who have absolutely repudiated Christianity, and who have concluded that the white man is an incorrigible "devil."

I have tried to stand between these two forces, saying that we need emulate neither the "do-nothingism" of the complacent nor the hatred and despair of the black nationalist. For there is the more excellent way of love and nonviolent protest. I am grateful to God that, through the influence of the Negro church, the way of nonviolence became an integral part of our struggle.

If this philosophy had not emerged, by now many streets of the South would, I am convinced, be flowing with blood. And I am further convinced that if our white brothers dismiss as "rabblerousers" and "outside agitators" those of us who employ nonviolent direct action, and if they refuse to support our nonviolent efforts, millions of Negroes will, out of frustration and despair, seek solace and security in black-nationalist ideologies—a development that would inevitably lead to a frightening racial nightmare.

Oppressed people cannot remain oppressed forever. The yearning for freedom eventually manifests itself, and that is what has happened to the American Negro. Something within has reminded him of his birthright of freedom, and something without has reminded him that it can be gained. Consciously or unconsciously, he has been caught up by the *Zeitgeist*, and with his black brothers of Africa and his brown and yellow brothers of Asia, South America and the Caribbean, the United States Negro is moving with a sense of great urgency toward the promised land of racial justice. If one recognizes this vital urge that has engulfed the Negro community, one should readily understand why public demonstrations are taking place. The Negro has many pent-up resentments and latent frustrations, and he must release them. So let him march; let him make prayer pilgrimages to the city hall; let him go on freedom rides—and try to understand why he must do so. If his repressed emotions are not released in nonviolent ways, they will seek expression through violence; this is not a threat but a fact of history. So I have not said to my people: "Get rid of your discontent." Rather, I have tried to say that this normal and healthy discontent can be channeled into the creative outlet of nonviolent direct action. And now this approach is being termed extremist.

But though I was initially disappointed at being categorized as an extremist, as I continued to think about the matter I gradually gained a measure of satisfaction from the label. Was not Jesus an extremist for love: "Love your enemies, bless them that curse you, do good to them that hate you, and pray for them which despitefully use you, and persecute you." Was not Amos an extremist for justice: "Let justice roll down like waters and righteousness like an ever-flowing stream." Was not Paul an extremist for the Christian gospel: "I bear in my body the marks of the Lord Jesus." Was not Martin Luther an extremist: "Here I stand; I cannot do otherwise, so help me God." And John Bunyan: "I will stay in jail to the end of my days before I make a butchery of my conscience." And Abraham Lincoln: "This nation cannot survive half slave and half free." And Thomas Jefferson: "We hold these truths to be self-evident, that all men are created equal. . . ." So the question is not whether we will be extremists, but what kind of extremists we will be. Will we be extremists for hate or for love? Will we be extremists for the preservation of injustice or for the extension of justice? In that dramatic scene on Calvary's hill three men were crucified. We must never forget that all three were crucified for the same crime—the crime of extremism. Two were extremists for immorality, and thus fell below their environment. The other, Jesus Christ, was an extremist for love, truth and goodness, and thereby rose above his environment. Perhaps the South, the nation and the world are in dire need of creative extremists.

I had hoped that the white moderate would see this need. Perhaps I was too optimistic; perhaps I expected too much. I suppose I should have realized that few members of the oppressor race can understand the deep groans and passionate yearnings of the oppressed race, and still fewer have the vision to see that injustice must be rooted out by strong, persistent and determined action. I am thankful, however, that some of our white brothers in the South have grasped the meaning of this social revolution and committed themselves to it. They are still too few in quantity, but they are big in quality. Some—such as Ralph McGill, Lillian Smith, Harry Golden, James McBride Dabbs, Ann Braden and Sarah Patton Boyle—have written about our struggle in eloquent and prophetic terms. Others have marched with us down nameless streets of the South. They have languished in filthy, roach-infested jails, suffering the abuse and brutality of policemen who view them as "dirty nigger-lovers." Unlike so many of their moderate brothers and sisters, they have recognized the urgency of the moment and sensed the need for powerful "action" antidotes to combat the disease of segregation.

Let me take note of my other major disappointment. I have been so greatly disappointed with the white church and its leadership. Of course, there are some notable exceptions. I am not unmindful of the fact that each of you has taken some significant stands on this issue. I commend you, Reverend Stallings, for your Christian stand on this past Sunday, in welcoming Negroes to your worship service on a non-segregated basis. I commend the Catholic leaders of this state for integrating Spring Hill College several years ago.

But despite these notable exceptions, I must honestly reiterate that I have been disappointed with the church. I do not say this as one of those negative critics who can always find something wrong with the church. I say this as a minister of the gospel, who loves the church; who was nurtured in its bosom; who has been sustained by its spiritual blessings and who will remain true to it as long as the cord of life shall lengthen.

When I was suddenly catapulted into the leadership of the bus protest in Montgomery, Alabama, a few years ago, I felt we would be supported by the white church. I felt that the white ministers, priests and rabbis of the South would be among our strongest allies. Instead, some have been outright opponents, refusing to understand the freedom movement and misrepresenting its leaders; all too many others have been more cautious than courageous and have remained silent behind the anesthetizing security of stained glass windows.

In spite of my shattered dreams, I came to Birmingham with the hope that the white religious leadership of this community would see the justice of our cause and, with deep moral concern, would serve as the channel through which our just grievances could reach the power structure. I had hoped that each of you would understand. But again I have been disappointed.

I have heard numerous southern religious leaders admonish their worshipers to comply with a desegregation decision because it is the law, but I have longed to hear white ministers declare: "Follow this decree because integration is morally right and because the Negro is your brother." In the midst of blatant injustices inflicted upon the Negro, I have watched white churchmen stand on the sideline and mouth pious irrelevancies and sanctimonious trivialities. In the midst of a mighty struggle to rid our nation of racial and economic injustice, I have heard many ministers say: "Those are social issues, with which the gospel has no real concern." And I have watched many churches commit themselves to a completely other worldly religion which makes a strange, un-Biblical distinction between body and soul, between the sacred and the secular.

I have traveled the length and breadth of Alabama, Mississippi and all the other southern states. On sweltering summer days and crisp autumn mornings I have looked at the South's beautiful churches with their lofty spires pointing heavenward. I have beheld the impressive outlines of her massive religious education buildings. Over and over I have found myself asking: "What kind of people worship here? Who is their God? Where were their voices when the lips of Governor Barnett dripped with words of interposition and nullification? Where were they when Governor Walleye gave a clarion call for defiance and hatred? Where were their voices of support when bruised and weary Negro men and women decided to rise from the dark dungeons of complacency to the bright hills of creative protest?"

Yes, these questions are still in my mind. In deep disappointment I have wept over the laxity of the church. But be assured that my tears have been tears of love. There can be no deep disappointment where there is not deep love. Yes, I love the church. How could I do otherwise? l am in the rather unique position of being the son, the grandson and the great-grandson of preachers. Yes, I see the church as the body of Christ. But, oh! How we have blemished and scarred that body through social neglect and through fear of being nonconformists.

There was a time when the church was very powerful—in the time when the early Christians rejoiced at being deemed worthy to suffer for what they believed. In those days the church was not merely a thermometer that recorded the ideas and principles of popular opinion; it was a thermostat that transformed the mores of society. Whenever the early Christians entered a town, the people in power became disturbed and immediately sought to convict the Christians for being "disturbers of the peace" and "outside agitators." But the Christians pressed on, in the conviction that they were "a colony of heaven," called to obey God rather than man. Small in number, they were big in commitment. They were too God intoxicated to be "astronomically intimidated." By their effort and example they brought an end to such ancient evils as infanticide and gladiatorial contests.

Things are different now. So often the contemporary church is a weak, ineffectual voice with an uncertain sound. So often it is an archdefender of the status quo. Far from being disturbed by the presence of the church, the power structure of the average community is consoled by the church's silent—and often even vocal—sanction of things as they are.

But the judgment of God is upon the church as never before. If today's church does not recapture the sacrificial spirit of the early church, it will lose its authenticity, forfeit the loyalty of millions, and be dismissed as an irrelevant social club with no meaning for the twentieth century. Every day I meet young people whose disappointment with the church has turned into outright disgust.

Perhaps I have once again been too optimistic. Is organized religion too inextricably bound to the status quo to save our nation and the world? Perhaps I must turn my faith to the inner spiritual church, the church within the church, as the true *ekklesia* and the hope of the world. But again I am thankful to God that some noble souls from the ranks of organized religion have broken loose from the paralyzing chains of conformity and joined us as active partners in the struggle for freedom, They have left their secure congregations and walked the streets of Albany, Georgia, with us. They have gone down the highways of the South on tortuous rides for freedom. Yes, they have gone to jail with us. Some have been dismissed from their churches, have lost the support of their bishops and fellow ministers. But they have acted in the faith that right defeated is stronger than evil triumphant. Their witness has been the spiritual salt that has preserved the true meaning of the gospel in these troubled times. They have carved a tunnel of hope through the dark mountain of disappointment.

I hope the church as a whole will meet the challenge of this decisive hour. But even if the church does not come to the aid of justice, I have no despair about the future. I have no fear about the outcome of our struggle in Birmingham, even if our motives are at present misunderstood. We will reach the goal of freedom in Birmingham and all over the nation, because the goal of America is freedom. Abused and scorned though we may be, our destiny is tied up with America's destiny. Before the pilgrims landed at Plymouth, we were here. Before the pen of Jefferson etched the majestic words of the Declaration of Independence across the pages of history, we were here. For more than two centuries our forebears labored in this country without wages; they made cotton king; they built the homes of their masters while suffering gross injustice and shameful humiliation—and yet out of a bottomless vitality they continued to thrive and develop. If the inexpressible cruelties of slavery could not stop us, the opposition we now face will surely fail. We will win our freedom because the sacred heritage of our nation and the eternal will of God are embodied in our echoing demands.

Before closing I feel impelled to mention one other point in your statement that has troubled me profoundly. You warmly commended the Birmingham police force for keeping "order" and "preventing violence." I doubt that you would have so warmly commended the police force if you had seen its dogs sinking their teeth into unarmed, nonviolent Negroes. I doubt that you would so quickly commend the policemen if .you were to observe their ugly and inhumane treatment of Negroes here in the city jail; if you were to watch them push and curse old Negro women and young Negro girls; if you were to see them slap and kick old Negro men and young boys; if you were to observe them, as they did on two occasions, refuse to give us food because we wanted to sing our grace together. I cannot join you in your praise of the Birmingham police department.

It is true that the police have exercised a degree of discipline in handing the demonstrators. In this sense they have conducted themselves rather "nonviolently" in public. But for what purpose? To preserve the evil system of segregation. Over the past few years I have consistently preached that nonviolence demands that the means we use must be as pure as the ends we seek. I have tried to make clear that it is wrong to use immoral means to attain moral ends. But now I must affirm that it is just as wrong, or perhaps even more so, to use moral means to preserve immoral ends. Perhaps Mr. Connor and his policemen have been rather nonviolent in public, as was Chief Pritchett in Albany, Georgia but they have used the moral means of nonviolence to maintain the immoral end of racial injustice. As T. S. Eliot has said: "The last temptation is the greatest treason: To do the right deed for the wrong reason."

I wish you had commended the Negro sit-inners and demonstrators of Birmingham for their sublime courage, their willingness to suffer and their amazing discipline in the midst of great provocation. One day the South will recognize its real heroes. They will be the James Merediths, with the noble sense of purpose that enables them to face jeering and hostile mobs, and with the agonizing loneliness that characterizes the life of the pioneer. They will be old, oppressed, battered Negro women, symbolized in a seventy-two-year-old woman in Montgomery, Alabama, who rose up with a sense of dignity and with her people decided not to ride segregated buses, and who responded with ungrammatical profundity to one who inquired about her weariness: "My feets is tired, but my soul is at rest." They will be the young high school and college students, the young ministers of the gospel and a host of their elders, courageously and nonviolently sitting in at lunch counters and willingly going to jail for conscience' sake. One day the South will know that when these disinherited children of God sat down at lunch counters, they were in reality standing up for what is best in the American dream and for the most sacred values in our Judaeo-Christian heritage, thereby bringing our nation back to those great wells of democracy which were dug deep by the founding fathers in their formulation of the Constitution and the Declaration of Independence.

Never before have I written so long a letter. I'm afraid it is much too long to take your precious time. I can assure you that it would have been much shorter if I had been writing from a comfortable desk, but what else can one do when he is alone in a narrow jail cell, other than write long letters, think long thoughts and pray long prayers?

If I have said anything in this letter that overstates the truth and indicates an unreasonable impatience, I beg you to forgive me. If I have said anything that understates the truth and indicates my having a patience that allows me to settle for anything less than brotherhood, I beg God to forgive me.

I hope this letter finds you strong in the faith. I also hope that circumstances will soon make it possible for me to meet each of you, not as an integrationist or a civil rights leader but as a fellow clergyman and a Christian brother. Let us all hope that the dark clouds of racial prejudice will soon pass away and the deep fog of misunderstanding will be lifted from our fear-drenched communities, and in some not too distant tomorrow the radiant stars of love and brotherhood will shine over our great nation with all their scintillating beauty.

Yours for the cause of Peace and Brotherhood,
Martin Luther King, Jr.

Appendix

Temple University's Policy on Academic Dishonesty

Academic Honesty

The students and faculty of Temple University are working together in a common endeavor: to seek the truth, to discover the truth, to speak and to publish the truth. It is an ancient and honorable endeavor to which teachers and students have dedicated themselves since time immemorial. Out of this long history of dedication to the truth has grown a specific set of requirements governing the ways in which we behave toward one another in the classroom and in which we may use one another's thoughts, words, ideas, and published research. As a Temple student, you will want not only to dedicate yourself generally to the pursuit of truth, but will also need to learn the specific rules which govern academic behavior at Temple University.

The most important rules are self-evident and follow inevitably from a respect for the truth. We must not take credit for research, for ideas, or for words which are not our own. We must not falsify data or results of research. We must not present any work under false pretenses. In order to be sure that we do not violate these principles, we must learn some specific rules. We must understand exactly what is meant by the three major types of academic dishonesty: plagiarism, violating the rules of an assignment, and cheating on an examination. The faculty of Temple University are confident that if we all understand these few simple rules, we will have no need to worry about academic dishonesty.

Academic Dishonesty

1. Plagiarism

Plagiarism is the unacknowledged use of another person's labor: another person's ideas, words, or assistance.

There are many forms of plagiarism: repeating another person's sentence as your own, adopting a particularly apt phrase as your own, paraphrasing someone else's argument as your own, or even presenting someone else's line of thinking in the development of a thesis as though it were your own. All these forms of plagiarism are prohibited both by the traditional principles of academic honesty and by the regulations of Temple University. Our education and our research encourage us to explore and use the ideas of others, and as writers we will frequently want to use the ideas and even the words of others. It is perfectly acceptable to do so; but we must never submit someone else's work as if it were our own, without giving appropriate credit to the originator. Some sorts of plagiarism are obvious. Students must not copy someone else's examination answer or laboratory report, submit a paper written in whole or in part by someone else, or have a friend do an assignment or take a test for them. Other forms of plagiarism, however, are less obvious. We provide below some guidelines concerning the types of materials that should be acknowledged through an acceptable form of citation.

(a) *Quotations.* Whenever you use a phrase, sentence, or longer passage written (or spoken) by someone else, you must enclose the words in quotation marks and indicate the exact source of the material. This applies also to quotations that you have altered.

(b) *Paraphrasing another's language.* Avoid closely paraphrasing another's words: substituting an occasional synonym, leaving out or adding an occasional modifier, rearranging the grammar slightly, just changing the tenses of verbs, and so on. Either quote the material directly, using quotation marks, or put the ideas completely in your own words. In either case, acknowledgment is necessary. Remember: expressing someone else's ideas in your own way does not make them yours.

(c) *Facts.* In a paper, you will often use facts that you have gotten from a lecture, a written work, or some other source. If the facts are well known, it is usually not necessary to provide a source. (In a paper on American history, for example, it would not ordinarily be necessary to give a source for the statement that the Civil War began in 1861 after the inauguration of Abraham Lincoln.) If the facts are not widely known or if the facts were developed or presented by a specific source, however, then you should identify the source for the facts.

(d) *Ideas.* If you use an idea or ideas that you learned from a lecture, written work, or some other source, then you should identify the source. You should identify the source for an idea whether or not you agree with the idea. It does not become your original idea just because you agree with it.

In general, all sources must be identified as clearly, accurately, and thoroughly as possible. When in doubt about whether to identify a source, either cite the source or consult your instructor.

When preparing a paper, you should ask your instructor whether he or she expects you to use footnotes, and whether all sources consulted should appear in a bibliography or only those from which you used material.

2. Violating the Rules of an Assignment

Academic course work is intended to advance the skills, knowledge, and intellectual competence of students. It is important, therefore, that students not behave in such a way as to thwart these intentions. When students are given assignments in a class or laboratory, the instructor will normally explain the rules under which the assignment is to be carried out. A student who does not understand the rules should ask the instructor for clarification. These rules are intended to make the assignment an educational experience and to make certain that the students' accomplishments on the assignment can be fairly evaluated.

Academic cheating is, in general terms, the thwarting or breaking of the general rules of academic work and/or the specific rules of individual courses. It includes falsifying data; submitting, without the instructor's approval, work in one course that was done for another; helping others to plagiarize or cheat from one's own or someone else's work; or actually doing the work of another person.

There are many examples.

If the answers to mathematics problems are in the back of the book, looking them up may produce correct answers, but it will not promote skill, knowledge, or competence. Or if the teacher says that you are not to use a dictionary for a foreign language translation but you use one anyway, you will not have participated in the intended reading exercise. In both of these examples, not only have you cheated yourself of academically useful work but you also cheat yourself of any helpful evaluation that the teacher might make. If instructors do not know what kinds of problems that their students are having, they cannot do much to help with those problems.

Another form of academic cheating occurs when work is submitted as if produced according to instructions when actually it is produced by some other means, or is simply invented. When students are given a laboratory assignment, it is assumed that they will carry out the assignment and that their reports will be based on their own laboratory work. A student should not make up data for a report or prepare a report without doing the assignment. If the assignment has called for the collection of data, perhaps through social or laboratory experiment, then the significance of the cheating can be great.

A special case of such cheating occurs when students avoid the expected work of an assignment not by drawing upon the work of others but by drawing upon their own work, already done for another course—for instance, by submitting a paper from one course to fulfill an assignment for another. This is academic cheating, because it frustrates the aims of the assignment. It avoids the development of skill, knowledge, and competence for which the assignment was made. When an instructor assigns a paper to be written outside class, he or she assumes that a student will prepare a paper specifically for that course. This does not mean, of course, that students should avoid building upon their previous work. All education, and especially education within a major field, assumes a continuous building upon what has been previously learned. For the purpose of course work, however, work that you have already done should be regarded as if it were the work of someone else. Specific use of that work must be properly acknowledged, and substitution of that work for a current assignment is a form of cheating unless specifically permitted by the instructor. If you wish to use a paper that you have prepared for another course, you should obtain permission from your instructor.

3. Cheating on an Examination

Examinations are intended to test your understanding and retention of the material covered in a course.

If you obtain help from other students during the examination, you have cheated. Thus, reading another student's answers while you are taking an examination is cheating.

When an examination is given in class, the instructor will usually assume (or explicitly state) that is is a "closed book" examination. If it is, students should not use notes or any other written aids in taking the examination. If you are unsure, ask.

When an examination is given out of class as a "take-home exam," it is normally assumed that you may use class notes, texts, or even material from the library that is properly cited. Your teacher assumes that you will complete the examination alone. You should not obtain help from fellow students in developing your answers and turn them in as if they were your work. Again, if you are unsure, ask.

Penalties for Academic Dishonesty

The penalty for academic dishonesty can vary from a reprimand and receiving a failing grade for a particular assignment, to failure for the course, to suspension or expulsion from the University. The penalty varies with the nature of the offense, the individual instructor, the department, and the school or college. Some colleges have additional policies, reflecting the unique training that they provide. Your instructor or dean will provide you with information regarding these additional policies.

Students who believe that they have been unfairly accused may appeal the decision of the instructor, according to the policies and procedures of the school or college. The student should first speak with the instructor. If that does not resolve the matter, the student should speak to the department's ombudsperson or chairperson. If the matter is not satisfactorily resolved at the departmental level, then the student may appeal to the dean or Grievance Committee of the school or college in which the course is given.

A penalty that is beyond the authority of the individual instructor, such as suspension or expulsion, may be imposed by the student's college. Faculty members who believe such a penalty is warranted must make such a recommendation to the student's dean in writing. The student's dean or appropriate college committee will rule on the case and inform the faculty member and student before the end of the following semester.

Students who are dissatisfied with the college's action may appeal the case to the Provost.

PASSED BY THE FACULTY SENATE, April 19, 1989

Notes

David Hume: *An Enquiry Concerning the Principles of Morals*

1. Benevolence naturally divides into two kinds, the *general* and the *particular*. The first is, where we have no friendship or connexion or esteem for the person, but feel only a general sympathy with him or a compassion for his pains, and a congratulation with his pleasures. The other species of benevolence is founded on an opinion of virtue, on services done us, or on some particular connexions. Both these sentiments must be allowed real in human nature; but whether they will resolve into some nice considerations of self-love, is a question more curious than important. The former sentiment, to wit, that of general benevolence, or humanity, or sympathy, we shall have occasion frequently to treat of in the course of this enquiry; and I assume it as real, from general experience, without any other proof.

2. Mons. Fontenelle.

3. Animasque in vulnere ponunt. VIRG. Dum alteri noceat, sui negligens, says Seneca of (Geor. 4, 238.) of Anger. De Ira, I. i.

Mary Wollstonecraft: *A Vindication of the Rights of Women*

1. Why should women be censured with petulant acrimony because they seem to have a passion for a scarlet coat? Has not an education placed them more on a level with soldiers than any other class of men?

2. Similar feelings has Milton's pleasing picture of paradisiacal happiness ever raised in my mind; yet, instead of envying the lovely pair, I have with conscious dignity or Satanic pride turned to hell for sublimer objects. In the same style, when viewing some noble monument of human art, I have traced the emanation of the Deity in the order I admired, till, descending from that giddy height, I have caught myself contemplating the grandest of all human sights;—for fancy quickly placed in some solitary recess an outcast of fortune, rising superior to passion and discontent.

3. For example, the herd of Novelists.

4. Vide Rousseau and Swedenborg.

Charles Darwin: *The Descent of Man*

1. "On the Limits of Natural Selection," in the *North American Review*, Oct., 1870, p. 295.
2. The Rev. J. A. Picton gives a discussion to this effect in his *New Theories and the Old Faith*, 1870.

Frederick Engels: *Socialism: Utopian and Scientific*

1. It is hardly necessary in this connection to point out that, even if the form of appropriation remains the same, the *character* of the appropriation is just as much revolutionized as production is by the changes described above. It is, of course, a very different matter whether I appropriate to myself my own product or that of another. Note in passing that wage labor, which contains the whole capitalist mode of production in embryo, is very ancient; in a sporadic, scattered form, it existed for centuries alongside slave-labor. But the embryo could duly develop into the capitalistic mode of production only when the necessary historical preconditions had been furnished.

Friedrich Nietzsche: *On the Genealogy of Morals*

1. *The Gospel According to Matthew* 6:21.
2. "Tartuffery" is a word of Nietzsche's coinage, after the comedy *Tartuffe* by Molière. The title character in the play is marked by a demonstrative and hypocritical religiosity, which he practices to swindle a gullible man out of his wife and estate.
3. This is a parody of Immanuel Kant's idea that one may *hope* were one cannot know.
4. The Greek word "pathos" comes from the same root as the English word "passive," and accordingly signifies a transient state of feeling that comes upon one, as opposed to an *ēthos*, a relatively stable disposition of character that one has some control over.
5. Nietzsche uses the French word "ressentiment" here, perhaps to convey a subtle difference from the German words for "resentment," or perhaps to characterize the French as more psychologically subtle. In any case, it is probably best to treat "ressentiment" as a technical term and infer its meaning from the text: It seems to be a sentiment, it is "reactive" in an especially "poisonous" way, and it has the potential to "become creative."
6. The German is "Sittlichkeit der Sitte." Nietzsche is playing on the relation between "Sittlichkeit," meaning "morality" or "ethics," and "Sitte," which can in the plural form mean "morality," but which originally meant "custom," "habit," or even "manners." The *Sittlichkeit der Sitte*, in any case, seems to indicate the outlook in which the authority of ethical standards derives from custom or tradition.
7. "Mnemotechnics" is a coinage of Nietzsche that comes from the Greek words *mnē*, meaning "memory," and *technē*, meaning "skill" or "craft"; "mnemotechnics" thus means something like "techniques for creating memories."
8. This principle is a variant of one attributed to Cato, the early medieval author of proverbs.

W.E.B. Du Bois: from *The Souls of Black Folks*

1. Revised from "Strivings of the Negro People," *Atlantic Monthly* (August 1897): 194–98. The verses are from *The Crying of Waters* (1903) by Arthur Symons.
2. Site of a Civil War battle of June 1862, near Richmond, Virginia.
3. River that runs through Du Bois's hometown of Great Barrington, Massachusetts.

4. In *The Autobiography of W.E.B. Du Bois* (1968) he reports that this incident took place during his high-school years.

5. An ironic rewriting of Exodus 2.22, in which Moses declares, "I have been a stranger in a strange land."

6. References to William Wordsworth's "Ode: Intimations of Immortality" from *Recollections of Early Childhood.*

7. In African American folklore, seventh sons as well as those children born with a caul, a membrane that sometimes covers the head at birth, are reported to have special abilities, such as predicting the future and seeing ghosts.

8. See p. 236, Dickson D. Bruce Jr.'s essay on the origins and meaning of double-consciousness.

9. A learned scholar.

10. Following their Egyptian captivity, the Israelites reached Canaan, the Promised Land, after forty years of wandering in the wilderness.

11. Refrain of the freedom spiritual "Shout, O Children!"

12. Macbeth 3.4.102–3. Du Bois symbolically represents the American character as guilty and blood stained, like the central character of Shakespeare's tragedy.

13. A delusive or misleading goal.

14. Secret society formed in 1866 by Confederate veterans with the stated intent of protecting white, Protestant interests. It rapidly became a terrorist organization responsible for widespread violence against African Americans.

15. Northern politicians and businessmen who entered the South following the Civil War. Portrayed as carrying their belongings in cheap, fabric valises (carpetbags), they were seen as enriching themselves at the cost of a defeated Confederacy.

16. Ratified March 10, 1870; it granted voting rights to men regardless of "race, color, or previous condition of servitude." Although the amendment was a moderate measure and did not outlaw qualification tests for voters, it allowed Congress to enforce the law through federal sanctions.

17. The results of the presidential elections of 1876 were disputed by Louisiana, Florida, and South Carolina, three states that backed Democrat Samuel J. Tilden against Rutherford B. Hayes. Some Southern Democrats threatened a "revolution" of secession from the Union. Republicans, in their attempt to mollify the Democrats, significantly reduced their support of the freedmen.

18. Mystical. The cabala, or Kabbalah, is a body of esoteric Jewish doctrines dealing with the manifestations of God. Written between the third and the sixteenth centuries, these books are difficult to interpret.

19. The Promised Land. Du Bois is reinforcing his identification of African Americans with the Israelites during their years of Egyptian captivity and their forty years of wandering in the wilderness.

20. 1 Corinthians 13.12: "For now we see through a glass, darkly; but then face to face: now I know in part, but then shall I know even as also I am known."

21. During the Enlightenment, philosophers such as Kant and Hume were convinced that certain races could be ranked hierarchically according to their psychological and moral characteristics as well as their bodily traits.

22. An attitude of deference or homage.

23. Toussaint L'Ouverture (1746–1803), leader of the black forces during the Haitian Revolution that overthrew French rule. After Napoleon tricked him into going willingly to France in 1800, L'Ouverture died there in 1803.

24. Literally, storm and stress (German). The term characterizes a German literary movement that valorizes emotional experience and spiritual struggle. Johann Wolf gang von Goethe, Du Bois's favorite author, was a leading figure in this movement.

Simone de Beauvoir: *The Second Sex*

1. *Franchise*, dead today.

2. The Kinsey Report [Alfred C. Kinsey and others: *Sexual Behavior in the Human Male* (W. B. Saunders Co., 1948)] is no exception, for it is limited to describing the sexual characteristics of American men, which is quite a different matter.

3. E. Lévinas expresses this idea most explicitly in his essay *Temps et l' Autre*. "Is there not a case in which otherness, alterity [*altérite*], unquestionably marks the nature of a being, as its essence, an instance of otherness not consisting purely and simply in the opposition of two species of the same genus? I think that the feminine represents the contrary in its absolute sense, this contrariness being in no wise affected by any relation between it and its correlative and thus remaining absolutely other. Sex is not a certain specific difference . . . no more is the sexual difference a mere contradiction. . . . Nor does this difference lie in the duality of two complementary terms, for two complementary terms imply a pre-existing whole. . . . Otherness reaches its full flowering in the feminine, a term of the same rank as consciousness but of opposite meaning."

I suppose that Levinas does not forget that woman, too, is aware of her own consciousness, or ego. But it is striking that he deliberately takes a man's point of view, disregarding the reciprocity of subject and object. When he writes that woman is mystery, he implies that she is mystery for man. Thus his description, which is intended to be objective, is in fact an assertion of masculine privilege.

4. See C. Lévi-Strauss: *Les Structures élémentaires de la parenté*. My thanks are due to C. Lévi-Strauss for his kindness in furnishing me with the proofs of his work, which, among others, I have used liberally in Part II.

5. With rare exceptions, perhaps, like certain matriarchal rulers, queens, and the like.—TR.

6. See Part 11, ch. viii.

7. At the moment an "equal rights" amendment to the Constitution of the United States is before Congress.—TR.

8. See Part II, pp. 115–17.

9. Or at least he thought he could.

10. A significant article on this theme by Michel Carrouges appeared in No. 202 of the *Cahiers du Sud*. He writes indignantly: "Would that here were no woman-myth at all but only a cohort of cooks, matrons, prostitutes, and bluestockings serving functions of pleasure or usefulness!" That is to say, in his view woman has no existence in and for herself; he thinks only of her function in the mail world. Her reason for existence lies in man. But then, in fact, her poetic "function" as a myth might be more valued than any other. The real problem is precisely to find out why woman should be defined with relation to man.

11. For example, a man will say that he considers his wife in no wise degraded because she has no gainful occupation. The profession of housewife is just as lofty, and son. But when the first quarrel comes, he will exclaim: "Why, you couldn't make your living without me!"

12. The specific purpose of Book II of this study is to describe this process.